The News
from Brownsville

The NEWS *from* Brownsville

HELEN CHAPMAN'S LETTERS FROM THE TEXAS MILITARY FRONTIER, 1848–1852

Edited by Caleb Coker

Published for the Barker Texas History Center
by the Texas State Historical Association

Printed in the United States of America.

Published for the Barker Texas History Center by the Texas State Historical Association in cooperation with the Center for Studies in Texas History at the University of Texas at Austin.

Number Two in the Barker Texas History Center Series.
Series Editor, Don E. Carleton.

Library of Congress Cataloging-in-Publication Data

The news from Brownsville : Helen Chapman's letters from the Texas military frontier, 1848–1852 / edited by Caleb Coker.

p. cm. — (No. 2 in the Barker Texas History Center series)

Includes bibliographical references and index.

ISBN 0-87611-115-0 (cloth : acid-free paper)

1. Chapman, Helen, b. 1817—Correspondence. 2. Frontier and pioneer life—Texas—Brownsville. 3. Officers' wives—Texas—Brownsville—Correspondence. 4. Fort Brown (Brownsville, Tex.) 5. Brownsville (Tex.)—Biography. 6. Brownsville (Tex.)—History. I. Coker, Caleb, 1943– . II. Title. III. Series : Barker Texas History Center series (Texas State Historical Association) ; no. 2.

F394.B88C47 1992
976.4'495—dc20 92-7443
CIP

Cover: Helen Ellsworth Blair Chapman by unknown artist, ca. 1838. Oil on canvas, 29½ x 24½ inches. *Courtesy of Benjamin M. Porter.*

Book design by David Timmons

CONTENTS

FOREWORD

The News from Brownsville: Helen Chapman's Letters from the Texas Military Frontier, 1848–1852 is the second volume in the Barker Texas History Center's cooperative publications series with the Texas State Historical Association. This series was established to encourage and support the publication of historical studies based mainly on collections in the Barker Center. Housing the nation's largest library of Texana as well as extensive archival, cartographic, newspaper, sound, and photographic collections, the Barker Texas History Center is the single most important resource in existence for the study of things Texan. A division of the Center for American History at the University of Texas at Austin, the Barker Center is open to anyone needing access to its resources.

Helen and William Chapman were important Texas pioneers who left an extraordinary record of the early days of Texas statehood along the Rio Grande. Recently, their descendants, the Cokers, the Porters, and the Freemans, donated an important group of the Chapman letters to the Barker Center. Those letters now constitute the Chapman Family Papers, a part of the Barker Center's permanent collections. The Chapman papers are an important resource for researchers interested in a wide range of topics relating to the history of the southern and southwestern United States during the nineteenth century. We are very grateful to the Chapman descendants for their dedicated efforts to preserve and make available this valuable collection.

Funds from the J. R. Parten Chair in the Archives of American History provided support for the publication of *The News from Brownsville.* Texas State Historical Association Director Ron Tyler and Assistant Director George Ward were unfailingly cooperative and supportive during this publications project, as was the Association's Executive Council. I look forward to working with them to publish other volumes in the Barker Center series in the near future.

DON E. CARLETON
Director, Center for American History

ACKNOWLEDGMENTS

THE BIRTH OF A BOOK, from conception to publication, is a lengthy, complicated process that reaches fruition only because of many individuals who generously contribute their time, support, and insights to the effort. Mabel Freeman Coker, my mother, and Philip R. Freeman, my uncle, both provided much encouragement, support, and help, as did my sisters and cousins, Helen Freeman Coker, Lavinia Lide Coker, Marion Porter Crane, John Alexander Porter, Benjamin Markley Porter, Lani Freeman Pugeat, Jeffrey Freeman, Anne Furman Dunn, and Claire Furman Smith. They all believed in the worth of the Chapman family letters and in my ability to edit them.

William R. Slaughter and Daniel L. Schafer, of the University of North Florida, were extremely generous with their time and offered many valuable suggestions. Curtis Tunnell of the Texas Historical Commission furnished helpful information, as did Anthony K. Knopp, Henry G. Krausse, Jr., and Kino Camarillo of the Brownsville Historical Association. Theo Budnik, a great-great-granddaughter of Charles Stillman, was also of great help.

There were many librarians who assisted my research efforts: Yolanda Gonzalez of the Arnulfo Oliveira Memorial Library at Texas Southmost College in Brownsville, Suzanne J. Stone (Duncan) of the Westfield Athenaeum, Margaret E. Rose, the Local History librarian at the Corpus Christi Public Library, Sylvia J. Taylor and Ann Lockett at the Santa Clara (California) Public Library, Carol Gilbert of the California State Library, the librarians on the staff of the New Orleans Public Library, the Jacksonville Public Library, the Clemson University Library, and the University of North Florida Library, as well as the reference staff of the Eugene C. Barker Texas History Center at the University of Texas at Austin.

The Barker Texas History Center has done much more than provide excellent reference facilities, however. Don E. Carleton, the director, and Katherine J. Adams, the assistant director, have offered encouragement and demonstrated strong interest in the book from the beginning. I visited the Barker Center to conduct much of my research of the historical background and discussed the project with both at length. Their guidance and help will always be remembered. Later, the Barker Center made possible the assistance of Janet G. Humphrey, who worked with me to polish the manuscript. I am very grateful for Janet Humphrey's insightful and creative recommendations.

Each of those mentioned was instrumental only in improving this book. Any errors or shortcomings are solely mine.

CALEB COKER
February 15, 1992

INTRODUCTION

IN SEPTEMBER OF 1855, Helen Ellsworth Blair Chapman, the wife of an army quartermaster, sailed aboard the Schooner *Major Barbour*, returning from New Orleans to Texas. In a letter to her mother, she observed that several of the sailors, in their idle moments on the Sabbath, read novels of the sort described by a ship's officer as "something very adventurous and exciting." She expressed concern, "How may they be nourished by the only food they are capable of receiving?" She briefly entertained the notion of writing a book herself to improve the situation. "Is it not possible to produce books exciting, captivating to such fancies and at the same time suggestive of something higher?" she asked. But like many who have thought of writing a book, she quickly dismissed the idea and conceded, "The spirit indeed is willing, but the flesh is miserably weak."[1]

Little did Helen know that she had already written such a book, a draft of which was safely packed away in Westfield, Massachusetts. Helen's mother had saved her letters written from the Texas frontier and the Rio Grande Valley. *The News from Brownsville* is a rich personal chronicle of Helen and William Chapman, of their daily life in Brownsville during its formative years from 1848 through 1852. During this period, the Chapmans witnessed and participated in the betterment and eventual evacuation of Matamoras, Mexico,[2] by United States troops in 1848, the establishment of the new Fort Brown, and the growth of its satellite settlement, which became Brownsville, Texas. While perhaps differing from the fiction Helen Chapman considered writing, this unique and spontaneous narrative of the

1. Helen Blair Chapman (hereafter referred to as HBC) to Emily Welles Blair (hereafter referred to as EWB), Sept. 23, 1855, Chapman Family Collection, Eugene C. Barker Texas History Center, University of Texas at Austin (hereafter referred to as CC).

2. Matamoras and Monterey rather than Matamoros and Monterrey, were the spellings commonly used by the U.S. Army at the time of the Mexican War. These spellings have been retained throughout the text.

Texas frontier in the mid-nineteenth century contains a wealth of information of interest to the general reader as well as the professional historian.

Helen Ellsworth Blair was born in Westfield, Massachusetts, on April 4, 1817, to William Blair, a prominent lawyer, and Emily Welles Blair. She was educated at Westfield Academy, a coeducational private boarding school. During her final year there, 1833, she was an "assistant pupil," helping to teach less qualified students. She completed her education in Philadelphia with four years at Mrs. Ashmead's, a private boarding school for young women.

In 1832 Helen Blair became acquainted with fellow student William Warren Chapman. He was born on January 31, 1814, and lived in nearby Springfield. In letters he wrote several years later, Chapman indicated that their decision to marry was made while at Westfield Academy.

William Chapman, the son of an armorer at the Springfield Armory, chose a military career. He graduated from West Point with the class of 1837, seventh in academic standing and second in military deportment with no demerits. His first assignment was at Fort Foster in Florida, twenty miles north of Tampa Bay. The Second Seminole War appeared to be nearing its end as he entered the theater of war. Within six months of his arrival, he was promoted from quartermaster to commander of the fort, primarily because of attrition in the higher ranks. Those whom the Indians could not vanquish, the mosquitoes did. Eventually William also fell ill to malaria, and the post was abandoned.[3]

Helen Blair, meanwhile, as William's fiancée, had moved south to be closer to him. She left Philadelphia in November 1837 for Savannah, Georgia, to teach "47 scholars."[4]

On May 8, 1838, William left Florida and traveled by steamboat to New Orleans and up the Mississippi and Tennessee rivers to Calhoun, Tennessee, to assist in removing 18,000 Cherokees to Arkansas Territory. Chapman's continuing illness mercifully cut short his service on the Trail of Tears. He was furloughed in late June and traveled to Savannah. Although Helen's original plan had been to remain in Georgia until the fall, the couple returned to Massachusetts together and were married in Westfield on August 29,

3. William Chapman's letters to Helen from Florida have been published in Edward C. Coker and Daniel L. Schafer, "A West Point Graduate in the Second Seminole War: William Warren Chapman and the View from Fort Foster," *Florida Historical Quarterly*, LXVIII (Apr. 1990),447–475.

4. Ibid., 59.

Framed photographs of Helen Chapman and William Chapman, ca. August 1838. Courtesy of Anne Furman Dunn.

1838. The following December, William was assigned to Fort Niagara in Buffalo, New York. In the cold of winter, he marched his troops from Albany to Buffalo. Helen accompanied him part of the way and completed the trip by stage.

The Chapmans remained at Fort Niagara until 1841, where William served during the Canadian border disturbances. During these years, they shared a double house with Dr. Robert Crooke Wood and his wife, Ann Mackall Taylor, the eldest daughter of Zachary Taylor. Their first house appeared marvelous to Helen's eyes. She wrote her mother that it had "every convenience we could wish," but neglected to say what those might have been.[5] The couple's first child, William Blair Chapman, whom they called Willie, was born in Buffalo on July 18, 1840.

Helen Chapman's familiarity with New York City dates from William's next assignment. He was transferred to Fort Columbus on Governor's Island in New York Harbor, where they lived until 1846. Although this post was not an especially exciting one, William took satisfaction in serving as an officer in the Second Artillery.

5. HBC to EWB, Dec. 27, 1840, CC.

Helen Chapman with her son William Blair Chapman (Willie), ca. 1846. Courtesy of Mabel Freeman Coker.

A promise of excitement accompanied Chapman's promotion to the rank of captain on May 11, 1846. Almost immediately, he left Governor's Island to join Brigadier General John E. Wool's column in San Antonio, Texas. He served as staff officer quartermaster for General Wool's army during the following eighteen months.

Doubtless the Chapmans kept up with the progress of the Mexican War. The contemporary general reader, however, might appreciate a brief synopsis of the action in order to understand better the historical context.

On March 1, 1845, three days before James K. Polk assumed the presidency, lame-duck president John Tyler signed a Congressional Joint Resolution inviting the independent Republic of Texas to join the Union. The twenty-eighth state formally entered on December 29, 1845. Prior to this time, Mexico had repeatedly warned the United States that annexation would be an act of war. Mexico claimed land north to the Nueces River, while the Republic of Texas considered the Rio Grande its southern boundary.

In order to defend its territory, President Polk sent General Zachary Taylor and his army first to Corpus Christi and then in March 1846 to the Rio Grande. Taylor's orders were to occupy a position on or near the river but to avoid conflict with the Mexicans unless a state of war existed. Traveling south from Corpus Christi, Taylor detoured briefly from his course to establish a supply depot at Point Isabel (now Port Isabel), twenty-five miles northeast of Matamoras in an inlet between the coastal barrier islands of South Padre and Brazos.

Tensions began to increase shortly after Taylor's arrival on the Rio Grande. He constructed a fort across the river from Matamoras, initially known as Fort Texas, and ordered a blockade of the Rio Grande to shut off the supply of war goods bound for the town. There were several skirmishes in April 1846, as Mexican troops assembled in Matamoras and prepared to drive the Americans from the disputed territory. Finally, on April 29, Taylor learned that the Mexican army, under the command of General Mariano Arista, planned to cross the river below Matamoras and capture the depot at Point Isabel, thus cutting off Taylor's supply lines.

Clearly, it was time to act. Leaving about 600 men at Fort Texas under the command of Major Jacob Brown, Zachary Taylor left for Point Isabel with the remainder of his troops. But because the Mexican army had been delayed crossing the Rio Grande, General Arista changed his strategy when he learned of Taylor's absence from Fort Texas and decided to attack there instead. The bombardment of the fort began on May 3 and could be heard from Point Isabel. Within a few days the American position became desperate. Ammunition was in short supply, and Major Brown, for whom the fort was later renamed, was mortally wounded on May 6.

In hopes of rescuing the command at Fort Texas, Taylor left Point Isabel with an army of 2,300 troops on May 7. They clashed with 6,000 of Arista's forces on the plain of Palo Alto the following day. Taylor's superior artillery prevailed despite his inferior numbers, and the Mexicans retreated at dusk.

Taylor's forces engaged Arista's men again the following day at Resaca de la Palma, a battlefield midway between Fort Texas and Palo Alto. This time, the defeat of the Mexican army was complete. Arista lost all his personal possessions, including his military chest and the heavy silver tableware from his mess. His retreat south of the Rio Grande was a rout.

Somewhat belatedly, on May 13, President Polk signed a resolution declaring that a state of war existed with Mexico. This allowed Taylor to pursue his enemy across the river. In command of 9,000 troops, he occupied Matamoras and other towns upriver in June 1846 and established Camargo as his main supply depot.

The next major event in the campaign for the northern Mexican provinces came in September. A fierce battle in Monterey left Taylor's army victorious. At the end of the month General John Wool led a column of about 2,800 troops, including Captains William Chapman and Robert E. Lee, from San Antonio toward Mexico.

After Monterey, a significant number of Taylor's troops as well as others, such as Captain Robert E. Lee from Wool's command, were sent to General Winfield Scott to pursue the war in the south. The remainder of Taylor's and Wool's forces combined amounted to 4,600 men. They soon defeated an army of some 20,000 under General Santa Anna. The battle, and the scene of William Chapman's only combat during the war, took place southwest of Monterey at Buena Vista on February 22–23, 1847.

General Scott's army landed on the Gulf Coast of Mexico in March and captured Vera Cruz at the end of the month. The army proceeded inland, winning battles at Cerro Gordo in April, Hill of Contreras and Churubusco in August, and El Molino del Rey and Chapultepec in September. The City of Mexico surrendered on September 14.

Negotiating the terms of the peace required several months. The Treaty of Guadalupe Hidalgo was submitted to Polk in February 1848 and

William W. Chapman and Willie, ca. 1849. This daguerreotype ($4^{1}/_{4}$ x $3^{1}/_{4}$ inches) was made at Brady's Gallery, 359 Broadway, New York City. Courtesy of Mabel Freeman Coker.

ratified by the U.S. Senate on March 10. The Mexican government approved the treaty on May 25 and the Rio Grande was established as the southern boundary of Texas. Five hundred and twenty-five thousand square miles, the area comprising Arizona, California, Nevada, New Mexico, Texas, Utah and parts of western Colorado, were ceded to the United States.

For the troops on the northern line, however, the months from March to November were spent in idleness. Beginning in August, William wrote to suggest that Helen visit him, first proposing New Orleans, then Matamoras, as her destination. Finally, in November 1847, Generals Taylor and Wool and their staffs left Monterey. They traveled overland to Camargo, where Wool remained, and Chapman continued with Taylor's party aboard a steamboat for Matamoras, arriving there on November 15. Colonel William Davenport was the military commandant in Matamoras, a city then under martial law, and Chapman became assistant quartermaster in charge of the army depot.

William was still imploring Helen to come to Matamoras in late December. At the same time, Helen was writing to her mother from Governor's Island that she expected to depart on the *U.S.S. Massachusetts* early in the new year. It is at this point that the Chapman's five-year sojourn on the Rio Grande begins.

The letters mentioned so far as well as those reproduced in this volume represent a small portion of the collection that arrived on my doorstep several years ago. Literally thousands of family papers dating from the American Revolution to the end of the nineteenth century comprise the record of five generations of an American family which originated in New England.

At random I chose a letter to read from the shipping crate. Immediately, it piqued my interest. My great-great-grandmother, Helen Chapman, had apparently stayed in the same Mexico City hotel that I visited with my daughter in 1984, 133 years later. As I continued sampling from the papers during the succeeding months, the outline of a story became more visible.

I began to focus on the letters written by the Chapmans between 1848 and 1852. They delineated a discrete chapter, not only in the lives of their authors, but also in the civilization of the South Texas frontier. They contained articulate expressions of the spirit blooming in mid-nineteenth-century America, Manifest Destiny,[6] providing as well a clear picture of the

6. The phrase "Manifest Destiny" was coined in 1845 by John L. O'Sullivan, who

Helen Chapman's parents, Emily and William Blair. Emily Blair's photograph was taken about 1856. William Blair's was made about 1850 by R. A. Lord in New York City. Courtesy of Mabel Freeman Coker.

events, the dealings, and the panorama of life on the Texas frontier. For instance, Helen's description of the first day she crossed the river from Matamoras to view the new town of Brownsville abuilding is so vivid one can almost hear the hammers ringing.[7]

When the military couple took up residence in Matamoras early in 1848, the border society, the people, and their customs, food, and language were so intriguing to Helen that she opened what soon became a torrent of correspondence to her parents and friends in New England. As quartermaster under the city's military rule, William was the city's "mayor de facto" and responsible for providing many of its municipal services.

When the U.S. Army withdrew from Mexico during the summer of 1848, Chapman was in charge of moving all its equipment and supplies

popularized it in the *New York Morning News*. It suggested that the territorial expansion of the United States was inevitable, given American political institutions, moral values, and character. See Wayne Andrews (ed.), *Concise Dictionary of American History* (New York: Charles Scribner's Sons, 1962), 580.

7. HBC to William Blair, Jan. 4, 1849, CC.

Harry Love: Army express rider, Rio Grande explorer, frontiersman, and Helen Chapman's friend. This picture was made from a photograph in Sutter's Fort, California, which was taken in the late 1860s, some fifteen years after Love left Texas for California. The butt plate of his revolver protrudes from his waistband in the cross-draw position. Courtesy of the California State Library.

across the river to what he called the "new" Fort Brown. The fort was to be a border post and the supply depot for other forts in the Rio Grande Valley. Chapman was responsible for the purchase of land and erection of government buildings, the care of thousands of mules and cavalry horses and military stores, the hiring of steamboats, and the contracts for providing a multitude of goods and services to the troops stationed at Fort Brown and along the Rio Grande. As such, he played an important role in the fledgling town of Brownsville. He was also an early proponent of the exploration of the Rio Grande as a transportation resource for the area.

Naturally, Helen Chapman spent her time in Matamoras and Brownsville in quite different occupations. Her letters reveal that she socialized and entertained frequently during those years, perhaps more often than she preferred. Dealing with a constant stream of visitors, managing a household and its servants, and caring for her family consumed much of her time. When her duties permitted, she found solace in writing and reading as well as studying Spanish. Her letters describe scenes of violence and despair, as well as moments of amusement, fascinating characters, and impressive settings. She expressed forthright opinions on a wide range of subjects which came to her attention, ranging from child care and healthful diet to slavery and temperance to Zachary Taylor's fitness for the presidency and the plight of Mexicans in the new state of Texas. In her letters are tales and vivid descriptions of a noted army express rider, gold seekers, Mexican funerals, an epidemic, a trip to Mexico City, and her own childbirth experience during a battle in the Merchants War. Helen Chapman's correspondence between 1848 and 1852 is indeed a valuable record of her life and the changes occurring in South Texas during this period.

We are fortunate that Helen Chapman was such an observant and literate woman. Yet she was also a product of her upbringing and the times in which she lived. The temperance and abolition movements which were ascendant at mid-century were often reflected in her letters. However, she thought independently on various social issues. For example, her notions on temperance were experiential rather than founded on mere adherence to a temperance society's ideology. There was much alcohol abuse on the frontier, and its effect on victims, their families, and society was often apparent to one viewing the scene through unglazed eyes. In contrast, her views on abolition were most likely secondarily obtained, because she had little direct contact with slaves or slaveholders until after the Chapmans left Brownsville. In this connection, however, it must be noted that she delved into the matter whenever she had the opportunity to discuss it with slaveholders. Most interesting, however, were her prescient notions of racism. These came from her observations of the enmity that existed between the American and Mexican populations in the fledgling state of Texas. Helen's frontier Texas milieu allowed her to observe firsthand the conflict between two races technically standing in perfect legal equality because of the Treaty of Guadalupe Hidalgo, which ended the Mexican War.[8] Perceiving as early as 1852 that, "The difficulty is in the race," vainly she hoped "that this dreary hate may be subdued between men who are living side by side as citizens of a common republic."[9] Having reached this understanding, Helen became one of the early advocates for the extension of full civil rights to the Mexican American population of Texas.[10]

She had the values of a mid-century New England Protestant, retaining an assumption of the inherent value of spiritual life from her Puritan forebears. In married life, her paramount duty was to her husband: in making a pleasant home for him and seeing to his needs. But it would terribly shortchange the Chapmans to imply that their marital relationship was based even in small part upon New England notions of Puritan duty. These letters offer tender proof of the Chapmans' continuing deep love and devotion to each other, as well as the charming aspects of their personalities. William remained ardently involved with Helen during their entire marriage, writing the most endearing letters of love and adoration to her whenever they were apart. After ten years of marriage, Helen proudly acknowledged that she had "every comfort a reasonable heart could wish within my reach and a husband as kind and attentive as a mother."[11] But it is also clear that her young son Willie was closely tied to the strings of her heart, and that her initial twenty-month separation from him contributed much to the hardship of frontier life.

In addition to family concerns, Chapman also felt a personal sense of duty toward her new community. She promoted schools, wrote to charitable groups for financial assistance for needy neighbors, appealed to missionary societies for a minister willing to serve Brownsville, and took in foster

8. This treaty granted to former Mexicans remaining in Texas after the Mexican War the full civil rights due American citizens.

9. HBC to Ebenezer Learned, Aug. 5, 1852, CC.

10. Several examples of Helen's efforts on behalf of Mexican Americans are included in the epilogue.

11. HBC to EWB, Sept. 7, 1848, CC.

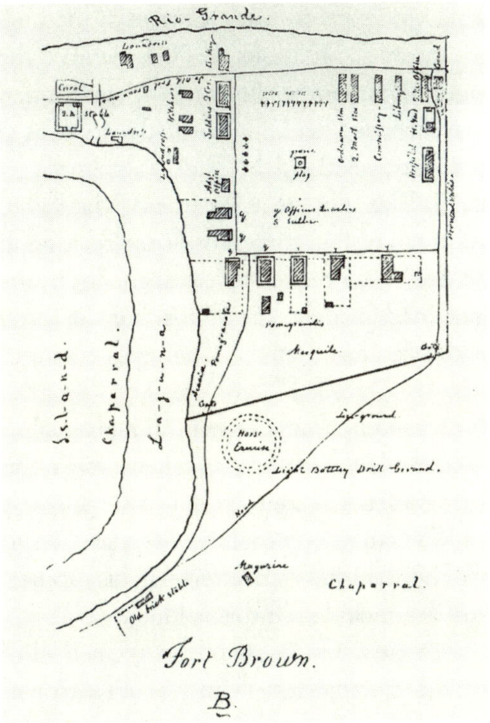

Left: This drawing of the new Fort Brown, which was located about 500 yards north of the original fort, was built by William Chapman. The $6\frac{1}{2} \times 3\frac{3}{4}$-inch drawing was attached to "Colonel J. K. F. Manfield's Report of the inspection of the Department of Texas in 1856." Courtesy of the Barker Texas History Center. Below: Fort Brown by unknown artist, ca. 1847. Engraving $3\frac{1}{4} \times 5\frac{1}{2}$ inches. From Capt. W. S. Henry's *Campaign Sketches of the War with Mexico* (1847).Courtesy of the Barker Texas History Center.

children. Her letters provide ample evidence of how a woman of the time exercised her moral suasion to improve conditions for the victims, the uneducated, and even the irreligious and intemperate of the Texas frontier.

The letters in which Chapman recorded her activities and responses to the scenes around her have themselves traveled widely. The Chapman family papers were originally stored in Emily Blair's home in Westfield, Massachusetts, where Chapman addressed much of her correspondence relating to Brownsville. After the Civil War, they were moved to a descendant's attic in South Carolina, where they remained until the late 1950s. For the thirty years before coming to me, they were stored at the California home of another descendant.

Despite this, they were well preserved, many written on high-quality, embossed Crane writing paper, and the handwriting was remarkably clear. Stylistically, the letters, particularly Helen's, were written in a surprisingly contemporary tone. Since most of William's correspondence concerned his business interests, only a handful of his light-hearted letters—to his mother-in-law, his son Willie, and Helen—are included in this volume.

Helen Chapman was a prolific writer. Consequently, a great deal of editing was necessary to reduce the original letters to a manuscript of manageable length. Therefore, this volume should not be considered a published edition of her letters. I have also deleted much material that was either trivial, boring, or irrelevant to the primary story: descriptions of minor ailments, weather, sewing, the storing of discarded clothing, information about Westfield, and similar matters. These deletions are unmarked.

In addition, I have occasionally moved paragraphs and sentences between letters. When I felt that the treatment of a subject would be enhanced by consolidating details from one or more letters, I transferred portions of the letters to the appropriate location. I have noted these instances with the source of the transposed material in footnotes. Some letters were undated. In those cases the letters were inserted into the text at the appropriate place as well as could be determined and were given an approximate date.

In order to give the narrative a sense of continuity, I have often run letters together without repeating the salutation and closing. The start of a new letter, written from the same location as the previous one, is indicated by a date in a standardized form.

Although Chapman's written English was commensurate with her education, she, like most letter writers, made occasional errors in spelling

Helen Chapman as she must have looked during her last visit to Texas in 1878. The 4 x 6-inch photograph was taken about 1877 by Rockwood Photographers, 17 Union Square, New York City. Courtesy of the Stillman House and the Brownsville Historical Association.

and used haphazard punctuation. I have corrected misspellings (except for "Matamoras" and "Monterey"), added punctuation where needed to clarify the text, and introduced paragraphs where there were none in the original manuscripts. The bracketed text and vertical-lined paragraphs are my words.

Finally, I have supplemented the letters and the story they tell with introductory commentary for each chapter and two important appendices. The first appendix replaces the innumerable footnotes that would have been necessary to identify all the military men and other individuals mentioned in the letters.[12] The second contains excerpted newspaper articles about William Chapman, the public figure, and about events mentioned or alluded to in the Chapmans' letters.[13] The frontier town's newspaper captured the flavor of Brownsville in inimitable journalistic style, reporting a combination of business, political, human-interest, and social news. Not everything in the press was to be believed, even in the mid-nineteenth century. But the articles provide a commentary on, and sometimes a contrast with, what Helen was writing to her mother. Each furnishes a view of the news from Brownsville.

12. See Appendix A for biographical information on military personnel and other individuals mentioned in the letters.

13. An asterisk denotes that a newspaper article relevant to the text will be found in Appendix B.

The News
from Brownsville

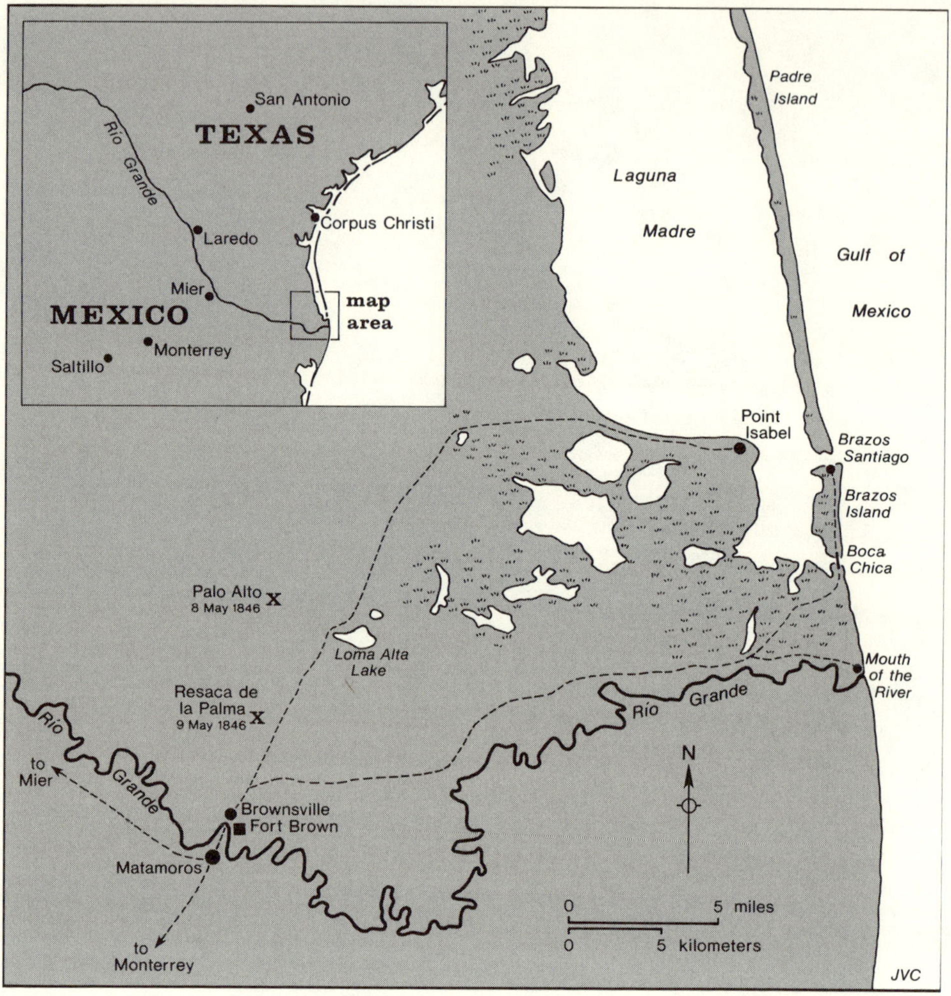
San Antonio
TEXAS
Río Grande
Laredo
Corpus Christi
Mier
MEXICO
map area
Monterrey
Saltillo
Padre Island
Laguna Madre
Gulf of Mexico
Point Isabel
Brazos Santiago
Brazos Island
Boca Chica
Palo Alto
8 May 1846
Loma Alta Lake
Mouth of the River
Resaca de la Palma
9 May 1846
Río Grande
to Mier
Brownsville
Fort Brown
Matamoros
to Monterrey
N
0 5 miles
0 5 kilometers
JVC

1.

REUNION IN MATAMORAS

January through March 1848

Helen Chapman was eager to rejoin her husband William after their twenty-month separation. His letters to her from Mexico had expressed his boredom with military life at the Buena Vista encampment near Saltillo and his loneliness for her. She agreed to meet him when his company returned to Matamoras, writing, "Shall we not be happy, my dear, dear love? You will have your reward, fear not!"[1]

Her daring adventure began on January 2, 1848, when she left New York on the *U.S.S. Massachusetts*, a steam packet equipped with sails. The ship carried clothing for American troops in Mexico along with several other passengers, including the captain's wife (Mrs. David Wood) and their daughter and another military wife (Sarah Chase), who was to meet her husband in New Orleans.

Helen wrote letters and kept a sea journal during the voyage of 17 days. Since the vessel made no port calls, her letters and journal were mailed home to her mother, Emily Blair, after arriving in Matamoras. A postscript requested, "Preserve my letters, they will be my only journal."[2]

My dear Mother, Aboard U.S.S. Massachusetts,

Sunday, January 2, 1848. We left the wharf [in New York] before 11 o'clock a.m. The day was rainy and somewhat dreary. We stood off towards the Jersey shore and though we strained our eyes eagerly for some signal

1. HBC to WWC, Dec. 21, 1847, CC.
2. HBC to EWB, Jan. 23, 1848, CC.

from [Governors] Island, we saw nothing. We watched the beautiful little spot as it receded in the distance, the church one of the last objects visible, and thought fondly of those who perhaps at that moment were inwardly praying for our safety. That little spot [Governor's Island] always seemed like one of the *Isles of the Blest* to me and never more so, than at that moment. I thought too of a more distant house of my fond mother and my darling boy.[3] This having one's husband in one part of the world and one's child in another is a sad thing. We stood leaning over the deck of the vessel for some time, watching the fast receding shores, when I said to Sarah, "This marriage vow means a great deal, does it not, Sarah?"

My home and heart's treasures were far away, and as we entered the [Verrazano] Narrows, I tried to interest myself in the whole scene before me. When we emerged into the ocean, the vastness and sublimity of the scene made individual life appear of less account. I thought less of our chances of danger or safety, and felt more sensibly the protecting care of Providence.

But these thoughts were only momentary. My experience following that time can be told in three words, sick, sick, sick. Oh! how sick—horrible, most horrible. . . .

The voyage, by Chapman's account, differed little from a modern-day pleasure cruise. Her seasickness ended quickly and she was soon lounging on deck, doing needlework, knitting, reading books from the ship's library, "talking a little harmless scandal"[4] with Sarah Chase, dining at the captain's table, and recording the ship's position in her sea journal at noon each day. She had an enjoyable trip, as the following journal entries indicate:

Sun. Jan 9. At anchor in the Bahama Banks. After a very fine dinner of roast turkey, boiled tongue, and plum pudding, Sarah and I examined the library and found a rich supply of books for our entertainment. All the standard British poets, Walter Scott's prose and verse complete. Burke, Hume, the English Drama, Swift, Fielding to Smollett. Spark's Biography and [Twiss's] *Life of Lord Eldon*. I mean to try and read. At this moment,

3. Helen's "darling boy" was seven-year-old William Blair Chapman (Willie), whom she had left in her mother's care.

4. HBC Sea Journal, Jan. 2–19, 1848, CC.

Sarah is reading Madam Calderon de la Barca's work on Mexico.[5] She says, "If Mary Prate gets hold of this book, she certainly never will go to Mexico. It gives such an awful account of scorpions, spiders and other things."

Tues., Jan. 11. My attempts to dress this morning were very ludicrous. First I was knocked against my berth, and then I was thrown upon the only seat of my state-room with no very gentle motions, but I at last succeeded in making a toilette that would pass very tolerably at sea and got on deck as soon as possible. Sarah soon followed and though neither of us felt very well, we went bravely to the breakfast table and after a cup of tea felt much better. We remained on deck some time, I finished *Florence Macarthy*, a very pretty story.[6] So I read a while in *Tremaine* and then we came into the cabin and sewed till dinner time. Sarah worked on her slippers, I on shirts. We had a dinner of roast duck, corned beef, roast pork, bean soup, baked beans, dessert of cranberry tarts, tapioca pudding, apples, nuts and raisins.

Late one night a week after their departure, while near the Bahama Banks, the ship struck an object in the water, broke the shaft of its propeller, and suffered a minor leak. Several days were lost while the crew shifted "the coal forward to lighten the stern." The shift in weight raised the propeller from the water and allowed the crew to remove it. Sails powered the ship for the remainder of the voyage. One afternoon, the women passengers decided to weigh and measure themselves and Helen was officially proclaimed to be five feet and one inch in height with a weight of 102 1/2 pounds. Toward the end of the voyage, the constant pumping and the noise of the carpenters engaged in repairing the leak caused some anxiety among the passengers, but Captain David Wood constantly reassured them that there was no danger.

Jan. 19. morn. Our calm was suddenly interrupted by a Norther.[7] Sarah and Mrs Wood remained up in the cabin trying very hard not to be sick, but feeling very much like it. I had a violent headache and took to my berth.

5. Frances Calderon de la Barca, *Life in Mexico* (New York: Doubleday, 1843).

6. Lady Sydney Owenson Morgan, *Florence Macarthy: An Irish Tale* (London: Longman, Rees, Orme, Brown, and Green, 1835).

7. Northers are the fierce, cold, often rainy storms that approach Texas from the north.

At half past nine o'clock, we anchored off the Brazos, driven in by the Norther. The Brazos at this distance looks like a very small fishing station and Point Isabel another.[8]

Jan. 19th. noon. Waiting for a steam boat to take us on shore and hearing a boat had started, we were soon on deck, watching its approach with no slight eagerness. Sarah first recognized Mr Chapman, and when she discovered beyond doubt that Mr Chase was not on board, she burst into tears. This distressed me much, for I really did not think she had thought it more than barely possible. However, she was very soon consoled by the information that the *Fanny*[9] was starting for New Orleans and had been detained to take her on board.

Mr Chapman quite astonished me. He wore a handsome full dress uniform—very nice linen purchased in New Orleans, his hair and whiskers worn as usual and no change except he wears a closely cut moustache which I think rather an improvement. He is somewhat darker, but otherwise looks as formerly.[10]

With Mr Chapman [was] also Captain Eaton and Major Weld of the 2nd Artillery. Captain Eaton looks precisely as he did in New York. I know not what idea the rest of you formed, but I certainly thought [that Brazos Santiago,] a place where so much business is transacting, must present a somewhat different appearance from the reality I found it to be.[11]

There was quite a heavy sea on the bar, and as the little dingy, impish-looking steamboat brought us near, pitching and tumbling, till at length it seemed to throw us on the sand, I could not conceive a scene more dreary. There is nothing but sand, blown into hillocks here and there, not a blade of grass or the faintest appearance of greenness. There is some shipping though none but very light vessels can approach the shore. A few rough board houses set down at random in the sand, looking much like very common barns as anything else, completes the picture of Brazos Santiago.

Mr Weld, a young officer stationed at the Mouth of the River, is tall and has a long thin face, slender figure and fair complexion. His hair hangs

8. Helen's vantage point was three miles offshore. The shipping channel, El Paso de los Brazos de Santiago, was only eleven feet deep, and large ships, like the *U.S.S. Massachusetts*, were unable to enter. Smaller steamships, called lighters, ferried passengers and cargo ashore. Point Isabel is now Port Isabel.

9. The *Fanny* sailed between Brazos Santiago and New Orleans stopping at other ports on the Gulf of Mexico.

10. HBC to EWB, Jan. 23, 1848, CC.

11. HBC to EWB, Jan. 23, 1848, CC. This text continues until noted.

upon his shoulders, his beard hangs on his breast, and his moustache twisted away partially from his lips, hanging upon his beard. Such is his outward [manner]. At the same time, he is gentlemanly and agreeable and a barber would make him a handsome man. [He] said, when he got completely disgusted, he went down to Brazos and after remaining there a little while went back [to the Mouth of the River] perfectly contented.[12]

I told him most people could find others more unfortunate than themselves, but I did not know where those at this place could go to look. Contemptuously, he replied, "They can go to Camargo. That is decidedly worse."[13]

On touching the shore, we walked through the sand, sometimes sinking to our ankles, till we reached the *Greenwood Saloon* where we were to dine. A high sounding name you will think for a rough tenement, but this is something more. Mr Lemon,[14] the proprietor who I consider to be a real genius, wishing to construct a hotel, and looking about for material conceived the lucky idea of transforming a disabled steamboat just ready to sink, into a land habitation.

Accordingly taking advantage of a Norther, he put on as much steam as possible and by the aid of wind and machinery, she was blown high and dry upon the shore and now sits as firmly in the sand as if she had never wandered over the waters. As in all high pressure boats, I believe the Ladies and Gentlemen's cabins are on the upper deck and you first ascend to the lower deck by stairs where are the kitchens, and store rooms. By another flight of steps you ascend to a sort of reception hall and enter from that the dining hall or gentlemen's cabin and really comparing it with everything around one, the effect is quite imposing.

On each side are the staterooms, now dignifying the name of bed room. Passing through, you enter the ladies' salon on each side of which are sleeping apartments also. There is some good furniture in it and Mr. Cossens of the *American* or Coleman A. Stetane of the *Astor*[15] could scarcely do the honors more gracefully than "mine host" of the Greenwood.

12. HBC Sea Journal, Jan. 2–23, 1848, CC; HBC to EWB, Jan. 23, 1848, CC, continues.

13. Camargo, a city south of the Rio Grande and 170 miles upriver from Matamoras, was a "Yawning grave yard," according to soldiers stationed there. Charles L. Dufour, *The Mexican War: A Compact History, 1846–1848* (New York: Hawthorn Books, 1968), 101.

14. In other correspondence, Lemon is spelled Lehman. Robert S. Leman was a successful merchant in Matamoras who later relocated to Brownsville, and became one of its early mayors.

15. The American and the Astor were the leading hotels in New York at that time.

A lady, in these regions, is still quite a novelty and the room was soon filled with all the officers stationed there. [Sarah] and I parted at the *Greenwood*. She to New Orleans in the *Fanny* that afternoon and I with Mr Chapman and Mr Weld to go to the Mouth of the River.

We rode in an ambulance, a coach and four as they laughingly termed it, drawn by four horses. When they started, it seemed to me they were driving directly into the Gulf, but they went on bravely and I soon got accustomed to the amphibious mode of conveyance. They drive directly through the surf because only there can they find a hard track, everywhere else would require struggling through loose sand.

Our drive through the surf extended to the mouth of the river eight miles away (I am particular about statistics to gratify Father.) We went immediately to Major Anderson's where we received a genuine Tennessee Welcome. The Mouth, as it is called, looks a little better than the Brazos, but not much. The houses are about the same. Major Anderson's house is the best and with a little good furniture carried with them from the United States, such as a Franklin Stove with a wood fire, it had quite a cheerful appearance. The two daughters bear it very well, but though Mrs Anderson makes an effort to be contented, it is evidently almost impossible. When this move was made, she had lived in Memphis twenty-six years scarcely passing beyond its limits during this time.

She is a quiet domestic little woman something like Mrs. Henry King.[16] The Major [is] fat, somewhat indolent, and pretty well contented with any place where he can be lazy, get a good dinner, and smoke cigars. The Andersons had a very nice tea in the Southern fashion, oysters, tongue, griddle cakes, hot biscuits, loaf cake. We slept that night in a room very comfortably furnished but merely with a covering of boards over the rafters. So I doubt not we had about a dozen rats dancing through the room all night. I felt a little fidgety but in all such matters, I am learning to make a grand effort and am determined not "to die a thousand deaths in fearing one."

Jan. 20. We departed early in the morning in the steamboat [*Whiteville*] for our home in Matamoras, 75 miles distant by water. The boats are small, of course, but quite comfortable, of high pressure and go groaning and whistling along in a way that would set everybody screaming on our Northern rivers. Running ashore is such a common occurrence nobody minds it and the boats seem to have a wonderful faculty of working

16. Mrs. King was a mutual friend in Westfield.

themselves off. The crookedness of the Rio Grande cannot be exaggerated. It is extremely muddy, the banks low, and utterly without interest and passing up this stream the question arises: For what are we here? For such a country as this why expend such blood and treasure? But a region quite as unpromising met the eye of the Pilgrims at Plymouth, and this is no way to judge. Therefore, I shall spare you in this letter at least, all crude fancies on political economy and tell you merely what I saw.

The [Rio Grande] is navigable to Reynosa and has been navigated as far as Mier (I was mistaken, boats run daily as far as Mier.) but with great difficulty.[17] As far as Reynosa it is easy and safe, there are no such difficulties as in the Mississippi and running aground, something that must of necessity often happen, is attended with no danger. Captain and Mrs Wood went up with us to see Matamoras.[18] Also Mr Taylor, nephew of General Taylor, and also Richard Ogden who is making a large fortune by trade.[19]

We arrived about dark and found our carriage waiting for us. This is a vehicle very much like the *Granville Stage*.[20] Having three rows of seats side curtained, so as to make it closed from the rain, which can be buttoned down or rolled up at pleasure. It was made in the United States, is on springs, drawn by two excellent horses and is very comfortable.

We drove directly to Mrs Hunter's[21] [in Matamoras] to remain until a fire could be kindled to take off any dampness that might be in the room. The first proposed arrangement had been to live in the same house with Mrs Hunter, but it was built of only one story and brick floors. This, Mr Chapman feared, would be unfavorable to my health and so produced apartments in the house of Donna Warneta (I spell the name as pronounced, the feminine of John), a rich Mexican widow lady.[22]

17. Reynosa is about 128 miles upstream from Brownsville, and Mier 70 miles farther. Both are south of the Rio Grande.

18. Apparently Captain Wood of the *U.S.S. Massachusetts* and his wife did not leave immediately for Vera Cruz, perhaps because of repairs being made to the ship.

19. Richard L. (Dick) Ogden was in business at the Mouth of the Rio Grande.

20. The Granville stage ran between Westfield and Granville, Massachusetts.

21. Maria Hunter came from a prominent Chicago family. Her adventures while traveling with the troops in northern Mexico had received frequent attention in the press (Paul Horgan, *Great River: The Rio Grande in North American History* [New York: Rinehart & Company, 1954], 737–738). Her husband, David A. Hunter, served as army paymaster in Matamoras. He, too, was socially well connected (*National Cyclopaedia of American Biography* [Ann Arbor: University Microfilms, 1967)] IV, 264; Horgan, *Great River*, 737–738). See Appendix A.

22. A reference to Dona Juanita Perello (sometimes spelled Parea). Helen Chapman had no knowledge of Spanish upon her arrival in Matamoras but soon gained proficiency.

Jan. 23. You must not by any means suppose that she desired it, but she is compelled to bear it as the bad fortune of war and really does it with a much better grace I fear, than I should under the same circumstances. The system is now in full operation of making the Mexicans bear the expenses of the war, consequently, no commutation for quarters is paid as formerly by the United States Army.* But to prevent the expenses from falling heavily upon individuals, the rent is paid by the Ayuntamiento or common [city] council of Matamoras so that the tax individuals have to pay is trifling.[23]

We are entitled to three rooms, but wishing to make her as little trouble as possible, Mr Chapman told her he would take only one large bed-room and the use of her drawing room in common with herself. We rather gain by this arrangement because we have the use of her furniture. It is one of the very best houses in the city, fronting the Grand Plaza and is by far the finest house I have ever had the honor to live in. It is of two stories, the ground floor rented for stores. You enter by a wide stone archway, the depth of the building lighted at night by a hanging lamp, into a broad piazza supported by heavy pillars and paved with brick. In this there is a staircase leading to the dwelling apartments and opening on the second story of the piazza also supported by pillars. From this piazza you enter the drawing room or salon, immensely large and very lofty, more so than I have ever seen and larger than any two parlors connected by folding doors that I know.

On the ceiling above, are three circular ornaments where chandeliers are designed to be hung and a great deal of ornamental work covers the walls. At one extremity of the salon is a door leading to my room, of the same height and width, but square, an immense room and as pleasant as I could possibly desire. A corresponding door on the opposite side, leads to her own apartments, two large rooms of the same size as mine. The whole width of the front must be great. She desires that some furniture in our room might remain and so we have a large mahogany bedstead of hers and two of the other articles. Among my comforts is a nice little Franklin stove, but the weather is so warm I have not desired a fire since I have been here and this is what they call "cold weather."

* An asterisk denotes that a newpaper article relevant to the text will be found in Appendix B.

23. The tax to pay for housing U.S. Army personnel and other war costs was, in fact, never collected. It is not clear how Dona Juanita and others were compensated. See *American Flag*, June 21, 1848.

Mr Chapman has made the most romantic arrangement for my comfort sending to New Orleans for a stuffed lazy chair, like mine in the parlor at home, a sewing chair of the same kind without arms, a Secretary's solar lamp and a quantity of things besides. This would seem extravagant but under the circumstances it is not so because [an] Officer's baggage comes free of duties. And two or three have offered to take the articles at the end of the year for the same price he paid in New Orleans. I must not forget to add that among his ample and really lover-like arrangements for my comfort, he has sent to New Orleans for house plants and flower seeds to cultivate on my balcony.

Mr Chapman has just come in and says that the front is at least 100 feet long. My room at least 22 by 22 and more than twenty in height, lighted by three immense windows or rather doors for there are no such windows as we have at home. The lower part of these doors is paneled, leaving the glass part about as large as the common windows. These open from the center out, like folding doors. The thickness of walls forms quite a recess. Outside of this glass door is a wire grating sufficient for protection but not close enough to exclude the prospect. Still outside of this are heavy wooden doors with very heavy iron fastenings.

In the parlors are found windows of the same construction opening on the front and one onto the back piazza. Along the whole length of the front and the end of the building which I occupy is a balcony wide enough for two or three to walk abreast, with an iron railing of handsome construction ornamented with brass. Mine is a corner room and the window opening on the south has no grating. This I keep open and can step any moment onto the balcony. This is a beautiful place to keep flowers. On the back piazza which is very wide you look out on a square paved court, on one side of which are the kitchen servants' apartments &c., a balcony connecting the upper story of this with the main building. There seems to be a dozen servants around the establishment I should think.

The drawing room is richly furnished. At the two extremities of the room, on one side of the doors are card tables of mahogany supporting very large gilt eagles, on one of these tables stand two large vases of French Porcelain filled with artificial flowers and covered with glass receivers, on the other stand similar vases filled with fruit. On the other side of the doors are sofas with a card table in the center. In the corners of the rooms are shelves supporting other vases and ornaments. On the mantel piece are large handsome vases and an ornamental French clock, besides a great many little things. There are four mirrors and four French paintings representing scenes in the history of Ulysses and Penelope. There are a great number of chairs in the parlor. A bookcase stands in one part of the room. With all this, however, it has not the comfortable look of an American parlor.

The Mexican ladies always stay in their bed rooms and how they pass their time is a mystery. They neither read, sew, walk or work and vegetate rather than live. Sunday evening according to the Mexican fashion accompanied by an interpreter, we paid our respects to Donna Warneta and were most kindly received.

She is extremely dark, of genuine copper color and about forty years of age, talks incessantly and is rather graceful. She has the reputation of being a very good woman and was very kind to the Americans, it is said, when kindness was needed.[24] Shortly after she sent me a box containing some choice dried fruit I believe. The box looks so pretty I dislike to open it and shall send it home if I get an opportunity. This morning she sent me a dish of sliced oranges dipped with sugar and cinnamon. They have delicious oranges here and I eat one every morning before breakfast. I never do so without thinking how I wish I could get some to you and the children.

We cross the Plaza (a square about but not quite as large as the Westfield Commons) to our meals and whenever I choose or the weather is unpleasant it is brought to my room. Our table is excellent, too good for me unfortunately. There is a profusion of game, very tender beef but not rich, plenty of vegetables, good tea, butter from the United States, and good bread. The cook is an American but the servants are Mexican. Our waiter glories in the famous name of Santa Anna. He is decidedly handsome and, indeed, these Mexicans have not bad faces. The little children are decidedly pretty.

I am now writing by Dick Ogden's secretary[25] which I can use, till I have my own and in which I have everything necessary for writing. This is one of my pet luxuries.

I have tried as minutely as possible to describe my situation to you and I think you will be gratified. I have everything for my comfort, the kindest and most attentive of husbands, abundance of leisure, and, thus far, good

24. Helen Chapman is possibly referring to the actions taken by the women of Matamoras to save the Texas prisoners of the ill-fated Mier Expedition of December 1842.

25. A secretary was a laptop writing desk.

health. Mr Chapman is so harried I only see him through the day at meals and in the evenings.

How is my darling Willie? Tell my dear boy, there is nothing but hot weather here, no fun sledding and Father would have no time to play with him or go fishing as he did at Governor's Island. He has so much business to do that he works hard from eight in the morning until tea time and often through the evening.[26]

We have two good surgeons, Dr McPhail and Dr Craig. Dr McPhail is an elderly man and is considered one of the very best in the Army.[27]

Jan 26. By yesterday's mail, I sent you a full letter giving an account of my journey and describing my situation.

Major Hunter went down to the Brazos two or three days since, and as Mrs Hunter felt lonely, I have spent much of the time with her. I promised to give you a description of her, but I find it difficult to do so.

She has not such marked characteristics for a heroine as I expected. She is tall, more so than yourself I believe, but more slender. Her dark brown hair is untouched by time, a rather thick, sallow complexion, common grey eyes, rather low retreating forehead. The features generally are rather strongly marked, particularly the chin and mouth. She has good teeth and a rather stiff figure. These are the traits at a first glance.

There is a great deal of character about the lower part of the face, the chin is square and firm and she is undoubtedly a sensible, energetic woman and one whose energy must show itself in some way and from the circumstances of having a private fortune, a handsome salary and no children, she has been wholly relieved from those cares which generally occupy the minds of other women and, thus, her life has passed alternately between frontier life, riding horseback, shooting, and hunting and fashionable life in New Orleans, New York and Philadelphia. Major Hunter is from the Stockton family in New Jersey and has a large circle of fashionable relations. She was from Illinois, married young and immediately translated into that circle. She has evidently been accustomed all her life to good society, but has too much spirit to be exactly a fine lady and might be thought wanting somewhat in repose.

Her hands are rather large and white, unaccustomed to labor entirely, but I was struck at once by the largeness of her wrist whether it proceeded

26. HBC to EWB, Jan. 26, 1848, CC.

27. Actually Craig was the older of the two and died in August 1848. See Appendix A.

from her mode of life or is the natural formation, I cannot tell. She is about 40 years of age and is very agreeable to me. She loves to talk and if people can amuse me, I would rather listen. She loves attention and loves to give advice. In the first I have no desire to rival her and I never hesitate to ask advice where people are capable of giving it.

We ride every afternoon, or rather I do, with Major and Mrs Hunter. Mr Chapman has not the time.[28]

She called for me yesterday afternoon to go to the Captain's office, (That is to say Mr Chapman's) an immense room of a building built by the Alcalde.[29] I cannot pretend to tell you what he has to do, only that he is busy from morning till night and has clerks, agents, and workmen, without number. At the office, he showed me Arista's plate,[30] now in his possession for safe keeping. It consists of one dozen silver dinner plates, two large platters for meat, 1 dozen table and tea spoons, two coffee cups shaped like china, with handles and chocolate cup. Also a large silver drinking cup. This was [the general's] camp equipage marked with his name, and worth about five hundred dollars.

About an hour since, I received a call from Donna Warneta, my hostess. She came accompanied by a French gentleman as interpreter. She was as usual profuse in her offers of service, pressing me to visit her often. Now don't feel, my dear mother, that I shall be poisoned with chocolate or fruits, for these people know that if they should harm either Mrs Hunter or myself, their heads and necks would very soon part company.

Donna J was dressed in a very fine French muslin, blue and brown with loose hanging sleeves, trimmed with lace, the neck of the dress rather low and her neck covered only with a pearl necklace, a diamond ornament being suspended on front. In her ears, she wore large diamond earrings, I should suppose very expensive, and a great many rings on her fingers and lace gloves. Over her shoulders was thrown a black satin shawl embroidered in

28. HBC to EWB, Jan. 23, 1848, CC.

29. An alcalde is the chief governing or judicial official of a Mexican town.

30. In his hasty retreat from the battlefield at Resaca de la Palma, General Mariano Arista had abandoned a set of heavy dinner plates of pure silver. William's duties, in addition to safeguarding the silver, were numerous. He had been appointed to collect all Mexican taxes, a sometimes difficult task (*American Flag*, Dec. 30, 1847, and Jan. 9, 1848.) In January 1848, when responsibility for the local schools shifted to the army, William was put in charge of their supervision (*American Flag*, Jan. 3, 1848). By February, he had put an "efficient" civil police force in place, seen to street cleaning and lighting, and planted trees in the plaza (*American Flag*, Feb. 2, 1848).

colors, in her hand she carried a very expensive French fan and a French embroidered handkerchief of the finest linen trimmed with thread lace nearly half a finger in width. She is from the interior, a woman of consequence, shrewd and sensible, and evidently thinks it good policy to "court the rising sun."

This city is infinitely more quiet at night than Westfield. No sound can be heard save the barking of dogs of which there are great numbers. The police are at present very effective and, indeed, I think [Mexicans] must be a very quiet people. I never hear loud voices, the servants around the house make no noise. The donkey drivers never seem to holler or make any fuss whatever. But it is a cruel sight to see how these poor beasts of burden are bound down by their loads. Sometimes you can see nothing but the heads and legs of the animals. The stores look full of goods but I have not yet been into them.

Jan. 28. Yesterday it rained hard through the afternoon and evening. At the present time the roads are almost impassable in consequence of the rains but Mr Chapman is trying to improve them.[31] * This is very unusual [weather] for the region and the people are predicting very abundant crops. Nearly all kinds of vegetables have started above the ground in the public garden and the green peas are ripe. People are bringing in fresh vegetables to the market. We have had radishes on the table. Yesterday at dinner we had lettuce, fresh cabbage, and carrots.[32]

The great difficulty here is the extreme dryness of the atmosphere and no means of irrigating the soil or indeed of procuring water in any way except by drawing it in barrels from the river. The taste of the water is rather pleasant, I think. The people here draw it in barrels from the river having contrivances in the heads of the barrels for letting in a rope and fastening at each end. In this way, holding in the rope, they roll the barrel over the ground or sometimes pull the rope over their heads and slip it down to the waist thus acting the part of a beast of burden.

The common people such as I see about the streets look better than I expected, the men particularly. There is something very picturesque in the blanket and sombrero. The dress of the women seems to be a chemise, the neck and sleeves fitted into a binding and a shirt of calico very often frilled around the bottom. It is so loose that the breast is very much exposed

31. At this time, martial law existed in Matamoras. Since the city was under the control of the army, the streets fell within the ambit of Chapman's responsibilities as quartermaster.

32. HBC to EWB, Jan. 26, 1848, CC.

and, indeed, some of the servants seem to have nothing over the bosom. They have a way of wearing their rebozos, which completely conceals these deficiencies of costume. It is thrown over the head, one end opened over the breast, the other carried straight across and thrown over the shoulder. The children are very easily dressed in simple tunics. Indeed, every day I see little boys and girls in the house and outside the doors running about just as naked as when they entered this world. [The Mexicans] have, I understand, a great many children.

Jan. 29. After tea this evening we had Colonel William Davenport, [Lieutenant E. E.] McLean, and Mr [Samuel] Belden, an American merchant, to visit us. The Colonel is Governor or Mayor *de jure* of the city, and Mr Chapman, mayor *de facto*. William's passion for planting trees is as great as ever. He is laying out walks on the Plaza and filling it up with ornamental trees.

The people of Matamoras seem very much pleased with the interest he takes in the city. The children have been crowded into close miserable school rooms, but he had other large apartments prepared with comfortable benches and desks and white washed walls and all things comfortable.* He holds a military commission, but his duties are all of a civil nature, paid $180.00 dollars per annum.[33]

There is quite a population of American and foreigners in Matamoras,[34] but no church of any kind except a Roman Catholic and that unfinished and in a miserable condition. I have had a call from the priest a short, fat, good looking man and a gentleman, but it is said a man of no principle. I cannot conceive of a better field for missionary labor. The church can do much to avert the evils of this war by following in the train of the Army, and especially in places that will be permanently occupied by Americans, laboring to bring them to a purer and better life. I notice that stores kept by Americans are open on the Sabbath and, indeed, there is nothing in the life of most Americans here to show that one religion is better than the other.

33. This sum was in addition to William Chapman's regular salary as quartermaster of the Army Depot in Matamoras.

34. Precise population figures for Matamoras at this time are not available. In 1840 there were reported to be 16,372 citizens in Matamoras, but the number had declined to 11,033 by 1850. Antonio N. Cavaleta, "The Twin Cities: A Historical Synthesis of the Socio-economic Interdependence of the Brownsville-Matamoros Border Community," in *Studies in Brownsville History*, ed. Milo Kearney (Brownsville: Pan American University at Brownsville, 1986), 162.

Jan. 31. By the same mail that carries this are [three] letters, one containing instructions to Father from William relating to his father's estate with money to carry out his objects,[35] another containing $500.00 to be spent in such repairs as you shall dictate as one knowing more of household conveniences than men, and a present from William of $500.00 in the form of a Treasury Note to yourself for your care of myself in sickness and your devotion to Willie.[36]

I know it will please you to learn that this is entirely a freewill offering, not given from the remotest suggestion of my own or any complaint of poverty.

As to the house, my dear Mother, you will see that William wishes the work done as well as everything else he undertakes, done well and completely, and would rather send more money than have it done badly.

Love to all and kisses to Willie.

Feb. 6, 1848. We sent you a very large mail last Monday and, since that time, I have not found opportunity to write a line. I study a little Spanish every day. I am beginning to get some insight into the language and hope that after a while I can make myself understood. Dona Juanita [Perello] is very kind and pronounces slowly, syllable by syllable, so that I may catch the sound.

Today she sent me some nice oranges, another Dona somebody, sent some more. My table is loaded with them, but I am unable to touch. I can possibly bear one orange in the morning, but not more.

On board the ship, and on first coming to the Officer's mess in Matamoras, I was obliged to live rather better than I ought, but I am getting back to the old system. Phyllis, our cook, makes very nice brown bread for me, cooks my meat dry, and gives me anything I wish. The mutton of this country is [poor], but roast beef is a standing dish and on this I dine principally. The great difficulty will be want of exercise, but I shall try to take as much as possible and try to fight against the almost irresistible inclination to indolence one feels in this climate.

35. William Chapman was employing his father-in-law, attorney William Blair, as a lawyer to buy the Chapman home in nearby Springfield, Massachusetts from his own father's estate.

36. Happy to be reunited after two years of separation, William Chapman wrote to his in-laws: "Permit me to present you with a five hundred dollar Treasury Note (which I wish you to invest in Westfield Bank Stock) in part payment for your invaluable daughter. Your affectionate son, W. W. Chapman, Captain, U.S. Army" (WWC to William Blair, Jan. 31, 1848, CC).

The secret of the difference in the destinies of the New England and Spanish Colonies may be read in their climate as well as in their religion. If the Puritans had settled in Mexico, they would have lost their Puritanism to a great degree. These poor peons are the most down-trodden looking race I have ever seen.

In the midst of so much that is sorrowful, it is pleasant to know that this war has been the instrument of letting the oppressed go free. By the law of Mexico, the laborer is virtually a slave while in debt to his employer and this, under the old order of things, was the bondage of a life time, but a large number of this class have been employed as teamsters and laborers by the Government at wages of twenty-five dollars per month with a ration and have long since paid off their debts and are now free men. A Frenchman in business here, a Mr Maxan,[37] says the rich would dislike excessively incorporation with the United States but the poorer classes would like it and feel safer under the present rule than formerly. But to those who see what Mexico is, the idea of holding it any other way than as a conquered province under martial law seems to be an absurdity.

They were laughing at the table the other day and some one said that English ought to be taught in the common schools for these are the nurseries of future congressmen. So far as I can ascertain by talking with officers of the Army, they are all agreed in the belief that the annexation of any part of Mexico will be wholly unprofitable and mischievous in every way. They say the agricultural resources of the country are nothing comparatively, and there seems to be an impression that the mines are nearly exhausted. I only mention this as I have heard it without knowing how much reliance can be placed upon it.

Matamoras is getting very much the appearance of an American town. You meet at every turn men from the States with the fresh energetic manner of those who have been born on a soil that yields its fruit only to those who earn it by the sweat of their brow. "Rough and ready" line of stages, "Dry goods & groceries cheap for Cash," an American Omnibus Hotel, and boarding houses, all show you the Yankees have gained a footing they will never lose.

As I heard the story the other day, the City of Matamoras sprang into existence by a sort of Queen Dido trick.[38] It seems for a certain

37. Felix Maxan was a mule contractor for the army.

38. Matamoras, in 1848, was a town of relatively recent origin. Originally known as San Juan

consideration the revenues of Tampico were sold to English Capitalists and when the bargain was completed before any revenue had been paid, the City of Matamoras, not containing a single house, was declared a free port and goods, of course, were entered at this point. This is a specimen of Mexican cunning. I give you the story for what it is worth. Doctor McPhail who told it is somewhat given to romancing and his statements have not quite the authority they would have if coming from Father.[39]

Walking out the other day I saw one of the melancholy results of this unfortunate war. Outside the enclosure of the Catholic burying ground there were at least a hundred graves placed closely side by side with here and there among them a wooden imitation of a grave stone with the name, and age lettered upon it. Two Mexican women stood near and to the question, "Soldendos Americanos?" the answer was "Si, Signora." There they lay the poor American soldiers victims of exposure, climate, and their own passions, more to be pitied perhaps than those who fell on the battlefield.

Thinking of their hours of pain, the absence of all gentle and soothing attention, their yearning for home, their youth, for I saw no age over twenty-one, I turned homeward saddened, and realized more than ever before, that I was a stranger in a strange land. The swarthy faces, the fig-tree putting forth its leaves, the orange, lemon and palm trees had made me less sensible of my situation than the graves of these American soldiers.

How you would pity the regulars and volunteers of the Army if you could see how they live in camp. There are five companies of the Tenth Regiment of Infantry [here] who are encamped a little distance from the city. The ground looks low and unpleasant. The tents, nearly all of them, are protected on one side at least, by a kind of hedge of canes or Palmetto, some of the more provident have completely surrounded their tents with this defense. There is nothing around which is pleasant to the eye and they

de los Esteros, Matamoras was a mere rancho with a chapel in 1765. By the 1790s, it was the small village of Congregacion de Nuestra Senora del Refugio. The village began to prosper and grow in the 1820s. In 1826, the town was incorporated as La Villa de Matamoros, named after Mariano Matamoros, a soldier priest martyred in the Mexican struggle for independence from Spain.

39. Dr. McPhail's version bears a passing resemblance to the truth. Emperor Iturbide allowed Congregacion del Refugio to become a port of entry in January 1823 in hopes of raising money for his financially distressed government. He then proceeded to impose taxes on imports high enough (43 percent cumulatively) to kill off any revenues. See Tom Lea, *The King Ranch* (Boston: Little Brown and Company, 1957), I, 29, n.9.

live month after month in that most fatal of all conditions, indolence of mind and body.

Surely nothing but the grace of God can restrain them under such a trial from intemperance and debauchery.[40] Many a poor mother who prays for the safe return of her boy will see him only as a miserable ruin and many a wife will commence a long sad life of suffering [at the close of this war]. And to see all this desolation, without the shadow of an equivalent reward. In Washington, they may invest war with poetry, but no one can do it here. Expenditures of immense sums of money, the loss of valuable lives and still worse, the wide-spread ruin of promising young men for territory which is not worth possessing are the naked facts that force themselves on the contemplation of men and women who see things as they are.

Feb. 8. The mail arrived last evening and you cannot conceive my joy in receiving your letter. It took a load from my heart to hear that Willie was happy and that you were all well.

You will have seen by the papers that Duncan has got himself into a scrape but from what I hear I do not think it will hurt him.[41] Was there ever such a ridiculous undignified order as that of General Scotts's? There is a report today that General Scott has been recalled but [the officers here] seem scarcely willing to credit it. They are inclined to think that if it is so, with only volunteer Generals in the field, that there will be reverses. By the mail last evening came a letter from Colonel Duncan. He is very bitter towards General Scott, and does not doubt that when an investigation takes place it will be for his advantage. He thinks *El Molino Del Rey* was the hardest fought battle.[42]

An officer in New Orleans [wrote that] the state of feeling had become such he believed General Taylor would be sent to take command. I could

40. Helen Chapman wrote a minister friend in Governor's Island suggesting establishment of a mission in Matamoras. She was concerned that "the circus, theatre, gaming and billiard tables, with bullfights to commence next Sunday, offered dangerous attractions [to American soldiers] where no alternative is provided" (HBC to Rev. John McVickar, Feb. 13, 1848, CC).

41. Colonel James Duncan was a personal friend of the Chapmans and had served under Zachary Taylor until his transfer to Winfield Scott's command before the battle of Buena Vista. Duncan at one point confessed authorship of a portion of the letters published in U.S. newspapers which deemphasized Scott's role in the capture of Mexico City. Scott responded by preferring court-martial charges against Duncan, General William Worth, and General Gideon Pillow, a political confederate of President Polk. In April 1848, after countercharges had been filed against Scott, Polk recalled him.

42. HBC to EWB, Jan. 1, 1848, CC.

not forget what you said about something happening to force General Taylor again before the people.[43]

The attachment to General Taylor's person seems universal, and many who do not give him credit for very great generalship or talent are sure of his unvarying firmness and honesty of purpose. His good sense seems to be undisputed and his conduct is unstained by any of the petty acts that have degraded almost every regular and volunteer general in the service. Mrs Hunter has known him intimately for years, living with his family at Baton Rouge, and has seen him constantly in the campaign. She thinks a residence in the White House would be excessively irksome to himself, and especially to his family. It is curious that military men generally, that is the reflecting and judicious ones, do not wish to see a military man made President.[44]

The last two days the weather has been sunny and pleasant. The officers are busy preparing a garden on grounds belonging to the Hospital. I have two large rose bushes, two orange trees and a variety of things on my balcony. Rose bushes flourish and bloom in the open air the whole year around. There are some very curious species of cactus growing wild in the neighborhood.

[In response to your letter,] do not feel anxious for Mr Chapman's safety. It matters little to most of [the Mexicans] whether the revenue is paid to the United States or to the Mexican Government. I have never felt more secure in my life though living in a Mexican family with my husband absent all day at the office surrounded ever by luxuries with no cares, and no labor. My time passes delightfully and the day seems too short for my occupations.

Remember me most affectionately to all. My health is very good and if we can be all preserved to meet once more in health and safety, I shall be very glad I came.

Feb. 13. During the past week, we have had some things to remind us that we live in an unsettled state of society. I do not know that I mentioned in any of my letters that we had two surgeons, Dr McPhail and Dr Glen, both distinguished in their profession, and both members of our mess. One morning we were shocked by hearing that the night before Dr Glen had been shot by a pistol in a gambling house. It seems the doctor, in a fit of passion, accused a [Texan] of cheating. He made some reply whereupon Dr Glen struck him with his cane. At this the Texan drew his pistol and

43. HBC to EWB, Jan. 1, 1848, CC.
44. HBC to EWB, Jan. 1, 1848, CC.

fired. The ball entered his side and passed round to the back. It was extracted, but there is some concern that it entered the chest and he is by no means out of danger. He has suffered extreme pain and I pray that in his solitude and suffering he may become a wiser and a better man.[45]

A duel was to have taken place day before yesterday between the captain of a steam boat on which we came up the river and another citizen of the United States.[46] There were three seconds on each side and the whole party had collected here in Matamoras for the purpose. Mr Chapman was well acquainted with the challenger. He then tried to bring about an accommodation and had resolved if this failed to induce Colonel Davenport to give an order for their arrest. He was happily successful and the parties have dispersed quietly. It was a load taken from my mind, for to know of such a duel about to take place [makes one feel like they are] a party to the crime. Captain Duffield, the challenger, is a very amicable pleasant man and has a wife and child in the United States.[47] On one of his trips down the river he brought me two hair pins of pure Mexican gold made precisely like the common steel hair pins, except that on the top is a knob about as large as one of the old fashioned gold beads. They are very pretty to fasten a cap with.

By boat the day before yesterday there was an arrival of some officers on their way to Monterey and Mrs Trevitt, the wife of Dr Trevitt, U. S. Army, on her way also to that place. She is a feeble delicate woman, younger than myself and has with her two little boys, one seven years old, the other four. Her husband thinks the climate of Monterey will suit her. She has a manservant and a nurse with her and seems pleased with her journey thus far.

Yesterday, we were out riding, Mrs Hunter, Mrs Trevitt and myself, and seeing a boat coming up the river we went down to the landing. Mr Chapman was already there mounted on Billy, his favorite horse, and prancing around in fine style. The scene altogether was picturesque and I wish I could give you an idea of it.

45. John Glen died the next day. William Chapman presided over the military commission which heard the case against Colonel Harrison W. Goyne in May. Their finding was excusable homicide (*American Flag*, Feb. 16 and May 24, 1848).

46. Duels must have occurred fairly frequently; the report of another appeared in the *American Flag* of Feb. 8, 1848.

47. S. B. Duffield piloted the boat that took the Chapmans from the Mouth of the Rio Grande to Matamoras. In August 1848 he was elected one of the first county commissioners of Cameron County, Texas.

One prominent object [before our eyes] was a laughing, stout-looking Mexican buying some turnovers from a little boy. [The turnovers] were very thin and filled with some kind of meat. These he held up to the light to see if they were filled properly and biting off the edge of one would throw it into the basket and try another. There was something so excessively good humored in his manner that Mrs Hunter and I at the same instant burst into laughter. [Laughter,] fortunately, is alike in all languages and the Mexican, understanding it perfectly, gave a perfectly irresistible grin of good humored mirth showing a magnificent row of teeth. Eating his turnovers and making a dancing sort of gesture, he seemed the very personification of indolent enjoyment and if you could have seen him at that moment, you would think that to him at least, it mattered very little to whom the revenue was paid.

Mr Chapman has in his employ about twenty Mexicans and on extra occasions as many more. If there be any secret feelings of hatred for the Americans, [they are] ably concealed. Going to breakfast this morning, I met a great many going to Mass and both men and women smiled as they passed and I think it must have been because I wore my silk Mantilla over my head like a rebozo.

The Mexican women are I believe the kindest creatures in the world. In 1843, when sixty Texan prisoners were sentenced to be shot, after every other means had failed, a subscription was raised in Matamoras of forty thousand dollars and the list sent on to the City of Mexico as a ransom for these men. The lady from whom Mr Chapman rents his office subscribed $5,000.00 from her own fortune. In the meantime, there was a change of government and the order was countermanded.[48]

Mrs Hunter and I walk about the streets with perfect freedom and naturally excite some attention. Mexican ladies seldom if ever are seen in the streets but the common people always pass us with a smile. The men also are smiling and really I cannot bring myself to have the slightest sensation of fear.

March 13, 1848. The days and weeks fly with a rapidity I never saw equaled. There are constant arrivals and departures from the United States

48. Helen Chapman appears to be referring to the threatened execution in 1843 of prisoners captured after the Mier Expedition. The women's proffered charity is not mentioned in other historical accounts of this incident. See, for example, Joseph D. McCutchan, *Mier Expedition Diary*, ed. Joseph Milton Nance (Austin: University of Texas Press, 1978), and Joseph Milton Nance, *Attack and Counterattack: The Texas-Mexican Frontier, 1842* (Austin, University of Texas Press, 1964).

and the port at the Brazos and they all generally stay a day or more at Matamoras.

A boat full came down[river] last night among whom was a German trader from Santa Fe going on to England to purchase goods on the supposition that the war will not be ended in under six months. He thinks it will be for the interest of the rich states, such as San Luis Potosi, and Zacatecas, that have not yet felt the pressure of the war, to gain time, by the excuse that a quorum cannot be assembled, and delay, in this way, the execution of a treaty until the Whigs come into power, thinking that from their opposition to the war and dislike to the acquisition of territory, they shall obtain more favorable terms. There is no nationality, no sentiment to make one state feel concern for the wrongs of another and on that account he thinks there will be no treaty, until those states are occupied. [In the meantime] things will remain as they are, neither at peace or at war.

If this be true, it will be a sad disappointment for the Army, for the talk is of nothing but the treaty, and speculation of when [we will] get out of a country that no one seems to love. Whatever may be the politics of the officers of the Army, so far as I can judge, they are invariably the most ardent friends of peace, and are unanimously opposed to the acquisition of Mexican territory, though they believe it inevitable, as it most surely is. The deed is already done, and the United States has already taken upon herself a burden as tormenting and as useless as Algiers is to the French. Mexico will have all the future advantages of the war, the Government may suffer, and the present generations may not be improved, but their children, it is probable, will realize its advantages. I wish I could make others feel, as I do, the importance of improving the American population in this country.

This German trader, Mr Speyer, an intelligent man, seems to have an utter detestation of the Mexicans. When some of us spoke of their kindness, he said, "Ah! You are in authority, you have power. Come under their authority and you will see the difference."

Another German gentleman, a Mr Stocknecht, who has been a merchant for twelve years in Durango, and who is now returning to Germany, talks about the people in much the same way as Mr Speyer.[49] [In his view,] the Government is excessively corrupt, [and] a government officer,

49. This is probably a reference to a Mr. Stahlknecht, a German cotton manufacturer from Durango. See Martha A. Sandweiss, Rick Stewart, and Ben W. Huseman, *Eyewitness to War, Prints and Daguerreotypes of the Mexican War, 1846–1848* (Fort Worth: Amon Carter Museum, 1989), 228.

by his dishonesty, can make himself exceedingly rich in the course of two or three years, and it is the universal habit to do so. Mr Stocknecht says there cannot be better soldiers than the Mexicans. Their perfect docility and indifference to life make them perfectly susceptible of discipline, but of their officers, he cannot speak with too much severity and disgust.

Mr Speyer told an anecdote worth repeating. At the time he left Chihuahua, they were making great preparations for the reception of the American troops, casting cannon and making shells. A German was employed in casting the cannon, and one day, being a "little glorious," he said to General Treas (the Mexican Governor), "General don't you think we had better put U.S. on these at once?"

The General pretended not to hear.

We may mourn over the evils of excessive civilization, but there can be little comfort in this animal sort of existence [led by Mexican peons]. As I have told you, even through the winter, the dress of the women is only a chemise and a petticoat with a rebozo when needed. Mrs Hunter tells me the chemise of the common people is only about half a yard in length, just long enough to tuck under the petticoat bindings. With such a dress, leaving the chest and bosom entirely bare, they wash their clothes by the river bank, or in ponds of water, by throwing them and squeezing them against a smooth board. They use a quantity of soap, and never boil them at all, merely washing and rinsing in the cold water of the river. Every day I see women in groups of ten or fifteen washing in this way. The children will be running around on the bank, many of them completely naked.

If we could believe them happy and really hardened to such exposure, the sight would be more tolerable, but such I fear this is not the case. I have been told by many who have lived here a long while, and who have also lived among Indians in the United States, that the mortality is very great among these people from a kind of galloping consumption. Dona Juanita, the lady with whom I live, tells me the same thing.

Mar. 14. I have just made a very simple dinner and am alone in my room. The day is such as you have at home in May or June and for a moment I [thought of] you in the old dining room with the south door open and wished I could be with you and feel the kisses of my darling boy. But when I get into such a feeling, I immediately employ myself about something and direct my mind entirely.

We have breakfast at eight and after that Mrs Hunter and myself take a walk. On my return, I study Spanish or write until dinner time, one o'clock, except when interrupted by company. After dinner, I sew awhile or read newspapers until 4 o'clock when we ride until tea time. In the evening, we always have company. Thus passes my time and I never knew it to go so rapidly.

The more I know of Mrs Hunter, the better I like her. She is rather dictatorial, and fond of power, but wholly free from littleness, that most tormenting of all faults to me. Two persons could not agree better and her conversation is very entertaining. She has lived among Indians and extreme fashionables in great style and in log houses and tents. She has strong sound sense, quick sympathies, perfect health, and is altogether a character.

She is a great favorite of General Taylor's and is just such a person as General Taylor likes. His prevailing characteristic, as well as hers, is sound political common sense. A great deal that enters into your life and mine would be Greek and foolishness to them. Whether they or we are the fortunate ones, I shall not pretend to decide. Certainly for all the wealth of the world, I would not lose that class of feelings that peoples my house of solitude with a thousand forms of beauty and brings the spiritual world into such intimate communion with them that the small trials of our pilgrimage have no power to vex me.

Mrs Hunter's super abundant energy amuses me. As it is, she has really nothing to do, but form plans for her brothers and sister's families, and take care of the Major. In him, there is a large development of the ideal, the moral qualities and the affections. He has the feminine, she the masculine qualities and she controls, not always very delicately too, I fancy. However, his chains hang very lightly, for she never annoys him with trifles, adapts herself perfectly to every situation, never frets at inconvenience, makes him perfectly comfortable, entertains company handsomely, and makes a delightful home for him.

She has told me a great deal about General Taylor, how he lives at Baton Rouge and his wife's habits. The furniture of their house is extremely plain and old fashioned, not she thinks from economy, but from perfect indifference to such matters, and frugal habits when young. For instance, the General and his wife were brought up on farms in Kentucky where sperm candles were almost unknown and at this day if you go into the house in the evening and Mrs Taylor happens to be alone, you will find her with a plain calico or gingham dress with an apron of similar material perhaps and knitting by a tallow candle placed in a tin candlestick while sperm candles stand in silver candlesticks ready for lighting. Some people laugh at this scene. Some call it [penurious], but to me it all has meshed rather pleasantly with their republican plainness and general worth.

Mrs [Ann] Wood,[50] the [Taylor's] oldest daughter, is very much like them, but Dick and Betty, the younger children, have been brought up under different systems and the young lady threatens very seriously to revolutionize the establishment. She is said to be very lovely, perfectly unassuming in her manners and seemingly unconscious that she is the daughter of a very rich and distinguished man. Nothing would please her father more than the union of herself and Major Bliss who is a man after the Major General's own heart, prudent with no meanness, sensible, correct, a scholar, devoted to his mother to whom he sends regularly $500 a year, but unfortunately not skilled in pleasing the ladies and not acceptable to Miss Betty whom he loves with the constancy and truth belonging to his nature.

She seems to have very many suitors, but from what I can learn Dick Garnett bids fair to be the happy man. His name almost describes him, for the Dicks are all of one stamp, irresistible to everybody, but General Taylor who regards him with no degree of patience. He is a lieutenant without property, with a good deal of talent, but not applied to any thing in particular, handsome, fond of dress, graceful, lazy, possessing all the dangerous qualities in which poor Major Bliss is deficient.[51]

The General's hopeful son [Richard Taylor] does not by any means satisfy him. He has been supplied lavishly with money, land and his education is completed, and he does not seem inclined to work. His father is exceedingly provoked. He seems to have no bad habits, but is lazy and knows there is no need of labor. This is the great reason for procuring a leave of absence and I believe he has purchased a plantation and established him upon it.[52]

50. Ann Mackall Taylor had married army physician Robert Crooke Wood. The Woods had been neighbors of the Chapmans at Fort Niagara in Buffalo, New York, in the early 1840s.

51. Major Bliss finally won the hand of the fair Miss Betty, Mary Elizabeth Taylor. She served as mistress of the White House during her father's tenure and was known for her intelligence, beauty, and grace. After William Bliss died of yellow fever in 1853, she married Philip Pendleton Dandridge (Zachary Taylor, *Letters of Zachary Taylor from the Battlefields of the Mexican War* [1908; reprint, New York: Kraus Reprint Co., 1970], x–xi).

52. Despite his father's doubts, Richard Taylor achieved success as a soldier in later life. Illness forced him to leave the Rio Grande Valley, and he ran a Mississippi cotton plantation until 1849. He attained the rank of lieutenant general in the Confederate Army in 1864 (ibid., xiii).

The whole merit of the style of the dispatches [Taylor's], belongs without doubt to Major Bliss. A rough sketch would be supplied by General Taylor and wholly remodeled by the Major. The letter [of condolences] to Henry Clay [whose son, Henry Clay, Jr., had died at the battle of Buena Vista] was written by Major Bliss. This I know, because he himself acknowledged it to Mrs Hunter. Mrs Hunter says the General has not a clear condensed style, but on the contrary takes ten times as many words as the Major to convey his meaning. Do not tell of this. Those in whose judgment I have great confidence think General Taylor would make an excellent president and I would do nothing to spoil his chances.

Mar. 18. I am at the office, and, having a half hour to spend before dinner, I cannot spend it any better than in writing to you.

[Wednesday] I went in company with several others to the battle grounds of *Palo Alto* and *Resaca de la Palma*. We started early in the morning, and carried refreshment with us. Captain Webb and Major Scott, U.S. Army, heard of our visit, and rode up from Point Isabel to meet us at *Resaca*, and thus we had the advantage of having the ground pointed out by one of the heros of these fields.[53]

Palo Alto, twelve miles distant from Matamoras, is an extensive level plain stretching as far as the eye can reach and unbroken by tree or shrub. It is said to be one of the finest battle grounds in the world, and looks as if it might be a fine theater for trials of skill. There could be no chance of dodging, no advantage of ground to either party. Almost every trace of the battle had been removed. Only occasionally you see the bleaching bones of horses on the grass, and probably some of men, but I rode on and [did] not enquire. The Mexican lines are still distinguishable by the broken appearance of the grass. I could imagine that men might meet in deadly contest in this field, but on returning to Resaca, I could scarcely bring myself to believe it has ever been stained with blood.

Without exception, it is one of the loveliest spots I ever saw and probably never looked better than at this moment. The season has been unusually rainy, and the verdure of the country at this time answers to [the greenery of Massachusetts] in June. Later it will have the parched dull look of July and August in the North. I say lovely because that is the only term to express the character of the scenery. The ground is broken into gentle

53. John Benjamin Scott was breveted major for his valor in these two battles. See Appendix A.

slopes, dimples, and glades, all of the softest character and covered with luxuriant green.

The chaparral is very beautiful, larger than what we should call shrubbery and yet not large enough to be called a wood or forest. I had an impression the ground was covered entirely with this low sort of underwood and that it was all of the same kind. But it is not so. You see long green glades covered with soft green grass, as smooth as a carpet and bordered by these woody shrubs, some almost rising into the dignity of trees, and containing most beautiful varieties of green. The acacia of a most beautiful yellow [bark] is green with graceful drooping foliage and the ebony is as dark and rich in color as our Northern Cedar and Hemlock.

In all these sunny little glades, in the rich verdure of the southern spring, and in the unclouded blue of a tropical climate, you have the far famed battle ground of Resaca [de la Palma]. The scene was so soft, so tranquil, that I could think of nothing but children at play, villagers dancing on the grass, anything but the mournful reality.

One of the long beautiful green vistas, with the broad shadows of the afternoon sun resting upon it was pointed out by Major Scott as the scene of the deadliest fighting. As we rode down to the spot, all along in relief against the green grass, were the blackened bones of horses and men, fragments of shoes, of woolen cloth, of harness, of capes, fertile proofs of a deadly encounter. They were mostly Mexicans who fell in that line and there they remained unburied, some were buried by our soldiers and some remained where they fell.

Major Scott served throughout the action with Colonel C. F. Smith and had much to say of his coolness and bravery. He repeatedly, during the hottest of the action, took out his watch and afterwards told the precise moment of time in which the important events of the battle took place.

Further on, returning, we came to a very beautiful spot, a large green open space which was the camping ground of General Arista where all his baggage and the booty was found. On the opposite side of the road are two large circular places where the turf has been turned up, and there lie the bodies of those who fell upon the field. Two large pits were dug and into these were thrown Americans and Mexicans. On the camping ground of Arista, are three or four graves, two of Sergeants and two, I believe, of Officers whose bodies have since been removed.

All along on the edge of the road, the day of the battle, fires were made and Mexicans employed in cooking for the feast, that should follow the victory. At one spot, Major Scott said, "We were dashing in full pursuit, when at this place, we saw Colonel Macintosh badly wounded in the cheek by a bayonet and scarcely able to articulate, 'Do you know where a surgeon is?'"

In the stern necessity of the moment, they could only say, "We hope you are not badly wounded, Colonel, the surgeon is at the rear." and pass on. His time, poor man, had not yet come.[54]

Fort Brown is considered a very good field fortification. I cannot pretend to describe it, and if I could, you could not understand it. Mr Totten is in command and we go over there often. Major Brown's[55] remains have never been removed from the premises and there is not even a head stone. If you could see the Fort, you would appreciate more highly than ever the bravery of the *Great Western*.[56]

54. According to one report, Colonel James Simmons McIntosh was bayoneted to the ground and was unable to move when finally rescued. He survived his wounds only to be killed in the battle of El Molino del Rey on September 7, 1847 (Dufour, *Mexican War*, 82, 264).

55. Major Jacob Brown, commander of Fort Texas, died during the siege of the fort on May 9, 1846. The fort was renamed Fort Brown in his honor. See Appendix A.

56. The Great Western was Sarah Borginnis, an Irish laundress, who achieved national acclaim for her services at Fort Brown. See Appendix A.

2.

THE PROSPECT OF PEACE

April and May 1848

Only the news of the most recent French Revolution, announced in the *American Flag* on April 3, 1848, could have taken precedence over rumors of a peace treaty ending the Mexican War. Yet developments in France lacked the immediacy of whisperings on the north bank of the Rio Grande. While Helen Chapman reported on the fine prospects for a city there, William selected the site for a new fort.

Helen continued to acclimate herself to her new surroundings. She learned more of the local customs, particularly the treatment accorded the dead and the expectations of the Roman Catholic clergy, studied Spanish, and socialized.

My dear Mother, Matamoras, Mexico

April 6, 1848. There is so much going on here and so much company that I am constantly employed and the weeks fly more rapidly than ever before. Of course, we can talk or think of little else here but the treaty[1] and the French Revolution.[2] It makes me shudder to think what may follow. Those who know best most dread to see the flame [of revolution] kindling.

In case of a war with England or any European power, Captain Sibley says it would be decidedly injurious because volunteers cannot meet the

1. The Treaty of Guadalupe Hidalgo, ending the Mexican War, was ratified by the U.S. Senate on March 10, 1848, but Mexico did not ratify the treaty until May 25, 1848, and Washington did not learn of the Mexican decision until June 9, 1848.

2. Louis Phillipe, king of France from 1830 to 1848, abdicated the throne because of widespread rioting. Louis Napoleon, also known as Napoleon III, was elected to the French presidency in December 1848 and led France until 1870.

veteran troops of the old world. He was stationed at Saltillo during the Battle of Buena Vista and saw the retreating troops. There were others who ran away besides the Indians and he, with others, is firmly in the belief that with a more determined and disciplined foe, the volunteers could not be trusted, whereas this war has created an idea that they are invincible.

There are strong hopes of peace with Mexico. Officers coming from General Wool's headquarters report that the Mexicans feel confident peace will be declared directly after the reception of the treaty. The Armistice went into effect about a week since, but everything goes on in the Americanized mode.[3] The schools are not disturbed. The streets are regularly lighted, the Plaza kept in order and all things quiet.

The collection of Internal Revenue is, of course, greatly diminished, collections only being taken on gold, silver and houses of amusements.[4] All the other revenue goes into the hands of the Mexicans and, instead of being expended for the public good, will probably swell the private wealth of a few individuals. The Armistice is generally regarded unfavorably by the officers on this line and is considered an unwise measure.

People who have lived here many years say that the inhabitants of this district were never so well off before. Mr Maxan, a mule contractor for the Government, who has just returned from a trip into [Mexico], says that large numbers of the rancheros are preparing to move onto the other side of the river as soon as the treaty goes into effect.

Returning from dinner a few minutes since, I stopped in the store below and had a conversation with a gentleman who has been in this country since the commencement of the war. He says he was at a tin shop and a man came in to order some articles manufactured. The master of the shop said that if he promised the things he should have to do all the work himself for he paid off his workmen (Mexicans) the day before, and he should see nothing of them again until that money was expended.

I went yesterday to the funeral of an infant. The open coffin was carried along at a rapid rate by two men, a little boy carrying the coffin lid. About half a dozen persons and a number of boys seemed to be of the company hurrying along without any order, accompanied by a fiddler who played a lively air, and a man who at every few steps threw up a sky rocket. On arriving at the church, the coffin (which by the way was covered with pink,

3. The armistice, entitled "Military Convention, for the provisional suspension of hostilities," was to remain in force during the period fixed by the Treaty of Guadalupe Hidalgo.

4. This was according to the terms of the armistice.

glazed cambric with a cross in white clothes nailed upon it) was set down on the ground in front of the door of the Sacristy.

The priest who looked completely brutified by excesses, and who was openly intoxicated, who lives with a woman publicly by whom he has five children, performed with the aid of an assistant such funeral services which consisted of a whining kind of chant and sprinkling the unconscious little tenant of the coffin with holy water.[5] The child was of the poorer class but was arrayed in all the finery its friends could procure. Shoes, a wooden moon or something like it in its little hands and a velvet cap on its head. After the sprinkling was accomplished, [the pall bearers] again took up the coffin and proceeded to the grave, still fiddling and shooting off the sky rockets. Here in Mexico, there is a curious blending of the ceremonies of the Roman Catholic Church with the Indian customs of the natives.

The sentiment is universal here that the death of a little child is a proper occasion for rejoicing and the sky rockets are considered typical of the ascent of the spirit to heaven. Mrs Hunter told me that the idea of the Mexicans in using music and sky rockets at the funeral of a child is to amuse the little traveler in his flight from Earth to Heaven. An American lady living at Reynosa who lost a little child in this country for whom she grieved excessively, was told by some Mexicans that her little boy was very happy in Heaven and that if she mourned for it God would be angry.

When the Armistice went into effect, the Captain [Chapman] was compelled to discharge some of his laborers and [the Mexican who drives our carriage] was among the number. The day after Major Hunter met him and asked him if he was going to bring the carriage around, he replied that he did not work for the Captain anymore and the tears came into the poor man's eyes. I pleaded to have him restored, I felt so sorry for him, and he now looks as happy as possible. What would you think to see Mrs Hunter and myself driving out alone with a Mexican driver. It does not often happen for generally there are gentlemen to go with us. We certainly lead a very easy pleasant life and I am thankful for so many rich mercies.

The Captain has hunted up all the soldiers' children and has got an English school together of twenty-five children.[6] How I wish I had some

5. Helen Chapman shares her characterization of the Roman Catholic clergy with other army wives and officers. See, for example, the writings of Theresa Griffin Vielé and Jane McManus Storms Cazneau.

6. On March 15, 1848, William Chapman ran an ad in the *American Flag* seeking a young man to take charge of an English school for boys. The same ad announced that a young lady had been engaged to teach the English school for girls.

books for them. I made a great mistake in not bringing some with me. Very few books seem to find their way here, except for the most miserable trash of the yellow covered literature, *Dancing Feather*, and such as that.

For myself, I do not feel the want of reading for my time is fully occupied without. At present, we have quite a large and pleasant society here. A few evenings since, I had a little party consisting of Mrs Hunter and twelve or fourteen gentlemen.

Captain Casey is now here waiting for a good opportunity to go to Florida. He is a fine man intelligent, agreeable, but in a hopeless decline. He is perfectly sensible of his situation and says with the greatest care, he cannot hope to keep above the ground more than a year longer. Captain Sibley, who came to relieve Mr Chapman not knowing of the countermanding order of the Quartermaster General,* is one of the finest men in the Army, a religious man and a perfect gentleman.

We have had until now Mr Churchill, the son of Colonel Churchill, Inspector General. He has just received an appointment in the Artillery, and seems to have no bad habits. His brother died at Point Isabel in all the horrors of delirium tremens. Mr Webster of the Engineers is also here, a cultivated intellectual man, and altogether the society is very pleasant. Here in a strange land, we all feel as if we belonged to one great family and associate together upon the same footing. All these gentlemen and others I have not mentioned are regular visitors either at our house or Mrs Hunter's.

When I have company in my grand Mexican parlor, with my solar lamp, silver candle sticks, cake baskets, cut glass and silver forks from New Orleans, I make quite a grand appearance and I know no one who enjoys these comforts of civilized life more than Mr Chapman.

Giving so much attention to Spanish, reading everyday from four o'clock to tea time and company every evening, you may imagine I cannot spare much time for sewing even if I had the strength. I prepare work and do those parts that I cannot get [someone else to do]. The rest [of the sewing] I give to Mrs Williams, a soldier's wife, whom it really seems a charity to employ.

She is from the northern part of the State of New York, has two children and came with the Army to Corpus Christi [in 1846]. Her husband was ordered with General Scott's command to the City of Mexico and she was left behind to support her children and herself as she best could.

On the whole living is expensive here for those who cannot procure stores from New Orleans. She has a room and her wood is furnished her by the Quarter Master. Everything else she has to procure by her daily labor and in the confusion of baggage in moving from Corpus Christi, she lost all her clothing. She is very handy and with her assistance I can get some wrappers made very easily. Yesterday she was here helping me make a lounge or, more properly, a sofa and William is so delighted with it he means to take the dimensions and send to you that you may get one [made] like it. It is for my bedroom and covered with turkey red like the parlor curtains.

Yesterday, Mrs Williams took a few mouthfuls of her dinner and then said if I had no objections, she should like to take it home to her children. The poor woman has seen much hardship in this war, but others have suffered infinitely more. She with many others listened with feelings better conceived than described to the firing at Palo Alto whither her husband had gone leaving her behind at Point Isabel. The next morning she was sitting up in her bed kissing her baby, when she heard the firing recommence at Resaca de la Palma.

Four women went on with the Army and were in the wagons during the battle. One of them whose husband was killed in the last battle sought out his body on the field, prepared it for the grave as decently as possible and watched by it through the night, her little boy sitting by her side. No entreaties could induce her to leave and there she remained until morning. She was pregnant and at the birth of her child, Mrs Williams says the child's face was of a dark purple color which the Doctor ascribed to her terror on that dreadful night. She has since married the hospital steward in Matamoras and the unusual color on the child's face has gradually disappeared.

A great number of women who have followed the Army have been left in utter destitution. Seventeen children were buried in one week at Point Isabel, one of whom was a little child of this Mrs Williams.

Mrs Williams tells me that the finery used in the decoration of the corpse is removed when the body is consigned to the earth, and that it is common to keep such articles and lend them about among each other for this purpose. She lives in the house of a Mexican woman and sees a great deal of their customs. So far as she knows them, she thinks them kind and honest though they are notorious it is said for their thieving propensities. They are more inclined to steal from each other probably than from Americans.

Tomorrow we are proposing to go down by land to Brazos [Santiago]. As soon as a treaty is signed, Matamoras will be in a measure deserted and a large city will spring up on the Texas side. Fort Brown is a healthy place and with good permanent quarters it might be made a delightful and beautiful station.

There are one or two deserted haciendas [on our route] where any quantity of pomegranates, lemons, oranges, citrus, figs and oleanders may be obtained. The mesquite and acacia of the chaparral are very beautiful and with artificial watering, things grow very rapidly. The [pomegranate] blossoms resemble wax and are very brilliant.

What would you think of a large magnificent oleander shading with its rich green leaves and beautiful flowers the most wretched looking thatched hut your imagination can conceive? Near it a fig tree extends its thick shade, the pomegranate with its beautiful scarlet blossoms, and the rich green of the orange and lemon trees form an assemblage of shelter such as the rich man in the cold north with all his wealth cannot procure.

Picture to yourself these profuse decorations around the hut of the Mexican and place under their foliage, squatted on the turfless ground, six or eight swarthy-looking creatures with wild tangled hair, the women nearly naked to their waist, the men equally so and five or six children running about with a kind of chemise to wear around the house or in a complete state of nudity. Some of them who make a little pretension to style will have a great quantity of chairs but still cannot resist the inclination to squat Indian-like on the ground. Such habits are undoubtedly injurious as much as we may talk of a state of nature and, [of course,] when they once get access to the brandy and tobacco of the white man, their fate is easily foretold. Captain Sibley says the impression created by this was in the minds of people at home.

We had a paper of late date from New Orleans last evening. General Scott's case excites great sympathy and though all acknowledge his weaknesses, yet all seem to think he has been shamefully treated by the Government. General Pillow will find that his petty little attorney tricks for notoriety are out of place with Army men.[7]

In Matamoras, (I do not mean in camp) the officers are all very temperate and regular. Indeed, they are so much with Mrs Hunter and myself, they cannot be in very much trouble. Ladies with all their faults, do certainly exercise a most favorable influence over men in softening their natures, preserving their gentlemanly habits and checking their excesses.

7. This is another reference to the dispute between Scott and Pillow, Worth, and Duncan.

Every evening, when I see the gentlemen carefully dust their feet, and talking rationally and acting like gentlemen, I feel that there is some good accomplished by being here. Major Hunter says if he were commanding general, he would encourage as many ladies to come into the country as possible.

I have had a little inclination to Asthma occasionally. Dr McPhail who has travelled in Europe and has had long experience says my disorder is due to spinal initiative resulting from sympathy with the womb and does not believe either lobe of my lungs is diseased.

Dona Juanita continues very kind, and keeps a large stick of wood covered in the night in case I should be sick and need hot water. I was told yesterday that General Cushing who speaks the Spanish language perfectly thinks her to be one of the most superior women he ever met. Her health is very delicate now. She is a great sufferer from nervous headache and dyspepsia. It is not strange, she exercises so little.

April 30. The *Telegraph*[8] has just arrived and again there is no letter from you. Mr Chapman says, "Tell Mother that if she will put a slip of paper into an envelope every Sunday containing the words, "All is well," I will credit her two dollars." These words only no more and no less and then as many letters as you choose. That two dollars he says can keep you a servant.

I sent you the communication sent to Dr McVickar. He has published a part of my private letter to him and signed my initials. For this I am sorry, I would have chosen some other paper than *The Churchman*, but I wanted his zeal and energy in the work.

May 5, 1848. I have decided to remain [in Matamoras] for the present. I do not think the heat here so trying as in New England during the hot months. There is a strong breeze from the sea, and neither Dr McPhail or Dr Jarvis (who is also stationed here) think it unhealthy. With my careful habits, and the presence of two of the best physicians in the country, I do not feel I am running into danger by remaining. Indeed, I could not reconcile it in my conscience to go away. We are so pleasantly situated and Mr Chapman enjoys so much the comforts of a home, that it would be cruel to leave him. I have the same decided conviction as to my own line of duty that I had when I decided to come here.

Colonel Paine of the North Carolina Regiment,[9] who passed down a

8. The *Telegraph* was one of the ships that visited the Gulf ports on a regular basis.

9. Robert Treat Paine's regiment had mutinied in August 1847 because of his inhumanly

few days since on his way home, says he thinks the sickness among the troops is owing to a change of habits rather than to change of climate and that if an Army were raised and kept in the United States, the mortality would be the same.

We were invited the night before last to Mrs Harmond's, the wife of an American merchant, a very fashionable and lady-like woman. It was only a small party made up of Officers and American residents.

Last evening Mrs Devine, an old American resident here who lives in great style, had a little party at which Mexicans and Americans were even invited. The aristocracy of Matamoras was assembled there and really they make a very good show. There is no difference of costume with the gentlemen dressed precisely as ours and the ladies, also the Senoritas, all carry very beautiful fans, some worth fifty dollars and more, and wear very costly jewelry. Some of them had invited me and I was introduced to others.

Their manners are graceful and exceedingly kind. Their mode of salutation is to throw one arm about the neck, not exactly pressing it, but going through the form. The sons of these best families are educated at Roman Catholic colleges in the United States and the daughters here in Matamoras go to Miss Bacon's school.[10] I should judge by the number of the children attending the common schools that it is very general to send them, and, in view of all things, I think the next generation must be wiser than their fathers.

When I arrived I was surprised to see Mr Chapman so handsomely dressed, knowing he had sent for no clothes from New York. It seems he gave a Mexican tailor a coat and pantaloons made in New York, to look at as a pattern, and with this only as a guide, he really succeeded in making a suit that could scarcely be told from the model.

An enormous Mexican woman asked me for the pattern of my dress. How she ever expects to fit it to her huge form, I do not understand. I was very glad, however, to give it. If they begin by imitating our vanities, they may end by copying something better. The Mexicans have a peculiar aptness for many kinds of labor. Their needle work is exquisite and they

harsh discipline. See William S. Hoffman, *North Carolina in the Mexican War, 1846–1848* (Raleigh: State Department of Archives and History, 1959), 20–21, 30; George Winston Smith and Charles Judah, *Chronicles of the Gringos* (Albuquerque: University of New Mexico Press, 1968), 424–431; Sandweiss, Stewart, and Huseman, *Eyewitness to War,* 59, 215–217.

10. Miss Bacon, from "the British Province of Upper Canada," had been operating a girls' school for some time (*American Flag*, May 15, 1848).

are capital imitators. They would make excellent workers in factories and are very docile and teachable. Poor creatures! They have taken a hold on my sympathies such as I feel they can never lose, and if my tongue or my pen can do any good when I return home, I shall aid them freely. I can never regard missionary operations with the indifference I have heretofore manifested. We may talk of increases of crime and increases of misery in a high state of civilization, but no evils can be comparable to those of ignorance and superstition.

The Mexican mother [suffers] the curse of our first mother. Her labor is all hard, washing in cold water by ponds so insufficiently clad, breaking up corn by hand, all make her burden hard. The whooping cough is among the children here and I am thankful I have it no longer to dread. The little orphans here in the house have it very badly. I never in my life have heard such whooping. One of them is worn almost to a skeleton. Many children of the poor suffer terribly in this complaint and undoubtedly may die. I am very often called to the window by the noise of the fiddle and skyrockets and find the same procession I have before described.

I had another visit from the priest of Matamoras. He is a gentleman in his manners, but a most disgusting flatterer. He is so notoriously bad, I have scarcely command enough of myself to be polite. I have taken a good deal of pain to ascertain the real character of the clergy in this line and from a variety of testimony, it seems to be evident that there has been only one good priest and he has lately died, the Curate of Monterey. All unite in representing him as a really good and consistent man, but the priest of Saltillo goes regularly from Mass on Sunday to the cockfight, and his place there is as conspicuous as it is at the altar. The successor of the old Curate at Monterey is said strongly to resemble his brother priest from Saltillo.

In Mexico, I suspect Roman Catholicism is seen in its worst form, loaded with ceremonies and unleavened by any mingling of Protestant faith and practice as in many other countries.[11] Such is not the character of the Roman Catholic clergy in the United States, and by the standards of their own church, such conduct is severely condemned.

I went into the church on Good Friday, the great fast day of the church. The image of the Savior was laid out in state covered with finery and display and surrounded by candles. In front of this was placed an image of the Virgin Mary dressed in deep mourning with the hands clasped as if in

11. Helen Chapman's New England background gave her a very limited exposure to Roman Catholicism, particularly as practiced in Latin America.

prayer. All round the room were kneeling men and women apparently in silent devotion. I bought one of the printed forms of indulgences issued to the people on that day and when I have time I will translate it and sent it home.

Love and kisses to my darling boy and Helen.[12] Oh! how I long to see him. May God watch over and protect him.

May 7. I have just been reading an extract from an English work entitled *Adventures in Mexico and the Rocky Mountains.*[13] It is amazingly written and perhaps as true as any book. Indeed, one loses all confidence in history to find what lies have been written about this war. The misrepresentation of facts and the false representations of character are received and circulated as truths to those who must depend wholly on testimony for their knowledge. One man gets the reputation of a "Bayard"[14] of whom the last thing that should be said of him is "sans reproache." Another gets from his flatness the reputation of wisdom in governing states and cities [of being] as wise as [the] leading polemicist when in fact he is narrow minded and wholly deficient in political sagacity.

Colonel Twiggs, who is appreciated as a model, is one such man who is one of the worst of men, though possibly a good fighter. One officer said he seemed to have a malicious kind of pleasure in wining young men and a most terrible responsibility was resting on him for the evil he had always caused. So much for the truth of contemporaneous history. I believe it is a solemn responsibility for anyone, however humble may be his sphere, to tell the exact truth and I have endeavored to do so in whatever I have written, but in matters of opinion, so many circumstances bias our judgments, it is perhaps impossible to give the exact truth.

I have said that Matamoras appeared to be orderly and well governed, but others say that there are robberies and disturbances of serious kinds in the outer parts of the city all owing to the insufficiency of the Commandant. I have written of things as they appear to me and others do the same. One would almost believe in the Theory of Ideas, seeing how differently the same object is seen by different minds.

12. Helen Pelletreau, a cousin from Southhampton, New York, was residing with the Blairs in Westfield while attending the Westfield Academy.

13. George Frederick Augustus Ruxton, *Adventures in Mexico and the Rocky Mountains* (New York: Harper and Brothers, 1848).

14. The original "Bayard" was Pierre Terrail de Bayard (1473–1524), a French soldier noted for his impetuous bravery, a Chevalier (or knight) *sans peur et sans raproche.*

The circus troupe has been out as usual today [Sunday] attended by crowds of men and boys. The great source of amusement seems to be with the clown who is sometimes mounted and sometimes on foot dressed in the most grotesque manner, his face frightfully painted—dancing and capering and making all sorts of ridiculous motions. This company is a miserable one and could not succeed in any village in the United States.

May 15. This week I have been unwell with one of my old turns of pain—Asthma. Dr McPhail is positive that it is neuralgia of the lungs. If this be so, there is some hope of outliving it. I am sure here my life is more favorable to the recovery of health than any I could lead. There is perfect freedom from care and labor, constant occupation and diversion of mind, company and long rides everyday.

Mrs Hunter and I were saying the first of the week, we wished some of the scenes in which we bear a part could be daguerreotyped for our friends at home. For instance, one on Monday last. As you cannot have the visible picture, try to imagine it. Two large carriages, or ambulances as they have been termed—the smaller one drawn by two large fine blooded horses from the United States, the other by four mules. The back seat of the smallest carriage, occupied by Mrs Hunter and myself—the other seats of both were filled with gentlemen. Behind them a strong escort of mounted Dragoons completely armed. The time Two o'clock in the afternoon and leaving Matamoras for a ride of seven miles up the river to pay a company of Illinois Volunteers encamped at that point.[15]* If I wished to daguerreotype our moment of starting, I certainly should wish to picture before you the Encampment.

The first objects that met our view on approaching, were two Mexican women—one employed in ironing on a board elevated on two barrels, the other at first sight, I supposed to be a child of twelve or thirteen years of age, but a nearer view showed that if not a wife, she would very soon be a mother.

Farther on along the edge of the wood we saw men in every attitude of lounging that could be conceived. Some in hammocks swung between trees. Others on a rustic bedstead made of logs and boughs laid across saddles and accoutrements lying about on the grass. Meat hung up to dry. Horses feeding and, indeed, everything you can naturally imagine to belong to an encampment. The men looked as if they had long ceased to care how

15. This would probably have been Santa Rita, Texas.

they looked and among them all I did not see one who looked fit to be seen.

The Captain of the Company came forward in a dark calico shirt and pantaloons, to offer us some peach brandy in a very suspicious looking tumbler. He is from Illinois but if not a Yankee is most surely the *Son of a Yankee*. I did not see a book or paper, but there were plenty of bottles and playing cards scattered about on the ground. An inactive army is a perfect hotbed of evil. And if they could see such scenes in Washington, I am sure they would take very vigorous measures to bring it to an end. An army of occupation will ruin our country, if it does nothing more.

At the risque of being bitten by wood tics, an insect that buries its head in the flesh, and produces a very painful sore, I left the carriage and talked awhile with the Mexican women. The youngest whom I mentioned calls herself Mrs Williams, the wife of a teamster,—and probably considers herself so,—but the connection will undoubtedly expire with the termination of the war. There will be an abundant sprinkling of the much vaunted Anglo-Saxon blood in the Sierras and valleys of Mexico. In families, you see every shade of color from the darkest Indian to the blue eyes and flaxen hair of the Saxon.

We have been on three or four such expeditions and next week are going to the Mouth of the River.

Love to all and kisses to my sweet boy.

May 18. Since I wrote you last, we have had considerable company in town and have had our hopes of peace again excited. The mail from Headquarters brings us late news from Queretaro of a favorable nature [concerning the treaty with the Mexicans.]

Mr Boultbee, an Englishman, and old resident of Saltillo is here now on his way to the United States. He considers peace as certain, though there may be some delay. He says the same irresolute and procrastinating spirit goes through every thing [Mexican], and that it is almost impossible to get a decision in the Mexican courts.

By an arrival yesterday, we had Dr Prevost, a young gentleman of great talents, moral character, and great powers of pleasing. His popularity is unbounded with both Mexicans and Americans, and with all these advantages, after mature deliberation, he has resigned his appointment, and is on his way home to make his final arrangements for settling in the interior of Mexico, to practice his profession. His choice is without doubt a wise one and he will not only make a fortune, but do a great amount of good. I wish from my heart that good men of commanding character and wealth, felt it more incumbent upon them personally to make "these waste places blossom like the rose."

The idea that only clergymen are required to go forth as missionaries is an absurdity. Physicians are peculiarly fitted for this office, for men are never insensible to their physical wants but often to their moral necessities and therefore he can gain admission everywhere.

Colonel Fay came down in the boat yesterday. In the same boat also came down a perfect original, an officer of the 16th Regiment from Illinois, a New Yorker originally and a complete specimen of a Yankee transplanted to the back woods. His memory is astonishing and he repeats whole cantos of poems without a blunder. Dr Prevost said his parting with the Army made him very sad, but this man kept him incessantly amused. Under an appearance of almost childish simplicity, he conceals shrewdness and sarcasm. He has too the genuine nasal twang. He calls the strap on the shoulder, a label, and says "When I got regularly labelled, I could associate with the high salaried and the high flung folks." There is a good deal of significance in the last phrase. I regret exceedingly that I did not see him. He arrived in the evening and left early in the morning so he had no opportunity to call on the ladies. All the officers met him at a party last evening at Dr McPhail's and they could talk of nothing else this morning at breakfast. They say his manner is perfectly peculiar and inimitable.

May 19. They are buying up land rapidly on the other side [of the river], and it is thought the immigration to the Rio Grande will be very great.[16]*

We expect to know positively in three or four days whether we are to have peace or war. Colonel Temple has the plan to move forward if hostilities are renewed. He is from Albany and is considered by all, myself among the rest, a most accomplished and fascinating man. This means more than if I had said it twelve years ago. He is like all the officers of that Regiment I know, a strong democrat, and is looking for the doings of the political convention with great interest.

Most of the officers of the regular Army [stationed] here are Whigs, I should think. There seems to be very little strong political feeling or rather they have no candidate for the Presidency on which their wishes have been fixed. General Scott is regarded by military men precisely as he is by

16. Cameron County, with an estimated population of 4,000, had been established in the latest session of the state legislature. The *American Flag* of May 17, 1848, predicted the influx of large numbers of new residents during the coming winter. It touted the lower Rio Grande Valley for its potential as excellent farm and ranch land.

civilians. General Taylor is thought to have less military genius but unsurpassed greatness of soul, wholly free from the little faults that obscure the glories of so many other generals. Colonel Duncan is sporting his laurels and will I fear throughout life. The whole Army censures him for espousing the cause of General Pillow.[17]

Injuries done by Mexicans to American citizens are tried by the Military Commission. For small thefts, flogging is often the sentence and some say disturbing scenes have taken place in the Plaza. There was a whipping that took place yesterday and I did not know it in time to get out of sight and hearing.[18] They say imprisonment is no punishment for in the American prison the Mexicans live better than they do at large. It is curious to see how much more energetic even in their vices our own people are than the Mexicans. The Americans will plan a bold, extensive and successful robbery; the Mexican will confine himself to petty theft.

I heard from [Sarah] Chase a few days ago. They have left the St. Charles Hotel in New Orleans and are now boarding at a private boarding house where they pay $100 per month. At the St. Charles, they paid $160 per month. Sarah has been a great deal into society and has passed her time very pleasantly. We pay, including washing and servant hire, $60.00 per month. Washing by the piece is a York shilling plus nine pence.[19]

May 20. This evening I have been riding with Mr Boultbee and his Mexican wife. She has a kind benevolent face as well as her sister. They are pleased with the idea of going to the United States and seem to look at everything with delighted interest. We rode to the river and for the first time in their lives they saw a steam boat. The Mexicans have a perfect horror of the Gulf and do not venture upon it except in extreme necessity.

Concerning the designs of the Government, the present intention is to retain in the regular Army a force of eighteen thousand. Of these, 14,000 will be kept on the frontier extending from the Gulf of Mexico up the Rio Grande and to the Pacific excepting a force in Oregon. This is pushing the Army altogether beyond its old stations and altering entirely the color of our fortunes. The Army may banish us to California.[20]

17. Helen Chapman's assessment of Colonel Duncan's situation has changed. In a letter to William Chapman, Duncan expressed his contempt for Scott and respect for Taylor (James Duncan to WWC, Oct. 30, 1847, CC).

18. Flogging was not banned in the military until 1851.

19. A New York shilling was worth approximately 12 ½ cents or pence. Thus, a York shilling plus nine pence would have been 21½ cents.

20. HBC to EWB, May 18, 1848, CC. News of the discovery of gold in California did not

Love to all and a thousand kisses to my dear boy. Oh! how I long to see him. I sometimes fear I am not doing my duty in allowing myself to be separated from him so much.[21]

Monday the 29th. We are all in most feverish anxiety to hear about the treaty and are looking every day for news with great eagerness. We think we must certainly hear by the tenth of June.

Captain Ogden has his head full of California and wishes Dick Ogden to go with him. The Ogdens are all money makers, spending it freely, fond of show and style, and heaping on their mother everything that wealth can procure.[22] It would take very little to give Mr Chapman the California fever, but he has promised not to apply for orders. If it be the will of Providence, we must make the best of it.

Last Sunday morning, I went to Mass for the first time. The service commenced a little before seven, and lasted a little more than half an hour. I went with no disposition to find fault, but rather to participate in whatever seemed to be worship. The service, in Latin, was muttered in so low a tone, as not to be audible, even by those nearest the altar. There was nothing imposing in the arrangements of this church. On the contrary, everything was poor and mean. On each side of the altar were two full length images, one of Jesus Christ, the other of the Virgin Mary. Directly over the altar was what seemed to be a shrine with a curtain in front made of embroidered satin. When the service commenced, this was raised and disclosed the Virgin and Child, each with crowns.

From the manner of the Priest, I should judge most of his petitions were addressed to the Virgin. His back was turned to the audience nearly the whole time, and praying as he did in a tongue unknown to them while partaking of what they deem most sacred elements, "the very body and blood of Christ," the effect must be what this remarkable church intended it should be, namely, to give the people the idea of a great proprietary sacrifice forever renewed by the Church, through her ministers.

To me it is frightful to see [such a priest] ministering in holy things, but

reach New York until August 1848. The troops were being sent to California as a result of the Mexicans ceding California to the United States under the Treaty of Guadalupe Hidalgo (James Trager, *The Peoples Chronology* [New York: Holt, Rinehart and Winston, 1979], 460).

21. HBC to EWB, May 18, 1848, CC.

22. The Ogdens traded under the name Messrs. Ogden and Mosby, located at the Mouth of the River. Advertisements in the local newspaper suggested that the firm sold "Groceries, Wines, Liquors, Boots, Shoes, Clothing, Segars, Sardines," and other frontier necessities (*American Flag*, Nov. 20, 1847).

though the Romanists believe a priest to be a *very bad* man that does not destroy the *efficacy* of his office. He is the earthly agent, appointed by the Church to dispense its heavenly mysteries and the *gift itself is not polluted by his unworthiness*.

Monday something happened to exhibit his real character most painfully. There was a great funeral of a Roman Catholic Gentleman, Mr Hugh Davine, an Irishman, very wealthy and connected by marriage with the first families here. The priest and his assistants robed in the most imposing garments of their order attended. Coaches hung with crepe, all the gentlemen of the place, many officers of the Army, Colonel Davenport, the surgeon, Major Hunter, Mr Chapman, and others, all provided with long mourning scarfs of the finest linen tied with crepe, wax candles and black gloves. No expense was spared. It was a great funeral, the funeral of a wealthy man.

Soon after the arrival of the guests at the house, I saw a miserably poor coffin having the appearance of an old packing box, carried along by four men toward the church. On close inspection, I saw it contained the body of a man and watched it with some interest. They set their burden down in front of the church, and waited some time to get a brief prayer muttered over it and a sprinkling of holy water, all that the poor can ever hope for. After waiting some time, with the uncovered corpse in the hot boiling sun, they seemed to think it would be vain to wait longer and again they took up their burden. As they passed this window, there was an appearance of most abject poverty about the whole arrangement and I thought of the contrast between these funerals of perhaps a Davine and a Lasarist.

I thought no more about it until last Sunday when a gentleman, a Mexican and a Roman Catholic, was talking about the very doubtful goodness of the Priest and, as an instance, mentioned that while returning from the grave of Mr Davine, the priest was accosted by the men who bore the other coffin, telling him there was a coffin at the gate, and begging him to bless the corpse with holy water. The priest repelled them rudely and angrily and said he was occupied and could not be disturbed. This was told by one of his own church.

On Sunday after Mass, I went to Miss Bacon's school room where we read the church service and a sermon. Miss Bacon is a woman of great energy and resolution and I believe she will yet succeed in getting a good school.[23] Her two cousins, Miss Williams and Miss Andrews, have joined her here and they intend to open a boarding school. Mr Boultbee, whom I mentioned in my last letter, says that if a lady would go to the City of Mexico, and open a young ladies' school, she could make an immense fortune in four or five years. There is only one school there and though their terms are ostensibly $500. per annum, with the extras they amount to $1000.00. The study of the English language is becoming like that of French, a necessary part of a fashionable education.

Love to all and kisses to Willie.

23. Helen Chapman's opinion of Miss Bacon was not shared by some of the men, including her husband. The reasons for their intense dislike was not clear, although Helen herself later referred to Miss Bacon as a "poor, worn out, old maid school teacher" (HBC to EWB, Aug. 28, 1850, CC).

3.

THE DAWN OF FORT BROWN AND BROWNSVILLE

June through September 1848

With the advent of summer 1848 came the news of the treaty formally ending the Mexican War. The Chapmans knew then that their days in Matamoras were numbered, but their future appeared uncertain. William's work intensified, since he was responsible for moving American military equipment and personnel north of the Rio Grande.

While Helen Chapman socialized with those leaving Mexico, she also responded to the news of Zachary Taylor's nomination for the presidency. She wrote to her mother at length about him from her unique perspective, relating stories and personal assessments from a variety of people who served with or knew him.

The summer was Helen's first exposure to the unrelenting heat and humidity of the lower Rio Grande Valley. She felt the "languor and debility" it created and understood the tradition of the siesta but claimed not to indulge.

My dear Mother, Matamoras, Mexico

June 4, 1848. There seems to be no doubt now that the treaty will be confirmed. We are all beginning to look seriously for a change of some kind. By my next letter, I hope I shall be able to tell you something definite as to moving. It may be William will be ordered far away where I cannot go with him and in that case I shall hurry home as fast as cars and steamers can carry me, but if [he is sent] to any healthy spot, I shall go with him.

Brazos Santiago, Texas, June 9. We received the official announcement of peace.* General Wool is hurrying matters as much as possible to get out of the country.

June 11. Last evening, I had a long talk with Major Anderson. His commission expired with the war, and as he has a large family, he, of course, feels much anxiety. He would like to be retained and ordered to the Presidio [on the Rio Grande near Laredo, Texas] with a view to permanent settlement. He is a Tennessee slave holder, but would gladly rid himself of his burden if he had the means. He says he cannot and never could sell slaves, that he should be thankful to live in a country where he could do without them, and if he were to become the inhabitant of a territory, about to be organized into a state, he would vote against the introduction of slavery. He thinks at Presidio hired Mexican labor would be more profitable than slave labor. He is a very good man, and I really hope he will be retained.

Later in the evening, we had some very fine music in Richard Ogden's room. He has sold out, and will probably soon start for California. In consequence of the peace news, we return to Matamoras tomorrow sooner than we expected. The moment we know our own destination, I will let you know.

Matamoras, June 13. We returned yesterday, the roads being so overflowed by the rains as to render our departure impossible Monday. Do not be alarmed if letters for some weeks to come are very irregular. Every [ship] that can possibly be used as a transport will be detained at the Brazos to carry troops home as they arrive [from upriver]. On account of the roads, we put the carriage on board the steamboat, and kept on the boat, until we were within 25 miles by water, and 8 by land from Matamoras, then we took the carriage. The place where we left the steamboat is called Arista's landing, being the place where he crossed with his army.

I was surprised to see the farms looked so well cultivated and the ranches looked more comfortable than they generally do. On this road, was a farm owned by an American gentleman, General Brewburn, who took an active part in the former Mexican wars, and owned a very large estate.[1] He

1. John (or Juan) Davis Bradburn, formerly of Kentucky, had been Mexico's commander and collector of customs in the port of Anahuac at the head of Galveston Bay. Conflicts with Texas colonists in 1831 and 1832, culminating in the arrests of Patrick C. Jack, William B. Travis, and Edwin Waller, resulted in what is known as the Anahuac Disturbances. See Walter Prescott Webb, H. Bailey Carroll, and Eldon Stephen Branda (eds.), *The Handbook of Texas*,

spent immense sums of money, married a Spanish Countess under the Empire and was a man of great influence. He separated from his wife and died a few years since. There is enough left about the estate to attract curiosity, and make one inquire about it, but it is little more than a ruin. His wife is still living in the City of Mexico.

We rode up the river with Mr [Samuel A.] Belden, an American merchant here, and Major Scott who was among the first to enter the country. Mr Belden thinks the people here are disappointed at the passage of the treaty, and would rather remain under the flag of the United States. There is said to be a very extensive organization for the establishment of an independent republic, in the three states of Tamaulipas, Nuevo Leon and Coahuila. There was a meeting in Matamoras on Friday evening among the citizens, as Mr Belden says, to consult on the subject.[2] They will find a great many American sympathizers without doubt, and it will be the Texas story all over again. As we entered Matamoras, we looked for the Mexican flag, but it seems the official notice has not yet been received. They are all ready to run it up the very instant the order arrives.

We see no difference here [in Matamoras]. It did not seem like war before and, consequently, it does not seem like peace now. Dona Juanita has made me a long visit this morning and is even more polite and kind than usual.

No orders have yet been received. By an Express last night from Monterey, we hear that the troops commenced their march on Monday. Thank God, they are on their return home, in time I hope to save many of them.

We understand that a large Mexican force is to be sent to this line, to prevent smuggling. I fear there will be constant disturbances. There seems to be a deadly feud between Mexicans and Texans, and they can scarcely be brought to regard each other as members of the same great human family. I am inclined to think the Texans are the worst of the two. Life seems to be but slightly regarded, and scarcely a week passes, that we do not hear

(3 vols.; Austin: Texas State Historical Association, 1952, 1976), I, 203; Nathaniel W. Stephenson, *Texas and the Mexican War* (New York: United States Publishers Association, Inc., 1921) 38–45; Virgil N. Lott and Virginia M. Fenwick, *People and Plots on the Rio Grande* (San Antonio: Naylor Company, 1957), 69–75.

2. This was an early meeting of a group that developed the Plan de la Loba, in which these three provinces of northeast Mexico would be independent as La Republica de la Sierra Madre. Their effort culminated in an abortive revolution led by General Jose Maria Jesus Carvajal.

of some daring outrage, some cold deliberate murder. These occur mostly on the other side and among Americans. This practice of carrying firearms and knives is dreadful. When the blood is heated and the passions raging, it is fearful to have an instrument of death at command. Those who are kept on this frontier will see the wildest kind of border life.[3]

June 16. I have just returned from Fort Brown. The mail arrived this morning, bringing a letter from you and one from Father. I cannot tell you how delighted I was to hear you and all were well.

I also received a Westfield paper and glancing over it, I find an editorial upon General Taylor. I am constantly hearing incidents in the daily life of this man, not only from his admirers, but from those, who are wholly incapable of appreciating his *peculiar kind* of merit. *Enemies in the Army*, he has none, but there are great numbers, who have no sympathy whatever with his remarkably simple *antique* character, if I may be allowed the expression. From these, I may reasonably expect to hear the truth and from all this mass of testimony, I have formed my opinion, and I give it to you for what it is worth.

Prominent in his constitution are *love* of *truth* and a *firmness so excessive* that it degenerates into *downright obstinacy.* He has profound contempt for all *shows and shams*. Simple as an old Roman, he seems to have I should think but little imagination,—little of that "divine life" that constitutes to some of us the glory of existence. Concerning this, however, I cannot judge. His sympathies are ardent as a child's, and in times of emergency, with an astonishing outward coolness, he seems in reality to have an enthusiasm that carries all before it. Captain [Amos B.] Eaton says, while admitting General Scott's *intellectual* superiority, that General Taylor possesses the *"Animus"* and the power of imparting it in battle such as he believes unequaled. The enthusiasm of his friends is boundless while with General Scott, it is different. I am on terms of habitual intimacy with very many of his warmest friends, but they do not speak of him with that *warm* loving admiration that General Taylor excites.

I should suppose such a man must have much imagination. Another peculiarity is his devotion to women, not as the term is most shamefully applied in modern languages, but that genuine antique sort of devotion that

3. The *American Flag* of June 14 warned Americans of the possible dangers of living south of the Rio Grande without protection from the military. American citizens would need to "look out for themselves" and "be prepared to defend themselves."

was a religion in olden times, when character was more fresh and simple. For the poorest camp woman, he would perform the same acts of courtesy, as for the greatest lady of the land. Devoted truly and fervently to his wife and daughter, he has unbounded faith in the excellence of women and this, though it may seem unimportant in the character of a public man, is not so. Men who sneer at women are not among the really great men.

As to his political course, it is not *politic* as the term is used to mean allegiance to a particular political party, because he is no more capable of being politic than Grandpapa could have been. This no-party system results I believe from his *love* of *independence*, another trait in his character. The *strong habitual pressure of military discipline* has kept him as a military man within bounds, but, *out of that capacity* to bind him to a party is out of the question. I believe he said at the commencement, that he would not be bound by any party *merely because he felt* so, because the control to which he had already been subjected, had been almost more than he could bear, and he was in a "great rage" to be free. Added to this, he is peculiarly deficient in all love of pomp and power, and at the moment probably *really* and *truly* desires rest and quiet. His statements concerning his ignorance of politics were made I believe without object, and in perfect good faith, a consequence of his uniform bluntness and sincerity. His ideal love for consistency is such, that he will keep to a resolution right or wrong and since he once said he would not be bound by a party, so he will continue to say even though by it, he should lose the Presidency.

I believe he now wishes to be elected, not from any love of the position, but because, from the conduct of the other candidates, he has an idea that he has been treated unfairly and this has roused his combative propensities, which are undoubtedly violent. Oppose him unjustly, and you rouse a slumbering lion. I believe he has a profound love of justice and if he was to be President, he would at least have the universal merit of forgetting his own personal interests. His prejudices, very likely he could not forget. It is certainly a curious game to watch. In the political system, with all its tortuous, but systematic evolution, he is a stray planet, a comet governed by wholly different laws, darting hither and thither putting the whole machinery into confusion. Whether he will ruin himself and others politically, or blunder into the right place, it is impossible to determine.

The troops are on their way down the river and are to be encamped at Palo Alto. Arrangements are making to evacuate Matamoras, but it will take some time. Until the Army is removed from Mexico, there will be much material for pleasant reminiscence, and I will write in this way anything that happens.

Matamoras, June 18 (Sunday). Another fandango as usual today. This was on the bank of the river and, walking out towards evening, we saw the party assembled. There was a temporary shed and awning, a liquor bar, stands with spirits, beer, wagons with heaps of watermelons, and musk melons of which the Mexicans are excessively fond and some other things.

There is one peculiarity in a Mexican crowd, its stillness. With the same number of our own people, or of Englishmen or Irishmen, you would hear shouts of laughter, curses, angry words, commotion in some way, but the men here I should think are taciturn. They seem to have a languid subdued look and the ball certainly had more the appearance of a religious ceremony. They are preparing this week for a great celebration, the Feast of St. John, which takes place on Thursday.

Returning home this evening we saw, in two or three of the huts, women dressing themselves for the evening dance. They manage somehow, though they wash in muddy, cold water, to make their clothes clean and it really seems quite a mystery to see them emerge from their dark, dirty dens with their white dresses and white satin slippers. It is amusing to see what a passion they have for this last named article of dress and also for silk stockings. A poor woman, if her whole wardrobe does not amount to five dollars, will manage to get these or, if not both, the slippers.

In one hut, they were erecting an altar for the festival. This was made up of pictures, images and an awning or canopy and anything bright and showy that could be procured. An enormously fat negro woman, who came into the country so early she does not know a word of English, was constructing a cushion covered with red silk in the form of a globe about as large as a baby's head on which she was fastening a profusion of rings and ear rings lent for the occasion. This was to be suspended from the top of the canopy.

June 20. We have a rumor that General Taylor and Mr Fillmore have received the nomination of the Whig Convention. It does not seem to me they could get a better ticket. Of course, I hear the two men, General Lewis Cass and General Zachary Taylor, constantly talked about and it so happens that I am living with intimate personal friends of both these men. Being so intimate, they might naturally expect some personal advantage from these nominations and that is one circumstance strongly indicative of the character of the two men.

General Cass's friends feel certain of snug berths under his administration, but General Taylor's friends have no such expectation. Dr Jarvis, a sensible observing man and who knew General Taylor long before he became a great man, says that such is the General's strict honesty and integrity, that if two men were to present themselves with equal claims and equal merits he would be very apt to give the office to the stranger through a fear that he might insensibly be governed by personal considerations. The troops are all on their way down, and we are all looking forward to change of some kind.

June 23. A mail with news of General Taylor's nomination. For the first time I am interested heart and soul in a Presidential Election. I fully believe General Taylor will make a better President than General Cass.

I was talking with Mrs Hunter, a few days since about General Taylor's views on slavery. She says she has often heard him talk about it and that he is strongly opposed to the extension of slavery into any new states and he laments that the bulk of his property is in slaves. It happened in this way. He inherited slaves and received a number by his wife, but he never intended to become a purchaser. It seems he placed eighty thousand dollars in the hands of merchants in New Orleans, and let it remain without interest for a year in order to secure shares in the United States Bank. The Bank, in the meantime, went broke, and these merchants had become so involved, that the only way of indemnifying himself for the large sum of money was to take possession of the Louisiana Plantation.

He is said to be so kind a master that the slaves have the warmest attachment to his person and he grants them greater indulgences than any of the neighboring planters. For instance it is a general custom to allow them half a day on Saturday to cultivate their own little patch of ground. General Taylor gives them the whole day. He has been told that his plantation would yield a much larger income, if he would make his people work as others do, but he replies that he would rather make less than be in danger of working them too hard. If complaints are made of an overseer, he is discharged at once.

You remember once I gave you an account of the [Taylors'] simple primitive mode of living at Fort Smith, Arkansas. Major Bliss writes that they are living in precisely the same manner at Baton Rouge, not the slightest change in the manner or appearance of the household.

Major Cass passed down river a few days since. He is a great man since his father's nomination and ordered a boat to New Orleans on his own responsibility. He arrived in the evening and passed directly down the river so I did not see him. Major Bliss says he takes such extreme care of his hands that he sleeps in gloves. The same gentleman says General Cass has the choked look of a high liver.

June 25. Yesterday was the closing day of the *Festival of St John* and the custom is for everybody that can procure anything in the form of a horse to ride for very life through the streets. These Mexicans have a wild look on horseback. They carry a very loose rein, use their spurs constantly, and put their animals to their utmost speed. I cannot conceive what natural connection there is between St John and this break-neck cantering, but there are other things quite as difficult to understand. We unconsciously kept the day by riding also but not on horseback.

A party of us went to *Palo Alto* and I again went over the ground cheerfully with Dr Jarvis, who was present at the battle. The two large pits at *Resaca* where the bodies were buried, which at my first visit were apparent by the appearance of the bare earth, are now equally apparent by the most rank vegetation, the earth is rich with human's blood and bones. Everything in the shape of a relic is removed.

I am told that at *Buena Vista*, arms and legs are found with the skin dried upon them and the clothing still on them. May God forgive us and bring good out of evil. Dr Jarvis says in one place at *Palo Alto*, he found a Mexican officer with the head completely severed from the body, and crouched under the legs, a little dog. He made every exertion to remove the animal and procured a teamster to assist him, but the dog became perfectly furious if any one approached him, and they were obliged to leave him. A hospital was established in the field for wounded Mexicans, but a great many crawled off into the chaparral and died. Dr Jarvis was appointed by General Taylor to inspect the Hospitals in Matamoras after the battles, and he says such horrible sights he hopes he may never see again. Some had a mat, but most of them lay on the bald dirt floor in such a state of filth and wretchedness as cannot be described.

The volunteers [of the army] are on their way down the river and some of them I fear are destined to fill prisons and penitentiaries or prey on society in some way. A half hour since, half of the 3rd Regiment of Dragoons arrived in town. The poor fellows are glad enough to be homeward bound. General Wool will be here in a few days and then we shall begin to think of evacuating Matamoras.

In Dona Juanita's room the other day, there were some Mexican ladies, and I said that if I had a nice little cottage on the other side of the river, the ladies of Matamoras must go over and visit me. They thanked me and said, "Oh, Yes, and then we shall take a journey into the United States." They laughed in the most gleeful manner possible at the thought, that by traveling across a river they could say they had been to the United States. They have much curiosity and would like to see new things, but are perfect cowards about all water conveyances. I should think far less of taking a voyage to China than they would of crossing the Gulf to New Orleans.

Dona Juanita's conduct is kind in the extreme. She tells me, even if the Major is ordered to the other side of the river, to remain here as long as I choose. Then she will take me under her protection and do everything in her power. Mr Chapman believes he shall be kept in the country. In a pecuniary sense, it will be to his advantage. He is putting up small houses and temporary buildings for the protection of property on the other side of the river, and many persons are making preparations to leave Matamoras and settle there.[4]*

On our own side, Saturday, we begged Dr Jarvis to write us a Whig song of General Taylor and this morning he read us one. We are going to have it set to music and published and I will send you a copy.[5]

July 2, 1848. The whole afternoon, there has been a rattle of carriages and vehicles of all kinds. Every thing that can be made a means of transportation has been put in use to carry everybody to another grand fandango or dance in the country. They are truly democratic entertainments, attended by all ranks. Another carriage, drawn by mules, was broken tonight, but I have not heard that any one was injured.

July 3. Mr Woodle,[6] an officer who belonged to Colonel Doniphan's Expedition, has just left. He has almost killed himself by drinking and,

4. According to a report William Chapman wrote in 1851, new Fort Brown was established on June 21 on a site which he had recommended in April (WWC to Quartermaster General Thomas S. Jesup, Apr. 25, 1848). The new fort was on higher ground only 500 yards from the original. The buildings, erected in temporary fashion to serve as a depot for army supplies being moved from Mexico, were fashioned from materials previously used in structures in Point Isabel, Brazos Santiago, and the Mouth of the River. The *American Flag* of June 24 predicted that the new fort would become permanent and foresaw a great trading center, perhaps named Athens, growing up around it.

5. Jarvis's rousing campaign ditty, entitled "Whig Song, for 1848," was published in the *American Flag*, July 1, 1848. Three stanzas alternated with the chorus: "Be ye therefore firm and steady, / Like your chieftain, 'Rough and Ready,' / And the victory is won; / A bloodless, yet a glorious one."

6. For "Mr Woodle," see the entry for Charles F. Wooster in Appendix A.

though a young man, looks as if stupefied by excesses. At the table, Colonel Doniphan was talked of and all the officers seemed to agree in the opinion that no honor was dear to him, but that, on the contrary, he was shamefully negligent of his command, putting himself out of the way, gambling and drinking, to avoid any trouble. His subordinate officers had all the cares and deserve the credit.[7]

What can we believe? The people of the United States are crammed with lies about the actors in the war. This reminded me of something Mrs Hunter said and it shows how guarded we should be in our language before children. She remembers distinctly when quite a young girl, sitting on the steps of General Cass's house with one of his daughters while studying her history lesson. The child asked her father some questions connected with her lesson and he, probably more in soliloquy with his own thoughts than consciously addressing her, said, "Oh! very likely there's no truth in it. There's no such thing as truth in history."

She says the thought immediately struck her, "What's the use of troubling myself with this hard lesson when General Cass says there's no truth in it," and she says she never after could feel the least interest in it.

We have just heard this evening that the General has received the nomination of the Democratic convention. Mrs Hunter is delighted and if she cannot see General Taylor be president, her next choice is General Cass. He also is an intimate personal friend of hers. General Cass procured Major Anderson's appointment and is very friendly to their family.

July 4. [Shortly] we go to the mouth of the river on a visit to Major Anderson. General Wool and his staff are here in Matamoras and will remain in this place and in the neighborhood until orders are received.[8]

Mouth of the River, July 5. Some poor fellows who have not been home for nearly three years are ordered direct by the overland route to California. One company, two days on the march toward home, were overtaken by an Express and their destination was changed to California. Does it not seem cruel? Major Washington when the order was given said, "It is our death

7. Colonel Doniphan led 850 Missouri volunteers west from Fort Leavenworth, Kansas, under General Kearny's command. When Kearny continued west from Santa Fe, Doniphan headed south to join General Wool's column. After battling Indians, Mexicans, and the cold for eleven months, Doniphan's expedition finally reached Wool in Monterey (John Taylor Hughes, *Doniphan's Expedition* [1847; reprint, New York: Arno Press, 1973]).

8. HBC to EWB, June 18, 1848, CC, continuing; Wool contributed to the Fourth of July celebration in Matamoras with a review and inspection of the troops (*American Flag*, July 5, 1848). Helen Chapman reported on the day's events in her next letter (below).

blow, but the fate of all and we must bear it." He has a wife and children in the United States. You would suppose this would be the time to make William think of resigning, but the thought is utterly abandoned.

I have so much to write about, but no time. I am hurrying this to send by the *Fashion*, on board of which are Major and Mrs Hunter. In a foreign country we cling to the few of our own race and language with a feeling we know not at home. I could not restrain my tears when she left and I feel sure I shall not soon see her like again.

Yesterday, the city was gay with flags.* The Mexican flag was run up for the first time with all the manifestations of rejoicing usual to such occasions, beating of drums, shooting rockets, and ringing of bells. In honor of this and American Independence, the United States flag, the Union Jack of Great Britain, the French flag and the Spanish flag were seen waving over the houses of the Consuls. The Mexican flag has an eagle with his talons on the cactus and in his mouth a serpent. At Fort Brown, a salute of thirty guns were fired, one for each state of the Union. In the course of time, it will be quite a fatiguing process to fire a salute.

July 6. Bocca del Rio Grande (Mouth of the Rio Grande) We came down Tuesday in an ambulance on the Texas side, with no other protection than a brace of pistols and a sword cane. We met with no adventure, however, and on our arrival at noon, found that the *Fashion* had just arrived from New Orleans bringing a mail from the United States. We ate dinner and immediately rode over to the Brazos to secure our letters and to ascertain the exact news.[9]

Our ride to the Brazos was made in a beautiful little carriage of Dick Ogden's which he brought from New Orleans and which was drawn by a pair of fine blood horses. You cannot conceive any thing more delightful than this ride on the hard beach. The fine invigorating sea breeze, the rapid forward motion of the carriage, the spirited canter of the horses, their hoofs beating regularly and quickly on the shore, the surf dashing and playing amid their feet, the tossing of their heads as if they too sniffed the ocean breezes make an assemblage of delightful circumstances it would be hard to excel. We drove immediately to the Post Office, but found that our letters had gone up to Matamoras.

The order is out for all government transports to proceed to Vera Cruz first conveying the Volunteers and all mustered out of the war to New

9. HBC to EWB, July 2, 1848, CC (resume).

Orleans and then conveying all the regular troops to this line to await further orders. I had supposed I should lose the opportunity of seeing all my old friends, but now, on the contrary, I shall be the first to welcome them. Oh! How glad and thankful I shall be to see them in safety once more.

Mrs Brice, the wife of Major Brice, Paymaster, has arrived in the steamer and will meet her husband in Matamoras. It is curious to see how people are received in this world. He is a very handsome man, but excessively lazy. Mrs Brice is a very fashionable woman in high health and spirits and always ready for amusement, all fun and energy. General Wool with his staff and all the officers here have just started for the Brazos on a tour for inspection and pleasure. The band of the 10th Infantry also goes with them. While in Matamoras, the regiment was reviewed and made a fine appearance. Colonel Temple is a graduate of West Point, and a fine soldier. The regiment is in fine order and discipline and this is their closing scene on the Rio Grande.[10]

Captain Irvin McDowell is under arrest, but has the sympathies of the whole army.[11] General Wool has made himself extremely unpopular and has quarreled with all his best officers. This is no secret. It is said the General is considerably frightened at McDowell's firmness and has tried to make him yield sufficient concessions to stop all proceedings which cannot succeed. All, who become obnoxious to the General seem to be sent to Camargo, the most uncomfortable place on the line, and, on this account, it is getting the name of Siberia, the place of banishment for state prisoners.

Last evening, we had a delightful bath in the surf. It was perfectly delicious and I wished so much that Willie was here to go with us. The water is actually warm and I should love for him to be in it. I did not feel the least chilling, but on the contrary a glow all over my body. Dr McPhail wishes me to bathe in the surf as much as possible. The climate of this coast, it appears to me, must be good.

Matamoras, July 9 (Sunday). There was a grand entertainment about a mile and a half from town, commencing at three o'clock and lasting until morning. We had a private invitation, but of course, would not go. There was a great crowd, horse racing, a monte table (gambling), the great amusement of the Mexicans—dancing, and a bar for liquor. Coming home early in the morning, the mules became unmanageable in one of the

10. HBC to EWB, June 18, 1848, CC.

11. Clearly, this incident did not affect McDowell's subsequent military career. See Appendix A.

carriages, and the consequence was that one young man, a clerk in a store, smashed his head, another broke his arm, another received dangerous wounds on the head and others slighter bruises.

Matamoras, July 11. Since I wrote last, I have made the acquaintance of a family who live in very handsome style. The gentleman is from Guatemala, rich and old, and his wife whom he married in Mexico, is still very young and at the time of their marriage was but twelve years and six months old. They had one child but it died. When we called at the house, there were a number of ladies present and among the rest, three sisters whose brother talks English. They have picked up a little from him and with their English and my Spanish, we made a very amusing time of it. They played on the guitar and piano, sung and really made themselves agreeable. Like the French, they have a great deal of manners. They laugh most merrily and Father would nearly lose his senses with their jabbering. It requires only a very small stock of Spanish to associate with them for they do all the talking.

I believe I have succeeded in making them like me and if I could only talk freely enough to tell them what we do in the United States, I should be a great favorite. They have great curiosity and it is astonishing what a mass of information Dona Juanita has gained in this way. Her brother, at eighteen, went to Paris and obtained his diploma at the Sorbonne and spent ten years in the different countries of Europe. You would be surprised at her knowledge.

I generally spend my whole morning in writing or studying Spanish. After dinner, I lounge awhile with some amusing book, but do not sleep as nearly every one else does, the Americans as well as the Mexicans. In this house after dinner, it is as still as midnight with servants and all, fast asleep. Luxurious habits increase rapidly upon people in this climate and I do not wonder that in a few years they lose their energy. Personal indulgence is so much thought of and money is thrown away in the most foolish manner upon eatables and drinkables.

Matamoras, July 12. If you hear from me less frequently, do not therefore conclude I am sick. Conceive if you can, what July is in this climate and you will see that journalizing cannot be very attractive. The truth is for years I have not felt so well. Everybody else is complaining of languor and debility, but I feel stronger than I did at the North.

All my leisure time lately has been employed in getting something ready to wear. Silks and even calicos are out of the question and this hot sun has faded out the only two muslins I brought with me. There is a French woman here, a dress maker from Mobile, who I believe will succeed very well in fitting me, but at this time she is sick. It is hard indeed in this climate for those who have to work. I went to see the poor woman yesterday and she seemed to have considerable fever. Her room was not like mine, airy and cool, and she had a quantity of promised dresses on hand concerning which she seemed much worried.

Since I wrote you last, the greater portion of the troops have passed down the river and embarked for the United States. The 10th regiment left on Sunday and we are now living in Matamoras without any military protection. Everything seems quiet, however, and we have no fears.

We are completely in the dark as to our destination. California and Santa Fe are at present the great bug-bear of the Army and if we escape those we shall be contented with anything. The moment we know I shall write, of course. It will be six weeks at least before the depot here and at Camargo can be broken up. There is an immense amount of public property to be disposed of and the quartermasters are all harried to death. Mr Chapman has scarcely sufficient time to sleep. He is putting up store houses on the Texas side and as soon as possible we shall move over. The old guard house in Matamoras occupied by the American troops is a curious looking place. It was a brick building and every particle of woodwork was torn out of it by the soldiers. It is now deserted, a mere brick shell of the house and the only trace of the war left on this side.[12]

There are, at present, to be five companies of artillery at the Fort Brown opposite Matamoras. On the opposite side of the river, the air is pure and fresh. There is always a fresh fine breeze from the Gulf and this year I have had no asthmatic symptoms. Dr McPhail is on the other side in Fort Brown. We have now here Dr Prevost, Captain Frasier and Captain Benham of the Engineers. Colonel Davenport and his aide, Dr Jarvis, Major and Mrs Brice with ourselves are the only persons left [in Matamoras]. Dr Jarvis and Mr McLean, the Colonel's aide, depart for the United States in a few days.[13]

Doctor [Jarvis] is one of the most entertaining men I have ever met, full of wit and humor, an old bachelor, but more dependent on ladies than almost any one I ever saw. I had a long talk with him last night about General Taylor and his opinion agrees with the one I had formed. Throughout his

12. HBC to EWB, June 18, 1848, CC.
13. HBC to EWB, June 18, 1848, CC.

whole career from Corpus Christi to Buena Vista, he was opposed in opinion by the best talent of the Army, but in every case his plans proved the best and were certainly successful. He thinks rapidly and generally correctly.

General Wool passed down the river about two weeks since. He spent two days in Matamoras and visited the Mexican ladies. One evening we were all in Dona Juanita's rooms and on her balcony the General and a very large staff, Mexican ladies and gentlemen, all mixed up in very delightful good feelings with the fine band of the 10th infantry playing in the Plaza. These people are fond of music and they were excessively sorry to lose the band.

Dr [Grayson M.] Prevost has returned to take up his residence in [Parras] Mexico. His friends did not oppose him though they thought the prospect dark. He is one of those men of whom we read in romances and belonging exclusively as I suppose to ideal creatures. Of extreme and delicate physical beauty, he is yet undeniably intellectual, possessing great moral and physical courage whom every body loves and of whom no one speaks ill. A man in whom the moral and the intellectual never for a moment lose their ascendancy. Yet with all this there is nothing effeminate. You feel there might be occasions that would draw out great force.

Indeed as I see more of the world, I find creation has much less to do with novel writing than observation. I have heard them tell of an old officer who is almost the counterpart of Major Bagstock and when the camp women went off, I saw two or three Mrs Mac Stingers.[14] I saw a famous Texan the other day a man familiar with the unrest and most trying time of Texas history, and he was well worth seeing. As tall as George Taylor, somewhat thin but very muscular, black hair cut close to his head, clean shaven, giving rather a Puritanical aspect to his appearance, his face completely burned with exposure, rather high regular features, a very deliberate rather drawling tone of voice were the characteristics of the outward man. He is going across the country with mules and a parcel of Mexican mule drivers, is dressed very respectably. Altogether he looks like a man to whom rain, wind, storm and tempest are all the same, firm and tough as oak.

14. The gouty Major Joe Bagstock and Mrs. MacStinger, Captain Cuttle's termagant landlady—a scolding, quarrelsome woman, are characters in Charles Dickens's novel *Dombey and Sons*, first serialized in 1847 and 1848.

In all my life I have never seen such odd specimens as I have seen for the last three months. I was amused the other day by a discharged Texas soldier volunteer trying to sell his horse. He "was glorious" and so, of course, must ride through the streets in a way to set children screaming and everybody running. While dashing along at this furious rate, he would shout at the top of his voice "Twenty five dollars, who'll say more, twenty five, twenty five going, Must sell, worth a great deal more, D —— d fine horse, going, going, saddle bridle and all, this horse has charged through many a battle, who'll buy?" Occasionally he'll stop and reiterate all this to some particular person, then give a sort of Indian whoop or scream, and dash off again through the narrow streets.

After all, these things cannot be described. An ignorant native of the town can as well imagine a bridge of ice as the sober inhabitant of a village in New England can realize such wild scenes as these. I want to describe to you the appearance of things in the other side of the river, but I must leave it for another letter. There is so much to say. General Wool is still at the Brazos. The weather is intensely hot, but healthy.

Matamoras, Monday, the 20th. I want to tell Helen [Pelletreau] of a lady whose grand characteristic is love of dress and company. She is the wife of Dr M ——[15] of the Army, a gentleman by birth and education and one of the best husbands ever known. The lady would be very pretty were it not for an appearance of languor and ill-humor, and when he married her at a western post, she was probably very young. Probably she was, at the time, surrounded by company and consequently in high good humor. The doctor fancied she was so young he could himself form her mind, but it has unfortunately turned out that she has but little mind to form.

Wholly without resources, she is not for a moment happy out of company. Indolent and luxurious, she has the dyspepsia complaint, namely, that everything makes her sick and yet she still eats everything. When General Wool was in the city, they spent the evening here and between eleven and twelve at night, she ate lobster salad, bread and butter, pound cake, candy, preserved figs, and other things, enough to kill anybody. She has a furious temper, and even her husband cannot control her.

While her husband was serving with General Wool, she remained with her father, but that very soon became too dull, so she started off to board

15. Helen later identifies Dr. M —— as Dr. Thomas C. Madison, assistant surgeon. See Appendix A.

at the Planter's Hotel in St. Louis, equal in expense to the Hotel Astor in New York. She ran into great expense in dress and, all at once, hearing that her cousin had decided to come to Mexico, she determined to go too, and started off without even informing her father. Thus, these two foolish women arrived in New Orleans and on every side were urged by officers of the Army to return, and not attempt such a difficult journey. But such people are always obstinate and come they would. She quarreled with her cousin on the war, very soon got tired and dissatisfied at Monterey, though pleasantly situated, expressed open contempt for the Mexicans and it was even said she told some Mexican ladies she did not like the Mexicans, and in short mortified her husband and disgusted everybody.

The journey from Monterey to Camargo was by land. On coming down the river, she was constantly complaining and annoying everybody, got into difficulty about a boat here and put the officers to great inconvenience changing the baggage. Her love of dress led her into constant absurdities. When General Wool and his staff went down to the Mouth of the River and the Brazos, Mrs Brice went down with them, but I declined. Mrs M ——— there made herself supremely ridiculous. Mrs Brice is a fashionable woman but always dresses appropriately. On this occasion, she wore a checked green gingham wrapper closed in the neck with a linen cambric ruffle, her hair plain and not a single ornament of any kind. On board the boat at dinner, the Doctor's lady made her appearance in a dark changeable silk, short sleeve, low neck and a red violet head dress. She has been married six years, but professes to have great delight in flirting.

By the time she got to the Brazos, her ill temper and silliness had so completely worn out the politeness of the gentlemen that they ridiculed her dress and manner without reserve. This is the picture of a frivolous woman, without any mental resources surrounded by everything to make life pleasant and an excellent husband, rank, a handsome income, and health if she would not throw it away. She has every blessing indeed, but instead engages in incessant whining, mortifying her husband and wearying everybody else.

Let Helen take this lesson to heart. Cultivate against a temper. Above all, remember that nothing is so ridiculous as overdressing, and if there be any doubt as to the kind of dress to wear, it is much better to be too plain than too much dressed.

Matamoras, Aug. 14, 1848. You are surprised undoubtedly at receiving a letter from Matamoras. One by one, they have all departed and I believe Mr Chapman and Major Sibley are the last officers in Mexico.[16]* All are crazy to get home and as Mr Chapman, so long as I will stay, is contented to remain, they have given him no order to go which is equivalent to an order to remain on the other side of the river.

The reason I have not written recently is because I have had a fever such as has been going through the city, a remittent, bilious fever of a very mild character which is in no case fatal. It confined me to my bed for 6 or 7 days.

I know you are bitterly disappointed that we do not return but this separation from Willie almost breaks my heart. It does not seem possible that I can live for months longer without seeing him and yet I am afraid he would not be happy here.

It is a wild place on the Texas side, full of gambling and drinking shops and all kinds of evil. Billiard tables, eating and drinking make up the lives of a great many. Gambling, they say, was carried to a frightful extent on the other line. Lonely married men who leave their families in the United States and come here to go into business become very intemperate. During the war it is said that married men had gone farther in dissipation than the unmarried. They cannot accustom themselves to the solitude of their own rooms. William's habits are perfectly good and I am satisfied my post is here, but my child! my child![17]

Wednesday, I go to the Mouth of the River to remain until our house on the Texas side is finished,[18] possibly in about a fortnight. At the Mouth of the River, it has been perfectly healthy the whole summer. It is believed there will be no Yellow Fever in Matamoras. Last year there was none on the Texas side. Phyllis, our cook, goes over this river with us. We shall take

16. When it became clear that William Chapman's departure from Matamoras was imminent, the Ayuntamiento, or city council, passed a resolution thanking him for his contribution to the city and granting him permission to cross to the south side of the Rio Grande at any time. The *American Flag* also gave him high praise for his accomplishments. (No issues of the *Flag* after July 29, 1848 survive. The New Orleans *Daily Delta*, Aug. 29, 1848, reported this story from the *American Flag*, Aug. 16, 1848.)

17. HBC to EWB, July 20, 1848, CC.

18. While Helen Chapman was traveling across the river, her husband was auctioning off the last of the government supplies which were not worth shipping to New Orleans (WWC to Quartermaster General Jesup, Aug. 15, 1848).

our meals with her. In addition, I have an excellent Irish girl to wash, sew and take care of me, no sinecure as you very well know.[19]

At the Mouth, I hope to tell you what is going on in Texas.

Mouth of the River, Aug. 23. I rise at five o'clock in the morning and take a salt water bath in my room accompanied by thorough friction with a bath towel. This takes me about an hour, I then walk in the corridors, and prepare a little work till breakfast at 7. I drink a cup of black tea and eat dry toast and baked potato or hominy. After breakfast, I take a ride on the beach of eight or nine miles and then study Spanish, write a letter, or prepare sewing till dinner which is very similar to my breakfast. I read, lounge or sew till between four and five when I dress myself and ride again on the beach until tea time. There is generally company in the evening, but they do not stay late, and we manage to retire between 9 and 10 at night. Before going to bed, my spine is rubbed hard until very red with volatile liniment. I am not obliged to take any medicine, except occasionally a little Asafetida.[20] It is not a very profitable life, but this summer was neither profitable or comfortable.

I bade adieu to Matamoras last Wednesday morning, the 16th, having lived there many weeks after the departure of the troops in the most perfect security and comfort. When I parted with my kind hostess, Dona Juanita Perella, she embraced me tenderly and told me to make her home my home whenever I went to Matamoras, and said every thing kind that could be said.

They are building a pretty little cottage for us at Fort Brown in a grove of pomegranates on land that, at the commencement of the war, was a beautiful Mexican garden. The house was not in a sufficient state of completion for me to live in so I came down the same day with Fred Ogden to Major Anderson's where I was most kindly welcomed. There are but few officers left and they are extremely impatient to get away. Major and Mrs Brice are staying here and so we have a very pleasant family.

The next day, Mrs Brice and I rode down to the Brazos and bought there numerous bunches of bananas just arrived on the *General Hamas* from Tampico. I wish you could see one of these bunches of bananas. It would

19. HBC to EWB; Aug. 23, 1848, CC. This Irish girl was Ann Mitchell. In business correspondence of Oct. 19, 1848, William Chapman sent a draft for $185.00 to a banking house in New York with instructions to have the five siblings and one in-law of Patrick, Mary, and Ann Mitchell, who were in his employ, sent over from Galway, Ireland.

20. Asafetida is a yellow-brown, bitter, malodorous resinous material derived from the roots of several plants of the genus *Ferula* and formerly used medicinally as an antispasmodic.

fill the circumference of a good size washing tub and is a heavy weight for one man to carry. The fruit is rich and delicious and everybody can eat them with perfect impunity except myself.

We saw Uncle Sam's wagons toiling along on the beach, some of the drivers asleep, one mending his shoe and others reading yellow covered literature. They are a dirty looking set and will be fair marks for the yellow fever if it comes among us. They put on a suit of clothes, wear them until they drop off and then purchase another.

You will undoubtedly hear by the papers, my dear Mother, that the yellow fever is at the Brazos. We have heard so within the last few days but many think it will go no further. It takes its most malignant form with persons of irregular life and laboring people who are not properly treated and cared for. Dr McPhail thinks it is easy to manage.

If Mr Chapman had insisted on leaving the country, he would not now have been out of it. The Brazos, the Mouth of the River, Matamoras, and Camargo have been great depots and a vast amount of property has been collected in these places. Major Sibley is still here preparing his papers. We must take our chances till next spring when I hope we shall go North, though such has been my feeling of good health here, I almost dread the northern climate. Major Sibley on coming down from Camargo said he never saw such an improvement in anyone's appearance as in mine. They all say the same.

Mouth of the Rio Grande, Aug. 26. When I wrote you last, we had just heard that the yellow fever was at the Brazos and everybody was sick. It turned out to be a false alarm entirely. The same fever is prevailing here as in Matamoras; bilious, remittent fever but mild and manageable. I continue exceedingly well. I have felt so decidedly the advantages of plain simple diet and regular habits that the richest delicacies do not tempt me to break my resolution. We have bananas, pineapples, everything good but "I touch not, taste not."

Mrs Madison, the doctor's lady whom I described to you was so sick and discontented that she left the country in the same boat with General Wool and everybody blames her. Her sickness was dyspepsia brought on and aggravated by her ungovernable appetites and laziness. Her whole life is to dress and see company and I never saw a woman more completely and universally despised.

The Major came down on Wednesday, having had a slight attack of fever, but he is now completely restored. The sea breeze is giving him a fine appetite and bracing him up completely. It does him good to get away a little while from business. He is often to bed late at night and always rises at four in the morning. I shall remain here at least a fortnight longer. Land and salt water are always healthy, I believe. All around Matamoras, there is rank vegetation and standing water, the great causes of disease in tropical climates.

Major and Mrs Hunter are in New Orleans, boarding at the St. Charles [Hotel]. Mrs Hunter visited General Taylor's family at Baton Rouge after her arrival in New Orleans. She remained there about a fortnight and reports that Miss Betty Taylor will become Mrs Bliss in November. From what I have formerly written you know precisely what kind of a marriage this will be. How few girls marry for what is our ideal at least of love. He has lost his mother very recently. She had long been very feeble and in his childhood was so affected by melancholia as to be unable to have care of him and he was brought up in extreme strictness by his maiden aunts.

Dr Prevost, in whom by this time I presume you take an interest, has gone on to the City of Mexico with Don Juan Lopez, our Spanish Consul in Matamoras. His papers are made out as an attache of the Spanish Legation and it will introduce him at once into the best society of Mexico.

I have a very handsome rebozo and I wore it a great deal in Matamoras. It pleases the Mexican ladies. During the last weeks of my stay in Matamoras, I took some of them out riding every evening at which they were greatly delighted. I took them over the river, showed them our new house and with great glee they called it visiting the United States. They addressed me as Dona Elena, sometimes Dona Elenita. I believe I have finally succeeded in pleasing them and I believe Dona Juanita really loves me. They are a kind affectionate race and worthy of a better fate.

We will send a paper which will give you some idea of what is going on in the new territory. It contains a very ridiculous puff about ourselves of which so far as I am concerned I feel ashamed and a little mortified but the smaller the paper the more perseveringly it will puff and the only way to deal with it is to take it quietly.[21]*

Dr McPhail has no thought for anything but his profession and about eleven o'clock every morning there will be a tap on the door, and "It's nobody but the doctor come to get your report, All well?" and sometimes

21. Chapman is probably referring to the *American Flag*'s article of Aug. 16, 1848.

he'll sit a while and again be off directly. The officers at Fort Brown are a very good set, quiet and orderly.

There are two colporteurs[22] who have come around since I came here. They brought a letter to the Major and he has done what he can do for them.

Sept. 4, 1848. I am still at Major Anderson's. The house is nearly ready and I shall return soon to Fort Brown.

An order from the Quartermaster General was received by the last steamer saying that as Major Chapman had expressed a willingness to remain on the frontier of the Rio Grande, he was ordered to do so and would be allowed to choose his post on the river. You may wonder, my dear Mother, that he should do so, but you must remember there are other posts far worse and that he might have been ordered to Santa Fe, Oregon or California. Captain [Leslie] Chase writes from New Orleans that a great many quartermasters have collected at the North and that they will probably soon be sent off on distant service.

By my coming here, the whole complexion of our life is changed. If I had remained at home, Mr Chapman would have gone to Washington City in January to remain there perhaps for years, perhaps to go from there on distant service. In Washington, he never would have been contented and not a thousandth part so useful. Moreover, it would have taken every cent of our pay and the interest of the little we have beside. Our acquaintances there [are many] and we could not live retired. Our position is such as to give us an opportunity to be very useful, and I trust we shall have the heart to be so.

As soon as I get into my new house, I will give you a description of that portion of the United States so rapidly springing into existence on the opposite side of the river. The great city of Brownsville in the opinion of its owners will rival even New Orleans.[23] If you and Father and Willie were only here, I could be contented to remain for life.

Sept. 5. This morning early Mrs Brice and I started for our usual ride [on the beach, but a steamer had arrived with mail]. I was so anxious to

22. Colporteurs are persons who distribute religious tracts.

23. The name Brownsville had been suggested for the new town in a letter tantalizingly signed "C" and published in the *American Flag* of June 28 (see Appendix B). Leroy Graf believes that William Chapman was the author; however, the style is more like Helen's (Leroy P. Graf, "The Economic History of the Lower Rio Grande Valley 1820–1875" [Ph.D. diss., Harvard University, 1942], 234). It is impossible to determine whether either wrote the letter. The town was not incorporated as Brownsville until Jan. 24, 1850.

prevent my letters from going up to Fort Brown that we rode over to the Brazos. What do you think of myself and another lady, not much older, starting off on this extreme Texas frontier and riding eight miles? We saw Major Thomas and some other gentlemen, procured some bunches of bananas and fresh limes from Tampico and returned well pleased, disappointed only in getting no letters.[24]

There is to be a regular steamer to Tampico and if I remain here through the winter, I shall go there. If my health requires any change during the winter, I shall go to Havanna. I do not think it will, however. I honestly think I like the summers here better than the winters so far. The weather is uniform and there are no keen chilling months.

Mr Chase sent over a lot of new books. We see every new novel published within a fortnight after it arrives in New Orleans, but unfortunately very little else. I can say with Coleridge, "Poetry has been to me its own exceeding great reward." It may be unfortunate for women to possess too much imagination, but I believe it more unfortunate to possess too little. In scenes where fancy is the only embellisher, we feel its need. I have felt the want of it most keenly in the ladies who I have seen here, not only for themselves but for my enjoyment. My mouth has been sealed and I have been compelled to restrain all my language to the most matter-of-fact character. I would sometimes for want of something else to do, read something to Mrs [Madison] that I had warmly admired, but before the piece was half ended, I would heartily repent of my folly. The existence of such women, except in constant excitement, drags heavily and with me the days are always too short for my occupation. Give me a little of the "*Mens Divine*" even if the penalty is head-aches and quivering nerves. The Extract particularly suggesting all this to my mind at this moment is called "*What is Poetry?*" by Leigh Hunt.[25]

Sept. 7. Mr Chapman came down the river yesterday on business, and today has gone to Pt Isabel. Two of the rooms are finished [in the house at Fort Brown], but the workmen have been taken off [the project] for buildings of more pressing necessity. I may stay here some time longer. It is considered healthier here than at Fort Brown and I have the salt water bathing. Dr Levely, a young surgeon of great ability, is here, but is going

24. Tampico is about 300 miles south of Brownsville on the Gulf Coast.

25. Hunt's essay "What Is Poetry?" was published in his book *Imagination and Fancy; . . .* (New York: Wiley and Putnam, 1845).

the way hundreds of others have gone, ruining his reputation and appearance.

I saw a sad sight a few minutes ago. Among the sand hills, only a few steps from the house, I saw a hole dug and shortly after a wagon with four men approached it and stopped. They took out a roughly made coffin, placed it in the hole, filled in the earth and departed. Religious ceremonies and all the decencies of Christian burial we well know are naught to the dead. Still you know not how painful it is to witness the absence of what long habit has made sacred and almost necessary. I understand he was one of the deck hands on the steamboat.

All deaths in the Army are recorded on the muster rolls but undoubtedly great numbers indirectly attached to the Army die in this way, and their friends remain forever ignorant of their fate. Among these same sand hills there is the grave of a Mrs Ferguson, the wife of a steamboat captain on this river. Her fate was a melancholy one, killed by the explosion of a boiler in this far off land and buried in the sand. She was a Northern woman and often when my eye rests on her lonely and desolate grave, I wonder if she had friends as loving and devoted as mine, to weep over her sad fate. But there are living women far more to be pitied.

It is pitiable to think how tenderly nurtured women are exposed to trials in foreign lands through the selfish thoughtlessness and wretched habits of their husbands. It is hard enough to suffer from these causes in one's own country and among one's own kindred, but here it is dreadful. I know of a lady who is obliged in Matamoras, to send out her little son, not more than thirteen years old, in pursuit of his drunken father. When men must go astray, think what a trial it is to send a child into the streets. Married men have what they call their frolics, out until nearly daylight in the morning and their wives will be at home all night trembling with fear.

I know of a lady from Massachusetts, not older perhaps than myself, of delicate constitution carefully and tenderly brought up, one of those characters who cling to others for support who suffers all this night after night. To add to her trial, she expects to be confined in January. Think of my lot in comparison with hers, every comfort that a reasonable heart could wish within my reach and a husband as kind and attentive as a mother.

Sept. 12. [William and the Brices] returned yesterday morning for Fort Brown. So I am alone this week with Major Anderson. My principal occupation is listening to him, and trying to entertain him. He is a good old gentleman very much like Grandpapa.[26] He is fed of the milk of human kindness, and has no fault except irascibility. He will blast out to his Negro boys just as Grandpapa would to cows or hogs. And if a stick should happen to be in his hand at the moment it would be dangerous but his wrath entirely evaporates before he can find anything. We have a great many talks about slavery and I get a great deal of information that may be relied upon. He says the fuss about the Wilmot Proviso[27] is only insuring bitter feeling to no purpose, for the only part of the new territory that can be possibly availing is that already included in Texas. He says he never has heard a Southern man even suggest the practicability of taking his slaves to Oregon, California or New Mexico.

On the Rio Grande, Mexican labor would be far cheaper and more serviceable. He says the condition of slaves has been materially ameliorated within a few years past. Formerly it was not an uncommon thing to see them overworked and insufficiently fed.

He was married the year I was born [1817], has had thirteen children, eleven of whom are living, was married in Virginia, his native state, and moved to Tennessee in about 1820 when there were only two or three loghouses in Memphis. He is a man of sound sense and good feelings and just such a man as Southern life cannot spoil but must of necessity injure. He has never been East of the Potomac, but will go over to Washington to settle his accounts and will go as far north as New York. I am curious to see what impression it will make upon him.

Sept. 13. I was called up last night at two o'clock to see the eclipse of the Moon and watched it through. Major Anderson and myself were the only star gazers in the land. The eclipse ended here twenty five minutes past 1:00 o'clock, a.m.

We are just beginning at Fort Brown a fall garden, from seeds planted now. We shall eat vegetables in the winter. Some vegetables are peculiarly fine in this climate, others will not grow at all. The sweet potato grows hard, fibrous and tasteless and runs out like an immensely long radish to the length of nearly half a yard. Cabbage, cauliflower and onions are peculiarly fine. The Mexican onion is famous, pure white, of delicate odor, tender and

26. "Grandpapa" was Isaac Welles, Revolutionary War soldier, who was born on April 17, 1761, and died January 31, 1839, in Westfield. Isaac married Anne Ellsworth (1772–1852) of Glastonbury, Connecticut in 1790.

27. The Wilmot Proviso would have prohibited slavery in any territory acquired as a result of the Mexican War.

of very great size. One on the table dressed whole would cover a dinner plate. Okra grows very fine. The pumpkins brought from Tampico are richer than our own in New England. Almost everything grows well, but generally much artificial watering is required. This is the great drawback to cultivation on a great scale. The soil is of great depth and richness. Corn is a very abundant product. Major Anderson has a little mill and he grinds his own meal and hominy every day as he requires it. When he leaves the country, he will give it to us, so we are supplied with hominy. Though in a remote frontier, we have none of the privations incident to such life except what relates to religion and education. Our physical wants are all abundantly supplied. Matamoras supplies us with everything actually necessary and New Orleans with every luxury we desire.

By a schooner from Tampico, we learned the yellow fever is raging there. The Mexicans soldiers sent since the departure of our troops are said to be dying under sheds and in any place they can find to lie down. You will undoubtedly hear that it is at the Brazos, but you may depend on hearing the truth from me. If it comes I will certainly write to you at once that you may be prepared for whatever happens.

Two Colporteurs arrived about three weeks since. I think the Texas side of the river an excellent field for that kind of labor. There is scarcely a good book on the Rio Grande except the lowest class of novels and unfortunately quantities of those. We are going to try to get a Sunday school started and then I am going to beg some books. I have been two or three times in my life such a successful beggar that I am emboldened to try again.

I am quite amused by a little article in the Westfield paper about going over to the [rail] cars to get a sight of the volunteers [returning from the war]. Tell all my friends that I have seen the Elephant, not in his improved condition after traversing two or three thousand miles of civilization but fresh from the camp.[28] All description is utterly vain. There is oppression, tyranny, injustice, and everything evil in the panic of war, but regiments are made up of men who would sell the shirts from their backs for liquor and seeing their miserable destitute conditions, it is hard to know where to fix the blame. The more I see of war, the more it seems to me unmitigated evil.

28. "To have seen the Elephant" was a common expression of the times, meaning to undergo a disappointment of high expectations. See Robert W. Johannsen, *To the Halls of Montezuma: The Mexican War in the American Imagination* (New York: Oxford University Press, 1985), 87–90.

My health is good and no prospect of increasing the numerical strength of the world. I have no time for more. God bless you all.

Sept. 15. I have a pile of unread books on my table and I hoard them with miserly care that I may not run out of reading. Since I have been here, I have been reading some books lent me by Major [J.] Gooch, the collector for the Port of Brazos Santiago. He resides in San Antonio de Bexar, but is a Massachusetts man by birth, and was educated in Williamstown College. He is fifty seven years of age, and has not been in Massachusetts since 1812. Would he not find it changed? He is prosy and dull and he seems so delighted to come and sit by me, and talk of the old Bay state that I have not the heart to neglect him. Our introduction was rather an amusing one. Riding down to the Brazos one morning, we stopped at the quartermaster's office. I occupied the back seat and two or three gentlemen were around the carriage, and instinctively I saw an elderly person on the steps, earnestly asking if any one had Harold Buliva's[29] last novel. I leaned forward and said, "I have it, Major."

In an instant, I perceived my mistake, and on being introduced, apologized, supposing it to be Major [Thomas] Eastland [quartermaster at Brazos Santiago]. But without hearing this, he commenced actually supplicating me in the most ludicrous manner for Harold. The inveterate novel reader spoke out in every action and gesture. He is a man of some political consequence I believe, but looks inefficient and has not been, I fancy, very successful. He speaks warmly in praise of the country around San Antonio, as do all others. Indeed, there is an abundance of water and it is perfectly healthy. I really felt sorry for the poor old man, and on my return from the Brazos, I sent off for the novel in all haste. You may judge how little of a novel reader I am, from the circumstance that Harold still remains unread. I am saving it for a choice morsel.

I do not think I ever thought so much of home as I do now. About 2 o'clock in the afternoon, I imagine Father coming home with the mail and sitting down perhaps to hear you read one of my letters.

A lady living here has just been confined who does know how to play on the piano, but who does not know how to cut or make a single garment. She was taken sick unexpectedly, and all was confusion,. Mrs Brice and I

29. Helen Chapman could only have been referring to the well-known author and playwright Edward Lytton-Bulwer (1803–1873). Bulwer's most recent book at the time was *Harold, the Last King of the Saxons*, published in 1848. Chapman apparently confused this title with the author when she referred to him as Harold.

had to commence some sewing in the night. She is a bustling, active woman, really kind-hearted, but no patience with inefficient and whimsical people. She knows exactly what to do in sickness, and, indeed, is one of the best ladies I could have been with. She was with the lady I spoke of, during her confinement and it would amuse you to hear her comments [which] were neither few nor charitable.

"How shameful is her mother, a poor woman herself, to bring up a daughter in this way."

"What a disgraceful looking house!"

"She had better leave her piano and learn how to sew."

[Mrs Brice] has almost too much energy and smartness to appear like a perfect lady, but her sound, practical bent and really kind heart are sterling qualities with me. Mrs Hunter was selfish and her sympathies exclusively given to her relatives.

Mrs Clayton, the mother of this sick lady who knows nothing but to play on the piano, arrived a few days after her confinement, and said, in Mrs Brice's presence, "What were you thinking of, Jane, to be so unprepared when you knew it must take place before long?"

"I think? Mamma. I think? Why I never thought in my life. I have always had you to think for me!"

This woman who has just been confined has money enough for the present, her husband will buy her a diamond ring costing $100, and gamble away or win a thousand at night, in play. Such riches of course are worth nothing and though she is a lovely, amiable, pretty creature, I know not what is to save her at some time of her life from extreme privation. [I relate this tale for Cousin Helen Pelletreau's benefit, not from] any feeling of unkindness, but from the best of motives. If she will only learn to sew handsomely, [she will never regret it].

Sept. 16. Today is the Anniversary of Mexican Independence from Spain, and they are celebrating it in Matamoras with a Grand Ball. Mr Chapman and all the other officers will attend. I am heartily thankful to avoid all the confusion and excitement by remaining here.

Mrs Brice returned last evening, delighted with her visit to Fort Brown and our new cottage. She visited some of the Mexican ladies, and they all expressed a great desire to see me. She says the streets look clean, the Plaza is very nicely kept, and the prisoners are working in the streets, something never thought of until suggested by the Americans, and apparently the utmost good feeling prevails.

I felt a little badly yesterday, and thought I would take some medicine, but in conversation with Major Anderson, I changed my mind. He was telling of a character (More common I suspect than we imagine.) who was always retreating before civilization. He would carry a little stock with him, turn it into the woods for pasture, clear a little spot around his cabin, and with about twelve days labor at his corn, actually kept his family in bread. The neighbors would help him haul his logs for burning. His whole time was spent in hunting, and from the sale of his venison, deer skins, and others, he bought everything to supply his simple wants. This was in Memphis at its first settlement and Major Anderson says he never saw a happier man. After the houses began to thicken, he started off with his stock and the last he knew of him, he was on the frontier of Arkansas. He says once one of this man's children lay seriously ill of bilious fever. The Major and his wife carried them medicines, but they steadily refused to give the child anything. To all appearance, devoted to the child, they sat by and watched it with close attention, but insisted on leaving all to Nature. They said the fever would turn off itself, so it did and the child got well. I am not prepared to follow his example, but undoubtedly we take and give much more medicine than is necessary.

Sept. 17. [Concerning the comment in your last letter about the Mexicans,] I am sorry you have so little faith in the Mexican nature for I have a great deal. The stories you hear are told by those who know nothing about them. I have very little confidence in my own opinions, because I am too easily pleased in everything to discriminate properly but all those officers who know them best and are most capable of forming an opinion, agree with me. If you could live here six months, your sympathies would be so excited for this abused, down-trodden race that it would pain you to hear such things.

Sept. 19. I am writing in almost darkness. There is another of those deluging rains that would frighten us if we did not remember the covenant written upon the bow of promise. It seems as if the windows of Heaven were indeed opened. It is not so sickly as it has been here. There has been very little sickness here, but at the Brazos and Matamoras considerable.

Mr Chapman came down from Fort Brown last evening in fine health and spirits as usual. I will return with him Thursday, and will then give you a description of the new Government Depot, and Brownsville. Our house is known by the name of Casa Grenado (pronounced Carsa Gran*ar*do) or Grenado cottage so named from the profusion of Pomegranates about the house.

The Independence Ball went off finely, I understand, in Matamoras. The officers were all invited to take part in the procession during the day. Seats were provided for them with the Ayuntamiento, or City Council and every possible civility extended.

When you feel disposed to murmur at our present conditions, Mother, be thankful it is not Oregon, California, or Santa Fe. We shall very likely have to take our turn at these places but every year delayed is a great blessing. After the line of steamers is well established to Chagres across the Isthmus, it will not be much of an undertaking to go to California.

Poor darling little Willie, he cannot conceive what a trial this prolonged separation is to me. I am going to write a letter to him, and do everything I can at this long distance to retain my place in his heart.

My dear little Willie, The Mouth of the Rio Grande

Sept. 17. As I cannot go and see you yet, but must stay and comfort your dear Father, I mean to write letters to my dear little boy as often as I can, and tell you about all the curious things I see.

I do not suppose my letters will be so interesting as Peter Parley's letters,[30] but I know my darling little Willie will love to read them because they come from his dear mother, who is thousands of miles away. I shall write very large and plain, and I hope by this time, you can read writing, and before very long, can begin to answer my letters. Your little hands would ache to write as much as I do, but one line from my darling boy makes me very happy.

If you carry your atlas to Grandpapa and get him to show you where we live, you will see we are a great way south from where you are living. Your geography tells you that there are three zones, the Torrid, the Temperate and the Frigid. The Torrid lies between the Tropic of Cancer and the Tropic of Capricorn.

Now if you look for that line across the Earth, above the Equator, which is called the Tropic of Cancer, you will find that Matamoras lies very near it; so near that the climate and the fruits are like those of the Torrid zone.

We have oranges, figs, lemons, bananas, pomegranates, and other fruits belonging to hot regions. Now I think I hear my darling say, "How I wish I was living with my father and mother to get all those nice things."

30. Peter Parley's letters were written by Samuel J. Goodrich. They have been charitably referred to as "the inanities of Peter Parley" (Allan Nevins, *Ordeal of the Union* [New York: Scribner's Sons, 1947], 108).

But remember, my dear child, if you were here you could have no great beautiful apples, no delicious peaches, and sweet mellow pears. You would have no great plum tree to climb and pick its rich juicy blue fruit.

Our kind Heavenly Father loves all his children and divides his rich gifts equally among all. To those who live in the cold north, he gives apples, pears, plums, peaches and berries, to those who live under a burning sun, he gives the oranges, lemons and figs.

We always think a great deal of what is difficult to procure and so as you only get these occasionally, you may think you would much rather have them, but I have heard gentlemen say when eating all these nice fruits, "I would gladly give away all these for one good apple," and you, I presume, would think the same.

But my dear boy it is of very little consequence what we eat or drink so long as we have wholesome food. We can eat all these things with a thankful heart but in thinking where we would wish to live, we should think of other things, more important. A little boy should want, if he can have good well-behaved, companions and playmates, a good school to get his education in and a good climate, to make him a strong healthy man. Now my dear boy, the place where we are going to live is new, and there is no school in the week and no Sunday School. The little children, I fear, say bad words, and do not behave well and I am afraid you would not like such hot weather, no ice for any boy to slide upon. So be contented, my darling child, and thank your Heavenly Father for giving you such a good, pleasant home. I hope you will make your teacher no trouble, get your lessons well and learn to think about them. I am glad you thought of expense about the house. People that do not think never can be useful or comfortable in the world.

"God Bless my dear child," is the constant prayer of your loving,

Mother

4.

"ONE HOUSE BUILT"

October through December 1848

Helen Chapman may have felt quite secure in her new home on the grounds of Fort Brown. Clearly she tried to convey this impression in her letters. Yet she could not disguise the fact that her surroundings were still quite primitive. Nor could she keep from her mother the news of some ominous events, such as a nearby fatality from yellow fever. She tactfully omitted mention of an Indian attack on their friend Harry Love, a scout and army express rider.[1]

For much of the fall, William Chapman's duties took him from home. Helen's amusing companion in his absence was a parrot that "screams out 'Hurrah' for a long while and then commences to laugh. When the children begin to cry, she always begins to laugh."[2]

Meanwhile, local citizens began to organize. Cameron County officials had taken office in September, and in December, local businessmen formed the Brownsville Town Company to lay out streets and sell land.[3]

Many amenities were entirely absent in Brownsville. Without a school or playmates and, especially important to Helen, with no church, how could a growing boy like Willie develop properly?

1. In September, Love was traveling with another American from Chihuahua to Fort Brown when they were set upon by a band of Apaches. They returned a "shower of arrows" with rifle fire and narrowly escaped by going into an arroyo filled by the recent rains. Although one of the horses was lost, the men survived (*American Flag*, Oct. 9, 1848, as quoted in the New Orleans *Daily Delta*, Oct. 21, 1848). See Appendix B.

2. HBC to Willie, Nov. 13, 1848, CC.

3. Jacob Lee Stambaugh and Lillian J. Stambaugh, *The Lower Rio Grande Valley of Texas* (San Antonio: Naylor Company, 1954), 91; Lea, *King Ranch*, I, 430.

How could the settlement claim respectability? Consequently, one of Helen Chapman's first efforts to bring civilization to the fledgling town was to encourage a subscription drive for a Protestant church. She hoped that the church's influence would curb the intemperate habits of the town's residents. She wrote more about her feelings toward drinking when alcohol was involved in two deaths that affected her deeply.

My dear Mother, Fort Brown, Texas

October 1, 1848. I have been at home ten days but too busy to [write]. I have been very much hurried with house cleaning, though I have had excellent assistance. We left the Mouth of the River in the midst of the Equinoctial Storm and it was well we did so for the wind blew so strong that there was great danger of an overflow.* Steamboats were kept in readiness and at the Brazos all the houses were deserted and so everyone took to the boats. At Boca Chica, our friend, Hughy McCarty,[4] was flooded out and fled with his wife and children to the Mouth of the River. Every house at these two places has been twice destroyed in these storms and people have reason to fear.[5]

I arrived here in a pouring rain but after the sun came out and I was able to look about me I was enchanted with the place. Our parlor is a large handsome room twenty feet square with four windows and two doors open onto piazzas on each side. Our bedroom is of the same size and we have a most convenient bathing room fitted for shower and plunge bathing. The most delightful thing of all, however, is the chimneys, real old fashioned fire places and the most charming wood to burn in them I ever saw. It blazes like pine and without any smoke. How you would enjoy it by the light of such a blazing fire and a fine solar lamp to set by the center table and read the *Knickerbocker Home Journal* and all the new works published.

If you could see us thus employed every evening, you would not think

4. Hugh McCarty was the toll keeper on the bridge across Boca Chica inlet or creek several miles south of Brazos Santiago at the south end of Brazos Island. A description of Hugh McCarty and his family are in Chapman's letter of November 21, 1848 (below).

5. The New Orleans *Daily Delta* reported on October 4 that the storm lasted from September 16 to September 23. Residents boarded ships on the final day. One ship, but no life, was lost.

it much like what you have pictured of frontier life. You undoubtedly torment yourself by thinking of us as in the middle of a wild turbulent population constantly subject to alarms and our pleasures poisoned by an unacceptable feeling of insecurity. But, my dear Mother, within the Government limits, no distracting causes intrude. He must be a bold villain who would attempt to pass a sentinel with loaded musket and into a place from where there would be no escape. Around our house and at the Government depot, it is as tranquil and peaceful as if there were no thieves, murderers and desperate men in the world. No one is admitted beyond the lines after eight in the evening and all who are not known are put in the Guard house. The office is in the same building so Mr Chapman is always at home. It is so unlike any thing I ever conceived of frontier living that I never think of it as such. We are expecting the troops now here will be sent away and new ones we understand are on their way.

I have been over to Matamoras twice and visited all of my Mexican friends. The new city of Brownsville is growing faster than I supposed any city could grow. How is my darling boy? How Willie would love to run around these pretty grounds, ride the pony, and play with the dogs and squirrels. This separation is very hard.

You may be frightened by seeing of the death of Captain Prentiss here from Yellow Fever. People are in doubt about the kind of fever it is. Dr McPhail says it would be called Yellow Fever in New Orleans. Whatever it is, we have both had it and so we are safe from a second attack.

Oct. 18. We left the Mouth of the River at a fortunate time. The tide has been constantly high since we left and the greater part of the ground is underwater. There has been no inundation here.

Mrs Brice has not yet come [from the Brazos] and I am the only lady within the Government grounds. I have not had time to feel lonesome. There are one or two families in the new town of Brownsville whom we visit and there is no need of feeling solitary.

Everything just now is in a state of transition. The old troops are going and the new are coming. Mr Chapman is surrounded by plans for building and is busy as usual. He is just the man for a new country and it may be the design of Providence to keep him in one.

Sunday, Oct. 22. In a house full of company and confusion, I am trying to finish my letter. Friday, three companies of the 1st Reg't of Infantry arrived here from Pascagoula. There was no house built but ours and that is running over. Only one lady came, a young married woman, Mrs Mumford,[6] I must tell you more of her hereafter. She is good tempered, amiable and inoffensive.

Oct. 24. The *Telegraph* arrived yesterday and brought a delightfully filled sheet from you mailed September 25th. Dear little Willie! I wish I could be present at some of those "chats." You know, of course, that he is in my thoughts incessantly. I would bear this separation patiently and even cheerfully, if I could feel certain that I am doing right.

My position is somewhat peculiar. We have prospered in worldly circumstances. I have everything I wish, without any necessity of calculating how it shall be acquired. I am relieved from all labor and yet in the only point upon which I am not indifferent, the gratification of my affection, I am forced to accept sacrifice and self denial. Whether I have a pine table or a mahogany, a silk dress or a calico, a rich table or one of the simplest fare are matters of the utmost indifference, handsome things come to me too late in life to dazzle my fancy, but to miss heart communion with you, the talk of my darling boy, his soft affectionate and carefree kisses, to lose his childhood is something about which I cannot be philosophical.

This Mrs Mumford is a pleasant, amiable little woman but makes herself almost ridiculous by her incessant reference to Aunt Jane. She was brought up by her Aunt, has never exercised her own judgment in the least, and since Aunt Jane can't follow her about the world, she is without helm or compass. She can sew very neatly what is already prepared for her, but as Aunt Jane has always cut out and prepared everything, her sewing even will not do her much good.

I mean to write of my little Irish girl [Ann Mitchell] who is not yet thirteen. The patient industrious child works for me all day and regularly after tea sits down in a room by herself to her own sewing, makes her chemises, her dresses, with some assistance from me mends and displays excellent judgment in managing her clothes. She cannot bear to be idle and I never have to tell her to work. I sometimes want to tell her not to set down so regularly at night, but I know it is for her good and I force myself to say nothing. [However,] I will not let her sit up after 9 in the evening. I shall keep her with me and after a while let her stay a few months with a dress maker.

6. Jennie Mumford was the wife of Ferdinand Mumford (see Appendix A). They were divorced in the Galveston district court in the early 1850s because of Ferdinand's scandalous behavior.

The poor child is an orphan and her story, though not an uncommon one, would make you weep. She has a patient plodding sort of industry and is thoughtful as all people are who are worth a cent.

> The following letter is from William to Helen Chapman at Fort Brown.[7]

Dear Ella, Point Isabel, Texas

Oct. 23. Captain Hunt will send for his wife and three children by this mail to sail from Boston to New Orleans. He says his wife will bring Willie out with pleasure. She is staying in Cambridge about a mile from Boston at the widow Nobles, Washington Street. What do you say to having Aunt Ann and Father take him to Cambridge and letting him come either with or without Aunt Ann.

> Helen wrote the following on the back of the foregoing letter from William.

My dear Mother, Fort Brown, Texas

Oct. 26. This letter from Mr Chapman was received only a few minutes since. It has made me half crazy. What shall I do? The idea of trusting my precious child to the wide ocean is something I have not faith to encounter. My fears may be wrong, but God in his mercy will pardon a mother's trembling for her only child. It is utterly impossible for me to come to any decision. I have been hoping that Providence would point out the path but it seems to give no sign. May God direct us all.

Ask the dear child himself. Perhaps God may give him the wisdom to make a right choice, and if you are satisfied as to duty, keep him if you think best. His father may be a little provoked at first, but he is too deeply

7. On October 24, 1848, Chapman was ordered to take over the quartermaster depots at Brazos Santiago and the Mouth of the River. At that point, the army had decided to maintain ten companies (two of artillery and eight of infantry, or 500 men) at the forts along the Rio Grande. Chapman recommended that the depots at Brazos Santiago and Mouth of the River be closed due to their vulnerability during storms and that Point Isabel and Fort Brown be the only supply depots, with Fort Brown acting as the distribution depot for the forts upriver.

immersed in business to make it a very serious matter to him. The father Willie remembers is not the father he will see again. Kind and affectionate, he will be, but so buried in business and other thoughts as to have little time for fondling or amusing him. He dresses often by candle light in the morning, goes directly to the office, comes in merely at his meals and is tired out at night and often writing until bed time.

There is no doubt about the healthiness of the place until July. Mr Chapman, in all probability, must remain for two years, so consider all these things. I have written to Mr Chapman that I cannot decide. I could a thousand times sooner hold out my right arm to be cut off. I could give up my attention to him.[8]

Helen

My dear little Willie, Brazos Santiago, Texas

November 21, 1848. I am at Brazos Island with your father, a place I presume that you would not consider very pleasant.

The island consists of nothing but sand. There is not a bush or a blade of grass on its whole surface. It lies on the great Gulf of Mexico, and is separated from the main land of Texas, by a little stream called Boca Chica. Over this piece of water, there is a bridge, and Hugh McCarty keeps the toll gate.

When we came down from Fort Brown, we stopped at Hugh's house. He has a new one, and seems very happy.[9] His curly headed little boy was dressed throughout in stout-red flannel. You will think this a very warm dress for such a climate, but there is a wind in winter from the north-west so cold that it makes everybody shiver.

[Helen Chapman had described Hugh McCarty and his son in an earlier letter.][10]

As I said before, Hughy owes his prosperity to General Taylor, but the power of turning it to account, he owes to his wife.[11] He is good natured,

8. Emily Blair apparently decided that Willie would remain in Westfield. He did not travel to Brownsville until early 1850.

9. The September storm had destroyed his old house.

10. Helen Chapman had described Hugh McCarty and his son in HBC to EWB, June 9, 1848, CC.

11. Theresa Vielé described Mrs. McCarty in 1852 as having sad eyes and a sad smile. She was not lonely as "peace was enough to satisfy her." She raised chickens to sell in Brownsville.

convivial and when alone cannot resist the common vice of his countrymen, but his affection and respect for her is such, that she keeps him greatly in check and when (as he sometimes does) he gets into a spice, if other means fail, delicate and feminine as she is, she does not hesitate to give him a sound whipping. He receives it meekly and is very steady a long while after.

His little boy is as much of a curiosity as he is, a complete little water duck, robust, hardy, handsome, though terribly sunburnt and with curly hair that would be called beautiful, if on the head of a rich man's child. When the seine is dragged into shore, he, with the rest, is in the water up to his head, and, indeed, is never out of it, except when sleeping and eating. It is a most graceful picture of free, unrestrained childhood. Seeing him almost fly on the beach, the water dashing up round his fat little legs, his head thrown back, and his long curls playing in the breeze. The most admirable exemplification of the cold water system I have ever known. So much for Hugh McCarty and his family, it may not interest you, but I wished to preserve some sketch and so I have introduced it here.

I have been rambling about on the beach all the morning, and have enjoyed it much. At one time around the bridge of Boca Chica, going and coming, I counted more than fifty wagons. Most of them are drawn by oxen. The driver of the leading wagon is the only one who feels it necessary to keep awake, the others tie their reins, throw themselves down in their wagons and are either asleep or in a dreamy condition but little better. Occasionally you see one of them reading a newspaper.

[The letter to Willie of Nov. 21 continues.] But I meant to tell you a little more about Brazos Island. This is the only harbor on this coast, and all the people and all the provisions are landed here. The mail came three days ago and brought a letter from Grandpapa saying you were all well. You cannot think, my sweet boy, how happy such news makes me. We have steamers, schooners, and other ships arriving every little while, sometimes a schooner comes in from Tampico loaded with fruit.

This morning, your father dressed himself by candle light, and sent off five vessels before breakfast. Do you think you will ever be so industrious as your father. I hope, my dear boy, you love to rise early and do not waste the bright beautiful mornings in bed.

See Theresa Vielé, *Following the Drum: A Glimpse of Frontier Life* (1858; reprint, Lincoln: University of Nebraska Press, 1984), 97–98. Chapman's description of Mrs. McCarty has been lost.

Your father has just got a very pretty covered buggy with two seats from New Orleans. It can be used with one or two horses. It is delightful to ride over the hard smooth beach and breathe the refreshing sea breezes.

We have a very nice house to live in, and if we had our dear little boy, we should be very comfortable.

A schooner came in last evening bringing us some late papers. We suppose that General Taylor is elected President. I am very glad of it, for I believe he is a good, honest man and will try to do his duty. I hope you learn well at school and make your teachers no trouble. God bless you, my dear boy,

Mother

My dear Mother, Brazos Santiago, Texas

Nov. 21. I have told Willie what kind of a place Brazos Island is, nothing but sand and the Gulf stretching out like the ocean before us. There is not a lady at the place except myself. Mrs Abadie [the wife of Dr Hilarian Abadie] is at Point Isabel, about half an hour's passage by water from this place, and Mrs Hunt, the lady with whom Mr Chapman proposed Willie should come, will shortly be there. Major Thomas, of the 3rd Artillery, is here, and Dr Madison, a good surgeon. The place is only to be kept up as a Port of Entry. At present, the Major is the only quartermaster on the line, and is here to ship stores, sell property and get rid of the cumbrous machinery kept up in war time.[12]

Heaven grant it may never be again the depot for an invading army. A year ago I should not have regarded a general war in Europe with half the horror I do now. It seems to throw men centuries back in civilization. I fear no wars can boast of greater atrocities than this with Mexico. On the other line, there was literally reveling in the Halls of Montezuma: among the common soldiers, the most debasing orgies; among the officers, such magnificent, but soul-destroying revels, as the luxurious wealth of Mexico could afford.

It makes my heart ache to think what wrecks of domestic happiness this war has made. Many a widow who remembers her husband as he was before the commencement of this war will be ten thousand times happier than

12. The previous quartermaster at Brasos Santiago, Major Thomas B. Eastland, had departed a week earlier. He was not well liked. The *American Flag* denounced Eastland as a "mimic hero and petty tyrant" (Nov. 23, 1848).

many a wife who sees her husband return, ruined for domestic life, accustomed to all the powerful excitements of every species of unlawful pleasure.

With the better class, of course, there was a longing for the quiet and well ordered life of home, but the larger class, the indolent, the luxurious, and the riotous, loved the freedom, the soft climate, the thousand allurements of Mexico. Dr Ten Broeck told me he believed if there should be another war with Mexico, three fourths of the volunteers would re-enlist. This seems almost incredible, but when you remember their sufferings here you must think how such men suffer in a severe and rigorous climate. They are men who hang about large towns picking up an uncertain subsistence by odd job of work, thieving very possibly, sleeping in garrets, or under sheds and never knowing where the next day's meal is to come from. After living for three years in a climate so genial that one can sleep outdoors without chilliness, procuring their daily allowance of food, often very poor to be sure, but very likely better than they ever had before, how are they to bear cold and hunger in a climate that tries even the hard working and provident. They might be vastly uncomfortable here, but they will suffer terribly there.

New England has always been a favorite station, but it is amusing to see how the officers here groan over the idea of going there. A banishment to Liberia could not be considered a greater hardship. Great strong men shiver in anticipation of those terrible winters.

Captain Walradt of the 10th Infantry Disbanded has just returned from New York. He could not live at the North and so has returned to settle here. He says the eyes of Southern men are directed with considerable interest to Brownsville and that it is believed it will become quite a city.

I never saw a place grow so incredibly fast. Time, health, or spirits have been wanting for me to give you such an account of the Texas side of the Rio Grande as I have wished. There are some men of property and influence, but most of them are mere adventurers and drinking shops and gambling houses are more abundant than anything else.

We supposed General Taylor is elected though we have not received positive information. All the troops at Pascagoula were delighted with the appearance of Miss Betty Taylor—so perfectly natural, unassuming and so unconscious that she is the daughter of a Major General and of a man who is candidate for the highest office his country can bestow. This unconsciousness cannot be feigned and is a strong family trait.

Did I ever tell you of reading a long private letter from General Taylor to Colonel Davenport in his own handwriting. I read it twice and with extreme care because I knew this to be the production of General Taylor alone. My conclusion was that Major Bliss had much less to do with the dispatches than I had supposed. If General Taylor could not give them to the world in the concise and elegant terms in which they were expressed neither could Major Bliss give in such dispatches any more than the skillful diamond polisher could create a diamond. The genuine one is in General Taylor's letters and it is not by any means so rough as I expected. There was no stiffness and constraint. The sentences were long and though, here and there, there might be repetition and a word too much, yet it was evidently the production of a man familiar with his pen and with books. I believe Major Bliss does little more than condense and touch up his sentences. Dr McPhail, who knew General Taylor in Florida, says at that time he used to write a great deal. One would find him in his tent writing page after page.

There is a gentleman in the neighborhood in charge of some salt works, Colonel Reynolds,[13] a man who has been nearly over the world, of standing and influence in New York, and President of the Bank of Galveston. He saw the letter in General Taylor's own handwriting and agrees with me in the estimate of his abilities. He says Mr [Henry] Clay is always his first choice, but he would be glad to see General Taylor elected, because he believes it will banish from the White House a set of political miscreants—men who would not dare come to General Taylor with their dirty political schemes.

Officers mention as something well understood that, in the famous Marcy letter,[14] when Major Bliss handed to General Taylor a perfected copy of his letter, after reading it, the General exclaimed, "But Major, you've left out what I said about the Fable."

"Yes, General, I thought that would scarcely answer."

"Ah no, Major Bliss, that's the best part of the letter, I can't have that left out," or words to that effect. I give it as common talk without vouching for its truth.

13. Colonel J. N. Reynolds and his partner, Judge Watrous, ran a salt works on a salt lake, thirty miles north of Reynosa, known as Sal de Rey (Leroy P. Graf, "The Economic History of the Lower Rio Grande Valley, 1820–1875" (Ph.D. Diss., Harvard University, 1942], 426).

14. Zachary Taylor wrote many letters to William L. Marcy, the secretary of war.

An enemy of General Taylor, so far as such a man can have one, but one who means to be just, says that, at the Battle of Buena Vista, the General actually *frothed at the mouth*, that he saw it with his own eyes. He also says, and it is undoubtedly true that in moments of *terrible* excitement, he swears awfully, but never when he is cool. This, among military men especially on the frontier and in wartime who swear habitually, is remarkable and shows the peculiar character of the man,—a man "of great rage." Such a man as Carlisle would glory; one, a "True Man," worthy of his beloved middle ages.

Nov. 22. Since I left Major Anderson's at the Mouth of the River in September, there has been nothing but confusion. There was only one house built at Fort Brown and every one had to live in that until other quarters could be built. It is delightful to get down to the Brazos and have a house to myself to be quiet. We return next week to Fort Brown to remain about a fortnight and then return here for a month or so.

Mr Chapman is overwhelmed with business, but it is of a kind he likes and will gain him credit. The clerks live with us and we have a professional colored cook. The expenses are divided at the end of each month.

We have a beautiful little carriage from New Orleans, and everything to make us comfortable.[15] The gentlemen say, "You must feel the want of ladies society." I do not say so but to tell the truth I am not at all sorry to get away from it for a while. I have plenty of books and that is the best society.

Mr Chapman places $400. dollars at your disposal to cover Willie's expenses. Love to all,

Helen

On November 24, Helen Chapman wrote a letter of condolences to Mrs. P. A. Levely of Annapolis, Maryland, whose son William had died of what was then called delirium tremens.

15. On November 21, 1848, Chapman wrote to Young, Blackwood, & Co.: "Yesterday the 'Barouche' and other articles were also received. I was somewhat alarmed when I first saw the name Barouche, lest the article might be out of keeping for a plain, democratic sort of a man,—but it was just what I wanted. It suits Mrs. C. to a 'T.' Your Mr Young, as Dick would say, must be a young man of certainly no young *taste*!"

My dear Madam, Brazos Santiago, Texas

It becomes my painful duty to write to you on this most mournful occasion. My acquaintance with your son commenced at Governors Island, New York when he first entered the Army and while there, his frank sincere manners, his brilliant promise in his profession, and his remarkable personal graces made him an object of universal interest. His amiability and social qualities strengthened the impression his first appearance had created, and when he left for frontier service, he carried with him the love of all.

He was associated with my husband on the march from San Antonio under General Wool and I had thus frequent opportunities of hearing from him. We met at Matamoras in July as old friends. After the departure of the troops from Mexico, I spent six weeks at the *Mouth of the River*, the station where the last months of Dr Levely's life were passed. While there, I saw him daily and I know, my dear Madam, it will be soothing to your feelings to learn that on every occasion when I saw him alone, his talk was always of home. After three years of perilous contact with the world under circumstances tending unhappily to deaden those earlier and purer impressions that careful training had implanted, it was easy to perceive that their influence was still most powerful over his feelings. In every allusion to his mother he spoke with the fresh and delightful enthusiasm of a boy. Your influence was certainly most powerful for in his mind you seemed elevated above the common faults of humanity. I think he was making arrangements to be with you by the last of December.

I afterwards returned to Fort Brown and the last time I saw him living was on a visit to that place about a month since when he seemed to be in his usual health. We have been at Brazos Island for the last fortnight, eight miles distant from the *Mouth of the River* and on Wednesday we learned of Dr Levely's illness. Wednesday evening we were told by Dr Madison, the physician in attendance that he was very much better. Thursday morning he was still supposed by his friends to be better though he expressed a firm conviction that death was at hand. He [asked] to see a clergyman but unfortunately in this distant land there is no minister.

I am told [he] made one of the most beautiful and fervent prayers that a mortal was ever heard to utter. He forgave from his heart all who had ever done him wrong and I believe he mentioned one gentleman in particular.

He prayed for his mother, for his immediate relatives, his friends, his comrades and the world. From all I could learn, he seemed not only calm, but perfectly resigned [to] the great change awaiting him.

It will ever be a source of regret that we could not see him in his last moments. We did not hear until late last night that his illness was dangerous. This morning early we rode over to the *Mouth of the River* expressly to see him, but were met by Dr Madison with the most painful and unexpected intelligence that we were too late. He died at 7:00 o'clock. About ten o'clock this morning, I saw him prepared for his last home.

According to his own request he was arranged in his dress uniform, the coat unbuttoned, and the arms extended by the side. The beauty of life still lingered and I never saw a countenance more natural. The fine manly figure lay extended on the couch, his hair curling as in life over his temples, and dressed as usual there was nothing to show the mournful presence of death but the marble paleness of those beautiful features. The expression was calm and placid and as I bent over his lifeless form I could not deny myself the mournful satisfaction of cutting some curls of his rich silken hair to enclose in this letter.

I know how worse than useless to a Mother's heart are all attempts at consolation. He has gone in the prime of his young manhood, such was God's will. The God of the Widow has given you this cup of anguish and his consolations will not be withheld. That He may be with you in this hour of agonizing bereavement and that we may all meet in a world where there is no more death and no more sorrow, is the fervent prayer of, Dear Madam,

Yours very truly and respectfully,
Helen B. Chapman

My dear Mother, Fort Brown, Texas

December 10, 1848. Mr Chapman is at the Brazos and about midnight last night, I was roused by a thundering knock at the door. The question, "Who's there" was answered, "The expressman with the mail." Two minutes after I had taken the letters, I was thankful that you all were alive and well.

About your ride in the rail cars, I was amused with Willie's impressions of travel. The ride to Blanford, Massachusetts was my first journey and it was long, very long before I got to New York to visit such grand places as Barnum's and the American. I look every day and more than once at his picture. To me it is very like him.

My feelings have been dreadfully tried of late in the death of poor Dr Levely of delirium tremens under circumstances painful and shocking. We did not know of his dangerous illness til the night before he died. We rode over early the next morning to see him, but he had been dead about three hours. The day was to me a dreadful one and on returning towards night, feeling I could not rest til the unhappy task was performed, I sat down and wrote a long letter to his mother. I mentioned everything consoling and avoided everything painful. The physician wrote that he died of a nervous affection of the brain. After I had accomplished all, I was half frightened at my own sensations. I had a tightening feeling about my heart and stomach and [decided] to leave such scenes to those more fitted to endure them.

Throughout the length and breadth of the land, War and strong drink are taking their thousands of innocent victims. Mrs Levely was expecting her son home in December. She is not only a widow, but poor and has no daughter.

We live literally "all along shore." One week at the Brazos and another here.[16] We have houses at both places, comfortably furnished, and rather like the variety. I must give you an idea of the way we travel. There are two roads, one via Point Isabel, the other by the Mouth of the River. Point Isabel is reached by a steamboat. It is about six hours ride in this direction and eight by the other. We travel in an immense covered wagon, called an ambulance containing three or if necessary four seats made either so as to roll up the curtains, or face them in such a way as to be perfectly impervious to rain. This is drawn by four strong fine American horses managed by an experienced driver, a "Yankee from the States." Of course, we can travel with just as much baggage as we please. To complete our equipment, there is a holster attached to the wagon holding a revolver and this, with a heavy cane containing a dirk, constitutes our preparation for defense. Neither the pistol or cane have ever been used and we do not anticipate any necessity for their use.

The road is perfectly level, and in dry weather excellent, but in wet weather, it is heavy. This road from Point Isabel is the same pursued by

16. William Chapman wrote, "I am now in charge of three posts, Brazos, Mouth of the Rio Grande and Fort Brown. By constantly traveling from post to post, I am enabled to perform all the duty required" (WWC to General T. S. Jesup, Dec. 14, 1848).

General Taylor [when he left Fort Texas to cut off the Mexican army on May 1, 1846]. It is perfectly solitary, with the exception of one or two little Mexican farms, and one house, a sort of tavern kept by an American of the name of Taylor.

We stopped at the Taylor house a little while, a rough board building built on the great plain of Palo Alto, not a large tree in sight, nothing but chaparral and not a glimpse of human habitation. The place and scene are good enough for the owner, one of the worst kind of slave holder, rabid against abolitionists, and dealing in slaves precisely as he would in cattle. He left Florida for the commission of some crime and here he is with his wife, a daughter and son, and his slaves. He is coarse and brutal, but his wife is a perfect lady, dignified, refined in feelings, of good family, educated and it is easy to see at a glance, possesses that innate something out of which ladies and gentlemen are made. [In spite of] the coarse, rude life that surrounds her, she makes no complaint, but has the appearance of a broken hearted woman in miserable health. Her daughter is coarsely molded like her father.

There is, as in all new countries, I suppose, a curious order of things, peculiarly so here perhaps, because men who are banished by crime from the United States can live across the river and still carry on business here. You may have heard of Judge Garland,[17] a gentleman of great learning, high standing and talents, who committed a forgery in Louisiana. He is living in Matamoras, with his mistress as his wife, by whom he has five children.

Colonel [Louis P.] Cooke, a Texan, who entered at West Point, but left and who held some high office in the State Government is also living in the same city, a fugitive from justice and is, if things may be called by their right name, a cold blooded murderer. He was tried and eleven jurors were against him but the twelfth refused to hang him. He was remanded and broke jail. There are many such men probably if the truth were known and no efforts made to make them better.

Brownsville just outside the Government grounds contains nearly 2,000 inhabitants. There are villages up the river quite thickly settled, there are numbers of inhabitants at the Brazos and Mouth of the River and not a single Christian minister. We are trying to do something and will have faith to believe we shall succeed.

17. This was probably Rice Garland, an attorney practicing in Matamoras.

My dear little Willie, Fort Brown, Texas

Dec. 14. In the last letter from Aunt Emmy,[18] there was a little one from you, my dear boy, and you cannot think how happy it made us. I read it first before reading the large letter and was glad to hear you have a new overcoat.

I did not mean to break my promise about the skates. I said you might have some when you were eight years old, but I cannot send a piece of money so far and you must ask your Grandpapa to purchase them. Your father thinks you are too young to wear skates and if you choose to wait until you are nine years old you can have something less dangerous of the same value in their place.

Did I tell you among our other pets of our goats and pretty little kids? The goats are very useful for their milk, which in coffee is almost as good as cream; the kids are playful, pretty little creatures as full of frolic as yourself.

The parrot screams, sings and does a great many odd things as usual. I think she is rather foolish for like a good many people I have known she screams, "Hurrah! Hurrah!" no matter what happens. If she hears other people make a noise, she makes one too, just as persons do sometimes at Elections and other great times. Never do a thing my child simply because others do it. That is no reason for a sensible man. Ask if it is right. God bless you, dear child.

Mother

My dear Mother, Fort Brown, Texas

Dec. 20. In my last letter, I told you of Dr Levely's death, and my feeling that in the future, I must avoid such scenes. But in frontier life, this seems to be impossible and the few collected together in such distant places, cannot shelter themselves under the plea of delicate nerves.

A week ago, I had to go through a scene almost as painful. I have told you of Mrs Mumford's arrival, but perhaps I did not mention that a few weeks after, Mr Page arrived with his wife, as Sutler or store keeper for the 1st infantry. They have been living with Mrs Mumford since their arrival. A week yesterday, we were all shocked by the announcement that Mr Page

18. Willie called his grandmother, Emily Welles Blair, "Aunt Emmy." His great-grandmother, Ann Ellsworth Welles, who lived in the Blair household, was called "Grandma-ma."

was drowned. The steamboat came up the river, with the intelligence that Mr Page took passage at the Brazos and was last seen on the boat, about midnight going down the narrow stairs by the wheel house. What rendered it almost certain that he had fallen overboard and was drowned was the circumstance that he went on board in a state of extreme intoxication.

I immediately rode up to Mrs Mumford's and was met at the door by Mrs Page smiling and happy, perfectly unconscious of the blow about to fall upon her. I passed on to Mrs Mumford's room and learned they had not yet found courage to inform her. Captain Mumford was decidedly unwilling that his wife, whose situation is delicate, should remain in the house when the communication was made. So she was placed in the carriage and the Captain and myself remained to break the intelligence to Mrs Page as best we might.

The scene was too painful to remember. God grant I may be spared such another. Her shrieks and screams could be heard in every direction and her affecting appeals to me, "Oh! Mrs Chapman, do you think he can be forgiven? Oh! he has not lived as he ought. It cannot, it cannot be!" screams still ringing in my ears. She is one of those women who seem strong only in their affections and though he was almost brutal in character, neglectful and rude to her, her love for him was almost idolatrous. She is helpless as a child. Her mother is poor and a widow. She has two sisters, widows who are supported by a brother having only the salary of a clerk. She has one sister married but whenever she stays with her she had to pay her board. Page has not left a cent and was in debt. Here is trouble.

I told you of the Taylor family at Palo Alto. Monday [Dec. 18], their daughter was married to a young merchant down at Point Isabel and we were all invited to the wedding. The groom was considered a worthy young man and for his sake and Mrs Taylor's, we went. The house is ten miles from Fort Brown and fifteen from Point Isabel. To accommodate the company and give them time to get home before dark in a country where night traveling is not particularly safe, the time for the wedding was fixed at 12 o'clock in the morning. Judge Bigelow officiated, he generally does very well because he uses a simple form suited to the latitude of Texas, but because Taylor insisted on his using the church marriage service, he made a good many awkward blunders.

It passed off well enough, however, and they were made securely enough man and wife. The poor mother lay in her narrow, comfortless bedroom, very ill. She has a bad cough, is much emaciated, and to all appearances her pilgrimage of sorrow is almost ended. I went in to see her and though I had seen her but once before, she opened her heart at once and disclosed such a depth of suffering as surprised me. "Oh! Mrs Chapman, I cannot live in this way. Nothing but my children brought me here and now that my daughter is to be married and my son going away to school what have I left? To stay here and keep a grog shop, to be giving liquor to these desperate men night after night, nothing but gaming, drinking, and swearing! Oh! it is murder, it is murder!" and her eyes grew wild and her weak frame quivered with agitation and this was in "the house of feasting." It was a sad scene indeed.

She talked at length while in the next room there was noise, laughter and, I fear, too much drinking. In her weakened suffering condition but one idea possessed her, to get away from that place and be with her married daughter in East Florida. It was perfectly evident to me that even without any organic disease, she would soon die in that place.

My dear Mother, I have given up my dreaming and have become a more practical woman. I have ceased to look for grand opportunities of usefulness, but have learned to use my energies, my position, and my influence in any cause where they may be made availing. So in this case I immediately took Dr Ten Broeck aside and told him that Mrs Taylor must go to Florida or she would die and that he and Dr Abadie must frighten her old brute of a husband into a consent. Dr Ten Broeck said he perceived at once that something was preying on her mind and I told him sufficient to convince both himself and Dr Abadie that the necessity was imperative. They both represented her case as alarming and are prepared to press it on her husband as her only chance for life. I talked to her son-in-law, a good hearted young man, and told him I hoped he would do everything in his power to encourage the step.

I must tell you something of Judge Bigelow,[19] the Chief Justice of Cameron County. He is the son of Deacon Bigelow of Colchester, Connecticut,[20] an elder in the Baptist Church. He came to Point Isabel at the opening of the war, and found it closed to all except such as could prove themselves to be in the employ of the government. So our Yankee enlisted himself as a carpenter and though he knew nothing of the trade, his good

19. Israel B. Bigelow, attorney at law, was a beef contractor during the Mexican War. He was elected mayor of Brownsville in March 1850 and served until November 1850 (*Rio Grande Sentinel*, quoted in the New Orleans *Daily Delta*, Apr. 6, 1850).

20. Colchester is fifty miles south of Westfield.

judgment in suggesting and his celerity in handling the plane, got him the post of boss or head carpenter where he earned his three dollars a day. We next find him in Matamoras keeping a grog shop, and making money by handfuls; then he got into some expedition by which he received a shot in the leg from a Mexican. Afterwards he went to practicing law and at length, by some hocus pocus, he gloried in the title of Chief Justice. I never spoke with him until the day of the wedding. Major Brice, who had become a little merry, came towards me, dragging along a large tall man of large frame well dressed with a head rather too small for his proportions, not intellectual but shrewd and calculating in expression. "Mrs Chapman, allow me to introduce Judge Bigelow. He has been desiring an introduction, but was too bashful to seek it."

The judge took a seat in front of me, and very soon got quite at his ease. He is certainly a "Cute Yankee." I suppose he has had only an ordinary education, but he really manages very respectably. You must know Mother that though very humble people at home "the Major and his lady" have considerable consequence in Cameron County and I try to turn it to practical purposes. He was saying they had succeeded in removing the county seat to Brownsville.

"Oh! Then Judge Bigelow," said I (I was careful to address him as Judge.) "You will have a handsome courthouse in Brownsville."

"I hope so," was the answer.

"But when are you going to get a handsome Protestant Church, Judge? You know a city can't pretend to much respectability until it has schools and churches."

"Yes Ma'am, that is a fact and I'll give fifty dollars to get a real good church, and a good minister, not one of your, ignorant set of men, but a real smart educated man."

"Certainly," I said. "But it needs someone of influence to start such a movement, and we want a judge to head the list."

"Well," he said. "I'll do it. Within a fortnight I'll have a subscription going the rounds. I had heard Mrs Chapman was in favor of having a Protestant Church and I'm very glad of it. We can't be respectable without it."

They have already started a subscription at the Brazos and I lost no opportunity of urging it upon them all. Dr Abadie says, "You shall most assuredly do it. Judge Bigelow was so delighted he would have started a subscription for a Pagan temple just as readily."

Mr Chapman laughed heartily and seemed much amused at seeing two such Yankees pitted against each other. In these cases you see the immense value of New England associations and principle.

A Yankee adventurer will become "all things to all men," to a degree St Paul never could have anticipated. He will cringe and crawl, have southern principles or any sort of principles, peril his soul in every possible way until he has wedged himself into a secure position. From that moment he becomes the master and then New England becomes the beloved and universal model. There must be churches, free schools, evening meetings and savings societies, not because it is right, but because they have such things at home and because they help to make a country respectable and prosperous.

In meeting with New England men, such as even this Judge Bigelow, when you once suggest these things, it is like communicating a spark to tinder, it arouses at once all these old and fixed impressions, the understanding is satisfied and he sees at glance precisely what is wanted.

If I had time to write all his talk I could convince you of the truth of what I mean. He started off as if at once, as if he had all his life been the determined and zealous advocate of all these measures. "It was only the other day," he said, "a friend of mine writing to me, asked me how many churches we had, how many schools, if we had post routes, a Post Office, and all those things."

"You were really ashamed, Judge, were you not that you must tell him we have none of those?"

"Yes, that is the truth, Mrs Chapman. Why a few years ago Houston was worse than this place, all sorts of iniquity going on on Sunday, just because people had no place to go to and now they have their churches, their schools, their evening meetings, their saving societies, everything they have in New England."

I never saw the contrast more strongly displayed than at the wedding between the uncultivated and the cultivated, the low-bred and the high-bred. There were the sovereign people of western Texas and there were the Officers of the Army brought up in the most finished refinement. There was General Whiting's son, young Ten Broeck from New York, Major Brice and others, all perfectly accomplished in manner. This I know is of secondary consequence and yet, when wanting it seems of great value. In all these gatherings you see the disproportions between the women and the men. There are no young girls at all, but there are no men worth having, but with few exceptions.

Mr Chapman has just returned from Matamoras where he has been with other officers to see the commanding General of the Mexican Army.[21] There are about five hundred troops in that city and the General, I understand, is a very gentlemanly man. He and his staff are to dine here tomorrow.

William Chapman's hand finishes the letter.

And they did dine and the way they got *corried* was a caution. I did not drink a drop, though I went through the form of drinking toasts with my usual grace. Helen has a little headache and desires me to wind up this letter, and it being rather long I hereby do it. All is well. I am off to the Brazos at 5 o'clock tomorrow morning: plenty of work, but Uncle Sam can only get 24 hours a day out of me anyhow. Kisses to Willie and love to all.

Yours Affectionately,
W. W. Chapman

21. The 300 cavalry and 200 infantry arrived in Matamoras in early December under the command of General Avalos (WWC to Gen. T. S. Jesup, Dec. 14, 1848). Chapman commented that smuggling was extensive.

5.

TRIALS OF FRONTIER LIFE

January through June 1849

At the start of her second year on the frontier, Helen Chapman found time to write her father to relate her first impressions of the Brownsville settlement. Her letter also provided a forum for her opinions on the extension of slavery, Manifest Destiny, temperance and the relative values of gold and the "welfare of the soul."

Gold fever virtually exploded in the early months of 1849.* Numerous parties bound to seek their fortunes made their way through Brownsville at the start of an overland route to California. Richard Ogden declared the advantages of what came to be known as the Gila Route, starting at Brownsville and traveling through Mexico to Mazatlan, where a voyage by steamer constituted the last leg of the journey to northern California.[1]

In addition to gold fever, another disease affected Brownsville in the spring of 1849. A cholera epidemic raged in Port Lavaca in January, New Orleans in February, and a month later it had reached the Rio Grande. Despite Helen Chapman's claims of good diet and "clean habits," she, too, was infected. Before fading out, the epidemic claimed one-third of the population of Brazos Santiago and 1,000 victims in Matamoras, about 25 percent of its population.[2]

Brownsville's attractiveness as a place to settle was further diminished by a different kind of scourge: raiding Comanches and Apaches. A number of lives were lost; others were carried off along

1. New Orleans *Daily Delta*, Feb. 1, 1849.

2. Extract from *American Flag*, Apr. 4, 1849, published in New Orleans *Daily Delta*, Apr. 12, 1849.

with livestock. An April attack at Santa Rita, a mere distance of six miles, must have been particularly frightening, but Helen did not see fit to write about it.[3] No doubt she felt relief that Willie had remained with his grandmother.

Another member of the Blair family, Helen's brother Welles, resurfaced after a mysterious absence of two years. Writing to William in April from Wisconsin, he reported that he had dropped the legal profession "entirely" and was "now engaged in farming." The intervening time he passed off as having been spent in the fur and lumber businesses of the West. "No one here knows anything about me," he wrote cryptically, "except what I choose to tell and that you may be sure is but little."[4]

My dear Father, Fort Brown, Texas

Jan. 4, 1849. I have been wishing for sometime to give you an account of the Texas side of the Rio Grande—its settlement, progress and prospects—but I have never been in possession of sufficient statistics to suit your *legally educated* tastes, and a statement prefaced by "they say" always passed with you for just nothing at all. But you must know, there is some difficulty in being precise as to localities and distances, in places never visited by surveyors' lines and in populations where no census is taken—and where people appear no one knows from what point, and disappear as strangely. Everything is fluctuating—and a terrible shipwreck is made of all kinds of principle.

I see Mr Brinsmade advances the sentiment that commerce as at present conducted is ruinous to individual and public honor.[5] I am afraid it is too true—here, an honorable man would scarcely believe the facts tending to strengthen such an impression. I am told that among the better class of merchants there are those, who will give *their oath* at the Custom House, that they have paid all the duties as required by law and at the same moment are smuggling in whole cargoes. This is, of course, among those

3. Extract from *American Flag*, Apr. 11, 1849, published in New Orleans *Daily Delta*, Apr. 26, 1849; extract from *American Flag*, Apr.18, 1849, published in New Orleans *Daily Delta*, Apr. 26, 1849.

4. Welles Ellsworth Blair to WWC, Apr. 9, 1849, CC.

5. The Brinsmades were a prominent family in Springfield, Massachussetts. The specific newspaper article Chapman refers to is not known.

doing business in Mexico. I could give you some amusing accounts of the way things are managed at the Custom House, if it were not lamentable to see such a wreck of public honor.[6]

If this valley is ever destined to great commercial and agricultural wealth as some suppose, so long as I live, I shall look back with vivid distinctness on the scene that first met my eye where the Government depot and Brownsville now stand. As soon as the order was issued for the evacuation of Mexican towns, the Major crossed to the other side, and aided by others in the selection, fixed on a high point of land a little above Matamoras for the Government buildings. A great many carpenters, excellent workmen, had been with the Army, some enlisted as soldiers, and soon the capital pay and boundless resources of Uncle Sam enlisted a Corps of American mechanics and laborers, as powerful in their way as the American Army. Then began a scene completely bewildering to the population of Matamoras.

Messrs. Stillman and Belden, two wealthy merchants from the North, bought all the land in the vicinity, in anticipation of its future value. It was just after the frame of a large store-house had been erected for the protection of Government property, that I first rode over to see my new home. I wish I could have daguerreotyped the scene for you, or could now give you any idea of what impressed me so forcibly.

The first step had been to cut a road from Matamoras to the river, and thence construct a ferry. The road led from one of the main streets, and this had been greatly improved by Mr Chapman before the Treaty. All the old Spanish streets hollow inward, instead of being elevated in the center—and, therefore, there was offensive stagnant water at all times. This was Americanized much to the delight of the inhabitants in the neighborhood—and it still goes by the name of "La Calle de los Americanos."

The ground chosen, occupied before the War as a Mexican village, is a pretty spot—not subject to overflow, perfectly level and free from chaparral. As I saw it that morning, the history could easily be read in the scene. Everywhere was bustle and animation—hammers ringing merrily—logs being prepared as foundations for other buildings—workmen in great number, all hurrying with their utmost speed—the new, fresh, comfortable looking buildings appearing in a contrast to the five or six ruined Adobe walls of Mexican houses that the ravages of war had spared.

6. This was a common practice with the customs officers in Mexico and probably one of their principal sources of revenue.

To make the scene unlike the thousand settlements throughout the wide West that are everyday breaking the stillness of forest and prairie, a train of *more than a hundred* huge four mule wagons had just arrived that morning from Camargo loaded with *heavy ordnance* to be shipped at the Brazos for the United States. It was a perfectly clear hot August day and this train was seen moving lazily along like a huge snake winding its path from Matamoras over the green prairie between it and the river. Numbers of wagons had crossed the ferry and parked where Brownsville now stands. The drivers were wild, reckless, ferocious looking men seemingly well-fitted for the frightful burdens they were carrying back to a place from whence they never should have departed. The significant *U.S.* was marked on every wagon and every box.

To make the scene still more unique, a company of mounted Volunteers had just come in from Tampico, so picturesque, so strange in appearance as in a lighter mood of mind would have amused one greatly. They had foraged their way across the country from Tampico in the broiling August sun of the Tropics, and certainly would scarcely be owned as descendants by our blue-eyed, flaxen haired ancestors. Each horse and each man was a study for a painter. Their own horses had been sold and they were mounted on miserable Mustangs having just life enough to carry them to the Coast, where their services would no longer be required. At each saddle-bow was hung pistols and a carbine, and when one looked at the men, it would be with an uneasy feeling that those fearful weapons would as readily be used in private quarrels as in public service. The horses looked as if they would give out before reaching the sea, and the men seemed in danger of being left in a very primitive condition as to raiment, before reaching their destination. Many of them wore large white Sombreros (or hats) of felt with a colored cotton handkerchief crossed corner-wise and sewed upon the top—this was tied by the ends under the chin and had much the appearance of one of those old-fashioned bonnets called gunboats.

These men had thrown themselves from their horses, and were lying about in the hot sun in every attitude of careless abandonment—some smoking—some cooking their messes—some eating the filthy compounds already prepared—the whole troop more wild and strange than anything you have ever seen.

I must except, however, the captain of the troop. He was a fine looking, square set, broad-shouldered man, and when Mr Chapman spoke to him from the carriage, he touched his cap and bowed low with the grace of a real gentleman. He must have been heartily ashamed of his command. Conceive all this grouping, with tents pitched in every direction—some light artillery, guns, and two or three pieces of heavy cannon lying about—the ruined walls of Mexican houses, with here and there the fragment of a fence, or something that showed recent habitation—the narrow and muddy stream of the Rio Grande, with a U.S. Steam Boat at the new wharf—the Camargo train still toiling along over the Prairie, and in the distance Matamoras still and solitary, looking across the river large and handsome. Add to this, side by side, with the athletic Americans, the puny-looking Mexican laborers, and you have the scene as I saw it that morning.

It was that of an *old race* passing away—a *new race* pressing on its departing footsteps—a new scene in the *history of the Country*, a *possession by conquest*. May it be long before this occurs again; but in the pursuing path, with the brain crazed by visions of mines of precious metals and quicksilver and with lands of inexhaustible vegetation, it is hard to stand still and go no farther.

I fervently trust that Northern men will fight to the last moment against the introduction of slavery into the new territories. If I were a Statesman, I would love to be carried dying to the Senate chamber to spend my last breath in this cause. I may be meddling in what I have not sufficient wisdom to comprehend, but it *does* seem to me there are great dangers in the future. They say no portion of the new territory, not included in Texas, can support slaves. This may have been true before the discovery of the Gold mines. Col.——— said to me a few days since (while talking of the possibility of being ordered to California), "I prefer being ordered across the Country because I want to take my negroes with me to dig gold." It is now the very land for slavery—but there are other dangers more remote, but to me not less certain.

I have told you before, that most unhappily the War lasted long enough to make the Conquerors love the land they had conquered. Most certain it is, there are longing and greedy eyes fixed on the "tierra caliente" of Mexico.[7] The rich valley of Tampico, the states of Zacatecas, San Luis Potosi and others are really so boundless in resources that language can scarcely exaggerate them. Men of the regular Army are so isolated from all business pursuits that nearly all places are alike to them, but volunteers

7. The *tierra caliente,* or hot land, of Mexico covers the lower-lying Gulf Coast lands stretching from Tampico, Vera Cruz, Chiapas, Campeche, and Tabasco to Quintano Roo on the Yucatan Peninsula.

whose means of living ceased with the War most certainly *did* covet those rich possessions, and the Army was no place to improve their moral perceptions. It was common talk they said, "The Mexicans are not fit to have such a glorious country—if it were only in the hands of the Yankees!"

There are also a large class of foreigners scattered over Mexico, who have amassed great wealth and would be glad to remain in the country if it possessed political consequence or stability, and if they could ever hope to acquire citizenship. This can only be done, I am told, by a public profession of the Roman Catholic faith—and even then they have few rights. These men have everything to gain by annexation.

One of them, a Mr Costa of Tampico, has just gone to New Orleans, expressly to agitate by printed statements, and in every possible way, the Sierra Madre scheme.[8] He dined with us at the Brazos, and his description of the inexhaustible agricultural resources of those states almost turned my head for the moment. He was born on the Island of Jersey, a British subject—of a Spanish mother and a French father—and now calls himself a citizen of United States. He is a gentleman—educated—talks Spanish better than English and must have considerable influence. There are more men scattered over the Republic of this class than is generally supposed. The Mexicans look for a new republic; the agitators regard it as the first step to Annexation.

One day at the dinner table, we had Colonel Reynolds of whom I have before written—talking of the immense supplies of salt and inexhaustible natural wealth of Texas. Then there was Dr Tobin, an English gentleman, a great traveller, and now President of a very rich English quicksilver mining company in San Luis Potosi. Everything he said might, for aught I know, be a great lie—but he is a finished man of the world and has that calm, simple persuasive manner of telling his wonders that you cannot help believing all for the moment. I believe, however, he is reliable. He says the mineral wealth of California can scarcely be exaggerated—that their company has agents there to ascertain the exact truth. He was on his way to England, with a view of greatly extending the operations of the company.

While all this conversation was going on, I thought the Spaniards could scarcely have returned to Old Spain with more dazzling descriptions of Mexican wealth than we are constantly having. The heads of those in the

8. This is another reference to the plot to make the three northeast provinces of Mexico an independent republic.

Army who penetrated to the City of Mexico have been most completely turned. Republican simplicity will seem tame after such almost Eastern magnificence.

If a man settles in a new country, he rapidly acquires a sort of love for it—if not disgusted enough to leave, he likes to speak well of it, and all the American merchants who come from the interior, and we see very many of them, all speak of the natural resources of the country almost as enthusiastically as Dr Tobin. A military man passing through the country, fatigued, disgusted, taking no selfish interest in what he sees, is scarcely capable of a correct judgment. If unimproved by industry and occupied by such a race as the Mexicans, what would an army think of the country, passing through any part of New England other than the valley of the Connecticut? And yet a man living on the spot would know that these mountains, rough and sterile as they seem to be, would all yield certain treasures.

Do not think *my fancy* is led captive—for I regard the possession of any land *south of that point where men begin to wither* under the heat of the sun as more of a curse than a blessing. But here, it is looked upon as certain that in a few years another great piece of Mexico is to be annexed to the United States—it is not deplored but on the contrary, the idea is rather relished. But think, my dear father, if any portion of the "tierra caliente" becomes included within the United States what an inexhaustible market there would be for slaves. It would be the great burial ground for the Old States—but immense fortunes would be made and men have never hesitated to peril life for money. It is only in mining districts, and those with rich luxuriant soils fitted for the cultivation of staple products that slavery can be profitable anyway. It is only in such countries where it can much longer be safe.

My horror of slavery arises not from a view of its suffering and injustice, for the world is full of sorrows—and perhaps take it all in all, the slave suffers no more than the freeman—it is from watching the workings of the system—seeing its influence upon the master and watching the slave.

But I meant to moralize less and tell you more of what is passing on this frontier. Some think this will be a great and prosperous region; others think that there are serious obstacles to its advancement. The soil is very deep and rich but water cannot be relied upon. As an offset to this, however, there are two crops in the year. So long as the American Tariff continues, there will be great facilities for trade, and for the coming years, large fortunes will be made.

Cameron County was laid off from Nueces, and includes the towns of Brownsville, Santa Rita and others of less note. Brownsville is by far the most flourishing town, and has received such a fair start that people of judgment think it cannot easily decline. Most of the houses are of a temporary character and the population is as motley as you can ever conceive—drawn together I believe from every nation on the globe. There are a large number of Mexicans, most of them from the laboring class. The proprietors, Stillman & Belden, have erected handsome brick warehouses at a cost of about three thousand dollars each. The price of brick I believe is rather cheaper here than in New Orleans, and the buildings I understand are fully equal to what could be built in that city at the same cost. Mr Lemon, another merchant of property, is building a goods store and Lewis Ogden has another, although he is about to sell out to go to California. There are three or four good brick dwelling houses—more in process of erection—and great numbers of an inferior character. There are great quantities of goods in the place, and sometimes business will seem to be dull—then again American and Mexican traders will come from the interior, and the town will be completely swept of goods. Mr Belden, very often in this way, sells off his whole stock.

There is an immense deal of smuggling—aided and abetted by the Mexican Custom House. A very respectable sum has been raised for the erection of a Roman Catholic Chapel and large subscriptions were made by American Protestants, not for the religion, but because it would be a popular measure and still more concentrate the Mexican trade at this point. I must not begin a fourth sheet. Farewell.

My dear Mother, Brazos Santiago, Texas

Jan. 14. Before the departure of the last steamer, we had a house full, Captain Babbitt, Mr Michler, and Mr Bryan, topographical engineers and Mr Whiting, a military engineer. Mrs Brice came in the same boat, and Mrs Caldwell with her family to join her husband at Clay Davis's landing.[9] All the gentlemen after temporary duty here will report to General Worth.[10]

9. Clay Davis's Landing, later known as Rio Grande City, Texas, was founded by Henry Clay Davis, who came to Texas in 1839.

10. Lieutenants Nathaniel Michler, William Whiting, and Francis Bryan were soon to lead exploratory expeditions to West Texas. On December 10, 1848, Secretary of War William L. Marcy ordered General William J. Worth, commander of the Eighth Military Department

The Cholera has made terrible ravages at Lavaca.[11] Out of 450 soldiers, 130 died. One officer fell a victim, Lieutenant Hanson, a fine young man whom I met last fall at Governor's Island. The residents of Lavaca escaped entirely, as did also the officers and their families. At the departure of the steamer, there was a complete panic in New Orleans. Major and Mrs Hunter are boarding at St Charles hotel and were very much frightened. It is indeed a frightful scourge but there has been no appearance of it as yet here.

On Wednesday, the 10th, we came down from Fort Brown, with Captain Babbitt and company. We stopped at the Ranch of San Martin[12] and I went into the kitchen to see the women. My dear Mother, you think you have known something of discomfort, I wish you could have seen the inside of that establishment, and yet it was one of the better class. The building occupied as kitchen is made of mud or clay, the floor of the same material and so rudely and imperfectly thatched as to afford no protection from rain. The fire was built nearly in the center, raised on two bricks, and the smoke escaped in whatever direction it could. They carry on farming to some extent, and there are many mouths to feed. Two women were squatted on the ground near the fire preparing tortillas. One, a woman perhaps sixty years old, was rubbing the corn to a fine paste on the stone used for that purpose, the other was flattening them out and laying them on what served as a griddle. On the other side of the fire, some slips of fried beef were broiling. A great portion of their food consists of this pounded corn and the labor must be immense. They are sensible of their own discomforts.

I said to them, "That is good exercise."

"Oh! no Senora, It is very hard, it makes our wrists very lame. In other places they have mills where they can grind their corn, and have no trouble with cooking but here it is nothing but work."

(Texas), to examine the country north of the Rio Grande from San Antonio to Santa Fe. On May 25, 1849, Lieutenant Whiting recommended to his superior that the "Big Bend" be thoroughly explored. However, he did not visit that area. His recommendation was based upon vague references made by earlier Spanish adventurers to vast territories in that part of Texas. See A. B. Bender, "Opening Routes across West Texas, 1848–1850," *Southwestern Historical Quarterly*, XXXVII (Oct. 1933), 116.

11. Present-day Port Lavaca is on Matagorda Bay, north of Corpus Christi.

12. San Martin Ranch, founded upon a Mexican land grant issued in 1828, lay between the Laguna Madre, a large tidal basin on the north, and the Rio Grande. It extended from the Gulf two thirds of the way to Brownsville.

This was on the American side of the river, and if such people were given a hand mill, I believe tortillas would very soon disappear. We frown very justly on the idea of Destiny being made the excuse for this rapacious invasion of our neighbor's rights and yet it is impossible to live among a people so morally, physically and intellectually degraded without feeling assured that a more powerful race must before long subdue them. My own opinions seem to myself either the result of intuition or impulse. If derived upon reflection, I am unable to trace the steps and give reasons for my conclusions. On that account, except in writing to you, I feel some hesitation in expressing my opinions, when at the same time to myself, they have absolute certainty.

I may seem visionary in saying that if I should live to an ordinary age, I believe I shall see the whole southern part of North America included within the United States.[13]

Your last letter has arrived safely. I did not suppose the Gold Fever had raged so in quiet little Westfield. I have a presentiment we are going to that distant, and by no means desirable, land. Do the right thinking and benevolent ever consider what an unhappy country that must be which is professedly given up to the thirst for gold? Nothing can save California, but the immigration of such men, as hold gold at its comparatively real value, light as a feather's weight in the balance with true honor, justice and all things affecting the welfare of the soul. To me Christian emigration is the imperative duty of the present age. I give you my presentiment for what it is worth. I have had others equally strong that have never had fulfillment.

Try to accustom yourself to the idea, dear Mother, for you may be called on to make the sacrifice. It is unnecessary to beg you to be prepared for any event for the whole course of your life has been such as to prepare you for all things. I know your anxieties. I know you have thought of stations so remote, as to seem almost like exile. I know you have thought of Cholera raging comparatively near us and have dreaded that we might be among its victims. I have written nothing of all this, for what could I say? Our lives are in God's hand.

Jan. 16. Sunday afternoon, we had a sick officer brought here, who was living very uncomfortably in his bachelor quarters and yesterday we had a house full of company.

13. The notion that at least some additional Mexican territory would become a part of the United States was commonly held in the late 1840s.

Richard Ogden came down from Brownsville, with Mr Stillman, a rich merchant who returns to his native state of Connecticut, after an absence of twenty one years.[14] His poor mother has pined so to see him that though very old, her friends had great difficulty in preventing her from taking this long journey to see him. He is grave and thoughtful, says very little, never talks even to his brothers, but upon himself buys, sells and sends off goods regularly. He is a most respectable man, addicted to no vice, and counts his gains of hundreds of thousands.

At the tea table, I said," I presume you have no intention of starting for El Dorado, Mr Stillman?"

With his grave passionless measured manner, he answered, "I think I may take a trip there in the spring." Undoubtedly he will and will go on to amazing wealth till he dies.[15]

A great many are going from Brownsville to California, by the land route in March or April. The weather is very unpleasant, incessant Northers, but my health remains very comfortable.

Jan. 22. To my disappointment [the steamer] brought us no letter from you, but as usual it brought company. Dr Jarvis among the number. The Doctor saw General and Mrs Taylor on his way. Mrs Taylor will not go to Washington in the spring [to attend Zachary Taylor's inauguration as president] and he suspects she may stay away entirely if she can manage to do so. Mrs Wood and Mrs Bliss will preside.[16] One of Mrs Wood's daughters, Puss, as we used to call her when she sent the book to Willie, I hear is growing up very pretty.[17]

Major and Mrs Hunter talk seriously of going to California and wish us to go also. We shall live at Brazos until summer on accommodation and so much the better. To all appearances we are to remain here for two years and yet I cannot feel in the least settled. It seems to me as if every mail brings an order to go somewhere. However this affects very little of my daily life. I cannot "make my hair white or black," and so I go on just as if I felt permanently settled.

14. Charles Stillman went to Connecticut, married Miss Elizabeth Goodrich at Wethersfield, Connecticut, on August 17, 1849, and returned to Brownsville.

15. The Stillmans and the Chapmans became close friends. The men engaged in many business ventures, including a sheep ranch, a silver mine, and the importation of Colt revolvers.

16. These are Taylor's married daughters.

17. The Woods had two daughters, Blandina Dudley Wood, born January 9, 1834, and Sarah Knox Wood, born in Florida during the Seminole War.

Mr Chapman returned last evening from Fort Brown after nearly a week's absence. Mrs Mumford is in an interesting situation. After such a report has been made three or four times, it will be considered very uninteresting. I am not! There is no prospect that Willie will have a rival. Indeed, that could never be. There seems to be a chasm about the child of one's youth that would be wanting to those born later in life.

My dear Willie, Brazos Santiago, Texas

Jan. 23. I have time for only a very few lines. We have so much company. We have had very rough unpleasant weather and if you were here the roaring of the sea, at first, would keep you awake nights. In Aunt Emmy's letter I told about our vegetables, so you see we know nothing about winter here. No fine sledding or sleigh rides. I think by this time you must have plenty of snow and I love to think of you running about in the cold healthy air with your pull boots, sack coat and warm mittens.

I suppose you have grown so much I shall hardly know you when I go home. The parrot talks as much as ever. I have bought some school books for Ann [Mitchell] and she is more pleased than you could be with toys. I think she will learn very fast.

My dear Mother, Fort Brown, Texas

Feb. 5, 1849. I have been at Fort Brown for the last ten days and shall be here for two or three more. This kind of life, traveling back and forth, is well enough, better perhaps for me than remaining in one place, but it sadly breaks up my journalizing. I have visited all my old Mexican friends in Matamoras and been very kindly welcomed.

Miss Bacon has had an examination at her school which many of us here in the Fort attended in the evening. There was a dance which I did not attend. There seems to be a great deal of friendly intercourse [between the Mexican and American populations]. General Avalos, the Mexican Commandant, is very polite and gentlemanly. There is another ball on the 22nd of February and I presume will be represented by both factions. Brownsville is constantly increasing at the expense of Matamoras.

I catch people on highways and by-ways and [have] lost no opportunity of saying church and schools. At last to my great joy, they have got a school started in Brownsville to be kept by a very excellent, and I should think, well educated young man, a member of the Methodist Church. He has organized a Sunday School and I trust this is the dawn of better things.[18]

My friend, Judge Bigelow, met me the other day and said, "Well, Mrs Chapman, I have redeemed my pledge. We have got a school started. Now the next thing must be a church."

What a strange year this has been! The strongest magnet in the world placed in that newly acquired distant region of California thrives tottering and pulling in the Old World, despotism and Marvelous driving thus and hither, to find shelter with us! If the mighty mass of beings can be molded and prepared for rational freedom, all will be well, if not, it is impossible to estimate how fatal may be the consequences.

I was amused with the remark of a gentleman in the Army, of Western birth and a Whig. He was speaking of Major Gooch, who is from Massachusetts and a rabid *Loco foco*, moreover a man of mean character, self serving, untruthful and boastful.[19] He said, "A *loco foco* from the East was of necessity a renegade, untrue to his education, and a seller of his birthright because the whole tendency of his early habits, his avocation, his religion, his culture, was of necessity *highly conservative*."

The expression was extravagant and yet this gentleman is not given to extravagant expression or opinions. He resigned from the Army when a young man of twenty five and until the opening of the War lived in Ohio where he was constantly associating with New England men. He came in as a Major among the new appointments. I am inclined to believe his remarks as applied to the *rabid class of democrats* is true.

Major and Mrs Hunter are living at the St. Charles [in New Orleans] at an expense of $60 per month. They have two rooms, a parlor and a bedroom. Mrs Hunter dresses very elegantly, the lace on her mantillas is $10 per yard and everything in proportion. She says since she left the country in June, she has spent over six hundred dollars upon her dresses and she cannot see much to show for it. Betsy Taylor, Mrs Colonel Bliss, told her she could see a great many things, her Valenciennes lace, for instance. We expect to hear by the next mail that Major and Mrs Hunter have gone on to Washington with General Taylor's family.

18. This is probably R. N. Stansbury (*American Flag*, Jan. 9, 1850).

19. Major Gooch was the tax collector from San Antonio. A *loco foco* was a member of a radical branch of the Democratic Party who was generally against privilege, banks, protective tariffs, and paper money. When they seized control of the Democratic nominating convention in 1836, their opponents in the party left the premises and shut off the gas (and, of course, the lights). The remaining Democrats used the new self-igniting matches, called *locofocos*, to light candles and continued the meeting.

Dr McPhail left two or three days since for Baltimore. We were sorry to part with him, but Dr Jarvis is considered equally good. During the Cholera, Dr Jarvis was in New Orleans and daily visited the Charity Hospital, 40 or 50 patients would be brought in the afternoon and, in the morning, he would see them all in the *Dead House*. There are no signs of its presence here yet.

God bless you all,

My dear Mother, Brazos Island, Texas

Feb. 20. In the midst of all kinds of confusion, I am trying to send you a few lines at least. The house has been overrun with company and now there is a lady here with a feeble baby and two servants. Another boat is expected tomorrow and that will bring another load perhaps. The California emigrants from Westfield arrived safely yesterday and passed us immediately to Matamoras.

You seem to have in your region, but an imperfect idea of our geography. The only seaport is Brazos. Small vessels can anchor at the Mouth of the River, but all vessels coming from the North discharge their cargoes and passengers at this island. Point Isabel is a point on the bay projecting from the mainland and distant about four miles by the channel from Brazos. The Mouth of the River is distant about eight miles and situated about south from Brazos Island. The course of the river is a little northwest making Matamoras nearly west from this place, twenty eight miles by land and sixty by the course of the river.

So you see, embarking for Matamoras and going up the Rio Grande to Point Isabel as the Westfield paper says is an absurdity. At the commencement of the war, the most absurd directions were sent out, showing a perfect ignorance of their positions. For instance, "you will discharge your cargo at the Wharf at Point Isabel on the Rio Grande," "You will proceed to Brazos Island touching at Point Isabel," &c.

The Harding Mining Company came to anchor on [Monday,] the 19th, but did not get on shore until the next day.[20] I believe nearly all called here. Young Fowler Hedge, Mr Barker, I believe, Mr Harding, Mr Clark[21]

20. This is probably a reference to the Hampden Mining Company, from Hampden County, Massachusetts, a group of forty-six persons who left New York in January 1849, landed at Brazos Santiago, and traveled overland to California.

21. Asa B. Clarke wrote a book of the experiences of the Hampden Mining Company, entitled *Travels in Mexico and California* (Boston, 1852).

and I believe one or two more. They all seemed in fine health and spirits. Mr Chapman will see them again at Brownsville tomorrow. I was delighted to see them and sorry they did not remain long enough to show them some attention.

Companies are constantly arriving here bound for the Gold Region. This company in particular has been praised for the fine respectable appearance of the men. I like the whole character of the movement in New England. So far from regarding coldly any excitement that carries young men of New England to the shores of the Pacific, my whole sympathies are enlisted and though I would prefer there should be some higher motive than the love of gold, I am thankful even for this.

In my former letters, I have tried to prepare you for the possibility of our going to California. I hope from my heart that we shall be allowed to remain in peace where we are, but it may be otherwise and I would not like such news to come upon you unexpectedly. In a month or six weeks our fate will probably be decided, and if we do go, we shall return home, of course, to say farewell.

I know you would not attempt even to induce me to remain behind, because there is no peace for me except in following steadily the path of my duty, however trying it may be. That it is the duty of every wife to go with her husband to California if he can take her I have not the shadow of a doubt and God help those men in that far region who are not restrained by the finer moral sense of women.

It is such a relief to hear you are all alive and well.

Helen

My dear Mother[-in-law], Brazos Santiago, Texas

Mar. 4, 1849. It is some time since I had the honor and pleasure of writing the above three words, or any others to you. The chief reason is that Helen does these things and everything else, so much better than I do, that I have a great reluctance to doing anything which she does, for fear that I shall suffer so immensely by the comparison. Whenever I can perform any act or labor which she cannot possibly do, I am exceedingly fearless and work without embarrassment.

It is Sunday evening. That good old season, which memory brings back, as the time when I was courting in a small village in the far North, a certain black eyed school girl, who then had no ringlets, or much hair of any kind on her well-formed intellectual head. Well, as I was saying, it is Sunday evening and tomorrow morning, in these parts, will be Monday morning, at which time a schooner will leave for New Orleans with a mail. The lady to whom I alluded, now the proud and happy mother of the finest boy, (although "I say it who shouldn't say it"), in the world, had intended to write, but being troubled with a slight nervous headache, a family failing, the only failing in the family, desired me most graciously, yet urgently, but with the sweetest smile in the world, such as no other lady could put on, to perform this pleasing duty for her.

My hesitation, rather conspicuous at first, was entirely removed by her promising to lounge on the red stuffed sofa, beside me, and not only keep me in countenances, but also supply me with ideas. At my other elbow sits Mrs Mumford, the sweetest little black eyed lady in the army, laughing at this family arrangement for writing home. With such influences around me, you see, Mother, I must do something; that my efforts may be pleasing to you, the writer humbly prays.

Helen wishes me to write on the subject of Cholera, and is the more particularly desirous that I should do so at this time, as she fears you may hear exaggerated accounts of its mortality on the Rio Grande.[22] It first made its appearance at Brownsville about ten days ago. Some 40 or 50 persons have died there, including four soldiers of the garrison at Fort Brown. None of the officers, or their families have been attacked. It seems to be confined mostly to the laboring classes; of 14 workmen employed on our new building, 12 have died. There were no new cases there today, and it is believed to be disappearing.

At the Mouth of the River, there have been but four deaths, and here, with a much larger population, but three. There was only one new case here today, for which in the absence of the Doctor, who had gone to the Mouth, I prescribed. He had all the symptoms, but I commenced in time by giving him a mixture of tincture of rum, tincture of camphor, peppermint and asafetida. One teaspoonful every hour. I put a generous mustard plaster on his stomach, which soon made its mark. Allowed him to take nothing but a little tea or rice water. His disease is checked and he seems to be out of danger. I mention this treatment as it may be useful to you.

22. Although the cause was not known in 1849, cholera is a bacterial infection transmitted by contaminated food or beverage. Early symptons are diarrhea, vomiting, and muscle cramps. Dehydration often results, which in 1849 was not treatable with intravenous fluids (*Encyclopedia Americana*, VI, 624).

People are under great excitement in this region, and you will no doubt hear most alarming accounts about us. Helen and I are perfectly well, but pay great attention to our food. We eat no vegetables except well cooked potatoes. Our food is mostly fresh beef, bread and potatoes. We have a good Doctor and plenty of medicine so that you need not be anxious about us. Dr [Ebenezer] Swift of Boston is our doctor.

9 1/2 o'clock at night. I have just been to see my patient with the doctor. He has considerable fever, produced by the reaction, is doing finely. He left him 1 1/2 grains of opium and 10 grains of quinine to be taken in an hour. The mixture I gave him today consisted of two teaspoons full of tincture of opium 2 1/2 grains. The proportions of the mixture were equal parts of tinc of camphor and opium (4 ozs.), asafetida 1 oz., peppermints (1/2 oz.). Love to Willie and all,

Your very affectionate,
William

My dear Mother,

I add a line to show you I am not disabled. I have a nervous headache. I have a great deal to tell you about the Californians, but cannot now. Do not be frightened about Cholera if you can help it. I am not frightened and do not feel more in danger now than at any time. We will let you know by every boat and you must not believe what you hear.

In case even the worst should happen you shall be informed directly. But it is strange how invariably it attacks the poor, coarsely fed, unclean in habits and uncomfortable in position. We have a fine large airy house, good food, pure air, good water and a good physician. Trust in God and do not be alarmed. Love to all and kisses to my darling boy. I am thankful he is in New England.

Helen

My dear Mother, Brazos Santiago, Texas

Mar. 6. I know your anxiety and it is useless to beg you to feel otherwise for you cannot help it. The Destroying Angel is among us and we have only to meet our fate with calmness. The doctor here thinks that any attempt to restore the saline substances of the blood by absorption is utterly impossible. You must use violent remedies or the patient dies at once in your hands and the physicians here seem to think that when Cholera is actually developed, there is no possible hope, the sinking is more rapid than you can possibly conceive, but it is consoling to learn that the agony is not long and even so terrible as has been supposed. There are intervals from pain and when the collapse takes place, the suffering ends. They all die calmly and in complete possession of reason.

But all physicians insist so strongly on diet. The simplest substances and in very small quantities. Food, that is not digested, instead of strengthening, weakens the body. There were no new cases of Cholera yesterday and it is hoped that it is on the decline. In Brownsville, the mortality has been dreadful. The position of this place is considered healthier as it has been found that on the very edge of the sea bathed in a salt atmosphere, the disease has not been so violent. I am glad you are in New England.

On the mantel piece of my bedroom stands a large bottle labelled *Cholera Mixture* ready for use in a minute. It is a sad looking object for it reminds us that the disease is here and though I feel no anxiety about myself, the least indisposition in the rest makes me tremble. I do not consider myself by any means exempt, but if my time has come I may as well go away in this as in any other way.

We see several parties of Californians almost every day when riding on the beach. We see them just at the commencement of their long and toilsome march through Mexico. The Westfield and Springfield parties with all the others since arrived will have to encounter Cholera at every turn. We hear it has shown itself in Monterey and Saltillo. God help them. It is a worse enemy than hostile Indians.

A few days since riding on the beach, I overtook a party from New York who were anchored the day previous in a schooner. They were all fine looking gentlemanly men. Two baggage wagons preceded them while they were on foot, all warmly clothed and each carrying a rifle. The countenance of one looked so familiar that it seemed I must have been struck at last by an irresistible impulse. I bowed. He smiled and bowed in return.

It is a hard thing to keep me within conventional bounds at all times and I longed to stop and talk with these men. If I had been ten or fifteen years older, I would have done so but I am among people who consider such a natural demonstration unlady-like and, moreover, people sometimes behave so badly in this part of the world, that it is not quite safe for a lady to depart from her reserve.

On returning over the beach, I, of course, met the same party again. There was no one in the carriage besides myself, except Mrs Mumford and the child, but as I approached this same young man, the wish to say one word at least to those poor fellows became so strong that I told Cline to stop the carriage and beckoned to him. He approached and I told him at first sight I believed he was someone I had seen before but I believed it was a mistake. He said his name was Valentine, that he had lived in New York City, but for the last two or three years in Massachusetts. Half a dozen of the others came up and stood about the carriage looking very pleased. They asked about the Cholera and I said I thought they would not be in danger if they kept good habits. The young man said, "This place doesn't look much like the North, does it, Ma'am. There's a great deal of drinking here."

I said, "Yes, and it is more dangerous here than in cold climates. You must remember you are New England men when you get to California."

They promised to do so. I wished them health, success, and plenty of gold and then we parted. Poor fellows! It was easy to see they had already begun to realize [the extent of] their undertaking. The beach of Brazos Island is about as desolate a spot as the eye can view, nothing but sand and the everlasting waves. Just starting on a journey with such an ocean [in view] would give one an idea of interminableness.

Mr Lehman, one of our merchants, was here in the evening and I was telling him my adventures with the New Yorkers. He was much amused and said he believed a number of them were sorry. He talked with a young man and among other things said, "Doesn't this country look wild to you after coming for the North?"

"Oh! yes," he exclaimed. "This is so different from Hartford. There, after I got out of the store, I could go to concerts and lectures, visit agreeable young ladies, and have everything so pleasant. It is so different here."

I am sorry I have not the young man's name. Stragglers from the different parties have already begun to return. Some I understand have already returned here and embarked for home. None, but the strong and muscular and stout of heart, should undertake such a journey.

Helen

My dear Mother[-in-law], Brazos Santiago, Texas

Mar. 16. Your kind letter of February 8th was duly received. I wrote you a hasty letter three days since, enclosing $300 in Treasury Notes. In regard to "securing the money expended on the house," do as you think best. I don't care a fig. Whatever you do is right.

As I wrote you a few days ago, I have no earthly doubt that [Welles] is living well in Wisconsin.[23] As the old woman said, "Didn't I tell you so?" Did I not say that he would some day come out all right. I shall write by this mail such a letter to that gentleman in Wisconsin as will bring him out, that he will either join you or me here, where no one would know him. Fear not, my dear Mother, although we have all suffered some, on the whole, we have reason to be grateful. I have great faith.

Eight days ago Helen was attacked with cholera, but it at once yielded to treatment and she is now out of danger and gaining strength fast. I did not mention it before or rather in my letter three days ago, because she was then not entirely out of danger, and by speaking of it and telling the truth, you might have been unnecessarily alarmed. I have been perfectly well, but am exceedingly careful in what I eat. I have seen every case here, and have prescribed for many in the absence of the Doctor. I have very been successful and am called Doctor as often as Major. We had no new cases yesterday and the disease is disappearing. It has entirely left Brownsville and Fort Brown, still some cases in Matamoras. We have cured every case here, when it has been taken in time and the patient has followed the direction of the Doctor.

The Westfield B boys called at our house and were in fine spirits with visions of gold before their eyes.

I know you would like a letter from Helen. By the way everything she does, says, writes or thinks is good. She can't be beat. I think so, and the masses sustain me. She is very sweet when she is sick. I told her last night that I wished she would get sick oftener. She then loses some of her energy and I have my own way more. I occasionally presume to spit on the floor when she is sick, a thing I would not dare to do when she is well.

Yours affectionately
W. W. Chapman

23. Welles Ellsworth Blair, Helen's brother, had been missing for several years. The Blairs hired an investigator of sorts, a lawyer, to search for him. He had recently located Welles near Oshkosh, Wisconsin.

| Helen added the following note.

Dear Mother,

I am lying on my back trying to write a line to convince you I am still alive. I am weak but they say entirely out of danger. I know you will be grateful and I trust my life is spared for some usefulness,

Helen

My dear Mother[-in-law], Brazos Santiago, Texas

Mar. 17. I wait until the last moment to write you. Since I wrote you yesterday, Helen has improved wonderfully. Today she has been able to "read, write and cypher," to say nothing of laughing at my jokes. You need have no fears.

Mar. 19. Helen had a fine night's rest last night, and this morning has got up for the first time since her attack, a week ago last Thursday. I am truly thankful to a kind providence that He has raised her from this dangerous sickness.

Three persons have died here after only five or six hours sickness. The disease now seems to be disappearing here, and I am perfectly well. It is raging terribly in Matamoras. 56 deaths last Friday. The fine breeze and salt atmosphere helps us here. Helen sends much love to all, and Father and Mother send kisses to our darling boy.

Mar. 24. Mrs Chapman, having resumed the editorial chair, I respectfully retire.

Yours affectionately
W. W. Chapman

My dear Mother, Brazos Santiago, Texas

Mar. 24. I cannot write much of a letter, but am anxious to show you I am able to write a little.

When I get well, I will tell you what I know of Cholera. The restorative powers of nature and judicious resting do more than medicine. Medicine, indeed, seems almost powerless. Doctor Swift says he would rather manage the disease at the North than the South.

We have bad news of the Californians. Night before last, a report came down the river that some belonging to the Massachusetts party had died of Cholera, but the Major called over the names of the Westfield people and none of those were among the number. Captain Hardin had been very sick, of what disease was not mentioned, but it was reported he was very much better.

This morning very sad news came down from Colonel Webb's party.[24] The whole organization is destroyed and numbers are returning. The men were so insubordinate they would not stand guard. In consequence of which a great portion of the baggage was stolen and also a portion of their money. But the worst of all is that the Cholera overtook them and twelve have already died.

Cholera is raging in Camargo, fifty dying in a day. In Matamoras there have been forty, fifty and sixty deaths daily, and the better classes lately have been the victims. Directly across the river at Brownsville and at Fort Brown, it has ceased entirely. It seems to go up the river, not on both sides at once, but by the shore. It has been bad here and at the Mouth of the River, but seems to have expended its force in both places. I feel like a person on whom a miracle has been performed. Women are much less apt to die of the disease, it is said, than men. You would be astonished at the emaciation one or two days, and even a few hours in the fatal cases, produces. I have begun to gain again and today on being weighed found my weight to be 86 pounds. At home, you remember, I weighted 97 before I began to gain flesh.

The house has been full of company. Californians [those bound for California] arriving constantly, but I have been shut up in my bedroom and have not seen them.

I have no strength to write in this letter about California. You probably know that if our lives are spared, we must go. So many miracles have been wrought in my favor, I doubt not I shall have strength to get there.

April 7. I am well enough to write you a long letter, but as usual the house has been thronged with company and the steamer is just about leaving. Major and Mrs Brice departed yesterday on the "*Fashion.*" We were sorry indeed to part with them. I have seen so many silly women, it is refreshing to meet a woman of strong sense and strong health like Mrs Brice.

Captain Mumford came in the *Fashion* and his amiable but foolish little

24. Webb was part of a California-bound expedition which also included naturalist John Woodhouse Audubon. Some in the party returned; others continued the journey. See John Woodhouse Audubon, *Audubon's Western Journal: 1849–1850*, ed. Frank Heywood Hodder (Glorieta, N.M.: Rio Grande Press, Inc., 1969), 50.

wife who has been staying here for some time was on the lookout at the top of the house.[25] In her childish joy, she ran down the whole flight of stairs to the ground and, as a consequence, she is still home lying flat on her back with a threatened miscarriage.

I am steadily and even rapidly gaining strength though my only food is about 5 tablespoons full of meat broth at noon with a bit of toast and a little rice. My breakfasts and suppers consist of a little toast and tapioca and a small quantity of goat's milk.

They have come for my letter and I must stop. The Cholera has been awful all along the line. Here at the Brazos we have lost one third of the population. In Monterey, it is raging.

Get ready for California. So far as anything in this business can be relied upon we are to go.[26] God bless you.

Helen

My dear Mother, Fort Brown, Texas

April 13. Tuesday [Apr. 10] we rode down to Pt Isabel, crossed in a steam boat to the Brazos and returned yesterday. Such rides do me great good and my health is really excellent. I believe I mistook my strength and attempted at times too much at home. The Dr is constantly cautioning me against any overexertions.

At Point Isabel, I was shown the spot where poor young Churchill in his frantic delirium jumped into the gulf. After his rescue, he quieted for a while but suddenly sitting up, he seized his sword, exclaiming, "I'll show you how to command a company," and fell dead on the floor.

Young Whiting is now at Pt Isabel and shows, but too plainly in his person, the fatal ravages of the destroyer. His face is very red, bloated, and his eyes heavy and lifeless. Those are agonizing sights to me, you well know, dear Mother, but in my mind there is more consolation in our poor [Welles's] case than in theirs. Both these young men had every advantage of rank, family and fortune. Gently and carefully nurtured, lavished safely and pleasantly into the world, they have made shipwrecks of all. Young Whiting is a grandson of General Macomb and was brought up in the most careful manner by a pious father and mother not merely so in name, but

25. This implies that there was a "widow's walk" on the quartermaster's house at the Brazos.

26. In a letter of April 6, 1849, William Chapman wrote to Colonel Hardee of San Antonio, "I am ordered to California!" This order was subsequently rescinded.

by parents whom all acknowledge to carry out in their daily lives, the religion they profess. Though young Whiting was expecting us, he evidently had not been able to restrain himself, and his breath smelled strongly. Of these three, dear Mother, all of the same age, one is in his grave, Whiting lives and our poor [Welles], it is to be hoped, is still alive.

Want of opportunity and time has prevented my writing about money matters as I have wished to do. I have encouraged William in sending home as much as possible, because I knew in that way only would it be safe. He has been entering into some little speculations here, that have proved very advantageous and I have felt anxious to secure a sufficient portion so that in case of the death of either of us, you would have enough to support Willie. Farther than this, I have no desire to lay up money. *Do not say to any one that William has been speculating.* If you wish to say anything, you can say that his pay has been very handsome, and his expenses while in Mexico, very small.

With the property now in Father's possession, and with $1800 in Mr Reed's hands,[27] you would be kept from want and my anxiety is in case of my death to secure some certain provision for you. Mr Chapman laughs at the idea and says as long as he lives Willie will be abundantly taken care of, but absent children have not the hold on a father's affection that those living with him possess, and if he should marry an extravagant wife and have a large family of children, he would find it exceedingly difficult to give you a sufficient sum for the proper maintenance of his child. Willie's separation from you is something I could not think of.

My wish is this, to go through some legal formalities for securing to Willie $5000 to be used by you for his support and education in case of my death. There are many reasons of great weight in my own mind to make this necessary and until I can effect it, I can not feel my worldly affairs so arranged as to make me die peacefully. If Father will draw the forms necessary for accomplishing this, I will get it done.

I hope it does not show an inordinate fear of the future in my anxiety to effect this. According to human chances, I feel more sure of life than I did 6 months ago. It is my disposition perhaps to make too many arrangements for the future. There is nothing prophetic in this. I am not

27. Colin Reed of Washington, Pennsylvania , was William Chapman's brother-in-law, the husband of Sarah Elizabeth Chapman. He was a business man of sound judgment and ability and William was involved in many ventures with him.

in the family way and it only results from my habitual wish to have every thing arranged.

Brazos Santiago, Texas, April 21. I lose no opportunity of writing though my letters must be very short. The physician is very much opposed to any mental labor, reading, writing or thinking.

The Cholera seems wholly to have disappeared from the valley of the Rio Grande. We fervently hope not to return. It was in Monterey at the last accounts.

The Major is at Fort Brown, but will be down this evening. I was intending to go with him, but was prevented by the unpleasantness of the weather. "But what of your health?" You will say. I believe I am gradually gaining but my emaciation and debility have been such, I shall be some time in getting back to my usual health. I need a journey, I may try a trip to Tampico for three or four days and see what that will do for me.

It is not likely we can go North before the 1st of July, indeed, it is our wisest course to keep back as much as possible and to make our departure late in the fall.

Love to see all and kisses to my darling boy.

May 5, 1849. Again I write at the last moment. I went up to Fort Brown last week to recruit my health and I think the change was beneficial. There have been heavy rains and the country is fresh and beautiful.

I went to Matamoras to visit my old friends and everywhere saw the destroying traces of the Cholera. They are enlarging the burying yard and almost every family is in mourning. All the old Mexican ladies died, among the rest my particular friend, Dona Ignacia Meridiola. The mother of Dona Juanita died and she herself was very ill. Dr Jarvis, in Matamoras during the epidemic, said he could scarcely pass a house where a body was not laid out for burial.

One evening while riding on the beach here at Brazos, we met a Mexican with his family on foot. They were from Matamoras and I asked the woman if any of her family had the Cholera. She said five had died with it in her house. It has disappeared and to those not actually bereaved it seems like a terrible nightmare.

I am recovering my former appearance and am now taking a preparation of iron. My mind partakes of the weakness of my body and I have no disposition even to read the newspapers. Dr Swift wishes me to avoid any mental effort as much as possible. He thinks all that saved my life was being slightly under the action of Calomel before my attack. I wish very much to give you a clear account of Cholera symptoms but I am not sure I have energy to do it. By all means attend to your bilious attacks and get your system regulated.

The rapid decline of strength in the patient is much more alarming than the violent spasms and cramps. Indeed, it is generally the case that those who die suffer the least. I had but three evacuations yet I was exceedingly more reduced than some who had twenty. Many who die never have a spasm and no more than two or three evacuations from the bowels. Calomel can sometimes be given in very large doses and, if the rice water discharges can be darkened by the flow of bile, the patient can be saved.[28] In the sinking condition of the system, perspiration is a bad sign and should not be encouraged. Highly concentrated nutrients, jelly, brandy, etc., are given where the stomach will bear them. After all, if one's hour has come it is not a bad death to die. It is terrible to the living but when I began to get better I often thought I never could have died easier. On Saturday and Sunday when in the greatest danger, I could have passed away without a struggle or regret and so it is with all.

Love to all and kisses to Willie.

Helen

My dear Mother, Fort Brown, Texas

June 8, 1849. We came up [the river] day before yesterday and I intended to write a long letter but was so tired I put it off til this morning, the last minute. I believe this moving up and down is well for me, but it breaks up all my regular habits and I seem to accomplish nothing.

You will hear all sorts of frightful reports about us and I know you must feel anxious. The Indians have indeed been here and committed their usual depredation.[29]* We travel, however, so heavily armed that we have no fear, and in the immediate vicinity of Fort Brown and Brownsville, there is, of course, no danger.

28. "Rice water discharges" is the term still used to describe the almost-clear stool from cholera patients.

29. In view of the many newspaper reports concerning Indian attacks in the vicinity, Helen was understandably trying to downplay the danger to her mother. This more or less confirms that Emily was also reading other sources to obtain news from Brownsville.

Harry Love came dashing up to the office last week, his horse covered with foam, bearing dispatches from Colonel Washington.[30] He is a perfect specimen of the *Border Dandy*, browned by exposure to wind and weather, of magnificent physical proportions, and altogether bearing himself with a dashing easy kind of grace that would astonish you. We had heard he had been murdered and the joy of his safe return was unbounded. He brings us accounts of the Indians ravaging the whole line above.

You cannot conceive what a weight is taken off my mind about California. I do not allow myself to regret or deplore any thing that *must* be and so I did not know how much I dreaded it till the order was countermanded.

My health is remarkably good, so good that I have been on horseback two or three times. My present plan is to start from here the last of July or the 1st of August in the company of Mr Douglas, one of the clerks who will take me to Wheeling, Pennsylvania. The Major, if he goes at all, will not go until later.

I have everything [to say] today and yet this morning, I cannot write a word. God keep you all from Cholera.

Love and kisses to Willie. God bless you all.

Your affectionate
Helen

30. Colonel J. M. Washington was the commanding officer of the Army garrison at Santa Fe, New Mexico. By his letter of January 31, 1849, Chapman informed Colonel Washington that Harry Love, the express rider, was to return directly from Santa Fe via El Paso to San Antonio. Following orders, Love traversed the Comancheria of West Texas alone and reported directly to General Worth in San Antonio with information "respecting the best route from Santa Fe to San Antonio" (WWC to Col. J. M. Washington, Jan. 31, 1849, CC). Presumably this information formed a basis for subsequent expeditions in 1849. Harry Love was reported dead in the *American Flag* on May 16. On June 2, the *Flag* reported, "It will be gratifying to many of our readers to learn, that there is strong reason to suppose that Harry Love, the well-known and daring express-rider, is not dead, as stated by rumor a short time since. We are informed that in Monclova, where he was said to have been murdered, nothing was heard of any such occurrence."

6.

PURSUIT OF CIVILITY

July through December 1849

Helen Chapman's contentment with frontier life continued during the summer of 1849. Although still recovering emotionally from her brush with death, she took pride in the growing evidence of civilization in the area, such as the Sunday school and the select school. Social life, too, was assuming a degree of predictability. An order of Odd Fellows was active in charitable work, and Brownsville's dignified Fourth of July celebration stirred its citizens' patriotism.

Women were vital to the appearance of any such culture and civility on the frontier in Chapman's view. Furthermore, women's duties included exercising their moral influence. Particularly in the absence of the church, women could exert a restraining force on the conduct of those who were otherwise adrift. Chapman regretted that many women lacked this sense of responsibility and the necessary strength of principle. The frontier needed women of "commanding and elevated character."[1] She, for one, felt equal to the task.

My dear Mother, Fort Brown, Texas

July 10, 1849. I cannot bear to disappoint you but I have almost concluded it is my duty not to go home this summer. My health is excellent and though I have, like everyone in this climate, considerable mental languor, I never had more physical energy. I want [to see] you once more. I have a longing for the old house and to see the bright sunshine pouring

1. HBC to EWB, Aug. 12, 1849 (below).

into the old south door of the dining room, but most of all I long for my child. I dreamed of him last night and his looks and tones were sweeter than ever. When thinking of this protracted separation, I fear that Willie will think that his father and mother do not love him as other parents love their children. There is no want of motherly tenderness in my nature, whatever may be my other deficiencies.

As for our plans, I can tell you nothing. I do not believe we are going to remain here but as to where our next home is to be in this vast republic, I have no pre-vision. Our destiny is the frontier and I am not sorry for there we are most needed. Poor little Willie. His letters made me feel bad, for [he] feared I would not go home. God bless you all.

Brazos Santiago, Texas, July 14. This is one of those days that makes one fully realize the heat of a tropical climate. There is almost constantly a strong fresh breeze that makes the air very comfortable, but this morning, there is not a breath and the sun pours down with a dry oven heat. It is not yet eight o'clock in the morning, but the sun has the full heat of mid-day in the North.

Notwithstanding all this, I am in almost robust health. The extreme dryness of this summer climate and unvarying temperature affects me most favorably. Others complain of extreme debility, but my habits are active and I seldom feel languor. This I ascribe very much to the regularity of my habits and the simplicity of my diet. I have broken away forever, as Willie would say, from the tramels of fashionable life and a woman of the world would consider my habits most absurd. I retire within half an hour of nine o'clock invariably, company or no company. I am generally bathed in cold water all over and well rubbed and dressed by five o'clock in the morning, never in bed after half past five. Even if I feel unwell, I make an effort and get up, but it very seldom is an exertion.

When dressed, I ride on horseback or if prevented, I walk until six o'clock when the heat drives me within doors. At seven precisely, we breakfast, mine consisting of boiled goat's milk with toasted bread. Occasionally I treat myself to a little piece of mush melon, but I make a light meal and drink no tea at breakfast. Is not this brave? Dr Swift says I have great vitality, and can thrive on less food than almost any one he ever knew.

I care about the house a good deal til dinner time, when I eat rice with mutton, meat soup without fat and without vegetables. I use no seasoning, but salt, and do not eat meat, but three times a week. I treat myself to one cup of tea at night sometimes a little toast and some times nothing. I eat no cake, no pies, no pudding unless a little bread or custard of the plain kind, and that in small quantities.

We ride every evening at five o'clock, until dark either on horseback or in a carriage. This is my life for the last three months; no reading, no writing, none but common and daily cares. I take no medicine and none seems necessary. I use an injection pipe.[2]

July 15. The steamer brought your letter of July 1, and it was indeed most welcome. You judge rightly that I have grown indifferent to many things once considered important. It is impossible to return to life from the very verge of the grave with precisely the same feeling as before. Besides my mind has been so occupied with great subjects, emigration to California, [Welles Blair's] unexpected appearance, the contemplation of a new phase of society that I can scarcely take interest sufficient in the commonplace affairs of life to be a very proper part in them. Moreover, death has been so busy that I seem only waiting my turn and thus I hold all things loosely. The war swept off half my old friends. Since that time, poor [Sarah] Chase is a widow.

[Colonel James] Duncan has vanished from the scene in the high noon of his fame.[3] His death really gave me a shock. I had watched his career with interest and I never dreamed it was so soon to end. But perhaps it is as well, his faults, and they were serious, will be forgotten now in regret for his early death and in admiration for his brilliant career. Had he lived longer, he might have outlived his fame, for as I remember him, he was wanting in many of the elements of calm, enduring greatness. However powerful a man's intellect, if without commensurate greatness of soul, he is necessarily short sighted. He has no calm trust in the far off future. Duncan was impulsive, too eager for present aggrandizement, to make a consistent and really imposing life. He was getting more and more involved in political schemes and, in time, the glory of the young warrior would have been lost in a more common and far less attractive character.

By your letter, I find you were anxious about us during the storm.* I forgot to tell you that most fortunately at that time we were absent at Fort Brown. It was fearful enough there, but here, it was most awful. Our house remained unharmed, though the torrents of rain forced their way into the

2. An injection pipe was a device used for enemas.

3. Duncan had died in Mobile, Alabama, on July 3, 1849, at age thirty-eight (New Orleans *Daily Delta*, July 6, 1849). See Appendix A.

house, covering the carpets and injuring the books. The wind seemed to whirl round and round in a way we never hear it in the colder latitudes.

This storm was very much out of season. August, September and October are peculiarly the hurricane months, and, during that time, we shall desert this house and live at Fort Brown. We shall move the end of this month. Here, the very ground is insecure. There, there is no more insecurity than in all places liable to such agitation of the elements. The houses are built of one story with reference to these dangers.

Fort Brown is really becoming a very comfortable place to live. Goods are there in great abundance and at prices I believe almost as cheap as in New York. The growth of the place is most astonishing and I am both happy to say with truth that the population is improving. A great many of the more desperate characters have either died of Cholera or gone to California. There are some very respectable citizens.

The Sunday School is flourishing and to me very interesting. There are about seventy scholars and a very liberal interest is displayed in its behalf. They have sent $150 to New Orleans for a library and the gentleman of the place feel interest in its success. Nearly half the children are Mexicans and they attend very regularly. Sometimes their appearance is very amusing. They make everything an occasion of dress and you would sometimes see them dressed out in white with ribbon streamers and their heads a perfect flower garden with artificial flowers. You very rarely see a bonnet among them. It is in these remote places and among such a population that you see the full value of this really great institution.

I asked Mrs Miller, a poor widow in Brownsville, if she would send her children to the Sunday School. She seemed delighted to do so and the following Sunday brought her daughter, a girl of sixteen, and a little boy of four years. The girl was put into my class. I gave her some of the Testament to read, that chapter in Matthew containing the Lord's prayer. She read quite well, with some hesitation at the long words, but when commencing with the verses "Our Father, etc." she read fluently and instead of saying "forgive us our debts," read "our trespasses."

I said to her, "You know that prayer."

"Oh! Yes ma'am," she said. "I never forget to say it every night."

"Your mother taught it to you, I suppose?"

"Oh! No, Mother can't read. I learned it at the Sunday School in Galveston. I was there three months and went every Sunday. There's where I learned to read."

When such children get books, they are talked of reading in the family, and good must necessarily be accomplished.

I think it is Miss [Fredericka] Bremer [the Swedish writer] who has some beautiful remarks upon those resting places in life when one is relieved from the extreme purpose of pecuniary care for one's family. The sympathies one almost necessarily lavished on the narrow circle of home take a wider range, the whole human family becomes brother and sister.

This I feel to be in some degree the case with myself, and coming to this remote frontier at such a crisis. The West has become the chief object of my sympathy. Until you cross the mountains and feel that magical change wrought upon yourself, you cannot conceive what the West implies. This infant giant, omnipotent almost for good or for evil, would at the first sight enlist at once and forever all the sympathies of your heart and kindle your poetical imaginations. You know how I love the refinements of civilization, how I shrink from coarseness of thought, action or language, yet I am willing to stay here and take this for the field of my earthly labor. It is no momentary feeling, but hourly strengthening. I am fully persuaded it is the great thought of my life. The West needs men of age, character, discipline and principle.

July 20. Every soul in the house, servants and all, is asleep this hot afternoon, and the house is as still as midnight. Whenever I find myself so situated, I am irresistibly inclined to write to you.

[Welles], poor boy!, writes of his solitary, unshared life. Has he yet to learn that some natures are forever solitary? Does this seem vain? It is certainly written in no such spirit for we are but as we were made, and it has always seemed senseless to pride oneself on anything not self-acquired. I have indicted and censured this feeling in others and you know I cannot make an excuse for solitary habits and keeping aloof from my fellow men. I try to force myself into compliance with all the proper demands of social life, still I cannot help a regret that there is a secret or inner life, unguessed, unshared, ever seeking consolation and ever alone. This will be the case with [Welles] and he may feel it more painfully out in the world than in his backwood's solitude.

Please pardon me, I myself am feeling wearied in one of my earthly trials. We have visitors in the house, good excellent people. I heartily wish there were more such in the world, but I must confess they are insupportably tiresome. They seem to be destitute of that kind of taste and knowledge that constitutes for me the glory and beauty of life. I dread their waking up for my talk is exhausted. They read nothing and when I spoke of the Hungarian General Kossuth, they did not know whom I meant.[4] I thought I would come down to a less elevated subject and made a remark to the lady concerning Lady Blessington's early life.[5] She did not even know of her existence. You may think such ignorance of the world we live in unusual and unpardonable. It is not so. It is too common for censure. There are some others, with whom you can converse pleasantly through all the regions of fact, but if you venture a little farther into a spiritualized region, they are struck dumb at once. Is it because men are so forever on the defensive in society that they never reveal themselves to each other except in writing? There, indeed, hearts answer to hearts.

But this is all idle retrospect and I should employ my time in telling you of other things. In my last letters, I had begun to tell you of Mr Richard Pilsbury, no common man.[6] He is now about sixty and has had a varied eventful life and one for which you would feel much sympathy. He has made and lost two or three fortunes, has traveled the world as a sailor, and in one of his adventurous searches after fortune, he lost his wife and six or seven children, all but two. Disappointed, embittered, "mad with the world," to use his own expression he buried himself in the wilds of Texas in a hut of his own construction, lived on such poor food as he could himself collect and prepare and I believe passed years in this condition.

He again emerged into the world and was sent to Congress as a representative from Texas. He was then about fifty-eight and while in Washington, faithful to an old and early attachment, he renewed the offer of his hand to a Miss Carpenter, a young lady in Maine of thirty two years of age. The unsuccessful younger man had been rejected; the Member of

4. Any follower of current events in 1849 would know of General Lajos Kossuth, the "responsible governor-president" of Hungary at the time. In April 1849 he had issued a declaration of independence from the Austrian Hapsburgs. Russian troops came to the aid of the monarchy in June (Helen Rex Keller, *The Dictionary of Dates* [New York: MacMillan Company, 1934] 121–122; Trager, *Peoples Chronology*, 463).

5. Lady Blessington in 1849 was the subject of the day's raciest international gossip. Born Marguerite Gardiner in 1789 of an impoverished Irish family, her scandalous escapades had long been followed in European society. In 1831, after her husband's death, Lady Blessington resumed her former position among London's elite, supporting her salon with her literary talents. She went bankrupt in April 1849 and fled to Paris, where she soon died. See Anne Crawford, *The Europa Biographical Dictionary of British Women* (London: Europa Publications, Ltd., 1983), 66; Sir Leslie Stephens and Sir Sidney Lee (eds.), *The Dictionary of National Biography* (London: Oxford University Press, 1921), II, 675.

6. Chapman is referring to Timothy Pillsbury. See Appendix A.

Congress was accepted. The family say, however, she had loved him from the first, but the opposition of friends parted them. If it was so, she married believing the dream of her young life was about to be realized, and I fear she has already awakened to a sad reality. He is one of the few men who have been something more than observers. He not only tells you of what he has seen, but he stamps on everything his own individuality.

He is also a man of fine feeling and generous impulses with a touch of the roughness of Western life, but not extending to his mind or heart. At the core, he is a gentleman and the most fastidious could not call him vulgar. He is large with black hair in which you do not observe scarcely a thread of white, eyes the strangest and most penetrating I almost ever saw. The pupil is immensely large leaving the iris scarcely more than a line around it. Such is the man who in his prime touched the heart of a very young girl in a secluded village life. He wrote to her from Washington and she very gladly received him as a suitor, but I think her romantic dream must have been a little shaken, to see the heavy, indeed, clumsy, elderly gentleman with fiery carbuncle nose that should have given her a suspicion of his habits, but his reputation, the real force of his character, his wealth and his rank, all blinded her and until married she could only realize that her husband was really in the downhill of life, his progress accelerated by high living and, worst of all, by actual intemperance.

She lives on a plantation in the sugar growing region of Texas, with none but slaves about her. To make it worse, though kind and devoted when himself, he is ugly and hateful when under the influence of liquor.

He has just been here on an electioneering tour and left a few days since. On his arrival, he made a speech in Brownsville, that was considered admirable, mingled with the people and won golden opinions. He went up the river and his brother-in-law, Lieutenant Carpenter, delayed having some company visit until his return. He came down in the boat dead drunk, having left all his clothes upriver at Davis's Rancho.[7]

They had to carry him from the boat, the next morning to a house in Brownsville where he lay for two or three days, until fit to be taken to his brother's. When finally restored to his senses, his shame and mortification were unbounded. He promised he would not taste another drop, but the night of his arrival here he was completely intoxicated. The next morning "Richard was himself again," when he took his departure. Anywhere else,

7. Davis's Rancho was another name for [Henry Clay] Davis's Landing which later became Rio Grande City.

it would seriously affect his election; here it should not for no one among them is sufficiently blameless to cast the first stone.

I have been waiting to give the children an account of the Fourth of July Celebration. The Government Hospital, a large wooden building, was used to deliver the oratory.

Everything was well conducted and there was no appearance of rowdyism, no stump oratory, or vulgar slang. I was most agreeably surprised with the whole proceedings and I assure you, my dear Mother, I never heard the Declaration of Independence read with such feelings before. It was the first anniversary of real American Freedom on this soil and to hear that great paper with its firm, calm temperate statement of wrongs, read in territory just wrested from the grasp of Mexico, seeing around me a crowd of men brought up under the daily influence of such principles, seeing them on the very verge of the Union and feeling how such notions of human rights must of necessity spread through the other so-called republic [Mexico], seemed to give me a feeling of Destiny, a kind of pre-vision that was overwhelming. At the close, "That as free independent States, we have," etc., my blood seemed to rush to my brain. I realized for the first time how good might come out of evil. Through blood, misery and moral desolation, this former part of Mexico is fairly launched into the great confederacy of States and the children's children will see only the blessing.

Parties have their origin as well in circumstances as in the constitution of men's minds. The West never can be conservative. How can men be conservative who have nothing to keep? Whose only hope is in "Progress."

Besides there is something in seeing barbarism and civilization side by side, that affects you strangely. You feel the irresistible necessity that one race must subdue the other and, where the moral precepts are not keen and delicate, they, of the superior race, can easily learn to look upon themselves as men of Destiny, impelled to conquer and subdue by the great design of Providence.

I am curious to see how [Welles's] Whig principles have been affected by these long years in the New Settlements. If, like me, he will acknowledge Radicalism just as much a necessity of a republic as the imposition of centrifugal force is a necessity of the earth, there will be more of the real genuine spirit of democracy in his nature.[8] But I suspect he will cling to the

8. It is doubtful that Chapman is referring to the political radicalism of Jeremy Bentham and John Stuart Mill. More likely, she means democratic sentiments, perhaps as expressed in the spirit of Jacksonian democracy.

Whig party just as he would throw the weight of his body upon the upper side of the coach when in danger of upsetting. In the same way men who love their country should try to advance the West, and build up institutions that are worth protecting. As in a family, a happy home will keep boys from roving, so a state completely furnished and comfortable destroys the desire of poaching upon neighboring Republics. As the states grow older they will in the same proportions grow conservative, and Radicalism will continue to retreat to the borders.

For myself, I confess, I have not the least fear about the size of a Republic if only the right kind of men are scattered through it. Knowledge and freedom are as subtle as light and heat. Nothing escapes their ambit. Slavery will fall before them and Romanism will exist only by showing its bright side.

The great danger of the West is "No Religion." The want of everything idealizing, beautifying, refining, the absence of strong moral restraints, and the urgent sense of right and wrong, when, in all times and places the hand is of necessity almost resting on the handle of a knife or the holster of a pistol.

The last time we came down from Fort Brown, I thought much of the influence of such things. Two or three times on the road, we met and passed horsemen. The roadways are infested with robbers and all men go heavily armed. Whenever we approach on these roads our fellow men, the invariable habit is to elevate the guns into a conspicuous position. See that the pistols can at any instant be slipped from the holsters and draw up; the sword and sword case into full view. The approaching party uses the same precaution, and thus gazing at each other, with apprehension and distrust, those meet for an instant and vanish, who are told to love one another. How different from the country salutation of happier places. How pleasant to live again in scenes, where you may meet quiet and peaceful people with a bow and a smile!

Without these precautions, there is real danger, and fancying what I should do in case of attack, I often realize painfully that I have not that shrinking horror of the shedding of blood I once possessed.

July 26. Our company went off this morning and I must confess to my great joy. I have sometimes an almost irresistible desire to turn people out of the house, lock my doors and get by myself.

We are going up to Fort Brown next week because we do not consider it safe to remain here during the hurricane months. The Major intends to make a tour of inspection as high up as Eagle Pass, and I shall probably go with him as far as Camargo. [If so,] I shall see Lieutenant [Charles C.] Gilbert who is stationed opposite Camargo at Camp Ringgold.[9] He is very highly spoken of, has good habits and seems to be a favorite of his regiment. You must ask among yourselves why I am not afraid to go out in a country so insecure. I do not quite understand it myself, but I can tell you frankly and honestly that I do not know what fear is. I seem to have made up my mind that no soft indolent drawing room life is for me, that though exempt from actual labor, I must constantly be thrown into circumstances requiring activity, decisions and fearlessness.

July 28. Last night the weather was oppressively sultry, not a breath of air, and with that kind of stillness that precedes a hurricane. In the night the wind rose and it began to lightning and rain. Fearing a gale, the Major got up and dressed but it passed over and this morning it is bright and pleasant as usual.

They have been having stormy times in Matamoras as you will see by the *Flag*.[10] The custom house is completely corrupt and the commandant, General Avalos, has been transcending his powers, and carrying matters with a high hand.

The prosperity of Brownsville depends mainly on success in smuggling and this seems to me a very uncertain basis for real advancement. If you believe the newspaper accounts, you will be terrified for our lives. This is unnecessary because the robbers, Indians or whites, are either too timid or too cautious to attack Government officers so well equipped. The impression is very general that there are more white than Indian ruffians on this frontier and that a very desperate gang are disguised as Indians. There is no law in such places and you find even justices of the peace who are themselves fugitives from justice. The riotous and quarrelsome outnumber the orderly and peaceful and so law is but an empty name. If you ask those families living on the frontier, "Can nothing be done to check this lawless violence?" you are answered, "Oh! they will purify themselves. All new places go through the same conditions. The rascals die and kill each other off, and make way for a better population. The pioneers are always of this stamp."

9. Camp Ringgold was a temporary cavalry post, established in October 1848 in Starr County. Its name honors Major David Ringgold, who was killed in the battle of Palo Alto. In 1849 its name was changed to Ringgold Barracks, and the following year it became a permanent camp (*Handbook of Texas*, I, 631).

10. This may be an indication that Emily Blair subscribed to the *American Flag*.

July 30. I do not remember telling you one amusing circumstance connected with the [Fourth of July] Celebration. As I told you several Mexican gentlemen of rank were present. The Alcaldes, Senor Manchaca, the representative in Congress [and others]. On joining the procession, our Judge Bigelow who is extremely civil (as all Yankees are) to those high in office, as a mark of respect, handed to each, the white ribbon badge containing the printed words, *Brownsville Sunday School*, in large letters. In happy ignorance of the language, and their consequent heresy, they did as they saw Romans do, and thus the novel spectacle was presented of a row of distinguished Mexican dignitaries, placed in seats of honor directly in front of the platform erected for the oration and publicly pledged by the white ribbon attached to their shoulders as supporters of the Sunday School.

To tell the truth, I do not think them sufficiently zealous for the honor of Rome to care a straw for its precepts or downfall. And so if they found it out, no great harm was done.

To bring my journalizing up square once more, I will say what I intended about Odd Fellowship [on the Rio Grande]. At the East, I gave it little attention, if I thought of it at all. It seemed rather absurd with all its mystery and parade. Here I have seen it under a new aspect and my conclusion is this: I would wish a friend or brother in civil life if his lot were cast among strangers to become a member of the Order.

The grand master [Benjamin Moses] is a man worth describing. In the prime of life and dressed in his regalia as I saw him the 4th of July, he is a remarkably handsome man.[11] He is tall, well-formed and the richly embroidered breast piece, or whatever it is, extending below his waist gave him a priestly and imposing appearance. But you would look at his face in a crowd. In a Northern Climate, his complexion would be fair, the forehead high, broad and slightly retreating, the nose rather large, finely cut and remarkably handsome. The eyes hazel and the mouth displays strongly the rare union of mirth and command. It may be from their good fortune in a leader that the Order appears to such advantage. Not only by his position, but by nature, he controls his fellows and his power is always used wisely.

At the Mouth of the River there is a little settlement called into existence by the necessities of the warehousing, it is not permanent and is

11. Benjamin Moses, also known as Judge Moses, was a magistrate and notary public at the Mouth of the River. "[A]ll the offices and honors that could be heaped on one individual" were concentrated in him, declared the New Orleans *Daily Delta* (Dec. 23, 1849).

composed almost wholly of young unmarried men. No physicians, no comforts belonging to organized society. There, the Cholera raged with the same frightful violence, as in all places on this frontier and the Odd Fellows were to each other, father, mother, brother, sister, wife and husband. The real spirit of love seemed to pervade their actions. It was not the cold enforced performance of a duty to which they were publicly pledged, but their time was freely given up. They performed for each other cheerfully the most laborious labors, bathed, rubbed, nursed with most tender care many of their number into life, performed every necessary office for the dying, buried the dead throughout the whole of that dreadful time, with all the ceremonies of the Order and religiously took care of their effects.

In old communities you do not see the advantage of all this but in this place, solitary friendless men may die alone and untended, their property seized by many unscrupulous people about them and their friends perhaps are never informed of their fate. The physician at the Brazos was so overwhelmed with labor that he sometimes could not go to the Mouth of the River for two or three days in succession. All he could do was to give written directions in all supposed cases and these men acquired such skill that the Doctor felt perfect confidence in leaving his patients with them. Though not an Odd Fellow, he expressed himself warmly in their favor.

So much for this: my testimony is humble but the humblest may together build up a strong support. If Welles is a member, or wishes to become one do not discourage him. Mr Moses, the gentleman I have described is a strictly moral man, perhaps religious. He has certainly shown its fruits here. He established an Anti-gambling society and in his capacity as magistrate had the moral courage to arrest two gentlemen, who were arranging a duel, and put them under heavy bonds. No other magistrate would have taken such a step and all honor, say I, to this prince of Odd Fellows.

Aug. 3, 1849. You will think my letters are all Jeremiads not over my own situation but over the evils about me. We are entitled by law to a Chaplain at Fort Brown and have been for several months. Yet we cannot persuade the commanding officer to take the necessary measures for procuring one. The chaplain is chosen by a Council of Administration composed of line officers, therefore, the Major cannot command a vote.[12]

Major [Giles] Porter has just arrived and he may be able to bring it

12. The army has always maintained a distinction between line officers, who bear the brunt of the battle, and staff officers, who function as administrators.

about. However bad society may be, there is also the grace of improvement and all men in their hearts really love order, neatness, domestic faith, the externals of devotion, at least, and all that builds up good society.

The history of the local Sunday School is an illustration [of] how rapidly good fruit as well as bad springs up on such a fresh rich soil. It commenced with four or five scholars, it now numbers more than seventy.

In the children's letter, I mentioned that there was one select school where the tuition is $2.50 per month. There are full 40 scholars, yet not ten of that number can really afford to go. The parents of the greater portion are very poor mechanics, living on their daily labor, many washer women are among the number, all living from hand to mouth. Yet the teacher tells me he has no bad debts. Is not this affecting!

I told you we had a new arrival, Major Porter. He has the reputation of being eccentric as all old bachelors are supposed to be. He is a fine reader among his other qualifications and talks it would seem in a good degree with quotations from Shakespeare. It is agreeable to hear him talk. He is not a person with whom you can converse for he is evidently impatient while another is speaking to him. However, when a person talks better than myself, I am very glad to listen and I promise myself much pleasure from his company.

He brings Lamartine's *Confidential Disclosures* and some other new books.[13] Passages throughout are of most wonderful beauty; yet there is something unsatisfying about Lamartine. It is all ornament, no structure and there is a kind of egotism about him that sticks me. He never completely loses sight of himself. He seems drunk with beauty, and should be transported to some rugged, bracing climate where he sees only naked strength and grandeur.

Have you noticed in the Home Journal extracts from Guyot's *Lectures on Comparative Geography*? They seem to me excellent, and the influence of climate on the human animal seems most correctly described:

"In the tropical regions," he says, "the power of life in nature is carried to its highest degree: thus with the tropical man, the life of the body overmasters that of the soul; the physical instincts of our nature those of the higher faculties: passion, sentiment, imagination predominate over intellect and reason; the passive faculties over the active faculties."[14]

13. Alphonse de Lamartine (1790–1869) wrote a number of books, primarily on French history.

14. Arnold Henry Guyot published *The Earth and Man: Lectures on Comparative Geography* in 1849 (Boston: Gould Kendall and Lincoln). One of the corollaries to the statement quoted

Mr Pilsbury whom I described to you and whose opinions are worth having says that persons who go from a cold to a warm region in the maturity or decline of life live longer for the change. After the natural heat begins to decline, the artificial heat required at the North is supplied in the South by the natural condition of the atmosphere: instead of being shut up in the heated rooms one can live in the open sunshine. All those faculties that wear upon the frame are subdued, life passes in a gentle dreamy state of repose, unnatural to vigorous manhood, but proper and suitable for the aged.

I think there must be great vitality to keep men alive under such ruinous habits of living [prevalent in the South]. The "dolce far niente"[15] of the poets, in plain English, is excessive idleness lounging on easy chairs and sofas with no faculty of the mind awake except [possibly] the imagination. Then all those villainous compounds, liquors, brandies, cordials, oceans of claret and a diet of the most peppery ingredients would seem to make such inflammable compounds that the only wonder is that they do not all [explode] every summer.

I have not seen much of the better class of Southern men, but I am inclined to believe that you see very few [fine] heads in the last latitudes as you do in the temperate [zones]. I hope some time to see them in the Senate and House of Representatives, side by side, but men generally here either approach the portrait of Mr Josh Sedley in Vanity Fair[16] or look dried up, heavy and bilious. I see no heads where the forehead and eye seem luminous with intellect and thought.[17]

By the way, do tell what is the opinion of the Whig Party as to the course of the present [Taylor] Administration. I see the *Union* and *Intelligencer.*[18] The last is dignified and says nothing, the Union seems actually insane, rabid with abuse. Is he as the Union says a mere tool in the hands of his Cabinet or does he exercise such power as the Constitution marks out for the Executive? Has he violated pledges?

here is that those who live in the temperate zones are more civilized and well adjusted. This was a prevalent notion of the times, and Helen Chapman tried to keep up to date.

15. *Dolce far niente* means delicious inactivity.

16. Thackeray's *Vanity Fair* was first serialized in 1847 and 1848. In the early illustrated editions, drawings of Jos Sedley show him as a fat, bilious man.

17. Phrenology was a popular pursuit in the late 1840s. This study attempted to correlate the conformation of the skull with evidence of mental abilities and characteristics.

18. The *National Intelligencer* was a conservative newspaper with Whig leanings, published in Washington, D.C., from 1800 to 1870. The *Union* was perhaps the *Washington Union*, which was published between 1845 and 1859.

Aug. 7. Yesterday I spent the whole morning in the store room and had a practical illustration "of the powers of life in nature."[19] A neat northern housekeeper would be perfectly beside herself with the ants, cockroaches, weevils, &c. with which the place is swarming. I examined some hominy and found it actually crawling with life. Flour is very much the same and it will not do to think of what one eats.

I am afraid I shall soon share in the general trouble about servants. Ann [Mitchell] who has been with me so long is possessed with the idea of learning a dressmaker's trade, and my cook is preparing to start for California. The other ladies in the country have been in trouble for some time. I being the only one who has had women servants, but I can always get a man.

Major Porter is really a beautiful reader. He read extracts this morning from Locke and Bacon and it really seemed like going to the fountainhead of Wisdom. Yet after all even in Bacon's writings you can see that he might be a courtier and ungrateful. In his beautiful language on friendship, he seems to have in mind the uses of a friend rather than the mutual delights such a relation would [provide] to a truly noble creature. On marriage too, the idea that single men should make the best churchmen because the charity never can overflow to all mankind, that must first fill a pool, does not seem to be correct.

It appears to me, we all hold the key to an exhaustible reservoir and if we once begin to give to another the love and the supply both increase infinitely. But for me to criticize such an intellectual giant as Bacon is too ridiculous. Of one thing, however, I am certain among common natures, single men and single women, often under circumstances to nourish ease, do become intensely selfish because the charity that is not required ever to fill a pool is hoarded up for themselves.

[I apologize for my] long letters, Mother. I suppose you are required to read them aloud. I fancy Father walking away before they are half finished. Grandmamma presumes, of course, that they are all very interesting, but wishes I would write about something and Helen Pelletreau would like a description of some parties even though they are Texas parties and Willie thinks nothing about them but waits only before dashing off to play to know if Father or Mother are well and when they are coming home.

I wish myself I could give you more amusing letters, but think how I am

19. Chapman is repeating part of the quote from Guyot she used in her letter of August 6.

situated, perfectly isolated in a sand bank, no neighbors, not the slightest incident to break the monotony of the day. When I get to Fort Brown, it will be a little better and if there is any gaiety I promise to describe it.

You may remember I wrote to you about Mrs Taylor at Palo Alto. Her husband is gone off to California. She has recovered and has gone to her daughters, to have some comfort I hope in her remaining life.

Aug. 11. It is two days since I have ended this. We are breaking up and my cook leaves this morning for New Orleans preparatory to her departure for California.[20]

Day before yesterday, I went to Point Isabel. We dined with a newly married lady, Mrs Garesché.[21] She is young, pretty, but wholly unfit for frontier life. I pity her from my heart.

Dr and Mrs Abadie are about leaving the country to our great regret. I called to see a Mrs King, the wife of a sea captain.[22] Her mother, Mrs Wilmer, a nice trim little old lady lives with her. You cannot conceive how delightful it was to me to see a house with an old lady in it. Until I felt the want of it, I did not know how necessary as pictures in domestic life were the presence of old people and children. In new places you seldom meet an old person and I have often felt a want without being able to discover it. But there I seemed at once at home.

My own health is excellent, far better than it was the last summer. I presume I am fully acclimated. God Bless you all.

Aug. 12. The Southwest has always been distinguished for its dissipations. Here you are asked to drink on every possible occasion and if they should get a church, I believe they would consider it as a necessary preliminary to invite a friend to take a drink before going to or on departing. During the eighteen months I have been in this country, I have seen only one, it may be safe to say two (of the last I am not certain), who refused to drink from principle or indeed, who refused at all. This was the Captain of the Steamship *Alabama*. I forget his name. Undoubtedly many among the hundreds I have met were strict temperance men at home, but this is the natural consequence of war and absence of social restraints.

As for myself, I am known far and wide as an uncompromising and

20. This cook is not identified. It is not Phyllis, who had been with them in Matamoras, because Phyllis is still with them in late 1851.

21. Mariquita Garesché a Parisienne by birth, was the wife of Lieutenant Julius Peter Garesché.

22. This is possibly Captain Thomas B. King of Point Isabel, Texas.

openly avowed enemy to drinking. At the North when invited to drink wine, I yielded so far to the usages of society as to raise the glass, bow, and return it to the table untasted. Here I refused the ceremony utterly.

"You know I am a teetotaler, Captain. Excuse me if you please," or "I'll pledge you in water if you'll allow me," or some remark of the kind with a smile always seems to be well received. It requires a little moral courage at first, but I was fairly frightened into it. I dare not leave the smallest degree of responsibility in this matter unfulfilled upon my own conscience.

In this plain question of ruin versus safety, I would not throw a feather's weight into the downward scale. The moral influence of women cannot be overrated and it is a mournful thought that their education has not yet been so conducted, as to impress them sufficiently with their own responsibility, or to give them such firmness of principle that they can withstand the torrent instead of being borne away by it. The best wife cannot keep her husband from intemperance, but if she be a woman of commanding and elevated character, she can prevent her parlor from being turned into a bar-room as is too often the case.

By the way is not General Scott's letter upon the Annexation of Canada a strange one?[23] I asked the question of Major Porter and he replied, "Not at all, for him perfectly consistent, for he has been crazy ever since first mentioned for the Presidency." I see the *Union* is frightened and indignant that a Whig should take up such a powerful weapon of its own party as Annexation. As for me, the more snow and ice they annex to the mammoth Republic the better.

Fort Brown, Aug. 15. I have sat down among the worst possible confusion to finish my letter. We arrived here at nearly midnight of the last day and I know you will be glad to hear that we are safely housed for the hurricane months. The weather-wise are predicting a great storm on account of the excessive ground swell of the ocean and some other signs. The weather is hot and sultry.

We came in a steamboat as the roads are impassable on account of the high state of the river. There are little Mexican settlements along the river

23. The New Orleans *Daily Delta* of May 16, 1849, reported a movement promoting the annexation to the United States of Nova Scotia, New Brunswick, Lower Canada, Upper Canada, Newfoundland, Labrador, and parts of Oregon not already annexed. Although the newspaper article Chapman mentions is unidentified, it is not surprising that Scott was a proponent of the action. He was very familiar with the northern forts, which he visited regularly during the Canadian border disturbances of 1838–1841.

called "Ranches," a little group of huts at which they collect wood for the use of the steamers. It lies piled up along the shore in the same way as along a railroad line and when the bell rings a group of Mexicans are seen running to the boat ready to throw in the wood and at the same time bringing their watermelons with them. This "little fragment of a world" unknown to them, visits them once a week and it leaves them as it finds them, poor [and] desolate. Those who travel on this river a quarter of a century hence will probably depict a very different scene. If all men were content with a tub in the sunshine, there would be an end to progress.

Aug. 20 (Mon.). The Major went down to the Brazos yesterday and I am here alone, very comfortably situated and in good health. Saturday we called on some of our Matamoras friends and were very warmly received. The city looks clean, no life, no energy. They are a strange people, these Mexicans, good hewers of wood and drawers of water, but low on motive power. So different from this side of the river. The ferries are in the hands of the Americans and when you cross to the other side you see a brisk competition among hack drivers and you are carried into the city for an American "bit" or a York shilling.

I must give you a specimen of manners among the "haut tow." We called to see La Senora Manitow, a very handsome woman, fat, fair for her race with perfect teeth, black hair untouched by time, richly dressed and as gay as a French woman. Her daughter was married about six weeks or two months since. Before the bride entered, we enquired for La Senora Longoria.

"Ah! pretty well," she said, "Complaining some of sickness at her stomach," at the same time she was making a curving motion in front of her own figure that we might fully understand the young lady was "Enceinte." Dr Jarvis, an unmarried man, was with us and she told this with the most joyous gaiety, adding, "such things she must expect, you know," bowing and smiling at the gentleman with a very coquettish air. We called to see Madame Farnaber who lost her husband by Cholera. Her parlor is of very immense size, very richly furnished and, since the death of her husband, draped in black. It will remain hung with mourning for a year according to custom.

The teacher of the school in Brownsville, was here the other evening and told me something of their debating society which I give you as characteristic. Two young men who were known as warm friends became excited and angry. Words got high and in the excitement one of the young men rose and tendered his resignation. The teacher, Thomas, tried to settle the difficulty. There are peacemakers even here. The young hotspur said that if there was a difficulty between them, it could be settled out of doors. This was thought to mean a duel, the belligerent prepared themselves to see a fight, and the peaceful tried to soothe the agitation. In the midst of the clamor about the resignation, an elderly man, a down easter and a kind of honorary member, rose and said, "Wal, I don't know who made this constitution but I know they was a damned set of fools anyhow. It puts me in mind of what a man said about this country, that it was jest like hell. There was only one way to git in and no way to git out."

This young man, Mr Stansbury, told me all his struggles and trials, hopes and fears.[24] He is a member of the Methodist church and has been brought up with severe notions of Christian decorum. At the same time his temperament is lively and social. The poor fellow is constantly mourning over what he deems his unfaithfulness to his Christian duties, a very tender conscience. It would be more natural for him to compare himself with others, and thereby think himself exalted in piety. He is constantly asked to take a drink, to go to fandangos and other places which his principles compel him to refuse.

Fort Brown, Aug. 24. The Major is at the Brazos and I am here in my very pleasant little home. Last evening I invited my Mexican friend Dona Juanita Perello to tea, in company with the wife of the American consul and two or three others. There is a beautiful little lake in back of the house, in the center of which is an island, and on this little piece of water, we have a pretty little row boat. We gave the ladies a boat ride by moonlight, and they seemed much delighted. Dona Juanita really seems to retain much affection for me and always receives me with open arms.

Last Sunday while on my way to a prayer meeting in Brownsville, I discovered dashing down the street, to my great delight, our dashing and favorite express rider, Harry Love. He had been sent by the Major to headquarters in Texas and also to Austin. It was a perilous journey and we had again been troubled by fears for his safety. But here he was again, safe and sound.

I wish I could picture him to your vision, as he came dashing down the street, well mounted as he always is, sitting his horse as if he were a part

24. R. N. Stansbury was employed as superintendent of the Sunday School in Brownsville, which had sixteen teachers, seventy-two scholars, and 720 books in January of 1850 (*American Flag*, Jan. 9, 1850).

of the noble animal he rides, his long black curls flowing in the wind, his chest thrown out, his expression cool, frank and resolute, his saber and spurs clashing, his clothes torn by the chaparral and covered with dust, one of Colt's revolvers, a six shooter, fastened to his side and an additional brace of pistols in his holsters. These are his usual accouterments, a saber, a Colt's revolver, and a pair of holster pistols.

Seven men stopped him at a distance of about sixty miles from this place to whom he said, "Clear the road, Gentlemen, or I must do it for myself."

The name ran through their ranks, "Harry Love" and they vanished into the Chaparral. He thinks they live in this neighborhood and were afraid of being recognized.

In describing the outward appearance of this daring, almost reckless, man, I can give you not the faintest conception of himself. I know nothing of his early history, but I presume he was not born a gentleman. There is, however, a kind of native nobility about him. His perceptions are quick and keen and his impulses are generous. He is not addicted to any low vices and has unbounded popularity both with gentlemen and the rabble.

"How do you do, Harry? What's the news? Just arrived?" and so on were the exclamations from all sides, as he entered the town. You cannot conceive what a wild, indescribable kind of grace such a man acquires who is also physically gifted, and whose home is in the saddle. He never breaks down a horse though his journeys are exceedingly rapid, because when he finds the animal flagging, he springs off, throws the saddle from his back, and lets him loose to graze. He, in the meantime, makes the saddle his pillow, and sleeps soundly anywhere under the open heaven. There is something actually awe inspiring in such complete faultlessness, and I could not speak with more deferential politeness to Daniel Webster than I do to him.

As we met in the street, I smiled and he took his cap from his head and bowed very low, but I was too glad for such a salutation merely and I held out my hand, with "How do you do, Mr Love? We are delighted to see you back again."

I assure you his whole manner as he reined in his horse and talked with me, might have been envied by the beaux of Broadway. The most perfect appearance and self possession without the least boldness or conceit. I saw him afterwards surrounded by gentlemen and his manner was precisely the same. We had good reason to be glad to see him, for he brought the Major's leave from General Brooke. He had a long interview with the General who expressed himself much pleased with everything we had done in this district.

Harry Love saw Thomas [Chapman] in Austin, Texas.[25] He has a large farm carried on in the Northern style and seems to be making money fast. He is employed by the Government as Quarter-master for five companies which of itself gives him a good salary. He writes that he has just sent his mother some money.[26]

I must tell you while I think of it of quite a touching little incident concerning our famous Harry. You know before he came down the river, he was reported and mourned as dead. But he came as usual and during that visit to Brownsville, he heard of the Sunday School. He expressed himself much interested in its success, and Lo! The next Sunday, he made his appearance, divested of all his border trappings and dressed in a handsome suit of black. They say he displayed the delight of a child and said he had not had an opportunity for many years of seeing such a sight.

The Sunday School continues to do well. We have a large library of over six hundred volumes and regularly receive papers. In my class there are two married women, both reading in words of one syllable, one is a Mexican, the other an American. The last named is about the size of Helen [Pelletreau], is *fourteen* years of age and has been married *three* months. She can read Spanish, but has no knowledge of her own language.

Aug. 30. The Major wishes Welles to apply for the U.S. Consulship at Matamoras. It is worth about $1,500 per annum and all the consuls in that city have grown rich by trade. The Major could give him some capital. He thinks if Bates and Ashmun would help him, he might get it.[27] There are several other applicants. I have merely time to suggest it. I think he had better make the application for it will do no harm, and it will satisfy the Major.

25. Thomas Finley Chapman, William's older brother, was born in Springfield, Massachusetts on July 20, 1812.

26. Eight months later, Thomas Chapman was still an affluent farmer, working 300 acres within one-half mile of the state capital in Austin. Among other things, he raised sweet potatoes, oats, pumpkins, melons, beans, peas, cows, hogs, and chickens. His reputation was that of a "gentleman, an excellent man and honest, some reports that lightly float over the scandal atmosphere to the contrary notwithstanding." In addition to his carriages and horses, Thomas Chapman somewhat apologetically owned "half a dozen negroes" who provided the labor (Ebenezer Swift to WWC, Apr. 27, 1850, CC).

27. William G. Bates (1803–1880) was a lawyer in Westfield (Westfield *Times and News Letter*, July 14, 1880). George Ashmun was a U.S. congressman from Springfield, Massachusetts from 1845 to 1851 (*National Cyclopaedia of American Biography*, VI, 430).

I did not mention in my last letter, that I might possibly go home in the fall as I would not prepare for you another disappointment. It is William's proposal to take me and, on his account, not mine. Of course, under such circumstances, I gladly acquiesce. I am busy with my preparations. We leave here on the steamer "*Globe*" on the 28th of September for New Orleans and go by the Southern route, Mobile, Charleston, etc., and shall hope to be there by the middle of October.[28]

Love and a thousand kisses to my boy. Tell him the parrot is screaming. God Bless you all.[29]

The *Globe,* in fact, left on September 24. From New Orleans and Mobile, the Chapmans traveled by train to Charleston, South Carolina. Another ship took them to Wilmington, North Carolina, where they boarded the train for Washington, D.C. While William went to Pennsylvania to visit his sister and brother-in-law, Sarah and Colin Reed, Helen proceeded to Westfield. It had been nearly two years since she had seen Willie; what a reunion it must have been!

28. WWC to Welles E. Blair, Aug. 30, 1849, CC.
29. HBC to EWB, Aug. 20, 1849, CC.

7.

"A RIGHT BUSTLING BUSINESS PLACE"

January through April 1850

The Chapman family closed out 1849 as a reunited threesome. Together with their son Willie, Helen and William left New York on the steamship *Ohio* on December 13. They spent Christmas and New Year's Day in New Orleans and departed January 10 on the five-day voyage to Brazos Santiago.

Brownsville had continued to thrive in the Chapmans' absence. *The Rio Grande Sentinel* had picked up where the *American Flag* left off. In early 1850 one correspondent wrote, "Buildings are going up every day; goods arriving, steamboats loading and unloading, and every person seems engaged to some useful employment. . . . Not yet two years old, and numbering 2500 inhabitants. . . ."[1]

The news was less rosy from Mexican cities which suffered insurrections and the Texas towns of Laredo and Roma (across the Rio Grande from Mier), which had endured Indian raids. Brownsville citizens responded to the latter threat by calling a town meeting. They appointed an agent to petition Washington, stressing that they felt essentially unprotected. U.S. troops were few, and when they had been ordered to lend assistance in the summer of 1849, they traveled on foot or in wagons "against an enemy whose movements are as fleet almost as the winds."[2]

Closer to Helen Chapman's heart was Hiram Chamberlain's organizing the First Presbyterian Church in Brownsville on February 23, 1850. The ceremony and services "were solemn and deeply interesting." Nineteen people joined the church at its

1. Letter from Matamoras correspondent to New Orleans *Daily Delta*, Mar. 9, 1850.

2. *Rio Grande Sentinel*, Apr. 10, 1850, as extracted in the New Orleans *Daily True Delta*, Apr. 17, 1850.

inception, including five (and Helen was among them) who reserved the right to withdraw when their own denomination established a church in the town.[3]*

Helen wrote of Willie's impressions of frontier life and thereby disabused those in Westfield of any notions that the Chapmans were living in luxury on the frontier. In April the Chapmans heard from an old friend, Dr. Ebenezer Swift, who wrote them from Fort Martin Scott in Fredericksburg. His message undoubtedly made them more appreciative of their lot in Brownsville. Of life at the remote post, Swift said, "I have been led to exclaim, 'Our suffering is intolerable.'"[4]

My dear Mother, Brazos Santiago, Texas

Jan. 20, 1850. I have but a moment to tell you we arrived safely Monday noon after a rough and unpleasant passage of five days. The first boat, the one we decided not to go in, made the passage in great danger. We have certainly great reason to be thankful not only for our health and safety but that all our baggage, everything shipped from New York has reached us without accident or injury. Not a piece of China was broken and nothing was injured by dampness. On our arrival, they gave us a warm welcome and seemed delighted to see us.

I do not very well know what I am writing for my head is turned almost among packing boxes, airing clothes, stowing away things, and more than all with such constant company. We have only boarding for ourselves and yet we are to provide for three people besides ourselves.

All this medley and hurley burley, though death to me, is a perfect heaven of delight to William. He is happy as a child can well be and really revels in the unpacking. [At the moment,] William is lounging in a most luxurious chair he has purchased for me at 25 dollars. He calls it my Asthma chair and it will indeed be most comfortable if I am compelled to sit up

3. *Rio Grande Sentinel*, Feb. 27, 1850, as extracted in the New Orleans *Daily Delta*, Mar. 9, 1850. The location of the church's first place of worship is not clear. Abbe Domenech, who visited Brownsville in 1850, suggests that Chamberlain initially held services at his house. See Abbe Emmanuel Domenech, *Missionary Adventures in Texas and Mexico* (London: Longman, Brown, Green, Longmans, and Roberts, 1858), 244–245.

4. Ebenezer Swift to WWC, Apr. 27, 1850, CC. This letter is not included in the text.

nights. He has purchased everything for me that a heart could wish and I cannot be sufficiently grateful for a lot so full of mercies.[5]

Willie is sleeping sweetly in his bed. To his nightly prayer, he adds after "God keep my little puppy safe," "And may he not die of joy when I go back." How you must long to see him, dear little fellow. I wonder now how I ever could have been separated from him. I could fill a long letter with Willie's sayings and doings. I hope after a while I shall get time to do so.[6]

We expect to go up to Fort Brown next week to visit at Colonel Bennett's. Brownsville is growing rapidly and real estate has risen greatly. Dr Baker is there, a Presbyterian clergyman from Galveston, and in one day procured on his subscription list $800 for a church.[7] A Roman Catholic chapel is already commenced. A Sunday school is established at Point Isabel. Altogether the frontier seems to be in a very flourishing condition. Willie pronounces it a better place than he had supposed.

I have no time for more and am really too tired to write. Best love to [all],

My dear Mother[-in-law], Brazos Santiago, Texas

Jan. 25. I believe Helen told you I had purchased an asthmatic chair for her in New Orleans. I now regret it, for she has converted it into a lazy chair. She is now sitting in it, the picture of luxury and ease, and says to me after I have been working hard all day, "Oh, you write to Mother, I am too busy." She is fussing over the fringe of some "company napkins."

We have been rather busy since our return in putting things to rights. The weather is charming—thermometer at 70 degrees—no fire this evening, living fair for poor folks and we are happier than we deserve to be. Every afternoon we ride in the new carriage with an elegant pair of black horses I purchased in New Orleans, and Master Willie, as proud as a young chicken cock, rides his little pony alongside with the servant.

5. HBC to EWB, Jan. 5, 1850, CC.

6. HBC to EWB, Jan. 5, 1850, CC.

7. Daniel Baker was one of the greatest evangelists of his day. His call to the lower Rio Grande in 1849 made him one of the first protestant ministers to be heard there. He covered vast distances, often under difficult conditions, in his mission to save souls and establish churches (Ernest Trice Thompson, *Presbyterians in the South, 1607–1861* [Richmond: John Knox Press, 1963], I, 428–430).

Willie is much fatter than he was, is in high health and full of life and fun with his kites, chickens, turkeys, dog, boats, fishing, riding, shooting, reading, playing cards with Mother, and eating which is by no means moderate. He supplies our table with fish of his own catching, and the other day caught one (a fine sheepshead) so large that he could not haul him in, and called to three boatmen to come and help him. I give him a cent apiece for fish, and eggs, of which he keeps a regular account in a book. I loaned him $10 to buy his pony with, for which I made him give me his note, with a promise to pay out of the first money he earned in the above way. I also allow him six cents for each chicken he raises. He seems to have quite a taste for making money and trading. I think he will be a merchant. I shall not object if he is at the same time a highly educated gentleman.

Day after tomorrow we go to Fort Brown to make an impression there. To give you a little idea of Texas life, the other morning while I was giving ammunition to my guards who were going to apprehend a murderer, a Presbyterian missionary just arrived from the old states on his way to settle in Brownsville called to pay his respects with a letter of introduction.[8] After I had secured and double ironed the murderer, I sent the parson, his wife, three children with one at the breast in my carriage to Brownsville.[9] I sent the prisoner to Brownsville yesterday after the parson to equalize the morals of the place.[10]

| Helen enclosed a note.

8. The Presbyterian minister was Hiram Chamberlain. The mention of the letter of introduction provides strong evidence that his arrival was in response to Helen Chapman's request to the Home Missionary Society for a missionary in April 1849. A Presbyterian minister had been found for South Texas by August 1849 who agreed to an annual salary of $600 to $800 (J. G. Junkin to HBC, Aug. 27, 1849, CC; see also WWC to HBC, May 4, 1851, CC).

9. Accompanying Chamberlain were his third wife, Anna Adelia Griswold and his four children: Henrietta Maria Morse (the daughter from his first marriage who later married Richard King, founder of the King Ranch), Hiram, Jr., Milton, and one-year-old Peter Bland (Lea, *King Ranch,* I, 63). However, the 1850 U.S. Census for Cameron County does not mention a Milton, but lists instead a female child, Caroline F. Chamberlain, age ten.

10. The prisoner was probably the locally notorious Dr. Kellogg. The *Rio Grande Sentinel* mentions that Kellogg "who, some months since commanded a party of robbers on the road between this place [Brownsville] and Point Isabel was lately arrested at Brazos Santiago, by Mr. Stevens, sheriff of our county" (Feb. 27, 1850; extracted in the New Orleans *Daily True Delta*, Mar. 9, 1850). See the introduction to the next chapter.

Dear Mother,

William has left me nothing to say even if I had time to write. I am really very busy getting things into some degree of order and preparing to go to Fort Brown.

Willie is very much improved by his journey. His troublesome night complaint seems to have left him wholly and he has a fine color. He is a great favorite and is considered exceedingly sensible. We have piles of new books, but I have not opened one.

The Western Presbyterian Board of Missions have at last sent in a missionary.[11] He seems to be a good man, but I think a good part of his time must be occupied in nursing the baby from the little I saw. He is one of the Doctor Clark sort of men and she I fancy may be one of the Mrs Doctor sort of women.[12] However, I am heartily thankful even for such aid. I prepared a second breakfast for them upon their leaving the boat, put up an abundant lunch for the road and sent them on their way rejoicing. I must close.

Best love to all, especially Grandmamma.
Helen

Helen Chapman commented on the status of the local economy in an undated and unaddressed draft.

[As to the development of local agriculture,] this might be done very speedily by the proper application of wealth and science. But whoever hears of a *rich scientific farmer* moving onto new lands of the West. The generality of those who come as farmers it is well known are miserably poor. They are fortunate indeed if they can bring with them a little stock, a few of the most absolutely necessary farming utensils and a little seed. Even among those better equipped, there is only a practical knowledge of farming on their own soil.

Much is said of lands so fertile that the farmer has only to drop his seed and nature rewards him with lavish abundance. This may be so in certain places, but there is generally a deadly miasma so generated by such fertility

11. See notes 8 and 9 above.

12. This was the Blairs' neighbor, Dr. Clark, a physician. See Helen Chapman's letter of August 1, 1850, for clarification on this reference, as well as for more information about the Chamberlains and their arrival in Texas.

that effectually checks all prosperity until this exuberance is exhausted. In general, Western land must be subdued to cultivation. In some places irrigation is necessary, in others, draining. Large and expensive contrivances are required for putting the land at once into cultivation altogether beyond the resources of individual enterprise.

There are no Government provisions for this. There are no benevolent men of wealth to take it upon themselves and so the small farmer can only after years of trial and disappointment succeed in making his own land productive. His neighbors are in the same condition, almost discouraged but forced by necessity to first experiment. In time they succeed, but often this is after many years of trial. The fresh influx of immigrants may increase the actual value of their farm, but [may also] increase their present distress because the production is altogether inadequate to the consumption. Freights are high because there is not sufficient trade for competition in land and water carriage and no return freight. They export nothing and so boats and wagons must return empty. Everything on a farm is acquired by slow and painful degrees. Provisions are high, fences are to be made, outbuildings to be erected with no money, no credit. How can farmers give money for schools and churches in this state of things.

Mechanics are a very mixed class, American and foreigners getting very good wages when any business is doing but are often thrown entirely on their former earnings if they have been fortunate enough to lay up anything. Rents are always high, and it is often difficult to find housing of any kind. The mechanic must buy everything and if he has a garden spot there are so many other things requiring attention, he has not time to work it. So he must live wholly on the daily proceeds of his labor. The poor mechanic cannot afford to give even time for the erection of public buildings.

The small retail merchant must live with the close strictest economy to maintain his plan. If he does a cash business, it is exceedingly small and he is almost sure to fail on the credit system.[13] The large merchant may be growing rich but not in money and generally finds it quite as much as he can do to meet his necessary payments.

13. For example, records of a partnership between William Chapman and Charles Stillman for the sale of Colt's revolvers to merchants along the Rio Grande in 1859 showed that the terms of sale were $25.00 with a 1 percent discount for payment within six months (Stillman to WWC, July 20, 1859, CC).

The condition of professional men is bad enough. They may be doing a great business, but it brings them no money, and every nerve is strained to prepare bread for their children.

The labor of procuring a support is not simplified by any division of labor as in older states. Each one must do everything for himself or it remains undone. The moral effect of all this is necessarily to make men selfish and men so engrossed present animal wants. The labor of bringing up a family under such circumstances is so great that except in solitary instances they succumb in a degree and become content with far less than would once have seemed possible.[14]

Chapman exercised her moral suasion when she solicited help for three destitute Mexican American children whose soldier father had abandoned them.

My dear Sir, [Draft, Feb. 8, 1850]

. . . All records that might have given some information of her husband's family were destroyed by an overflow of the river in Reynosa [Mexico]. In my interviews with her I could only learn that her husband's name was William Gourlaye, that he had a brother, James Gourlaye, and when letter was last received that his mother and sister were living. She believed him to be a native of the City of New York, but it is not probable she had any idea of his birthplace.

Mrs Gourlaye is a person of pleasing appearance and has the manner of the better class. Her three children are all girls, the eldest about twelve, the second ten and the youngest eight. The children of their mixed marriage are very bright and possess considerable personal beauty. They are more American than Mexican in appearance and are very intelligent. At the close of the war, we made a memorandum of such meager information as we could collect and gave it to Dr Jarvis of the Army who promised to use every exertion to discover the family of Mr Gourlaye. He did so but unfortunately nothing satisfactory could be discovered. He succeeded in finding a cousin who knew the brothers and said that when he last heard of James Gourlaye,

14. Neither the specific date nor addressee of this letter is known. Helen Chapman retained a partial draft in her possession.

he was on one of the rivers in the Southwest. He had previously been with the Army. This is the extent of our information and it is, of course, useless.

The peculiar misfortune of these children is in the extreme poverty of the family and in the condition of the mother. It is said by those who have long known her that her mind has never been exactly right since the loss of her two children by the Indians. Her health is miserable and her head is often in such condition as to render labor impossible. Poverty presses upon her so severely that I believe she would be perfectly willing to part with her children, and it has been suggested that there might be a danger of her selling the eldest, to a fate that we should shrink from naming.

When first mentioned I rejected the idea as monstrous and impossible, but I find those better acquainted with the demoralized condition of Mexican society think otherwise. We cannot judge fault of a woman thus situated and thus it is our especial duty to "Judge not at all."

Elina (Helen), the eldest, interested me so much that I sent her to Miss Bacon's English school thinking that she might perhaps be prepared for a teacher in her own country. The terms are high, five dollars per month, but with the aid of fifty dollars received from some friends in Pennsylvania to whom I mentioned the circumstances, she has continued in the school until this time. Miss Bacon whom I mentioned is a lady from Matamoras and a member of our church. With great liberality, she has received within the last six months the two youngest children into the school without any expectation of reward though her circumstances are such as to render any additional labor to herself a very great sacrifice. One might endeavor to undertake to teach ten American children with American habits of industry than one Mexican with the injudicious and capricious indulgence they receive at home. The three children are now at school and learning their father's language. The question before me is: What is to be done with them? What shall they do after receiving this faint awakening of intellect, be thrown back again into their poverty or must means be found to withdraw them.

I know not how it appears to others, but to me it seems that the children of an American citizen left orphans in a foreign land should be considered as children of the Republic, and that American Consuls might have some authority to act in these cases. The love of adventure carries our citizens to every quarter of the habitable globe, and I believe, if we could but know, we should be overwhelmed at the suffering and destitution experienced by the families of these adventurers left helpless among people talking a different language and having no common sympathies. Cases here have come within my knowledge of harrowing interest and having almost the wildness of romance in their details.

I know, my dear Sir, that this plain statement is all sufficient to arouse as much sympathy in your own heart as I could possibly desire. Without knowing myself what can or [should be done, I ask for your assistance].[15]

My dear Sister[-in-law],[16] Brazos Santiago, Texas

March 13. We are living as usual in two places and both are to be arranged. Willie has a very decided contempt for the externals of frontier life. The house we occupy at Fort Brown is an old building used during the War, rough in construction as they all are and white-washed.[17] It has been enlarged by the addition of a back building in which we manage to have our dining room, kitchen, etc. This is entirely unfinished as yet over head, the rafters and roof, all displayed. One morning at breakfast, Willie raised his eyes and exclaimed, "Well, I declare, this is a strange kind of house to live in. If my Aunt Emmy had such a place as this, she would use it for a wood-shed." Another time he exclaimed with great energy, "I despise such houses, they are just fit for barns and stables." He has a great idea of magnificence; and these rude arrangements seem very displeasing to his eye.

Earlier he said but little of home, that was true only, while the excitement of a new scene lasted. He now talks a great deal of everything connected with it: evidently thinks Aunt Emmy the best and greatest woman that ever lived; the old house and trees, the finest in the world; Westfield, the greatest place; and Charley and George Cox surpassing all other boys that ever lived. That is his home and this is a kind of pilgrimage.

Poor boy, it is but the old illusions and he must someday soon experience the same awaking that all have known on their first return home.

15. Helen's aid to young Helen Gourlaye perhaps contributed to her eventual success in life. William Chapman, visiting Brownsville in 1853, reported that she had married a Lieutenant Manuel Romero of the Mexican army (WWC to HBC, Sept. 22, 1853, CC).

16. Helen Chapman is writing to Lucy Bartlett, who had married Welles Blair after his return to Westfield from Wisconsin in the fall of 1849. The newlyweds were soon to move to Kenosha, Wisconsin, to farmland William Chapman had purchased with land warrants the army issued to veterans.

17. This building was old in the sense that it had been used at either Brazos Santiago or Mouth of the River during the Mexican War, but it was a new building at Fort Brown.

I could fill a sheet very amusingly with his sayings and doings. On board ship one night a large group of us were on deck, among the rest were three or four young girls who were talking very fast and some were all talking together. Willie sat very quietly a little apart with a Mr Fisher and myself, and with all his grandfather's deliberation, he remarked, "The Persians have a saying, that ten measures of talk were sent down from Heaven and that women took nine."

"Where did you get that, Willie?" said Mr Fisher.

"Among the golden sands in the *Massachusetts Cataract.*"[18] was the answer. It caused much merriment you may conceive, especially as it was said with such a grave thoughtful, unconscious air.

He is disposed I think to be quite a politician and his ideas are altogether more radical than his Aunt Emmy would approve. He is decidedly in favor of taking Cuba because he sees it a desirable place, very jealous of England and believes that in case of war, the United States should interfere between Russia and Turkey. He has a most religious belief in the entire invincibility of the Yankee nations, and is altogether a promising young sovereign of the Republic.

This morning he was studying a lesson in Geography in which China was mentioned. He berated England soundly for all her injustice, and then said, "England is getting great islands all over the world. Why don't we get some? I wish the Americans would go and take Japan and give them fits."

"Give them what?" I exclaimed.

"Give them fits." Isn't that a blazing little radical for you. If you should question all the boys of ten years throughout the country you might be startled for the conservatism of the future.

I am sorry I have no time for more. I must write a line to Mother. Do wish love to [Welles],

My dear Mother, Brazos Santiago, Texas

March 15. When I begin to write I always wonder to myself why I did not talk more when at home and yet it seemed then as if we had gone over everything.

18. The *Massachusetts Cataract* was a small newspaper variously published in Worcester, Boston, and Taunton, Massachussetts from 1842 to 1853. It was also published under other names from time to time, such as the Worcester County *Waterfall* and *Temperance Standard.*

I often think it is well I brought Willie away for he would have increased your care. As for the dear little fellow, he is learning a great deal of good and evil very fast. His health, I think, is decidedly improved. He has seldom any trouble at night and there is more robustness and firmness about his appearance. He rides on horseback very well and is a most successful fisherman. He seems to have a great deal of principle and people call him a remarkably well behaved boy. I have not put him to much study not only because I did not consider it desirable but also because I had not time. I am beginning now to look through my confusion and I believe I can teach him a great deal without injuring him.

Willie is studying his lessons barefooted. As a treat, he runs about on the gallery without his shoes and stockings. He talks much of you all and prays every night for Bruno [the dog].

March 21. If *you* are full of cases and ten thousand different employments, I can sympathize with you most fully. Until now, I have been obliged to sit down and let everything go. The house at Fort Brown has been full of carpenters, masons and workmen. Things have been moved and removed dozens of times, and I have said repeatedly, "Blessed are they who have little." I am tired of the sight of trunks and packing boxes. The necessity of keeping up two establishments greatly increases our care and labor. The worst, however, is at an end and I hope we shall have some enjoyment.

I have quantities of matter to write about but my head is full of household matters. Tomorrow we go up to Fort Brown. I am very well, perfectly free from cough and asthma. The weather is beautiful, mild and clear. Willie I think enjoys it [here], and is not in the least homesick though devoted to you all. I am getting him fitted up as fast as possible in thin clothes for he rebels stoutly against wearing thick ones, and, indeed, for a fortnight has abandoned his flannel and woolen pants. This afternoon he and his father go fishing.

I believe I have told you of the arrival of Mr Chamberlain, the Presbyterian clergyman. He teaches in the school and I think will procure a very comfortable living. A church was organized and the Sacrament of the Lord's Supper was administered on the following Sunday. There was a little knot of us, but certainly when kneeling before the altar of our beautiful churches in New York to receive these sacred emblems, I never felt the solemnity of the occasion as [I did] here, when sitting on a board bench and receiving them from a plain pine table. I was one of the number who joined the church, on condition that when an Episcopal church is organized I shall have liberty to withdraw. A Methodist clergyman has arrived, and an Episcopal clergyman in Galveston wishes to come. The daughter of Mr Chamberlain has opened a female school. So the prospect is very encouraging. The wife of Mr Chamberlain was a Griswold from Hartford. I think her father was a farmer living in the vicinity.

We are both of us delighted that the *Westfield News Letter* will not be discontinued. It is a most welcome paper to us, not only because it is well conducted, but because it supplies *your* deficiencies in the way of local news.

I wish you would get the straw bonnets that are perfectly *use*less at home colored and have ready to send to me by the next trip of the *Alderman*. Bonnets are in great demand here and they are so soon ruined by the climate that one must change often. Whatever I ask of you in this way draw from my little stock of money at home.

Judge Bigelow has paid back all the money [we] advanced to Mrs B[igelow], and she is living with him in a nice little box of a house. Lumber is dear in this place and Willie surveys the house with ineffable contempt. Passing her house on horseback, the Major said, "There is where Mrs Bigelow lives, Willie." "That!" he exclaimed, "Why it's no bigger than our old b ——— house before it was thrown down." "Do you call these trees? They're nothing but bushes." "I'd like to see some real good green grass, this looks like grass at a distance, but it's nothing but weeds." These are some of Willie's commentaries on the Valley of the Rio Grande, and I give them to you for what they are worth.

Helen

8.

SOCIAL ORDER AND DISORDER

May through September 1850

No town of 2,500 could exist without a certain amount of scandal. Brownsville in the summer of 1850 exemplified this axiom. One woman, overcome by jealousy, attempted suicide by dosing herself with arsenic and laudanum. Two gamblers engaged in an "affray" during which one was killed; he had just lost all his money dealing at monte.[1] Even the distinguished Israel Bigelow "exhibited his pugilistic powers" twice in one week, the second time reportedly getting the worst of it. An abundance of mosquitoes and barking dogs as well as a plethora of prostitutes marred Brownsville's vigorous growth.[2]

Of greater consequence were a number of assaults on the rule of law and order in the town. Several thieves stole $3,000 from a merchant, although some of the money was later recovered. The infamous Dr. Kellogg escaped from jail and was shielded from rearrest by the "unprincipled rabble who had gathered around him."[3] Two accused murderers were lynched by a jury of their peers without being subjected to the niceties of a trial. The *Rio Grande Sentinel* indicated that in Bill Hardy's case, Brownsville citizens convened something akin to a meeting and voted to hang him. Francisco Flores's jury, however, more closely resembled a mob.[4]*

Both the Mexican General Francisco Avalos and the Indians preyed upon the local populace. Avalos's banditti reportedly

1. New Orleans *Daily Delta*, June 12, 1850.
2. New Orleans *Daily Delta*, Aug. 6 and 20, 1850.
3. New Orleans *Daily True Delta*, July 10, 1850.
4. Extract of *Rio Grande Sentinel*, July 17, 1850, in New Orleans *Daily Delta*, July 23, 1850.

appropriated $55,000 from the American consul at Monterey and lesser amounts from other travelers, while the general himself attacked a Frenchman in Matamoras.[5] During the summer he was also accused of impregnating a Mexican woman and kidnapping a female slave and her child who had escaped from their Brownsville owner across the Rio Grande.[6] Indians were active in May near Laredo, in June near Rio Grande City, and in July near San Antonio Wells.[7]*

Elections for state, district, and county officers took place in August 1850. Much was at stake, since the men elected to judgeships would rule on land titles which had been disputed for two years. Fraud and vote-buying prevailed. At one location, where eight people lived, more than ninety votes were cast. A Frenchman visiting Brownsville at the time wrote, "Tables are placed in the streets, garnished with bottles, full of whiskey which is liberally distributed to such as take a ticket bearing the name of a certain candidate. Those who had formed no opinion drank freely in both camps."[8]

By mid-August, however, the Washingtonia Society, a temperance group, began to make inroads in the locals' habits. "The drinking houses are not doing much; . . . you hear nothing but temperance, temperance, from morning til night."[9]*

In other positive developments, an ice business opened, and a new sidewheeler, the *Grampus*, was put in service, running between Brazos Santiago and Brownsville.[10] Most encouraging, very few deaths resulted from disease which had so predominated a year earlier.

5. The actual amount taken is not definitely ascertainable from available sources. Various accounts place the sum anywhere between $33,000 and $55,000.

6. New Orleans *Daily Delta*, June 12 and Sept. 4, 1850; extract from *Rio Grande Sentinel* in New Orleans *Daily Delta*, July 10, 1850.

7. New Orleans *Daily Delta*, May 20, 1850; extracts from the *Rio Grande Sentinel* in the New Orleans *Daily Delta*, July 9, 1850.

8. New Orleans *Daily Delta*, Aug. 20, 1850; Domenech, *Missionary Adventures,* 241–242.

9. New Orleans *Daily Delta*, Aug. 20, 1850. Washingtonians, operating under the aegis of the American Temperance Union, signed a pledge agreeing to total abstinence (Thomas C. Cochran and Wayne Andrews (eds.), *Concise Dictionary of American History* [New York: Charles Schribner's Sons, 1962], 932).

10. New Orleans *Daily Delta*, Aug. 29, 1850; Lea, *King Ranch,* I, 58.

My dear Mother, Fort Brown, Texas

May 3, 1850. It is late in the evening and we have the first moment, in two or three weeks, of quiet and solitude. I have just seen Willie to bed and now with my pen in my hand and the room cleaned, I have that confused, bewildered kind of feeling that you can so well understand. We have had the task of putting two houses in order and have had constant company.

The last was something unexpected. Among our fellow passengers in the *Ohio* were a Mrs Morris and her daughter, Kate, a young girl of sixteen from New York and going out to New Orleans to spend the winter.[11] They arrived more than a fortnight since. They seem delighted with their visit and I really believe if the season were not so far advanced they would stay much longer. They leave a week from tomorrow on the *Globe*.

The Major is scheming as busily as ever and believes all his affairs to be going very smoothly. We do seem to be wonderfully prosperous but "in the day of prosperity consider." Major O'Brien seemed to have as fair a chance from life as Mr Chapman and yet he has gone![12] I never have known Mr Chapman so affected by any death.

Willie continues very well and grows rapidly. He rides every day on horseback and is not fatigued by a distance of eight or ten miles. His figure has improved and I think a firmer life for a while will be advantageous. Tonight when I said I should write to you, he said, "Tell them to write about Bruno. I want to hear about him, and tell Aunt Emmy that I want to get back to Westfield. Texas doesn't begin to be equal or half equal to Massachusetts."

May 12. Mail after mail has been sent off and I have not sent even a line. I have been bewildered, confused, hurried, driven and know not how the time has gone. Our New York company goes off tomorrow and then I hope to procure a little quiet. There has been company late at night, picnics, and all sorts of excitement.

On the 9th of May 1850, there was a picnic to Palo Alto, 12 miles distant.[13] Willie accompanied the party on horseback and made the

11. Mary A. Morris and her daughter Kate were the wife and daughter of Francis Morris of 85 Nassau Street in New York City.

12. Major John P. J. O'Brien had died on March 31, 1850. See Appendix A.

13. This celebration of the battles of Palo Alto and Resaca de la Palma was held on May 8 and 9. According to one account "All the ladies of the city and garrison graced the occasion, and a colation of eatables and drinkables was done ample justice to." A ball concluded the festivities (New Orleans *Daily Delta*, May 18, 1850).

distance going and returning (24 miles) without fatigue. He is altogether beyond having his horse led by a bridle rein and really rides extremely well. He is growing rapidly and is very much browned. People generally think Willie cut out for a lawyer. I have a companion for him, a little girl of his own age of whom I will tell you when I can get some quiet.

My dearest Valeria,[14] Brazos Santiago, Texas

May 28. Your letter was received this morning and I am so delighted that I am losing no time in [again] placing you in my debt. How was it that you wrote, my dearest Val? Were you threatened with the loss of your darling coffee or banished to your chamber til the task was completed? But whether by your mother's sweet kind of compulsion or your own good will, I am most sincerely grateful.

But I must tell you that I have recently had a visit of a month's duration from two New York ladies, fellow passengers on the outward passage of the *Ohio*. We were introduced to them by a mutual friend at the wharf on starting and afterwards became more intimate while boarding at the *Veranda*.[15] I never should have thought of inviting strangers to visit me here because I do not consider the inducements sufficient but they came to New Orleans for pleasure and to see something of the world and evidently had a great desire to see a new phase of life in Texas.

They gave such decided hints of their wishes that I proffered an invitation which was readily accepted and accordingly they arrived the middle of last month and left two days since on the *Globe* apparently delighted with their visit. Part of the time was spent here and part at Fort Brown. Sarah knows what a desolate looking spot the Brazos is and will exclaim how could they pass the time there? But Sarah never saw this house, at that time in progress of erection by Major Eastland, large, high and cool with five chimneys and a noble piazza running the whole four sides of the building. We have plenty of seafood and sea bathing with the most unlimited personal freedom, lords of all we survey though it is only a sand beach.

But do not think I had the presumption to rely wholly on these advantages. The visitors were mother and daughter. One about thirty five,

14. Valeria Merchant had been a friend since the early 1840s in Buffalo. She was a relative of Captain Charles Merchant.

15. The Veranda was the hotel where the Chapmans stayed in New Orleans.

the other fresh from *Madam Chegaray's*[16] and in all the unsophisticated freshness of "Sweet Sixteen," I did the wisest thing I believe that I could do and sent for two young gentlemen from Fort Brown. Mr Jarvis from New York, a brother of Doctor Jarvis, U.S.A. and Lieutenant Gibbons of the Fourth Artillery. Mr Gibbons is a true gentleman, lively, agreeable and though not exactly handsome has an agreeable face and like almost all the officers of the Light Artillery companies rides admirably. He has, moreover, the advantage of a very fine figure.

I had also Rebecca Bennett, daughter of Colonel Bennett, Paymaster, who is also nearly sixteen. It was most amusing to see them. The girls presumed in their character of schoolgirls to say and do a thousand things that would not have been allowable had they been older and the gentlemen for the same reason felt none of that constraint and fear of commitment that they might have done with acknowledged young ladies.

There were gay times I assure you. A horseback ride on the smooth hard beach in the morning, a ride in the carriage in the afternoon, while in the evening, reading and conversation left no time unoccupied. We all went to Fort Brown in company and the unusual sight of ladies visiting the Rio Grande for pleasure set everybody on devising schemes for their amusement. The officers gave them a dance and on the 8th and 9th of May there were picnics to the battle fields. A strange place for a picnic you will say but so it was.

On the 8th a large party rode down to *Palo Alto*, a distance of twelve miles, and returned to *Resaca de la Palma* in the afternoon where we dined. Willie accompanied us on horseback. On the 9th we went to *Resaca de la Palma* with the Light Artillery Company where a salute was fired at twelve a.m. We had dinner on the grounds and returned somewhat fatigued but very well pleased.

It is amusing how ladies love to visit in a garrison. No matter how rude the accommodations, it is all the same. The gallantry of military men supplies every deficiency and really I do not wonder for taking them, all in all, they are the most delightful men in the world. You speak of your present quiet and repose as in delightful contrast with your previous floating existence. My dear Valerie, the Army is not the only place where women live such lives. Indeed as society is constituted in this country, no woman can ever imagine her destiny.

16. Madame Chegaray's School was a fashionable school for young ladies and was highly regarded by military families.

I have learned much since I have been on the frontier that once was never dreamed of in my philosophy. I have seen wives of merchants, lawyers, clergymen, all professions, suffering hardships and drifting about from places far more than we have ever seen and without any of the alleviating circumstances that always attend military life. I have seen women thrown upon this frontier under most trying circumstances and I know they look with envy upon us who are sheltered within the walls of a garrison. There is this difference between being *in* the Army and *out* of it.

In civil life, men seem to think their wives must share their fortunes, good or bad, as a matter of course, but in the Army men seem to appreciate the sacrifices and really feel very grateful in consequence. Especially on the frontier, it seems a general sentiment that women, for the sake of their men, deny themselves the comforts and elegancies of life and on this account the men are called upon to extend to the women every possible care and kindness. There is a true chivalrous feeling that I see no where else and which to me far more than counterbalances any slight annoyances that occur in this kind of life.

But what I once should have called miseries, I laugh at now. For instance, a mouse once put me into a very lady-like state of nervousness, but not much more than a year since, I slept in a weather-boarded loft where real rats held their revel all night long and now a whole regiment of them would not disturb me. According to my present rational ideas upon such subjects, I do not think that ladies accompanying officers of the Artillery or staff to any frontier post unless it be to New Mexico are in danger of anything worthy of the name of privations. The Artillery posts must necessarily be in easy communication with the necessary comforts of life and staff officers, if they anticipate any length of service, can generally make themselves tolerably comfortable. With the Infantry, it is different. They really do have a hard time of it.

The officers here are nearly all married and all the ladies that I have seen are refined and intelligent women. Some of them unfortunately have been bred in cities and seem altogether too delicate for the rough life awaiting them. One who has gone to the new post, Fort Merrill, a Mrs Grainger, is a bride, one of the sweetest prettiest little creatures I ever met.[17]

17. Fort Merrill, established in March 1850, was on the Nueces River in present-day Live Oak County. It became a marginal post in 1853 and was abandoned in 1855 (*Handbook of Texas*, I, 629).

At Fort Merrill, the site of the post had not even been selected when the order was given to erect huts. Until they were finished, their only shelter was a tent. They had not even hospital tents, nothing but wall tents. Think of a whole family, babies, servants, and all, crowded into a wall tent. Four ladies are at Eagle Pass.[18] The two who went last must also live in tents and the wife of the commanding officer is the only one who has a home. And what kind of house, think you. A new home with a wood floor, no windows, only board shutters and when too cold to keep windows and doors open, they must shut up the castle and light candles. This, of course, will only be the case for a while but building materials are transported with great difficulty and such must be their mode of life for some time.

[Having said this much,] I would again repeat my own invitation [to visit], but believe everybody laughs at the idea of making a visit on the Rio Grande. I do not think so as regards ease and comfort, but those who judge this place upon what it was during the war, of course, cannot help but think otherwise.

I hear occasionally of Charles [Merchant] and see his name often in connection with Indian forays. May Heaven preserve him from the fate of poor Lieutenant Hudson.[19] He lived with us for six or eight months and was a very estimable man.

My dear Mother, Fort Brown, Texas

June 8, 1850. Mr Chapman went to the Brazos yesterday to sell off property and break up the Post. He will be absent until Saturday night, perhaps longer. I am not alone for in the room next to my sleeping room is Captain Mumford, and on the other side of the parlor is Colonel Wilson.

Mr Chapman is one of the most ample providers ever known. I have free command of money and I could give Aunt Betsey a good home almost without feeling it.[20] Even with a good deal of company and not much

18. Chapman is probably referring to Fort Duncan. Camp Eagle Pass was established during the Mexican War, and a town sprouted around it. The camp was discontinued with the building of Fort Duncan in 1849 several miles away. The fort's location on a Mexican trade route made it significant during a variety of border disturbances during the next sixty years (ibid., I, 280–281, 624–625).

19. Lieutenant Walter Hudson had been killed during an encounter with Indians, reportedly by a woman he had spared (Vielé, *Following the Drum,* 233–234).

20. Elizabeth Welles Pelletreau was Emily Blair's sister. She lived in Southampton, Long

economy, we could keep house as cheaply as we board now. You understand, my dear Mother, that I cannot save what we need not spend. It comes and goes freely. Household expenses are not regarded in the least and so long as William has no troubles, he does not care.

My dear Mother, Brazos Santiago, Texas

June 19. I sit down to write a few lines, but so worn out, body and mind, that I can scarcely hope to be intelligible. There has been one constant scene of confusion and excitement since I wrote you last. We were at the Brazos getting a little rested from the fatigue of the New York company when news arrived that Doctor Prevost had arrived in Brownsville with his intended bride, her father and mother, and a friend.

This was Tuesday morning [May 28]. We had an immense wash out on the line and were obliged to pack up in the greatest hurry, take the clothes, rough dry, and before 10:00 o'clock, we were on the road to Brownsville. We arrived just at night in a pouring rain, put the house in order and, at 9:00 that evening, had a wedding in the parlor.* The Presbyterian clergyman officiated, Doctor Prevost having vainly endeavored to secure the services of a Roman Catholic priest. Doctor Prevost is the son of General Prevost, one of the first gentlemen in Philadelphia. His wife is a Mexican lady and no Mexican priest would marry them on account of his being a protestant. They remained nearly a week, five of them and during that time we gave a grand party, our first and I fervently trust our last. They say 150 persons were present for supper. I have no time for particulars.[21]

As a finale to this, my cook got drunk and thinking for a fortnight to come at least I should be free from company, I let her go away thinking I could get along with Ann [Mitchell] and her aunt, a recent importation from Ireland. I was worn out and longed for peace.

Just at this juncture, the Steamer *Corvette* came down the river and news

Island. Her husband Albert had recently died, and at the time her future was uncertain. See HBC to EWB, Dec. 22, 1850, CC, below.

21. Dr. Grayson Prevost married a woman from Parras, Mexico, identified only as "Anita." A Brownsville correspondent reported, "Through the efforts of our kind host and hostess, the affair was made a very merry and pleasant one" despite the presence of General Avalos (New Orleans *Daily Delta*, June 12, 1850). Chapman had to maintain at least the pretense of good relations with Avalos because of the frequent interactions between Mexican and U.S. authorities.

was brought us that a lady and infant, Mrs Brewerton,[22] was on board and had a letter of introduction to Major Chapman. She was consigned to our care by her husband and there was no help for it. We were just about starting for the Brazos, so we brought her with us. She leaves this evening but I hear some more people are coming down. It is in vain, however, to hope for anything like solitude.

Doctor [Prevost] gave Willie a pony. By the way, Willie is becoming quite a successful speculator. He has sent two ponies to New Orleans and sold them at such an advance that with some other little sums collected in various ways, he has now $70.00. Seventy dollars! He grows rapidly and seems remarkably well. The weather is very warm and Willie burdens himself with as little clothing as decency will permit. He gets his lessons pretty regularly and does much better than one would suppose living in such a hubbub and confusion. Love to all.

June 26. I thought by this mail, I should certainly be able to bring up my journal to the present, but instead of that, I am again writing at the last moment. When well enough to do anything, I am very busy with sewing. You know I have a little girl to sew for as well as Willie and though I can get some assistance, all the cutting and planning goes through my hands and brain.

I have never the felicity of telling you that we are alone. Colonel Bennett is spending the week with us, a worn out "Bon Vivant," the victim of good dinners and choice liquors, exhausted at an age when he should be in his prime. I do not suppose he is more than forty-five and yet his physician knows that he may die at any moment. For two or three years, he has had sensations of fullness after eating, gastric pains, but he went on eating, as thousands do, eating and drinking, til suddenly about three months since, he was startled from his security by a hemorrhage of blood from the stomach. He vomited nearly two quarts and ever since has been subject almost daily to violent pain and distress in the region of the stomach. Dr Jarvis says his stomach is precisely like a worn out sack, the slightest imprudence may at any moment bring on another turn of bleeding.[23] It is literally worn out and nothing but extreme care can prolong his life.

He does not know the extent of his danger and, even if he did, his habits of self indulgence are so confirmed, I do not believe he could deny himself.

22. Mrs. Brewerton's husband was Lieutenant George Douglas Brewerton. See Appendix A.

23. These symptoms suggest a peptic ulcer.

He thinks he diets, and I will tell you how. Last night for supper, he ate heartily of fried fresh fish, with tomato catsup, finishing with sponge cake. On going to bed, he asked me for some sponge cake to take away the taste of his medicine. I suggested that currant jelly might answer his purpose better and gave him a plate containing two slices of sponge cake and two spoonsful of jelly. After swallowing his pills, he devoured the whole to destroy the taste. This morning he ate fried fish and buckwheat cakes with Stewart's syrup. This noon, he ate stewed oysters, fried fish, with catsup, rice and syrup. Sage pudding, and water melon. This evening he had one of his distressed turns.

This is his dieting and is about of a piece with men's dieting generally. This gentleman is a widower, and has made proposals to a lady who has the subject at present under consideration. Dressed and in friendly spirits, he is a handsome man, though the expression of the mouth is too voluptuous, does not look in ill health, though somewhat sallow, of rather a noble presence, respected, rich with but one child and added to these advantages, his rank as a colonel of the Army, makes it very possible she may accept him. What a terrible take-in it will be!

Willie is very well, gets his lessons regularly and is a great reader. Books of adventure and travels especially delight him. He received your letter and for a time was inconsolable for the loss of Bruno, but he seems reconciled now and, in his prayers, has substituted his new dog, Dickey, for Bruno.

We have a tempting array of new books on the table, but I do not indulge myself in much reading. The Major thinks Miss Bremer's "*Lighthouse*" is very beautiful.[24] I have only glanced through it. When she speaks of Elina [one of the characters] and others like her, she says "They all are souls which are waiting for their Pentecost." I could not but think of Lucy [Blair] and pray that her Pentecost might soon come. "For what purpose is this life? Why do I live?" are questions through which she is still struggling.

Dear Mother[-in-law], Brazos Santiago, Texas

July 2, 1850. I have been intending for some time to write you about Willie, and I have been the more desirous of doing so, because my opinion

24. Swedish author Fredrika Bremer (1801–1865) was a reformer and champion of women's rights. Eleven volumes of her books were translated into English in 1844–1845 (*Encyclopedia Americana*, International Edition [Danbury, Conn.: Grolier, 1989], IV, 502).

of him has so materially changed since I first saw him in Westfield, after an absence of three years. While at the North, being constantly on the move, and my mind occupied by a thousand things, I only observed him casually, and had no opportunity of noticing his intellectual and moral culture as I have since done.

But now I can most honestly say that I never saw a boy of his age who was his equal. He is the most intelligent, sensible, manly, truthful, handsome, and affectionate boy I ever saw. He sometimes uses bigger words than I, his father, but always with correctness. He is a great reader, and often amuses himself for hours with a book when other children would be restless for play. He strives to do nothing wrong and frequently lectures his father and generally backs his arguments by saying, "Aunt Emma, I know, would think so."

You undoubtedly have the first place in his loving heart, though a half year has elapsed since he saw you. He almost daily declares that there is no place like Westfield, that he wishes to live there, to have a barn there for his pony, to own a piece of land there, which he will purchase with the money he has saved, and so forth. No Scotchman is more attached to his highlands than Willie is to his "house" in Westfield.

He is a great temperance boy, and I really believe that nothing can ever shake his principles on this subject, they seem so strongly rooted. He often lectures men upon this subject, the observance of the Sabbath, profane swearing, and similar matters. I never thought I could love a child as much as I do. Helen and you know how strong that is. He is a great happiness to us and we desire no other company. He gets his lessons daily and learns very quickly.

He has grown tall, is filled out, and with his sunburnt face is a beautiful boy. He has a beautiful pony, which was captured at Buena Vista, and rides daily. I wish you could see Helen on her handsome bay pony and Willie on his, riding with me along the beach on a charming evening, after a hot day.

We are all very happy, and now that [Welles] is found, Helen has no cause of anxiety. Her health was not good after her return from the North, but now it is much improved, and she rides horseback every evening.

I think [Welles] and Lucy will do well in Wisconsin. I believe I wrote you that we had purchased another 160 acres of "heavily timbered" land about two miles from his farm. I also sent him today a soldier's land warrant for 160 acres for him to locate, take possession of, and cultivate or lease. If I should be as successful in some of my private businesses as I hope, I will send him in the course of a year some ready cash to operate with. Since I saw you last, Mr Reed [William's brother-in-law] and myself have divided $2500, the profits of our Mexican wool trade, and I have over 50,000 pounds here now ready for shipment to the North. Mr Reed is astonished at its paying the Dutchman's *one* percent (100 per cent).

We go to Fort Brown tomorrow to spend the 4th and shall return soon after. Helen and Willie join me in much love to you and all,

W. W. Chapman

My dear Mother, Fort Brown, Texas

July 17. The mails have gone by almost without my knowing them and indeed I have known nothing but a sensation of heat and inability to do anything. I have not been really unwell but my time has gone just like that of everyone else in these burning climates at midsummer.

Willie continues perfectly well and is now going to a Spanish school, kept by Mr Monsaloatge, the missionary of whom I wrote.[25] He likes it and I think he is learning well.

There is no more important practical knowledge than that of French and Spanish and I am anxious that he should learn them. He only attends in the morning for the present, the afternoon being too hot.

July 18. Yesterday I went to see a Mrs Lawrence whose husband, a young lawyer, died of intemperance a few weeks since. At the time of his death there was not a penny in the house. They were in debt and had nothing of any consequence to eat. The poor lady is trying to get a living by taking in sewing. My heart aches for her and I have given her some sewing because she must have help. She says her grandmother brought her up to do everything for she said nobody knows what may happen to you before you die.

We are expecting another couple from the interior of Mexico, Parras, to be married. A Mister Chapman, an English gentleman who has been for years living with a Mexican woman after the fashion of the country. He has been wishing for his children's account to legalize the connection but has had no opportunity. A foreigner can only marry by renouncing his protestant faith. It is rather an odd sight to see a man and woman with a family of children stand up to be married. But "Better late than never," certainly. Love to all.

25. Ramon Monsaloatge was a former monk who had broken his vows and married.

My dear Mother, Brazos Santiago, Texas

August 1, 1850. I am at the Brazos again, and am trying to resume my old habits of writing. Since my return, a great deal has happened peculiar to a new country, that is worth describing, but I have lived in a hurry and confusion and was in no mood to be a chronicle of passing events. Someone says a journal should always be written from memory and I believe there is some truth in the suggestion.

When we first returned in January, we found that the Reverend Mr Baker was up the river on a Missionary tour. He spent a few days with us on his return, and seemed fully sensible of our wants.

Mr Baker was for some years pastor of a church in Washington City of which John Quincy Adams was Elder. He had the manners of a man of this world, and had the dress and appearance of our Eastern ministers except that his manner was more free and less professional. He was full of anecdotes and in his sermons was exceedingly practical. He was considered a man of great usefulness. Before he left the country, Mr Chamberlain to whom I alluded before, arrived with wife and children.

You know how delighted I was at the arrival of a missionary, but I must confess when the Reverend Mr Chamberlain arrived, my hopes were somewhat dampened. They landed in the morning, and came immediately to the house to wait until the carriage and mail were in readiness. At a glance, it was easy to see that he was among clergymen, what Dr Clark, our old neighbor, was among physicians. He looks like him, without possessing that decidedly benevolent physiognomy which if I recollect right, Clark possessed. Mrs Chamberlain had a rather languid, fretful, fine lady air. The eldest daughter was a bright, intelligent, pretty girl, and the other three were large healthy children, but undisciplined.

The lady immediately began with apologies for their appearance which I considered decidedly unnecessary and then continued with complaints of the boat, the hardships of the passage and the assertion that "if she could have had any idea of what she should suffer, nothing could have induced her to come." All said with the languid drawling sort of tone of a spoiled woman of ease and fashion. There was a baby in arms, of course, and whenever it cried which was very often, the father immediately took the child as a matter of course, so that it was easy to see that instead of poring over theology in his study, he held the Office of Baby's Arms, and I believed I was prepared for many imperfections but it was impossible with regard to the wife, not to have many misgivings. I might after all the disagreeables of a sea voyage, a delicate situation, have felt as she did, but I certainly think as the wife of a missionary, I would have controlled my language. The Missionary Society gives them only $200.00 [26] For the rest, they are dependent on the people and under such circumstances, should keep their expenses at the lowest possible limit. But the lady, as a matter of course, is display, wears a white drawn bonnet trimmed with lace and has a jaunty (I do not know if the word is legitimate) air, that we never see in wives of clergymen at home.

There was every disposition I think to do well for them, but their expectations, or rather hers, are so large that people are becoming wearied, and I do not believe he can get a support another year. The stores and warehouses of Brownsville are of brick, large and handsome, but the owners of these, and the main supporters of the church, those who have families, live in very small unpretending houses. Lumber is so high and titles to land so involved in litigation, that people do not like to expend much capital in this way. But with great liberality, they have subscribed for a nice brick house, the rooms to be of good size and everything comfortable.[27]

The utmost delight and gratitude ought certainly to be expressed for such conduct [on the part of the supporters of the church], but instead, Mrs Chamberlain said to the Major, that she was sorry the rooms were not larger. She wanted a parlor like Mrs Chapman's. To feel the force of this speech, you must know there is no parlor in the country of the size or furniture of mine. There are six windows and it requires more than fifty yards of carpeting. It is furnished in New York style and like no other place. We do not wish to seem extravagant, but we are the oldest residents in the country and have been gradually accumulating. The house is an old building, used during the war and though with repairs presenting a fine appearance, altogether larger than we should think of building. A room of that size at the present price of lumber would cost an immense sum. You can see how thoughtless and inconsiderate was such a speech and how unpopular.

26. It had been understood that the total annual salary should be $600 to $800 (J. G. Junkin to HBC, Aug. 27, 1849, CC).

27. Vielé reported that the subscription collected for a church building had been used by Chamberlain to construct a parsonage to which he held title (Vielé, *Following the Drum*, 109). Abbe Domenech echoes these comments, adding that Chamberlain had "alienated the minds of his co-religionists by equivocal conduct in a rather serious case" (Domenech, *Missionary Adventures*, 245).

Mr Chamberlain would like twelve hundred dollars beside his house. It will be hard to procure this, and, moreover, his manner is not popular.[28] He is prosy and monotonous in the pulpit and does not [talk] with the men like Mr Cravens [does]. He looks feeble and dyspeptic, is undoubtedly worried and annoyed at home and altogether is much to be pitied. It is a great mistake sending a man of such character and with a large family to a new place. A younger woman and man could live about among the parishioners and get a living almost without their feeling it.

This is the case with Mr Cravens [the Methodist minister].[29] He is a widower, lives in a little room built off from his church, and takes his meals among the brethren. In this way he is constantly among the people. Rough savage looking men will seek him out when they would never venture to the house of the other ministers. A Western missionary should never be out of the way. Mr Cravens was here a few days since, on his way to Alabama, to be absent three or four weeks. He has over fifty members and his church, in every respect, seems flourishing. He is a working man, and is in the midst of everything. He has organized a Washingtonia Society and has drawn in some very hard cases.[30]* One case he mentioned was really affecting. A Scotchman stopped him in the streets and said, "Can't you do anything for me."[31]

"Yes, my friend. Go and sign the pledge, come to church every Sunday, and go regularly to work every day in the week. Consider it an insult if a man asks you to take a drink. It is an insult to you, for it poisons you."

The man promised. About a week after, this man came with a pail of nicely filtered water, saying that he filtered more than he wanted for his own use, and that if Mr Cravens would accept it, he would like to bring him a

28. One visitor to the area noted that Chamberlain's "discourses were for the most part diatribes against the Pope and Papacy, subjects highly relished by the Presbyterians" (Abbe Domenech, *Missionary Adventures*, 245).

29. Neamiah A. Cravens was initially unable to find a place to preach, but he secured funds to buy a lot and erected a church sixty feet long and twenty feet wide. Seats and a pulpit were installed, and Cravens partitioned off ten feet at one end for his bedroom and study. The first services were held on May 12, 1850. The offering that day raised $100, the balance due on the building. Hiram Chamberlain was present and aided in the dedication. The building was then proclaimed to be the "first Protestant church built on the Mexican border" (Olin W. Nail, *The First Hundred Years of the Southwest Texas Conference of the Methodist Church 1858-1958* [Austin: Capital Printing Co., 1958], 64–65).

30. Thirty-five members had joined by August 1850 (New Orleans *Daily Delta*, Aug. 6, 1850).

31. HBC to EWB, Aug. 20, 1850, CC (commencing).

pail every morning. There was real kindness in the act, for it is quite a laborious performance to filter the Rio Grande water for drinking. Not long after, he brought two very handsome pitchers saying he wished one to be used in the church and the other to be used in Mr Craven's room.

You can see by this little incident the character of Mr Craven's popularity. They love him. Up to the time of his leaving, the men have been perfectly sober.[32]

Aug. 15. We are full of company again. Mr and Mrs [John W.] Phelps are spending ten days, or a fortnight at least, here with three children and two servants. Dr Jarvis is also here so we have eight persons in addition to our own family. The weather is intensely hot and I am sick of the very sight of food.

In *The Life and Correspondence of Andrew Comber,*[33] in a letter where he insists upon the necessity of exercising the nervous system, Comber says, "Scarcely a day passes in which I do not feel positively grateful for being obliged to exert myself and to do many things and see many people that were I left to inclination, I fear I should often neglect, &c. &c., the more you force yourself to active communications with others and the more you exercise your mind and encourage your friends to rouse you up, the more certainly and speedily will you acquire strength of mind and health of body." This was addressed to a lady suffering under a complication of nervous disorders. The kind of life I lead may be the means of keeping me alive, but I am very positive it is not beneficial for children and instead of being positively grateful, I can only be resigned.

The weather is extremely hot. I can write no more in such a hubbub and with much love to all, especially Grandmamma, I must close my letter.

Aug. 20. I consider Willie's position almost unfortunate inasmuch as it wants altogether this element of hardship and calculation. The son of a very rich man could not be surrounded with more appliances of ease and what makes it worse, the position is entirely a false one. Here at the Brazos, where we stay most of the time, we live in a kind of feudal state. The Quartermaster's department is separated by a very high wall from the collection of sheds that compose the village. There is only one entrance through this wall at which a sentinel is posted night and day.

From these outside people, we are as entirely separate as if we lived in

32. HBC to EWB, Aug. 20, 1850, CC (ending).

33. George Comber (1788–1858), *The Life and Correspondence of Andrew Comber* (Edinburgh: MacLachlan and Stewart, 1850).

separate worlds. I do not think Willie has ever been outside the gate except with me or his father to ride on the beach. It has never been forbidden, but I do not think he has ever thought of such a thing. Belonging to the yard and in his father's employment are 125 men, many of them very respectable and earning their $125. to $150. per month.[34] Some of them have families, but so strong are the distinctions of rank in these cases that there is no approach to equality and among them all it is "the Old Major" and "the Little Major." They are devoted to his amusement, and as he is really amiable and winning, they do ten times more for him than what they might consider enforced service. Such a condition of things could scarcely happen anywhere else.

Here we have no equals in social position. I mean, of course, at the Brazos, not up the river, and the effect upon his mind cannot but be unfortunate. When he first came here, he was certainly intoxicated and displayed some disposition to imitate his father's quick authoritative manner, but I checked that in the outset, made him wait upon himself, forbid the southern habit of calling him Master Willie and Young Master, made him say to the men, "Will you please" on all occasions, and now I see nothing of it. Notwithstanding, however, there is great danger of his thinking the world was made for Caesar.

He is very good about spending money and yet, as he himself saw, when talking about Captain Hunt's boys, and their eagerness to spend "I do not spend money, mother, do I?" (but after thinking a moment) "I don't know why I should for I have everything I want, it seems to me." But it is no more than justice to say, that his wants are reasonable. Not a particle of candy, nor a toy or anything for mere amusement, except firecrackers on the 4th of July, has been bought for him since his arrival. His father will have a good table, but pickles, sauces, tea, coffee, hot bread, meat at night, everything that will injure him, Willie relinquishes with a very good grace. He is very anxious himself to avoid ill health and such ugly sores as children have often in this country. I believe he has heard himself called handsome, and I think he has rather too much pride in his personal appearance.

His appearance is peculiar, I believe. In New York, he was thought to be a Spanish boy, and his complexion attracted attention everywhere. Such a rich brunette complexion is unusual. I think he has a great taste, much

34. Helen Chapman has overestimated the wages paid, perhaps by as much as $100 per month, according to the payroll records (Quartermaster's Payroll Report for Fort Brown, October 1851, CC).

more than I had at his age, for beauties of scenery. He has read to me pieces of descriptive poetry that I should not suppose a child could appreciate. Children's books seem no longer to have any interest for him. His great delight when the mail arrives is to sit down with me, and get me to find pieces for him to read. He very often brings pieces to me that he especially admires. Haloolah, Mardi, *Life in the West*, by Ruxton, and books of that kind, he perfectly deserves.[35]

He is in many respects a very lovely child,—full of sensibility and enthusiasm, intelligent, affectionate and conscientious. At the same time I often fear that there is by nature a want of the sterner and bolder qualities. The excessive care lavished upon him has undoubtedly rendered this more apparent, and the circumstance of his position all seem to increase the evil. As General Taylor said in dying, "I have endeavored to do my duty."

We were all shocked and overwhelmed by the news of General Taylor's death.[36] He was a man for great occasions only, and the ship of state appears to me without a helmsman and every instant nearing the breakers. There are few men who, like General Jackson or General Taylor, have power to impose their individual will in great crises.[37]

The young men of Brownsville are drinking themselves almost to death and I often thank God that [Welles] is not here. The temptations of young men in southern cities exceeds all you can imagine and I cannot but think [Welles] is far safer where he is. There is an elegant drinking establishment in a beautiful brick building completely furnished and rendered as alluring as money and taste can make it. We have had some horrible executions and when I have time I will try to tell you of them.[38*]

But I have spent too much time over this moralizing. But I must first tell you of one present that I do enjoy exceedingly, that of a very pretty barouche from New York. Mr Chapman had such a grand opportunity to sell the one we brought with us to a Mexican gentleman, that he parted with it, and sent to the same carriage maker for another. I never step into a carriage of my own without a thrill of thankfulness to God, for having

35. Authors Haloolah and Mardi remain mysteries, but George F. A. Ruxton (1820–1848) wrote *Life in the Far West*.

36. Taylor had died on July 9. The news reached Brownsville by express rider on July 21. Ten days later nearly the entire town turned out for a service in his memory. William Chapman (and presumably Helen) did not attend because he had business at the Brazos (New Orleans *Daily Delta*, Aug. 6, 1850).

37. HBC to EWB, Aug. 25, 1850, CC (and following paragraph).

38. This is undoubtedly a reference to July's lynchings.

surrounded me with so many blessings. It is not that I care in the least for show, and that this seems to gratify it, but I believe it results from my vivid impression of the longing I had for a ride when sick years ago. Oh! what a luxury it seemed to ride every day as some did and how it seemed to me that bright summer day as if I must have that *one* indulgence. As well as you all loved me in those days, there was no money in the house for any such indulgence. The plan was abandoned, but Uncle Charles sallied out and returned after a while with an old buggy and an old horse. I had my ride, and I know no carriage, however luxurious, with horses of the noble breed and training can ever give the *woman* such pleasure as did that rickety old establishment to the *child*.

Aug. 25. We have a family of seven persons and one young gentleman staying with us waiting for the boat. I am tired and half worn out. When the guests are all gone and the house is quiet, I will write a long letter to you.

We are now once more the last family belonging to the Army at Fort Brown. Captain and Mrs Hunt are leaving the country. Colonel Bennett's family left by the last steamer. Love to all.

Aug. 28. I was sorry not to hear from you by the last mail and learn how you are living though the hot weather. I hear it has been extremely hot at the North and here the heat has been greater than I have ever before known. I believe my last letter was not written in very good humor. I was nearly worried to death with company, annoyed by the heat and my nerves were out of tune.

I have had more trouble with servants this summer than ever before in my life. After my great party when Doctor Prevost and his Mexican family were visiting, I came home one day, expecting dinner ready to be served. I found nothing cooked and the cook was smiling and happy, sitting on the doorsill gloriously drunk. I was obliged, of course, to send her away and the next one I hired knows nothing, not even how to cook a beef steak. She washes and irons well and learns readily whatever she is taught, but she is careless and untidy and tries me in various ways. Her good temper is her best qualification, and she gets along well with the children. I have another excellent girl who relieves me very much. I have been in capital training for the last two years to keep a boarding house and I have added that to my known means of getting a living.

Directly after the departure of Mr Phelp's family, Miss Bacon, a poor, worn out, old maid school teacher came down to recruit pupils. It was very much against the Major's will that she came at all and I am constantly occupied in keeping the peace. She is not agreeable, she is pedantic and in trying to say witty things she generally ends in being rude. The men all hate the sight of her, though some are more careful than others to conceal it. In opposition to all of her unfavorable characteristics, I must say she would give away her last copper to anyone who needs it, she denies herself almost the necessities of life to send home everything she earns, she devotes herself to an intemperate, worthless brother and works patiently without seeing an end to all these difficulties. She is one of the kind of visitors I love to have and for whose comfort I would labor with the greatest delight, but Alas! for those who are not endowed with the gift to please. The Major will do anything for her in the way of procuring drafts or something such as that, but will not be annoyed by her presence. Poor Woman! It would seem as if my home should be her especial place of refuge. Her lot is precisely what mine would have been if God had not made it to differ.

Another missionary arrived a fortnight since about whom I feel very hopeful. He is sent by the Presbyterian Board of Missions to Brownsville to labor among the Mexican population. He will also open a Spanish School. Monsaloatge, I think, is the name, a Spaniard and a converted monk. He brought a letter of introduction to the Major from Doctor Baird of New York. He has one of the sweetest, most benevolent countenances I ever saw and when I watched him caressing and fondling his little girl with such tenderness, I thought, how cruel to condemn a man with such affections to a solitary life. His wife, I am sorry to say, looks feeble and delicate, but I am most happy to add, contented. They spent a day with us and seemed much pleased with the attention we gave them.

We look anxiously now for congressional action concerning Texas. On the Rio Grande, so far as I can learn there is no such bellicose spirit displayed as in other parts of the states. How any southern man of sense can be a *Disunionist*, I cannot conceive. It is the salvation of the South to cling to the North. I firmly believe, however, the end must and will come. These abolition lecturers who inflame men's minds can scarcely exaggerate their stories of individual wrongs.

I must tell you something that happened the other day entirely out of the life you know of. You have heard of Padre Island, a long sandy shore stretching up the gulf and as we wrongly supposed wholly uninhabited. Mr Chapman coming down the river the other day met a Mr Singer, quite a well informed, respectable man and to his great surprise found that he was living only about three miles up the island.[39] He has married off one set of children and is now bringing up a second set. They started for California but were turned back by cholera. Not knowing what to do, the wife proposed they should go over to Padre Island and try to pick up a living. They did so, pitched their tents and seemed contented. Two or three days after, Mr Chapman proposed that we should make them a visit. We went in a large boat [and] carried a table, dishes, meat, sugar, and tea as well as servants and children. The water was so low the boat could not reach the shore and we found Mr Singer waiting with a little kind of hand cart to which was harnessed a little old donkey. The end of the cart was pitched down to the level of the boat and after two or three tumblings on the part of our live load, we were landed safely at the cabin. Their house had been build by the joint labor of their hands and all their furniture consisted of wood thrown by the waves upon the shore. The children are beautiful and perfectly healthy. The wife is a great, strong, muscular looking, good humored woman and helps him regularly with his outdoor work.

The mail is about closing and I will tell you more of my visit when I write next. My health at present is very good and I think I am gaining flesh. Willie is well and seems very happy. Love to all.

Your affectionate,
Helen

39. This was John V. Singer, the fifty-seven-year-old brother of the inventor of the sewing machine, and his wife, the wealthy Johanna Shaw of New Orleans. The Singers bought Rancho Santa Cruz on Padre Island, the site of an early mission, from the heirs of Padre Balli. They renamed it Las Cruces Rancho. They had six children on Padre Island. They were forced to leave the island at the commencement of the Civil War because of John Singer's Unionist sympathies (Verna Jackson McKenna, *Old Point Isabel Lighthouse: Beacon of Brazos Santiago* [Harlingen, Tex.: Port Isabel Press, 1956], 20).

9.

FAMILY BURDENS

October 1850 through February 1851

Harry Love returned to Fort Brown in late August 1850 from a five-month journey of exploration up the Rio Grande.* He had undertaken the trip on William Chapman's orders to discover how far upriver navigation was practicable. After an exhausting and danger-filled adventure, Love found this point to be about 967 miles above Ringgold Barracks. This finding so encouraged the *Rio Grande Sentinel*, that it optimistically envisioned a "complete revolution in transportation." Goods could be delivered to the Great Plains via the Rio Grande, provided that more forts were established in Texas to offer protection from Indians.[1]

Conflict between Mayor Israel Bigelow and the Brownsville city council over finances, specifically the mayor's salary, precipitated a crisis. The council voted to hold another mayoral election in September. Meanwhile, one newspaper reported, "Everything is uproar and confusion. Real estate is falling every day and merchants are leaving. . . . Indeed these are what may be styled starving times. Money is scarce."[2] Robert S. Lehman succeeded Bigelow as mayor.

1. William W. Chapman, "Report of Exploration of the Rio Grande, made by H. Love . . .," and following editorial, *Rio Grande Sentinel*, Nov. 27, 1850; See Appendix B; Jane McManus Storms Cazneau reported that the Love Expedition reached a point on the Rio Grande 200 miles below El Paso, although it is more likely that the "Grande Indian Crossing" at Lajitas, Texas, was the upper terminus of the trip, according to a ranger at Big Bend National Park (Jane McManus Storms Cazneau, *Eagle Pass or Life on the Border*, ed. Robert Crawford Cotner [Austin: Pemberton Press, 1966],178; Gus Sanchez to Caleb Coker, Dec. 17, 1990, interview).

2. New Orleans *Daily Delta*, Sept. 25, 1850.

Helen Chapman did not write to her mother about these events in the fall of 1850 and early 1851. Nor did she keep her mother informed of the violence in the town.[3] Rather, she was occupied with the care of her three foster children. They joined her family for varying reasons and stayed differing lengths of time, but Chapman took pleasure from the simplicity of their wants and her part in overcoming the disadvantages of their earlier experiences.

My dear Mother, Brazos Santiago, Texas

Oct. 1, 1850. Yours of September 15 was received yesterday. I am glad to hear Father and Grandmother continue to improve.

I have been wanting to tell you about the little girl in my family and about the dwellers of Padre Island. I have at present a little girl [Lizzie Millett] from New Orleans here on a visit.[4] She is ten years of age, mild and lady-like in her manners, well brought up and apparently very well principled. I shall keep her till next spring at the latest.

You will think it strange that I am filling the house with children, but I sacrifice my own loss of quiet to Willie's interests. He reads altogether too much when alone and tends after the fashion of the family devouring everything written in his way. Stories and travels seem to be the favorites thus far and I try to put in his way such as seem least exceptionable. He has been reading Miss Edgeworth's novels lately and I have been looking over them myself. They seem to me only fit for children and are not comparable with Mary Howitt's.[5] He reads the *Cataract* and Westfield papers with great interest.

While upon [the subject of news]papers, I am reminded to caution you against belief in all the lies of letter writers from Brownsville to the New Orleans papers. In one of the last, I see it mentioned that Major Chapman

3. See, for example, New Orleans *Daily Delta*, Sept. 10 and Oct. 15, 1850, and Jan. 10, 1851 (quoting from the *Rio Grande Sentinel*, Jan. 1, 1851); *Rio Grande Sentinel*, Nov. 18, 1850.

4. Lizzie Millett was an orphan. Helen wrote to the child's grandmother, Mrs. M. Carroll, in New York City, for instructions. Mrs. Carroll acknowledged the letter and was willing to care for her, but appealed to Helen for funds to pay Lizzie's passage to New York (Mrs. M. Carroll to HBC, Oct. 15, 1850, CC; WWC to HBC, Sept. 22, 1853, CC). Lizzie had a younger brother, Johnny, mentioned in HBC to EWB, Jan. 6, 1851, below.

5. Both Maria Edgeworth (1767–1849) and Mary Howitt (1799–1888) were much-published British novelists.

caught four runaway slaves when just within reach of the Mexican coast and sent them back to New Orleans. I do not know when I have felt more annoyed. It is a lie from beginning to end and he had no more to do with the transaction than my father.[6]* The facts were simply these. Captain [E. N.] Anderson who commands the U.S. Steamer, *Mentoria*, on his way up to Brownsville from the Brazos when near the mouth of the river saw a boat containing four runaway negroes who were making their escape into Mexico. He captured them as his own individual act and sent them to New Orleans, claiming his reward, I suppose.

We, as Northern people retaining all our Northern feelings and principles, felt a profound pity for these poor creatures who had made almost superhuman exertions to obtain their freedom. Captain Anderson sent to the Major to know what he should do with these negroes. Mr Chapman sent word to him that it was no affair of his and he had nothing to do with it. Captain Anderson is from Tennessee, the son of a slave holder, and has no scruples in the matter.

Poor creatures, my heart ached and bled for their hard fates, but for those whose misfortunes it is to live in slave states, there is no help but to suffer in silence. The more I know of slavery, the more horrible it seems to me and darker and darker grow the clouds that hang over the future. I have heard slavery discussed by slave holders, by military men who have lived long in the South and regard it only in a political aspect, by women, by free servants, by persons who merely tell incidents without any excitement or sympathies, or any abstract notions of right and wrong and, in every light, it is fearful and ominous.

I do not remember if I have told you of any of our friend, Mrs Singer's talk about slavery. She has lived nearly all her life among the great sugar plantations of Louisiana. The planters are mostly French and the proportion of whites is very small compared with that of the colored and mixed population. Mrs Singer has owned slaves herself, her mother has a large number and she buys and sells with as little thought as if the transactions were in cattle.

These planters are seldom married men. Their wives are chosen from among their slaves. "What do they do with them," I asked, "when they become old and ugly?"

6. William Chapman wrote the New Orleans *Daily Delta* to contradict the story (Oct. 11, 1850). The author of the article, an unemployed Brownsville printer named J. M. West, later apologized to him (New Orleans *Daily Delta*, Oct. 12, 1850).

"Oh! sell them and get plenty of others," was Mrs Singer's reply.

"But what becomes of the children?"

"Oh! They are sold too. A man will sell a whole family of them at once."

Reflect a moment what a condition of society this will in time create. The mother's condition fixes that of the child. This is law. If the mother be a slave, the child is a slave even though the African blood be scarcely discernible.

These slaves have only a Christian name, Sally, Tom, or something similar. They change owners frequently, are separated in infancy, know nothing of their own birth, who was their father, their mother, their brother or relations. Incest must be a thing of everyday occurrence and committed unconsciously. The following incident Mrs Singer mentioned as having seen herself, and indeed the occurrence is not uncommon.

In company with another woman, she went into the auction room for the sale of negroes in New Orleans and while there, two very fair beautifully dressed girls came in with a yellow woman. Mrs Singer supposed them visitors with herself and was not undeceived til she saw them step upon the block. The yellow woman began to cry and one of them said, "Oh! Don't cry, Mother, if Father has no more feeling than to sell us, I don't want to live with him, but I'm not going to be sold to any man to work for him, implying that she expected to be bought for a wife. Two young Frenchmen, brothers, immediately secured them at a thousand dollars each and took the mother with them.

There is much in the external personal signs of degradation to keep the black race humble and patient, but how will it be with those who by a long continuance of this social system retain only such a slight tinge of African blood as is supposed to heighten European beauty. Think of being surrounded by beings from whom you are trying constantly to exclude every ray of knowledge.

While I was waiting on the other sheet of material for the carriage cushions, Miss Bennett, a sister of Colonel Bennett, Paymaster, came in to make a call with a little black child, Charlotte, about six years old whom she pets and caresses very much as you did Bruno [the dog]. She sat in the bedroom with me, leaving Charlotte in the parlor with the children. She sat very contentedly til she heard the children asking the child if she knew her letters and afterwards pointing out the letters to her. She said, "I really believe they are teaching that child her letters." I merely laughed and made no effort to stop them, so there was no help for her but to jump up and carry off the child to prevent such an imminent danger.

I never see this child without a feeling of profound pity. She is like hundreds of other black children, the victims of a selfish unreasoning caprice kept about the parlor as a plaything. Her affections and taste cultivated by refined associations and yet she is liable at any moment to be brought to the Auction Block and knocked off to some hard, unfeeling task master. It would have been ten thousand times better to let her run wild with the animals til old enough to work in the fields.[7]

I have told you before of her master [Colonel Albert G. Bennett], a man whose stomach is worn out, whose affairs are embarrassed and who may die at any moment.

There are a good many sickening things about us. These exaggerated stories of Brownsville prosperity have drawn hither a great many people without any means or substance. Provisions are high and there is really a great deal of poverty. Men are reeling about the streets, shooting people dead in their insane fury and violating all laws, human and divine.

Last evening riding out in the country, we passed a party of Mexican horsemen and as they rode by, I noticed that one of the men was strapped by the body across the horse, the legs hanging on one side and the head on the other. He was dressed in his usual clothes and on my calling the Major's attention to it, he said it was probably a dead person. On returning to the city, we found a crowd surrounding a dead body, the same we had seen on the horse. I had one sight of a figure stretched on the ground and a mangled bloody mess where had been his head. I felt heart-sick and I longed to get away from the frontier. It seems the man had been shot by the Sheriff that afternoon while escaping on what was believed to be a stolen horse. He would not stop, so the Sheriff shot him down.* No one seems to blame him and perhaps in these new places such acts are terrible necessities.[8] It is impossible to appreciate these blessings of law and order, til deprived of them as we are here. You must remember, however, that we are not actual sufferers from all this confusion. Inside the garrison, we are

7. *Uncle Tom's Cabin* had not yet been published.

8. The Brownsville correspondent to the *Daily Delta* wrote that a coroner's jury ruled this a justifiable act. He raised the troublesome issue of whether the deputy had jurisdiction over a crime committed in Mexico allegedly by a Mexican citizen. Since no arrest warrant had been served, he questioned whether the shooting was, in fact, justified (New Orleans *Daily Delta*, Oct. 11, 1850).

in a different world from those living in town. No thief or murderer ever ventures within range of a sentinel's musket.

Willie is studying Spanish and I believe making very good progress. I am taking lessons myself of Mr Monsaloatge.[9] I have no time for more by this mail.

Oct. 13. Willie and I are alone at the Brazos, the Major will remain at Fort Brown until Wednesday. At present, we are all well, but both my girls have been down with Dengue Fever, or breakbone fever, as some call it.[10] Willie was a little sick for a day or two, but nothing worth mentioning.

The Major has had remarkable health all summer. I left part of the family at Fort Brown coming down here for a few days thinking the sea air might make me feel better. This fever has been a real epidemic, going through families and affecting everybody more or less and the Point Isabel doctor says it has much the character of bilious influenza at the North. The summer has been intensely hot and this fall there have been great quantities of rain. The day is precisely like a spring day at the North, soft, still and pure.

No work is allowed within the yard on Sunday and I believe there never was such a good set of men. There is always great eagerness to get into the government employ on account of higher compensation, better accommodations, and above all, the security of payment, a great consideration in such a state of society as this. They are, therefore, picked men and they know they are in extreme danger of losing their places if they are ever known to go upon a frolic. It is a very rare sight to see a man belonging to the [quartermaster's] Department intoxicated and any riotous, noisy behavior is altogether unknown. The military regularity of their labor does very much to keep them sober, and if you could see them, you would come to the conclusion that absolute power is a very good thing, if it can only be placed in very good hands. Here it contrasts so strikingly and so favorably with the confusion and weakness of civil affairs. In Brownsville, the city government is in the hands of the rabble and the most miserable work they make of it. Wickedness of all kinds abounds and there are scarcely righteous men enough to save it from destruction.

9. See HBC to Dr. Robert Baird, Feb. 3, 1851, below.

10. Dengue fever is a mosquito-borne, viral disease that is completely incapacitating during its acute phase but almost never fatal. It is characterized by extreme stiffness and pain in the joints (*Encyclopedia Americana*, VIII, 704).

Mr Cravens, the Methodist Minister, is really doing some good. Mr Chamberlain with his slow and old fashioned jog trot preaching is not even looked at. Do you read "Franchesca's" letter in the New Orleans *Delta*?[11] She has the right idea of the kind of minister wanted [on the frontier], men who have force and eloquence even of the rudest kind, men who will make themselves heard even by shouting in their ears if they can do nothing more than drown out, for a moment at least, the clamor of gross sensual pleasures and for gold.

Our churches are what Willie very naturally calls barns, but our drinking shops are really elegant buildings, fitted up with everything attractive and forming a most dangerous contrast to the cramped close, cheerless looking dwellings of most of the inhabitants.

Another young man in town has just been given over by his physician and must die another victim. Next door to me at Fort Brown lives young Henry Whiting, a son of General Whiting, one of the best of fathers and one of the best of men. He was brought up in the most careful manner, but he is weak and is killing himself with drink.

I have not yet heard from Lizzie's friends in New York. I have been separated from her a week and really begin to think I am fond of her. She is such a cheerful useful little creature. There is one good thing about her if her lot should be cast with us. She is very small and her feet [are also].

Willie wishes to send Helen [Pelletreau] something by the next trip of the *Alderman*, but is puzzled as to what to send, and so am I.[12] There are no pretty goods here as formerly. [The local merchants] buy for the Mexican market and it is impossible to find a print that will wash. There is no gingham, no cashmere. My time is spent chiefly in preparing, sewing, cutting and fitting, attending to the housekeeping, and teaching the children. I have everything arranged so that I accomplish a great deal.

Nov. 1, 1850. I am very well. The servants are getting well, and everything seems prosperous.

Annie [Mitchell], whom I brought up from Brownsville, is here for a few days getting ready to be married. She is a pretty, graceful girl and I have the satisfaction of feeling that she begins her married life knowing

11. "Franchesca's" letter in the New Orleans *Daily True Delta* appeared on Oct. 1, 1850. Its author was a Mrs. Willis, a correspondent from San Francisco who kept New Orleans and much of America abreast of what was happening in the Gold Rush city.

12. The *Alderman* regularly sailed between New York and Brazos Santiago. The schooner was owned by a brother of Charles Stillman.

sufficiently of everything. She can cook, wash, and iron, and sews beautifully. She has strong sound sense and an admirable judgment about her dress, no desire for ornament, but likes everything neat, plain, and simple.

The young man's name is Alfred Bennett, formerly in the Major's employ, but now a journeyman printer in Brownsville earning from fifty to sixty dollars a month. He is now secretary of the Temperance Society, has a good knowledge of Spanish and is quite intelligent. He looks like a gentleman and, though poor, is above Annie in position and education. She is, however, as I have told you, a very remarkable girl and has the step of a queen. During the time she has been with us, she saved forty-five dollars, every cent of which was sent to Ireland, to bring out the other children without a hope of ever receiving a dollar in return.

But the family all arrived safely this spring, and with the exception of the two youngest, are earning their own living. Mike, the oldest, is working in the Quartermaster's Department at $25 per month and a ration. He has paid Ann the whole sum he borrowed, and we are spending it to set her up in housekeeping. She belongs to the Methodist Church, and some evening week after next, we are to give her a wedding. The whole family are now here, eight in all, and it does one's heart good to see how healthy and happy they all look. The other sister who came out with Annie is married to a wheelwright and house carpenter, and it is really amusing to see what a transformation they have effected since May in the *raw material*.

I do not know if I told you, how Ann begged to go over to New Orleans to meet them. I refused for some time, thinking it foolish, but at last consented. I found out after she had left, that her anxiety was to get them made a little decent, before they were seen here. She took all the money she could raise with her and on her arrival found them with a crowd of immigrants renting a room and buying some bread each day. They were bare headed, bare footed, almost naked. She went to work and really I never saw such a sum of money go farther. She had friends in New Orleans who wished her to stay with them, but she was so fearful they would find out about her family that she stayed with the family in all their dirt and discomfort. She went about town getting each of them some things absolutely necessary, set the Irish women to work, made each of the children sunbonnets, palm leaf hats, and frocks, got shoes, jackets and pantaloons for the boys, and when they arrived, though she was terribly ashamed of them, I thought they looked remarkably well. She sat up nights and worked her fingers to the bone. All this was done in two days, the time of the steamer's stay in New Orleans and by a young girl of sixteen.

Willie is very well and happy and acts as if he fully intended to go home next spring.

Nov. 5. I told you of the arrival at Brazos of Mr Monsaloatge, a reformed monk with his wife, child and wife's sister. The child, a girl was two years and a half, very pretty, very winning and graceful in her ways and always about her father. She seemed not to know of her mother's existence. In the course of conversation, it came out that the woman was a second wife and step-mother to the little girl.

They left the child with us a little while just at evening. She began to cry and the Major walked up and down with her on the piazza. She fell asleep and lay in his arms. When her father returned, Mr Chapman, in his jesting way, said a great deal in praise of the child and told Mr Monsaloatge that he had better let him keep the child. A great deal was said in his earnest enthusiastic kind of way, but it was all in pure jest.

To our surprise two or three weeks since, Mr Monsaloatge came down and made a serious offer of the child, revealing a tale of domestic unhappiness that would affect the hardest heart. The mother died soon after the child's birth. For a year he took the sole care of it himself and then married, he says, solely for the sake of the child. But his wife bestowed no care upon it and even seems to hate it, is jealous of any attention he bestows on her himself and he thinks after his wife's confinement the situation of the child will be much worse.

He says if he were to die his wife would cast off the child at once and, as much as he loves the child, he would be willing to part with it to those who could bring it up in comfort and happiness. His devotion to the child is undeniable and what we saw of the family on their first arrival confirms his story. Mr Chapman told him that he was very likely laboring under a mistake as to his own circumstances that he had no sure means of support except his pay and probably could not be able to give a child anything on her marriage. Mr Monsaloatge replied that he expected nothing of the kind, that he was miserably poor himself and that all he desired for his child was a good home. The Major said he would give him an answer on hearing from the friends of the little girl now living with us.

Angeline Julie Monsaloatge was born in Paris. Her mother was a Frenchwoman.

Dr. Jarvis replied from Fort Brown to Helen Chapman's request for help in treating William Chapman's case of dengue fever.

My dear Mrs Chapman, November 10, 1850

Your note of this morning I have just received and I take the earliest opportunity to answer it. I do not think you should entertain any serious apprehension from the mere fact of the Major's head being affected. This seems to be the principal symptom in all the recent cases of the Dengue (which is doubtless the Major's complaint) and is much more severe in this particularity than in the earlier cases that occurred here. It, however, lasts but a short time and soon disappears with the other symptoms characteristic of this annoying illness. In most of the cases under my treatment at the present time, I have to cup them freely in both temples and also in the back of the neck, then purge them with Blue mass and extract of alocynth, say 20 grs. of the former and 5 grs. of the latter followed by a dose of castor oil and mustard footbath. These means generally suffice with warm drinks to induce perspiration and relieve all the symptoms.

The Major, being of a full habit, may require considerable depletion and I would keep him on thin gruel alone at least while he has this fullness of the head and fever. I should doubt the propriety of giving him opium which you allude to in your letter where there is any great disturbance of the brain. Cold applications to the head may also prove beneficial.

I am in hopes, however, by the time you receive this letter that he will be much better as to render all this advice unnecessary. If he is able to travel I would recommend by all means his coming up. This change of air will benefit him.

I do not mean to convey the idea that we have not the dengue here at present. This last Norther seems to have developed it full in our garrison, but since its subsidence the cases seem to have diminished.[13] There is only one officer besides myself fit for duty in the garrison. Major Giles Porter and his man Tom, Lieutenant Gibbons and some 12 soldiers are down with it. Lieutenant Garesché is sick with a catarrh and Lieutenant Holmes with Rheumatic, leaving Lieutenant Whiting the only officer for duty besides

13. There had been a severe norther from November 6 to November 8.

myself in the garrison. In town the disease has nearly, if not entirely, subsided.

My brother went according to your wishes to see Mr Monsaloatge and found him better and sitting up. He told him what you desired in reference to the child with which he appeared to be highly gratified. I understand from Mr Stillman that the *Grampus* will not be up for some days, the *Comanche* having gone down to the mouth for her load.[14]

If the Major should feel able to ride over, he might come up in the latter boat. The moment he gets here I will take him under my special charge and in some measure endeavor to repay his attendance upon me in my recent illness from the same tormenting disease. I hope he will not prove so crass as our "Old Major."[15] His disposition, at no time very amiable, is now something like that of a mad dog, snapping and snarling at everything that comes in his way, but as old Samuel Wells[16] would say "Its his nature" to do so.

Aunt Margaret and Whiting are now the only 2 persons in our group who have escaped the dengue.[17] I found the former this evening sitting in a room, doors and windows closed the latter with double curtains and a fire that would have roasted alive a dozen John Rogers, with a thermometer out of doors standing at 70 degrees of summer heat. She tried to induce me to come in but I had no idea of being roasted alive or barbecued and therefore declined. In answer to my inquiry as to the cause of this great application of caloric, she replied that she kept up the fire to keep away the dengue. In her case the remedy was as bad as the disease or at least the preventative.[18]

14. Both steamboats were owned by M. Kenedy & Co. and commenced service in August 1852. The company was owned equally by Mifflin Kenedy, Charles Stillman, Richard King, and James O'Connell. The *Comanche* had the shallower draft (Lea, *King Ranch*, I, 59).

15. Major Giles Porter was "eccentric as all old bachelors are supposed to be" (HBC to EWB, Aug. 3, 1849, CC). In 1853 and in 1857 Porter was acquitted in a court-martial on charges that were never made public (WWC to WBC, Dec. 17, 1852, CC; Lea, *King Ranch*, I, 142–145).

16. Dr. Jarvis's inside joke refers to Samuel Welles, a seventeenth-century ancestor of Helen Chapman. The quote is remarkable because it had been passed down in the Welles family for six generations.

17. These are Margaret Vernon of Brownsville and Lieutenant Henry M. Whiting.

18. Ironically, the remedy Miss Margaret chose to pursue was probably an excellent mosquito repellent.

Express to the Major my sympathy, but I trust that in a day or two he will be able to relish a cigar as well as a joke.

Yours truly,
N. S. Jarvis

My dear Mother, Brazos Santiago, Texas

Dec. 13, 1850. Your letter of November 17 was duly received. I am sorry you have suffered so much anxiety on my account from not writing often enough. The truth is I have known very little health for the last year. On my return from our trip to the North, owing to fatigue, excitement, the breaking up of my regular habits at hotels, the violent transition from heat to cold and from cold to heat, all combined produced the most severe attack on my lungs I have ever experienced. There was some inflammation of the lungs and pleurisy probably and I do not think they have ever regained their former strength. Before I had a fair chance of recovery, I had all the fatigue and excitement of the Morris's visit, then Doctor Prevost's wedding and the great party. About that time I had a complete loss of appetite, not a feeble one but no hunger, no desire. This was a poor preparation for the overpowering heat of the last summer which was greater than has been known for years. I felt myself losing strength but still remained quite comfortable. The hot summer was succeeded by remarkably cold Northers, chilling us almost to death. The consequence was universal sickness.

The Dengue or Breakbone fever has been a regular epidemic attacking nearly every one. I wrote to you that both the servants were sick. After that the Major was taken ill, and the sickness of all the rest was nothing compared to his. His brain was very much affected, his mind wandering and running from subject to subject with lightening rapidity, very much the state of mind it seemed to me that precedes delirium tremens.

I was here at the Brazos with no physician nearer than Point Isabel. Part of the time the wind was blowing so furiously that no boat could reach the Point. I spent one night in this way, unable to keep him in bed following his every motion with intense anxiety. At daybreak, we dispatched a boat for the Doctor and about 9:00 o'clock he arrived. His symptoms were alarming and if the weather had been hot it might have been impossible to save him. As soon as possible, we took him up to Fort Brown and most gladly and thankfully I put him in the care of Doctor Jarvis.

There was an incessant strain upon my nerves until I saw him well and strong and you will not wonder that when that moment arrived, I found that I was myself sick. I have had no fever, but asthma and a violent cough. With the hope that a change might benefit me, I came down here three days since leaving the children at Fort Brown. The effect has been almost magical and my cough is rapidly subsiding.

Dec. 15. I have improved very much within the last two days and, indeed, feel as well as ever though rather weak. Willie has wonderful health and is really a very handsome boy, too much so perhaps. He is growing very tall and straight. His teeth are becoming white and handsome, his complexion dark but very clear, his hair rich and glossy and withal the same pure thoughtful child-like face that he had with you. The defect in his face is the smallness of his chin, unimportant as a matter of beauty, but I fear indicating some deficiency of will.

Willie is a great favorite with the gentlemen and Judge Bigelow gave him twenty dollars the other day on condition that he should expend it on sheep. Mr Reed has sent him a fine Cotswold sheep of great value here. Willie and I, between us, have a flock of about seventy or eighty. They are considered very productive property, the increase is so rapid.

I have received a letter from Lizzie's grandmother, another tale of suffering. She expresses the utmost anxiety, however, to have the children with her and the present arrangement is to send them next June in the *Alderman*. At present, Lizzie is exceedingly useful to me and if I could be sure that her support would not come upon my hands for life, I would like to keep her a while.

We have taken little Angeline. "How can you undertake this with your health," you will say? But I am fortunate in having one of the best girls in the world to take care of her and Lizzie constantly amuses her.[19] She is, moreover, a brave resolute thing, accustomed to being knocked about. Her health is good and she asks only God's gifts, the pure, fresh air and the sunlight to make her happy. She eats bread as pampered children would eat cake. She knows nothing of delicacies and, of course, never cries for them. The children all live very plainly, no matter what is on the table and Willie also has astonishing self control. When I leave him at Fort Brown, they say he is just as careful as when I am with him. In my next letter, I will write more of Angeline.

19. This is a reference to Jane Anderson of Bilgooly Kinsdale, County Cork, Ireland.

Dec. 21. I still continue very well. We expected to go over to New Orleans on a new boat to hear Jenny Lind, but since the old steamers are still to be kept running, I think we shall not venture.[20]

By the last steamer came John James Clark, consigned to us by Mr [Colin] Reed. He has been with Mr Reed ten years ever since his arrival from Scotland, of which country he is a native. The result of his long trial in a store is that he cannot be a good salesman because he is so honest. He has the most uncompromising antique kind of generosity with ever so much Scotch obstinacy. He cannot call a poor article "first rate," but must on all occasions call white, white and black, black.

Mr Reed has sent him off to see if we can do anything with such an unmanageable piece of humanity. He is to be a clerk until he can do something else and he is to live with us. He is twenty-six and I am not sorry to have him with us. He is poor and has orphan sisters in Scotland to support. On the vessel, he had sheep in charge and, feeling the full value of money, he took care of them himself. In consequence, he got the nickname of "the Shepherd," and it must be confessed that he has rather a pastoral appearance. He will be called green and all that, but as for me I reverence God's image in such a character. I am glad to have him with Willie for much of his time is necessarily spent with the clerks.

Mr [Samuel] Jarvis, the other clerk, is a perfectly exemplary young man, not one who perhaps would stand the furnace heat of temptation like our Scotchman, but who certainly does not want opportunities for wrong doing. His tastes are delicate and refined. He is a gentleman by birth and education and never guilty of any excess or any improper language. As they are so much with us, they could not be better chosen on Willie's account. Jarvis is handsome, intellectual, a great reader and has something remarkably spiritual and beautiful in his countenance.

John Clark has rather a sharp, long, attenuated, care-worn face and a good intellectual development and benevolent expression. To me, Mr Jarvis carries in his face the prophecy of an early death, the other that of a life of toil, hardship, and struggle. Both will be clerks till they die and both will cling to the strong arm that now directs them with the helplessness of children.

Where is the difficulty? I have described the front of their heads, the back of them tells the secret. They both want *animal force.*

20. Jenny Lind, the "Swedish Nightingale," and her tour of the United States during 1850–1851 consumed as much newsprint as any other news item in America during those years.

I thank Heaven they are here, instead of [Welles]. They are safe from their temperaments, he would be in constant danger. Poor young Whiting has just had a terrible attack of delirium tremens. If it had happened in the summer, it might have proved fatal. In this climate, it generally ends with inflammation of the brain or bowels and death speedily ends the suffering. I can see the evils of California here on a smaller scale. Drinking, gambling, poverty, suffering widows and children, a city growing too rapidly with no land cultivated and no ownership of soil and rents kept up at a most ruinous rate.[21]

I have written so much because I know you are very anxious to hear about Willie's companions.[22]

If I had time, I would like to give you a picture of our domestic life. The servants seem very fond of the children and do their duties very well. We have bright fires in the evening, a center table covered with books and papers and more than all, the spirit of love and contentment. Willie often says, "What happy days these are, Mother."

It would be rather an advantage to Willie, I think, to stay here another year. This boating and riding on horseback is bringing out his physical energies admirably. His form is becoming erect and firm, while his great activity prevents the bilious disorders to which older persons are subject. He has admirable opportunities for studying Spanish, French and even Latin.[23]

I believe I promised to say something more of little Angeline. It seems to me, she has rather a stout frame. She has the pale Spanish complexion, but healthful. Her hair is at present light, her forehead well formed, her eyes are large, very dark, and what may really be called magnificent. The eye lashes are rather longer than usual, but not so long as Willie's. Her mouth is very pretty and her teeth are the most beautiful I ever saw. Notwithstanding these favorable points, I doubt she will grow up handsome. Her father's features have remarkable symmetry and beauty, the outline is beautiful, but it seems to me, hers will have too much breadth. So much for her appearance, it is impossible to tell you much of her mind.

She is wide awake, cheerful, exceedingly observant and a perfect little French woman in her love of dress. Soon after she came to me, I fitted on a little red dress of the same color as the one I gave Helen and looking

21. HBC to EWB, Dec. 13, 1850, CC (commencing).
22. HBC to EWB, Dec. 21, 1850, CC (resume).
23. HBC to EWB, Dec. 22, 1850, CC.

down upon it, she threw up her hands with most amusing gesticulations and exclaimed. "C'est Magnifique!" She has lived without the companionship of other children and has some peculiarities. She has had such a training in poverty that if ever so much disposed to pull a thing to pieces, I tell her "it cost money," and she ceases in an instant.

Dec. 22. I ought to feel deeply grateful that I am able at the commencement of a new year to send you some money and yet I feel more like writing a lamentation than a Thanksgiving. I think of poor Aunt Betsey and contrast my situation and even yours with her real and pressing needs, yet I am utterly powerless. In the present condition of things, it is utterly impossible to apply to Mr Chapman. The local demands on his purse are heavy. He has the whole burden of his mother's support and her expenses are considerable. In addition, he has sent two thousand dollars to [a business associate] which though in the form of a loan is to all intents and purposes a gift. He has had some rather considerable losses and though he would make any exertion to gratify me it would be wrong of me at this time to make the request. It is astonishing how he bears all these demands not only as something that cannot be helped but cheerfully and, indeed, acts as if giving were a pleasure. "The Lord loveth the cheerful giver."

I have Mr Chapman's promise of anything I can save from the next year's pay and I may be able to furnish a little. If I should go North next summer, I might reduce my expenses so as to accomplish something but that is all uncertain.

As is the case with most interesting businessmen, the more he extends his business operations the less money he has to use and I think he would find it difficult to loan even two or three hundred dollars at this time. I do not know what Aunt Betsey can do. I sometimes think if she could [move] her family and live with you, it might perhaps be better. An irresolute, timid, unenterprising mother, it appears to me, cannot impart a favorable character to boys. There is nothing hopeful in living under such influences.

If I could give Aunt Betsey any article of personal property that she and her children might retain, I would gladly do so but I have no disposition to have any money swallowed up in the farm without some security of payment whenever a division is made.[24] Cannot Father write and ascertain

24. See Chapter 8, n. 24. Albert Pelletreau's estate was being probated. Aunt Betsey had sold off the income-producing farm animals for living expenses, a course Helen deemed improvident, and was low on funds. It appeared that the home place would have to be sold to pay creditors of the estate and to make distributions to other heirs.

positively if any money were loaned for repairs and re-stocking the farm, whether there is any power in the executors of the estate to give security for the loan to be repaid whenever a division [of the estate] is made.

Jan. 5, 1851. I was terribly frightened in this attack of fever [that afflicted William last month] and with very good reason. In those nights of anxious watching, I could not but think of the condition of three families at least in case the worst should happen. The only property for which a thorough business man would give three cents on a dollar is that contained in the real estate in Springfield and Wisconsin. There is not one dollar of income that would not cease with his life. Much more has been made but it is "cast upon the waters" and is depending solely on the life, success and honor of those who hold it.

From our manner of living, there is a general impression that we are rich, but it is all uncertain and by removal to an expensive post where there was no means of increasing his income or by [his] death, this would cease at once.

The Major is very sanguine that he will, before he dies, become a very rich man. I think the chances are about equal that he may become very rich or find himself all at once without a cent. I do not allow it to give me uneasiness. I can do nothing, except by constantly urging moderation and caution. Habits of self indulgence increase very rapidly upon men in these hot climates and I have many fears of violent fever or of broken health. You will not mistake me as referring to any thing except excessive eating and the use of tobacco. When nature can bear no more, the unfailing resort in this country is *Blue Mass and calomel*.[25]

One of us is incessantly scheming to grow rich or rather to make money, the other in some way to improve the condition of those less fortunate. Our point of union is in our benevolent emotions.

Jan. 6. I am alone at the Brazos with one of the servants and my little Angeline. The Major went up on Friday with the rest of the family leaving me here. [Don't] feel anxious about Willie being separated from me in this way. They all say he is as careful in my absence as in my presence to fulfill all my wishes and then I have a treasure in John Clark to assist me in his upbringing.

At Mr Reed's, he [Clark] merely ran home to his meals and then back again to the store. John [prefers] to stay in a warm cheerful parlor to eat

25. The first was a common laxative; the other, an antidiarrhea medication.

instead of hurrying out of the house to a cheerless office and he and Willie are already good friends. He is in John's care during my absence and I feel easy about him.

Christmas day he [Willie] was bent upon making a kind of New England Thanksgiving. There must be pies of mince, apple, peach and pumpkin, a turkey and to crown all a chicken pie and also nice fruit cake. To enjoy them fully they had to be of my own making and I determined to gratify him as much as was in my power. The cooking was all successful and the chicken pie was pronounced excellent. I had a raging headache all through the operation, and after the dinner, I was compelled to go to bed.

However, I [had] told [Willie] he might invite four or five boys. I determined, however, that Willie should suffer no disappointment. He was to tell their mothers that we would keep them until eight or nine o'clock and then send them home with our own man. They all arrived and there was a terrible racket. Willie ran in very often to kiss me and console me and about seven o'clock he declared to me, "I must confess I shall not be sorry when eight o'clock comes." Before eight o'clock some of the boys got wrestling and he sat down, all the time watching the clock. [At the appointed time] Willie started up and cried, "Come boys. It's eight o'clock, time to go home," and the house was quiet ten minutes after.

It seems to me that [the three other] children thrown into my care within the last year are striking examples of peculiar training.

Little Johnny was not two years old [when he came to live with us]. He had been under the care of a camp woman of a wild and lawless life but whose extreme suffering completely shut out from all her old practices while he remained with her. She was a woman of much character and God only knows through what trials she may have arrived at such a fate.

She was with the Army in Mexico from first to last, exposed to all kinds of hardship and her life alternating between the rough carnivals of the camp and attendance among the wounded and dying. She could not have been all evil for she evidently in her own way loved the child and when he came to me, his body was clean and pure. His system healthful and not a trace of the neglected child in his whole appearance. The curiosity in the child was the perfect subjection into which she had brought him. There might be a dozen such children in the house and no disturbance. He would eat with a hearty relish whatever was given him, never cry or cry only slightly when hurt, was pleased with the lightest trifles, perfectly neat in his habits, and, indeed, compared with other children in these respects, a perfect wonder. You would have thought him probably too quiet, too gentle, would wish to hear a louder and more ringing laugh, bolder movements and evidence of a more unfiltered nature.

His quietness resulted from his loneliness, I think. When able she would go out washing leaving him with some bread and water tied up to the window that he might amuse himself looking out and be in no danger from fire. He was a romping merry little creature before he left me but no more difficult to manage than at first. He is far away and I can only pray for the little darling now.

Lizzie shows me the force of impressions made upon the mind before the age of seven years. As you are aware, she arrived in this country between the ages of seven and eight, had no intercourse but with Mexicans and at the end of three years retained but a very slight knowledge of her own language. By want of any links of association, she seemed to have lost to a certain degree the memory of her previous life, and after becoming a member of our family, I noticed that these old associations seemed gradually reviving as her knowledge of the language returned. Names suggested objects and she often surprises me now with details concerning things in New York. She describes the outside of the churches, a habit of her aunts sitting in the parlor with the blinds closed looking at people returning from church (a great habit in cities), taking a walk on Sunday afternoons, the furnishing of her grandmother's house, the talk of the family, but she has no recollections of going to church or Sunday school.

The great desire of the mother was to dress them handsomely and this is the most decided trait they exhibit. She remembers going to a Day School and says that she could read long words in the spelling book, but she has lost it all. I have [been] teaching her to read, but she takes little interest in it. She will have tact, taste, management, industry. Her family affections are strong, and she may make a very useful woman.

The last specimen, Angeline, between father and mother, has kept up through her little life an incessant battle for her rights. She has a positive commanding way about her, plants and stamps her little foot and breaks into a long unceasing scream until her wish is accomplished. A cry from her was like an arrow straight to her father's heart and immediately gained for her all she wished.

Though a little afraid that I might not be able to gain her affection, I determined to subdue her at the onset. In the first place, every one [in attendance] received strict orders to give her nothing she cried for and every instance of disobedience was punished on the spot. She was rather distant for a while, but she now begins to realize that her situation is improved. She has all she really needs to make her happy without a battle and, strange to say, hangs about me continually though the rest do much more to amuse her. She has ceased her crying altogether and obeys promptly.

Jan. 15. There will be a gleam of hope for Aunt Betsey. You know how I dread to make applications for another poor relation from the fear that requests of this kind would financially embarrass the Major. Last Sunday, in the most accidental manner, my trouble about poor Aunt [Betsey] all came out in a gush of tears, partly pride and mortification, mingled with some much better feelings. You know I am never guilty of the meanness of crying for effect. I shed tears because the Fountain is overflowing.

The Major quite laughed at my trouble, and in the most charming manner possible, as if it were a mere trifle, gave me two hundred dollars to spend as I choose for her use.

He is really the most noble hearted and generous man in the world and I sometimes think he will be rich before he dies. He spends his income in such princely benevolence. William mentioned all things seem to work favorably. Some money came in unexpectedly so that he did not feel it in the least.

I have written to Aunt Betsey enclosing a check for fifty dollars and have not mentioned that any definite sum remains in my hands for her use. I thought it better to write to you first. I have the money in my possession, $150, ready to send at whatever time and whenever you may think best. I have perfect confidence in her economy, but not in her calculations. I really wish she might seem to be doing something for her own support if only for its moral effect on her children.

Willie is doing well. Angeline is a great favorite with the Major and a very good child.

Helen Chapman wrote to Dr. Robert Baird to raise money for the school taught by Ramon Monsaloatge.[26]

26. This letter was printed in the *Christian Union*, a publication of the American and Foreign Christian Union and later drew contributions from readers, such as Ebenezer Learned of New London, Connecticut (Ebenezer Learned to HBC, Aug. 12, 1851, CC). Apparently, Mr. Monsaloatge's school had failed in part due to opposition of Catholic priests.

My dear Reverend, February 3, 1851

Among a very ignorant and consequently bigoted population, Mr Monsaloatge labors at a great disadvantage. They have not only a horror of his heresy, but by his marriage, they seem to consider that he has violated vows of peculiar sacredness. [He wanted to serve in one] of the more liberal South American states and with his talents and information, his influence might have been greater among a people more intellectually developed. A certain degree of enlightenment must precede proselytism and from what I read in the *Christian Union* and other journals I infer that the South American republics are altogether in advance of Mexico. Certainly they are in advance of frontier populations such as we have here.

I need not assure you, dear Sir, that the failure to establish a school in Brownsville has been a source of extreme regret. So long as Mexico remains in this distracted state, there will be [a disregard] for crime on both sides of the river that is unknown elsewhere and a lawless vicious population of our own as well as of the Mexicans along the whole line of the frontier.

I have tried to ascertain whether the failure of Mr Monsaloatge's school arose from the priestly opposition or any deficiency on his part and I have been inclined to think that it arose mainly from the first cause aided possibly by some want of patient, laborious perseverance on his part. In this, however, I may do him great injustice.

A friend at Laredo, a place above Brownsville on the Rio Grande, tells me that he does not believe a protestant school would be attended at that place, but that a Roman Catholic school could be assembled at once.

I know, my dear Sir, that your society is powerless in this matter, still it will do no harm to impress upon the religious world that in regions of this character, the school master must precede or rather accompany the Bible. Without him, the distribution of this and all other good books is literally casting away pearls of wisdom.

Notwithstanding these discouraging circumstances, I would like to see the experiment fairly tried of good Protestant English schools all along the American bank of the river. I really cannot understand the apathy that prevails on this subject.

There is no hope that for years to come there will be any system of public school instruction in Texas. Private school teachers cannot give themselves a support and place the price of tuition within reach of the masses. It follows, therefore, that they must remain in ignorance unless help comes from abroad. As a means of restoring pure religion to a Christian nation and a means of preserving peace between two republics already watching each other with jealous hatred and eager covetousness, there should be a chain of well appointed primary schools all along the line of the frontier. They should be supported by Government or by private benevolence until they can sustain themselves. No one doubts the necessity for a chain of military posts. Can anyone, who realizes the necessity of intelligence in those entrusted with the blessing of a free government, doubt the equal necessity of a line of schools. Of what possible use will it be, to send Bibles, tracts, and other books to people who cannot read.

My dear Mother, Fort Brown, Texas

Feb. 10. Your letters of the 9th and 19th of January were received two days since. I tremble to think what news the next mail might bring [of the health of Father and Grandmamma].[27] However I may have believed myself prepared for changes in that beloved home, I feel now that they would come upon me with unexpected force. I am disturbed at what I recollect of the general tenor of my letter enclosing the draft [to Aunt Betsey].

There were reasons to justify me, but they are no longer in existence and I beg you to use money as freely as is desirable. If this should prove to be my dear father's last illness, it would be a most distressing thought that any alleviation has been withheld that money might procure.

I write in great haste at the last moment. I have been very busy fitting out Lizzie for her new home. She has been adopted by Captain Porter, a very excellent man without children who also takes her little brother.[28] Mrs Evans, another excellent person, has taken Fanny so that all the children are provided with a comfortable home without sending them to their poor grandmother in New York.[29]

It was a terrible trial for Lizzie, but I felt that unless I could keep her for life it would be a cruel kindness to keep her any longer. She will grow up in the sphere of life best suited to her abilities and you cannot conceive what a relief it is to my mind that they are provided for. The father is considered a harmless monomaniac.

27. The letters said that both Helen's father and her grandmother, Anne Ellsworth Welles, were ill (EWC to HBC, Jan. 9, 1851, and Jan. 19, 1851, CC).

28. This was possibly Major Giles Porter, the commanding officer at Fort Brown.

29. Apparently Lizzie, Fanny, and their brother were children of a soldier and a camp follower. Fanny never resided with the Chapmans.

Angeline is a great comfort to us, a play thing for the Major and a most interesting object of care to me. I do not feel the anxiety about her when she is out of my sight that I did for Willie yet I have an almost equal pleasure in fondling and caressing her. Little Willie is very well as is also the Major.

I have one excellent girl from Cork, another from the county of Waterford who is not so skilful but who is very willing and devoted. I have good reason to speak well of Irish girls.[30]

God Bless you my poor mother. I wish I could be with you to nurse my poor father and comfort you. Good night, dear Mother, best love to all,

Feb. 19. A boat arrived last evening, but nothing from you. I am, as you must know, exceedingly anxious [to hear of Father's health].

How I wish I could be near you to comfort and assist. Love to all and may God keep you in health and safety till I can go home again.

Your loving,
Helen

30. The two Irish servants are Jane Anderson and Mary Nugent, who came from Waterford County, Ireland.

10.

TRAVEL TO MEXICO

March through June 1851

Various vague ailments troubled Helen Chapman in March 1851. But in spite of that, when army business required a representative from Fort Brown to visit Mexico City, she agreed to go along on the trip, hoping to improve her health.

While in the capital city, Chapman saw the local sights and socialized with other Americans living there. Her astute observations resulted in descriptive letters to her mother and husband, many of which are not included here. She sympathized with the local women who had so few diversions available to them, with the impoverished Indians who had been oppressed for so long, and with the typical Mexican citizen who seemingly had "no national honor, no prosperity, no life."[1]

The inefficiency and *mañana* philosophy of the Mexican bureaucracy lengthened the trip into June. Meanwhile, Chapman's family was changing. The oldest generation was giving way to the youngest.

My dear Mother, Brasos Santiago, Texas

March 5, 1851. Yours of February 20 relieved me very little, but was better than I expected. I wish that I could relieve you, but at present I should be rather an encumbrance than otherwise. I am in my old condition, run down, no appetite, no energy. Under such circumstances I know neither you nor Father would desire my presence.

1. HBC to EWB, Apr. 24 and 29, 1851, May 22, 1851, CC.

It seems to be decided by others more than myself that I am going to Vera Cruz and the City of Mexico if I can get there. [Willie] wishes me to go because he thinks it may improve my health. It is very possible that the rarefaction of the atmosphere caused by its great elevation may prevent my approach. I can certainly go as far as Jalapa. Mr Jarvis, the Major's chief clerk, is going on business connected with the Government and it is arranged that I shall go with him.[2] He was there before with the Army [during the invasion of Mexico], has a perfect command of the Spanish language and we go with facilities for seeing the best society of the Capital. My old friend, Dona Juanita Perello gives me letters to her brother who is a Senator in the Mexican Congress. We have many letters [of introduction and safe transit] and, if I could only feel at ease about home and have a tolerable degree of health, I should have every prospect of a delightful journey. I mean to keep a journal if possible. Annie [Mitchell Bennett], my old servant, goes with me with her husband's consent and approval.

Do not let this that I have written add to your trouble, my dear Mother. I am not so feeble as you have seen me many times before. I expect to be absent two months.

Helen

Dear Mother[-in-law], Brasos Santiago, Texas

March 16. Yours of February 19th is just received, and in the absence of the other and best branch of the family, it becomes my pleasant duty to answer it. I must, however, be brief as I have many letters to answer.

Helen sailed yesterday morning for Vera Cruz in the Schooner "*Major Barbour.*" We have had a favorable wind since she left and I think she will be there tomorrow evening. I have hopes that she will be greatly benefited by the journey. She went well fitted out, with the Governor (Ann, now Mrs Bennett) in charge, and letters of credit for $3000. She has been gradually improving in health for the last two or three months, and I am in hopes that she will be herself again when she returns.

2. Government attorneys had asked William Chapman to obtain specific information in regard to original Spanish land grants on which the government's claim to the federal land at Brazos Santiago were based. One Leonard Dobbins had disputed the claim and sued. The necessary documents were available only in Mexico City. Samuel Jarvis was sent to obtain the evidence for Chapman.

Helen has letters from General Avalos of Matamoras to General Arista, the President of Mexico, and to all the commanding officers at every city and town from Vera Cruz to Mexico, with a request to each to furnish her with a mounted escort. Helen, as good as she is, goes in some for grandeur in her latter days.

Now, Mother, please don't laugh about that *Silver mine*.[3] For the end is not yet. I went into it with my eyes wide open, fully knowing it to be a perfect lottery, heads I win, tails I lose. It will be just $1,000 lost, or a "Pile" made. One of the six owners returned three days since from the mine. From his report, I would not take $9000 for my interest. I might take 10,000, simply because I like quick operations. The Capital is to be $350,000. Don't deny yourself any comforts for you have had your share of trouble in this world. At least enjoy yourself until the silver mine bubble bursts! Mother! Obey orders! or I will certainly cut you off without a picayune.

[Willie] is writing by my side and will give you his own views of matters and things. Love to [all].

Yours very affectionately,
W. W. Chapman

My Dear Grandmother, March 16, 1851

Why do you not write me about my little playmates. I want to hear about Charley Cox and Emerson Davis. My little pony died, but I have another. I have three dogs. I have a Chihuahua dog, it is about a foot long. It never will grow any larger. Lieut. Thomas gave it to me. He came from Santa Fe. I have also two Scotch Terriers whose names are Scot and Nel. I have not many playmates and so I take great comfort in my dogs. Mother sailed on the 15th for Vera Cruz. I asked mother to get some things in Mexico for my little playmates in Westfield. I have a perfect little model

3. Chapman had invested in the Santa Rita Silver Mining Company. This passage suggests that he put $1,000 into the venture. The mine was the Jesus Maria Vallechille in the Mexican state of Nuevo Leon, which Charles Stillman mentioned in a letter to his brother of July 1851. According to Stillman records, shares in the mine sold for $1,000, and the venture was eventually capitalized for $4 million, which means that there were 4,000 shares outstanding. Apparently, the scope of the project grew significantly between March and July, and the original six owners referred to must have increased to a much larger number of shareholders. The mine supposedly struck a rich vein the next year. Shares in the mine were later traded in New York (Chauncey Devereux Stillman, *Charles Stillman, 1810–1875* [privately printed, 1956], 15–16).

Brig. I am learning Spanish. I felt a little bad when Mother first went away, but I have got over it now. We go up to Fort Brown tomorrow to stay three weeks. We will then come down and go to an island that has gull eggs upon it. I have a special Cotswold buck. I have 40 sheep.

From your affectionate grandson,
Willie.

My dear William, Vera Cruz, Mexico

March 19. We are here safe after a passage of very beautiful weather. We came to anchor last night too late to enter [the harbor]. My head is giddy and I have no strength. Indeed during the voyage, the only two connected ideas of which I was conscious was that I was a great fool to leave such a comfortable and happy home and joy that Willie was not with me to suffer that horrid sickness. The poor little fellow would have wished himself with [you] and Jane and Mary many a time.[4]

I cannot too strongly express my sense of Captain Arnet's kindness.[5] I was miserably sick from the moment of leaving to the time of coming to anchor and he nursed and provided for my comfort as no Captain ever did before. Ann was unable to do anything for me and the Captain held my head and did everything a man could do for my comfort. The schooner was far more comfortable than a steamer and fortunately in this case as rapid.

The health officers have made us a visit, but the Custom House officers have not yet made their appearance. I hope they will not unpack my trunks for they never can get it packed again. [Looking across the harbor, we see] the United States Ship of War, *Albany*, is sending a launch to us.

Diligence Hotel.[6] We had no trouble with our baggage. Before leaving the schooner, Captain Fauntleroy, Purser of the U. S. Ship of War, came on board with a midshipman. He is a large, noble-looking man, a grand specimen of a Naval Officer and seemed agreeable to me if only because he was a countryman.[7]

My room is fitted out in American style and so far we are very comfortable. Vera Cruz is a much handsomer town than I had supposed,

4. These are the servants Jane Anderson and Mary Nugent.

5. Fred Arnet captained the *Major Barbour*.

6. "Diligence Hotel" was the series of hotels providing accommodations along the stagecoach route from Vera Cruz to Mexico City.

7. HBC Journal of trip to Mexico City, Mar. 15–27, 1851, CC.

very neat and the antique look of the buildings increases its interest. At this moment with a most delicious atmosphere, it is hard to conceive how Vera Cruz can ever be unhealthy. We took on board some of the Orizaba Oranges and they seemed to me the finest and sweetest I had ever seen, not so large as the Louisiana [oranges], but sweeter.

Ten thousand kisses and blessings for my beloved boy. Tell Jane not to let Angy forget me, but talk to her about Mother and the pretty things she will get her in New Orleans. God bless the little darling.

Let the girls hear what I have written. Tell Mary I want to hear when I return that she has been singing Irish Jigs and "I'm Afloat" all the time I have been absent. Tell her it's altogether more agreeable to sing "I'm Afloat" than to be afloat. Tell Jane I have perfect confidence in them both and it is a great comfort to think the house is in such good hands.

The following are excerpts from Chapman's journal of her stagecoach trip to Mexico City which commenced on March 20 and ended on March 27, 1851.

Thursday, the 20th. Captain Fauntleroy urged us to remain another day and visit the ship. We saw much of him and found him very agreeable. He laughingly told me that he had that morning announced my arrival in Vera Cruz in a letter to the [Navy] Department. I have a great pride in the appearance of Officers of the Army and Navy in a foreign country and he is one in person and manner certainly to gratify such a natural pride.

He gave me his arm to the carriage. The door was shut and we found ourselves with a Mexican gentleman and his two daughters rattling through the city and I seemed to breathe more freely when I passed those heavy walls between four and five in the evening. Our mode of conveyance at first seemed ludicrous. The coach, the mules having been taken off, was pulled into a box car and drawn by two mules over the Rail Road about seven miles in length. It goes through a dismal country, sandy and full of pools of standing water. Our fellow passenger, the State Treasurer, says that in the making of this little piece of road, the work of Yankee enterprise, 3000 laborers died of disease. It grew dark while we still moving over the plain through clouds of dust.

After leaving this [rail]road, we rode over the open plain and it was dark before we commenced the ascent of the mountains. My night at Vera Cruz had been a poor preparation for wakefulness in the stage[coach], but I struggled bravely against my drowsiness wishing to see by the brilliant moonlight any object of interest on the road.[8]

We passed the Hacienda of Santa Anna,[9] its white columns gleaming in the pure light but unfortunately just before arriving at the National Bridge, I fell into a deep sleep and did not awaken till suddenly blinded by a glare of light.

I found myself in the wild and savage scenery of Plan del Rio, gazing on a scene that for picturesque and strong effect, I had never seen equaled. You will remember that here the Mexicans made their impotent effort to stop the passage of General Scott's Army by blowing up the noble old bridge, killing in the attempt eight of their number. The invincible troops immediately cut a road down into the chaparral and without a day's delay, the Army found itself on the opposite side of the gorge.[10] Strange enough and as a very good proof of Mexican character, the ruined bridge still remains a monument to their folly, and the road cut by the conquering Army is now the traveled stage road to the Capital. Down this same precipitous descent, we came tumbling with lightening speed and, ascending the opposite bank, looked back. We had passed the rugged and apparently impenetrable barrier surrounding us, heightened in effect perhaps by the brilliant torch-light and still more by the living features of the picture.

It was at 4 o'clock of the morning and in an old house just at the entrance of the bridge, the rancheros were holding a fandango. A great many teamsters and muleteers must have joined the company for I never saw a more uninhabitable looking region. Within we heard a wilder kind of music, the beating of drums and a melancholy kind of chant in which the dancers accompanied the music. Without, in the yard, were little tables on which were placed different kinds of liquors, around which were crowds of dark, swarthy figures in their sombreros and gay blankets adding greatly

8. The party traveled along the National Road, the route followed by Scott's army four years earlier.

9. Antonio Lopez de Santa Anna (1795–1876) was the Mexican commanding general who opposed American forces beginning with the battle of Buena Vista. He was a master of political intrigue and from 1832 until a few years before his death was either dictator of Mexico or hiding in exile.

10. This was a plan which Captain Robert E. Lee conceived and implemented. Lee had joined General Scott at Vera Cruz. His engineering skills, which enabled the army to traverse the rugged mountain range between the Gulf Coast and Mexico City, contributed greatly to the army's success, and brought him praise and quick promotion after years of relatively slow advancement (*World Book Encyclopedia* [Chicago: World Book, Inc., 1989], XII, 177).

to the picturesque effect of the scene. Occasionally a lady, accompanied by her cavalier, in her camisole, gay petticoat and a man's straw hat would step out from the ball room and refresh herself at one of the tables. In the house she was certainly fashionable in her dress perhaps clad with not sufficient lightness for she wore her ribbons very gracefully draped about her person.

Altogether the hour, the military associations of the spot, the nearness of Cerro Gordo,[11] the wild character of the scenery, the dark picturesque form of these night revelers so completely excited my fancy that I had no further need of sleep and at daybreak first caught a view of the cold snowy peak of Orizaba and a little later saw it bathed in a rosy light while all around was seen in the cold gray dawn.[12]

We passed the spot a little farther on where the dead of Cerro Gordo were buried and our Mexican travellers told us that passing that spot two months after the battle, the effluvia was almost intolerable.[13] At the next station for changing horses, I saw a little muchacho make his toilet with an expedition that would set Willie an example in the morning. He was lying on the floor and waked by the noise of the coach probably concluded he should get up and see the fun. So jumping up he poked his head through the hole of his blanket, shook out his hair, and our young ranchero came out already dressed to receive us. The stage road passed very near Cerro Gordo, indeed over one corner. Mr Jarvis pointed out the hills where parts of the forces were stationed.

We came to Encero just at daybreak in time to have a fine view of the Peak of Orizaba bathed in sunlight while all below still lay in the gray dawn. Here too at Encero, in a pleasant rolling country, we saw another of Santa Anna's residences with its handsome chapel and offices.

[March 21.] At nine in the morning we reached Jalapa. Soft lovely green hills surround the little town, all richly cultivated. Perote[14] and Antabee frame [the] background. There does not seem to me to be a spot of level ground on its surface. The descents are so precipitous and the roads so steep that carriages are never used. No, the only conveyance is the sure footed little mountain ponies of the country. The whole appearance of the

11. Cerro Gordo was the site of one of the major Mexican War battles, fought on April 18, 1847.

12. Pico de Orizaba, also known as Citlaltepetl, is a volcano of 18,700 feet.

13. Approximately 1,500 were killed or wounded.

14. Cofre de Perote is an extinct volcano of 14,048 feet fifteen miles west of Jalapa. It is sometimes known as Nauhcampate'petl.

town is neat. The abundance of fine water, the absence of dust, the wild profusion of flowers and fruit make it unlike any other spot in the world. The roads and lanes are festooned with flowers. Every house, however poor, seems to have a large garden filled with orange, fig, bananas and other trees. The dwellings are all of one story and, though differing greatly in internal decoration, preserve a very democratic exterior. The town is very old and where walls are crumbling into ruins, the luxuriant vegetation is forcing it way through every crevice. One would not for the world have it tarnished by repair.

[*March 25.*] [After Jalapa] there is a constant succession of lovely scenes until we arrived at the volcanic region, which contrastingly was all the more desolate for the scenery we had passed.

As we approached San Miguel and saw its old church pointing with its spire to heaven, it seemed a lovely valley emblossomed among hills, [but] before we had time to take in half the beauty of this mountain region, we were whisked up another lofty mountain, over an interminable range of hills and valleys until we felt almost giddy at the elevation.

This too we left behind, ascending to a blasted volcanic region that looked as if cursed by Heaven. Far around there was nothing but volcanic rock with scarcely the faintest sign of vegetation. It has the appearance of turned up earth baked in the sun. All this desolation was the work of volcanic action in the Cofre de Perote, in ages long gone by, for not the faintest record of any such eruption remains.

At La Hoya, in the midst of the severe wildness, there is quite a collection of huts, but how the people live there is a mystery past comprehension. After leaving La Hoya, the scene gradually became less desolate and at Las Vigas, elevated above the region of all but pines, the terrain has considerable beauty. The inhabitants all looked healthy.

Arriving at the great plain of Perote, we came in view of the solitary peak of Pesano, a lofty isolated mountain rising from the level plain, and still we had the lofty snow covered summit of Orizaba and the Cofre de Perote to see. It was dark before we entered Perote, and dark when we left in the morning. I was not sorry to lose sight of the castle, but altogether fully pleased with the town there.[15] As we anticipated, the only actual source of discomfort is the cold which is really severe.

15. Perote was the site of the prison where members of the Mier Expedition were incarcerated until 1843.

The inn is thought a strange place according to our ideas of comfort, with no sitting room, no fire, the windowless bed-chamber, all are dreary enough, but the rooms are clean, the bedding nice, and as at all of the *Diligence houses*, we found the usual accommodations for bathing. Off the stage routes, this very necessary luxury is often missing. Our supper was excellent and that long ride through the bracing mountain atmosphere destroyed all our fastidiousness.

[March 26.] The next morning after taking a cup of chocolate, we left at three o'clock accompanied by our armed escort. The air was bitter cold and though abundantly provided with warm clothing, we all shivered with cold. At a short distance from Perote, we saw large icicles.

The inhabitants were commencing to plough their fields, the soil of which is said to be excellent and under good cultivation. After leaving the plain, we still continued to ascend mountains through a country parched and dry from want of rain and through clouds of dust.

As we drove into Amozoc, I think the last town before reaching Puebla, my eye was at once attracted to two large magnificent flowering trees rising far above the dome of the church in regular cones and around its sides with flowers of a very brilliant red. As we drove around the plaza to the Inn, the stage was, as usual, surrounded with beggars. I had already given away everything I had about me, and bursting away from the wretched crowd while the horses were being changed, I ran across the square to the church to have a nearer view of those magnificent trees. Two or three of the passengers followed, equally attracted by a sight so beautiful.

On entering the enclosure, we found them to be Cedar trees, the gentleman said a hundred feet high, but to be within bounds, I'll say seventy-five, standing on each side of the principal entrance, of great age. Around each tree, twined lovingly, was a gigantic trumpet creeper with its rich dark flowers and foliage. Both grew together, the rich laurel-like leaves of the vine with the still darker hues of the cedar, so completely intertwined from base to summit that they seemed as one. Beautiful images of strength and beauty, there they stood, living altars, pointing to heaven in their fresh unchanging beauty. I loved to think they were the work of some gentle hearted monk of the olden time, altars on which heaven must have smiled and which the sun and dews of heaven must have loved to nourish in eternal beauty. It must have been a heart still overflowing with human affection, a heart that the cloister never could chill into forgetfulness of earthly love, that suggested the beautiful thought of this planting in their infancy together, the cedar and the vine.

As we approached Puebla, the roads became fine and the country seemed highly cultivated. We came within view of the City of Churches (Cholula) about four in the evening and the scene is probably more agreeable to the eye of an American than that of other Mexican towns. There is more life and animation. The hotel was crowded and though we had time for a walk around the city, we were much too fatigued and were compelled to rest before dinner. The streets through the night were very noisy. We rose very early and after a cup of chocolate were again on our way at four in the morning.

[March 27.] Nothing can exceed the magnificence of mountain scenery in Mexico. After leaving Puebla, we passed the grand snow crowned Popocatepetl[16] and the white mountains beyond. [They] were a beautiful sight to see. The sun rose behind the corpse-like summit of La Malinche,[17] and baked the white peaks of Iztaccihuatl[18] in rosy light.

The Indians have a tradition that La Malinche (as they call the fair Indian interpreter of Cortez, Dona Marina) was buried on the top of the mountain which bears her name, and the idea was suggested probably by the peculiar arrangement of the rocks on the summit. When I was first told the legend and its peculiarity was pointed out, I noticed it directly, but could not feel certain how far the resemblance was aided by my fancy. The appearance is that of a gigantic woman stretched out as for burial, the arms crossed, the head slightly inclined to one side and the chest elevated. The limbs and feet are as distinctly defined as the head. I was strengthened in my belief of the resemblance being positive by the remark of a most unreal, apoplectic looking gourmand of a Frenchman who after asking the name of the mountain exclaimed, "The top was very peculiar, it looked like a person laid out to be buried."

At a certain point in the road while ascending the mountain, we approached so near Popocatepetl and the White Woman [La Malinche] as

16. Popocatepetl is a volcanic peak of 17,887 feet in the Sierra Madre Oriental range southeast of Mexico City.

17. La Malinche is a dormant volcano of 14,636 feet in central Mexico on the Puebla-Tlaxcala border lying sixteen miles northeast of Puebla, Mexico.

18. Iztaccihuatl is a dormant volcanic peak of 17,342 feet in the Sierra Madre Oriental range southeast of Mexico city.

to read distinctly on their sides the limit of pines, of barrenness and eternal snow. Beyond the certain summit of the volcanos, the Friar's peak, the Indian guides refuse to proceed. Their ideas of a volcano are associated with very painful images of supernatural terror and this is certainly by no means the most surprising of their fancies. We saw distinctly the naked perpendicular cliffs of Iztaccihuatl, at least 1000 feet in height.

At Rio Frio, 10,119 feet above the level of the seas, we stopped for breakfast. The breakfast was a very good one, but the pure mountain air of these elevated regions had so exhilarated my spirits and braced my nerves that I believe I could have eaten the coarsest Mexican cooking even after having caught sight of the cooks. I believe I told you how delicious to me was the smell of the pines. At this point, our journey seemed nearly ended and we soon began to descend the mountain at a speed perfectly frightful before one becomes accustomed to the sureness and safety of the mules. We strained our eyes to catch a first view of the valley of Mexico, and when it burst upon me through an opening in the mountains, my first thought was of the scenes in Pilgrim's Progress, a view of Heaven to the Pilgrim. I do not think this can be the point at which it is usually noticed by travelers. It is more distant, seen but for an instant, and as you again plunge into the new raw mountain passes, it seemed unreal. After traveling here through lovely mountain passes solitary as in the infancy of Nature, all at once through this astonishing purity of atmosphere you scan to catch a glimpse of hill, lake and valley, dome and spire, distinct yet faint and seeming to me as if painted on the sky.

You may think all this the effect of air on an over-excited imagination, but [these] are my first honest impressions, however wild they may seem.

For us [in the United States], the vicinity of a great city is marked for miles around by large towns and their ring villages, highly cultivated fields and busy population, so that the effect was strange [in Mexico] going over such a barren country and all at once finding ourselves rolling into the streets of a great city, swarming with life. The effect is greatly heightened by passing all such mountain barriers and then finding ourselves in a scene where the architecture is all strange and foreign, the appearance of the people equally so, the consciousness of our extreme elevation, the thronging associations of the scene, all conspired to make us feel ourselves in a new world. The feelings are not to be described but I believe you can sympathize with them and you will readily understand that when we [arrived at the Diligence] hotel in Mexico [City], I was so burdened, so excited and so confused that I could scarcely grasp my own feelings, much less describe them.

Helen received this letter from William in Mexico City.

My dearest Helen, Fort Brown, Texas

March 23. The "*Yacht*" brought a long letter from your mother, which I answered for you in my most cheerful style. Father and Grandmother were both much better. Aunt Betsey's farm was to be sold and she was coming to Westfield at least on a visit. Mother's letter was dated February 19 and commences thus:

"I received a letter from Betsey two days since saying the place was advertised for sale. They should probably break up by the first of April and saying she had received a draft of fifty dollars from you. She seems nearly solemnly impressed with a grateful sense of your kindness to her and with the thankfulness to God that there is a home here to receive her where her services are needed."

Angeline and Willie are both very well and I supply your place better than I thought I could. Everything goes on like clockwork in the house. This I suppose you are ready to doubt, but I can tell you there is a great difference between my being a looker on and head devil. Your constant example of real goodness has made a better man of me; I now only need occasions to bring me out. I play cards with Angy and Willie, ride with and amuse them in various ways. Doctor Jarvis wishes to be remembered. Regards to Mr Jarvis and Mrs Bennett.[19]

Ever your affectionate,
William

My dearest William, Mexico City, Mexico

March 29. I intended to write a long letter, but all day yesterday I was waiting for ink. You will think it is a very foolish reason, but in a Mexican Hotel, you are treated to Mexican promises and very little else in the way

19. WWC to HBC, Mar. 30, 1851, CC.

of attendance. Importunity and perseverance were not wanting on my part yet the ink was not forthcoming. Mr Jarvis was out most of the day putting his business in train.

The journey from Jalapa was a hard one and the other passengers, strong, robust men, seemed worn out and exhausted. I bore the journey better decidedly than Mr Jarvis or Ann. Ann complains of headache, has had bleeding at the nose and evidently suffers somewhat from the thinness of the atmosphere. I find no difficulty even in going up stairs.

Captain Mugarietta is here at this moment.[20] He sends "muchas memorieas" to Colonel Bennett and you and all other friends. [Two other] gentlemen [Messrs Glover and Mather[21] have] just left and I have written this at intervals in the greatest confusion. Tell Mrs Stillman, if she sees Miss Bacon, to tell her to abandon all idea of coming to Mexico.[22] I do not think one could succeed without a capital that would be a comfortable little independence at home. Miss Bacon, I know, will not doubt the sincerity and friendliness of my advice.

There is a little boy about twelve years of age here at the hotel running about with a little Chihuahua dog. I never see him that I do not have an aching longing to see my own beloved boy. Love to all who inquire, not forgetting the kindest remembrances to Jane and Mary with ever so many kisses for little Angy. How many times I have wished for Doctor [Jarvis]. How many old corners we could explore together! I drag the poor captain about till he is half worn out.

We have been absent just a fortnight, my dearest William, and I fancy you have scarcely had time to miss us. To me, it seems months, passed pleasantly it is true, yet still with many a yearning for home. Every pleasure I experience I am wishing so much that you could share it with me. I have

20. Captain Mugarietta served as their guide in Mexico City. He apparently knew William Chapman and Colonel Bennett well and may have served in Matamoras. Captain Jarvis, for one, was happy to have his assistance. He wrote, "I have found Captain Mugarietta who has proved himself exceedingly kind and he has interested himself with the various officers in the departments to make the various searches required. It will be a tedious business, but if the documents are to be found at all I will get them. I cannot yet tell how much of the proofs can be found. I should not know how to begin were it not for Mugarietta. He has secured an audience for me with the President whom I am to see on Monday next. Great ceremony is required on such occasions, Mexico being more like a monarchical government in its display than a republic" (Samuel Jarvis to WWC, Mar. 29, 1851, CC).

21. Captain Glover was the former U.S. consul from Tampico whose $55,000 was confiscated by General Avalos. He was in Mexico City attempting to recover it.

22. Miss Bacon arrived, despite this caution. See HBC to WWC, May 25, 1851, below.

no time to write how I long to see you. You must imagine all that the fondest and most devoted love could say. Good bye and God bless you.

Your loving,
Helen

My dear Mother, Mexico City

April 1, 1851. [On Sunday] we accepted an invitation to join a party of Mexican ladies and gentlemen to what they termed a breakfast in the country. It was at a place called *Napoli*, a few miles from the city, over a beautiful road passing through the *Paseo*, by *Chapultepec* and other places that were famous in the War. The hour was set for half past eight in the morning and I supposed we were to breakfast about eleven and return soon after. But Mexican ladies are famous for long delays at their toilette and it was noon before the whole party was assembled and passing through the city gates. There were as many as thirty five in all, but it was made up of only two or three families. Old ladies not so young looking as Grandmamma before she became disabled, married women with their children, even the babies and an old woman half nurse, half friend of the family, young ladies and young gentlemen. All seemed pleased and happy, affectionate and loving towards each other and altogether it was to me a very pleasant sight. They are universally devoted to this kind of amusement, yet for some reason, they go but seldom and when they do, never seem to know when to get home, as I found to my sorrow.

On our arrival we found a large building to which was attached a race course, a ten pin alley, an amusement I believe introduced by Americans and very popular among the Mexicans, and a target for shooting matches. The parlor to which the ladies were conducted was very handsomely furnished with Brussels carpet, mirrors, pill tables and center with marble tops, rosewood sofas, and easy chairs with cushions of blue damask.

After a little while we were taken round to see the premises, shown some animals that I had never seen before, among others, the Buffalo. The Mexican ladies and gentleman seem to have their separate amusements and the ladies really seem very happy by themselves. They talk very fast with great animation and all together.

About two o'clock in the afternoon, we had breakfast and Heaven preserve me from such another, not that it was not very good, but such a profusion and as it seemed to be the fashion to taste all the dishes, I was fearful of committing a rudeness by refusing. Everything is all separate. You have a fresh plate even for a dish of fried potatoes and the more solid dishes come last. After becoming sick and wearied with the sight of food, they brought me roast beef, turkey, ham and I know not what besides. Some of the dishes were purely Mexican, They insisted on my trying some of their famous "*Chile Colorado.*" I believe it is a nicely prepared dish and for those whose throats have been thoroughly seasoned with peppers, tea and hot drops, I presume it is very palatable. Having had no such preparatory training, I believe I praised it with rather tearful eyes.

There was great merriment. All talking at once, champagne corks popping, toasts drunk with great spirit, a wild eager sort of animation. However, it was a peculiar aspect in which to view them, a break in their [daily] existence, an effervescence as temporary as champagne.

Then commenced dancing and waltzing to piano music, and I, at last, made up my mind that they were intending to make a night as well as a day of it. They danced until night and then they had tea or what they called tea. They make excellent coffee and chocolate but tea is more often drunk by themselves.

After tea they walked about awhile, as if never to depart for their homes, but at length, we were packed into the carriages and driven into the city.

Helen

Samuel Jarvis wrote William Chapman on his progress, April 2, 1851.

Dear Major, Mexico City

I was in the archives of the War Office all day yesterday searching for the documents. I have found several of the Acts [requested by our attorneys] such as the General Colonization Law and some others, but have not yet found any establishing the military post or custom house. As the documents are in three different departments, War, Hacienda, and Relations, it is likely to prove a very much longer operation than I expected especially as the papers in the latter department were thrown into irreversible confusion by our troops who destroyed great numbers of them.

Mr Smith to whom I showed the letter of Basse & Hord says that it will take 6 months but if I can't do it in a month or less I will give it up.[23] Mr and Mrs Smith, Mrs Hargraves and others have called on Mrs Chapman and have been very kind.[24]

I am preparing copies of the laws required and expect to find something in the archives of the Commisssioners of Colonization. The *grants of Balli and Jaimes* I have not yet found though the gentleman in charge of the Dept of Interior is searching for them.

We are stopping at the Hotel Diligencias and have four rooms. Our expenses per day are $2.00 each and $1.00 for Ann and the passage to Vera Cruz from here in all about $140.[25]

Give my regards to all and believe me yours truly,

S. M. Jarvis

My dearest William, Mexico City

April 6. A gentleman goes to New Orleans tomorrow and will mail this letter at that place. Captain Mugarietta has been very polite and kind. With him, we have visited the Paseos, the Alameda, a public rancho intended to be for Mexico City somewhat as Hoboken is to New York. And lastly "*The Church of our Lady of Guadalupe*," very beautiful and in better taste than any church we have seen. The old chapel on the hill interested me much more. On our return we found the road lined with Indians returning to their homes on the hills.

On Friday, we called at Mrs Hargraves in company with Captain Glover, also at Mrs Smith's home and the house of an old Spanish General with whom Mr Jarvis lived during the war. That evening, Mr and Mrs Smith called and invited us to visit with them on the following day the Hospital built by Cortez. I was very happy to do so, but I returned excessively fatigued.

23. The firm of Elisha Basse and Robert H. Hord represented the U.S. government in the Dobbins lawsuit.

24. See Appendix A for Buckingham Smith. Mr. Hargraves was a wealthy American businessman living in Mexico City. His wife came from Philadelphia. The spelling "Hargraves" is the prevalent one used in Helen Chapman's letters. However, in some instances she spelled it "Hargous." A Peter Hargous, an American financier, was in Mexico City at the time promoting a railroad across the Tehauntepec Isthmus between the Gulf of Mexico and the Pacific (Miguel Covarrubias, *Mexico South* [New York: Alfred A. Knopf, 1967], 167).

25. Samuel M. Jarvis (hereafter referred to as SMJ) to WWC, Apr. 7, 1851, CC.

I find it difficult to procure the kind of food that suits me. With a market loaded with every delicious vegetable in the world, they have none on the hotel table but potatoes, beans and cabbage. Their meat is cooked up with such a quantity of lard it is unsafe to eat it and altogether I miss the cooking at home. Ann mourns over Mary's biscuits, cookies, etc. They have only two meals, breakfast, from eight to ten o'clock, and dinner, either at four or six in the evening. We dine at four but half the time I take some simple thing in my room.

Ann counts the days till we shall again be on our homeward way. It will be a happy day when I again see the old sand hills of the Brazos. Home is home, however homely.

Because Ann is counting the days to get home, you must not imagine she is useless. On the contrary, I do not know what I should do without her. She finds her way into the kitchen and manages to pick up enough Mexican to make known our wants and perseveres until they are supplied. The whole attendance of the house consists in a man coming in the morning with a little whisk, such a thing as a broom is unknown, who flourishes it round the center of the room making a terrible dust and then retires with no dusting, no filling of water pitchers or any of the usual work of a bed room. They promise everything when you can get sight of them and do nothing.

Your loving,
Helen

My dearest Ella, Fort Brown, Texas

April 7. I wrote you last Sunday and the Sunday before.

I hope, my own dearest Ella, that you are by this time in the City of Mexico. As it takes 14 days for a letter to go to the City of Mexico from here, I have some doubts whether this will reach you there.

[As to Brownsville news,] Mrs Falco was married last night. It was a beautiful affair, a magnificent supper of meats, fruits, preserves, cakes, and wine. A select company were present, Mr and Mrs Phelps, Charles Stillman, Mrs Sharman, Mr Chamberlain and family, Mrs Kingsbury, Mrs Maxan and others. All the officers except Mr Garesché. Major Porter and Mr Gibbon were not invited. The bride looked sweetly. The younger Miss Chamberlain was bridesmaid; Garey, Groomsman. Leman and Mag Vernon were also present.

John Clark [William's clerk] thought that some one was watching and following him all one day and night and wished to leave at once on the *Meritorius* for the States. I made him sleep at our house and take his meals with us and the next day he got entirely over it and concluded it was imagination. He has now no wish to leave.

The children and servants are all well and we get along finely. Regards to the Captain.

Yours ever affectionately
William

My dearest William, Mexico City

April 9. I must tell you how my time is divided. I retire and rise early, generally about half past five and, as early as I can procure it, take a cup of chocolate with a piece of bread. Mr Jarvis is not often ready to walk before seven and about that hour we go out to walk on the *Alameda*, in the fruit and vegetable market, to visit churches, or wander about the city. We breakfast at half past nine, or even later. Mr Jarvis goes out about eleven in the prosecution of his business.[26]

At four we dine. If I do not go out after dinner, I amuse myself in watching the curious and animated scene below from the balcony.

This morning before sitting down to write, I walked on the Alameda with Captain Mugarietta and Mr Jarvis. I have made another engagement at twelve to visit the "*Hospital of Jesus*," with Mr and Mrs Smith.[27] They were here last evening and have shown themselves very polite and kind. Mr Smith's situation is unpleasant. His salary is altogether inadequate and it is impossible for him to live so as to command respect of the Mexicans.[28] I suppose the rent of a decent house would cost more than his salary. He seems to be a pleasant, intelligent man and has considerable curiosity with regards to Mexican antiquities.

26. At this point Jarvis had met with Mariano Arista, the president of Mexico, who was a friend of William Chapman, Mr. Aquille, the minister of hacienda, and Dr. Galvez, the director of colonization. Each received him courteously and promised cooperation.

27. The Hospital of Jesus, where Cortez's remains were first deposited, is located several blocks south of the Zocalo.

28. The New Orleans *Daily Delta* noted on January 18, 1851, that the American legation to Mexico City was being maintained at the expense of a private American merchant, possibly Peter Hargous. The implication was that the merchant was receiving some illegitimate benefit from the arrangement.

[Evening] I went this morning with Mr and Mrs Smith to see the *Hospital of Jesus*. Afterwards, we visited the *Monte Pio*, the old palace built and inhabited by Cortez. Also the church adjoining where Cortez's remains were reputed to have rested for a while until through apprehension of violence they were removed to Europe.

Very kind regards to all enquiring for me. To the girls, good wishes and kind remembrances as usual, to Angy, kisses, and to Willie, everything that the fondest mother can say. Oh! how I long to hold him close to my heart once more.

Dearest Willie, do you miss me any? I do not mean little Willie but yourself. What a happy meeting it will be when we are safe together once more.

God bless you all,
Helen

My dearest Ella, Fort Brown, Texas

April 13. I heard from you, from the City of Mexico much sooner than I expected. I was delighted with your and Captain Jarvis' charming letters and more particularly to hear of your good health. Remain as long as you continue to improve from the climate. Everything goes on finely at home and you need not hasten back on that account; so dearest Ella stay as long as your health, or any other cause, may render it necessary. Do as you think best in everything and then you will please me.

Mrs Gonzales and Mrs Leman have each presented their lords with little ones. Mrs Gonzales two days since and Mrs Lemon today. Doctor [Jarvis] waited a few days to accommodate them, obliging is he not? However the two fees, $100, will help to pay the expenses of his three months trip at the North.

Willie, Angy and the Doctor join me in much love to you and the Captain. I sent [Alfred] Bennett his letter [from Ann]. He is well and looks very nice with a new hat.

Ever your affectionate,
William

My dearest William, Mexico City

April 18. This morning early, after my customary cup of chocolate, I am seated to make a beginning; the time for endings is very dubious.

Yesterday, Holy Thursday, I was tired almost to death. I rose early and stood on the balcony all the morning to see the world of Mexico on foot. This is to be seen only one day in the year. On all other days, in the courtyards of the wealthy, carriages stand ready, the horses or mules ever harnessed to the carriage, the coachman waiting, and so they remain from daybreak till midnight.

At ten in the morning, every vehicle, horse, mule and burro must disappear from the streets and then such a throng of pedestrians crowds the walks, as I never saw before. Crowds of richly dressed ladies, leperos, Indians, children and beggars, jostle each other in most democratic equality. At ten o'clock, Mr Jarvis and I followed the crowd of church pilgrims. First to the six churches of "*San Francisco*," the convent built in 1535, then to "*La Profesor*" the fashionable church of the city, to the *Cathedral* and half a dozen more that I cannot remember.

On Holy Thursday, the wealth of the church is all displayed in order to render more effective the mournful tragedy of Good Friday. There is much sameness about the decorations of all the churches; a profusion of silver plate, gilded oranges, a plant in pots with a gaudy profusion of yellow blooms, numberless bits of silver suspended and quivering on slender vines, make a gay, showy and rather tawdry scene.

[At] one of the principal churches of San Francisco, we saw a procession of monks, and, at the first glance, I thought them the ugliest men without exception I had ever seen. They moved enveloped in such a cloud of incense and I from my kneeling position had not the best opportunity of examining them critically but so far as was possible I tried to discover whether their features were really heavy and altogether unintellectual or whether it resulted from their deforming style of dress, and shaven heads. I am certain that a handsome man would be as completely shorn of his beauty as Sampson of his strength by this frightful arrangement of the hair.

I returned from my pilgrimage about one in the afternoon, tired to death with the impression on my mind of a child's show made up of silver plates, oranges, images, etc. From the balcony about three o'clock, I had a fine opportunity to see the magnificence of [Mexican] dress. Their richness of costume could not exceed my expectation, but I certainly was not prepared for the display of so much good taste. Mrs Hargraves was raving about the beauty of ladies on the *Paseo*.

April 19. I close with an account of the day's ceremonial of Holy Thursday. In the evening, Captain Mugarietta went with us to see the display by candlelight. We visited *La Profesor, The Cathedral, The Sagraniam, Lorito, Santa Catalina, L'Encancian* and the *Three Churches of Santa Amerigo.* We were out until eleven at night, and you may be assured I came back tired enough but very glad that I had gone. There is much beauty by candlelight. Immense silver candles lit large silver vessels, but it was impossible to enumerate in such a blaze of splendor.

On Friday, I spent part of the morning with Mrs Smith, and while there saw Mr Forstall, the Agent of Barring & Brothers, a very acute, sagacious man.

I had written so far when the bells that since ten a.m. the day before yesterday have been silent, all at once commenced ringing vociferously and at the same moment there was such a discharge of rockets as would have set Willie nearly wild with delight. This was at half past nine on the morning of Saturday, the great ceremony of *burning the Judases.* They (the Judases) are carried about the two previous days for sale, made of all sizes, some as large as life, as hideous, as grotesque, as black, as frightful as Indian fancy can create. I shall carry a small one to Willie as a specimen. These images are combined with fire works and hung on ropes suspended from balconies, tied to dogs' tails with some ingenious contrivances and all set blazing at once.

Saturday Evening. We walked down to the Plaza, and such a crowd of human beings I never saw before. The whole square was a dense mass of heads. Towering high above all, were carried the Judases, some with heads like hogs, some with forms like nothing in air, earth or ocean. At one in companionship with the Devil, by no means harmonious, however, for their hideous heads were constantly butting furiously against each other to the great delight of those around. A baby elevated on the shoulder of a blanketed Indian, I very innocently mistook for a Judas, but fortunately the mother remained in ignorance of such a horrible mistake. I was curious to see such an immense crowd so quiet, no loud angry voices, no drinking, no noise but rattles, people talking pleasantly, babies crying, and even these but seldom for they seemed as much delighted as the older babies.

Temporary houses of refreshment had been erected in the center of the square and altogether the city presented the idea of some joyous festival and this on the most solemn fast day of the year. If there ever be such a thing known as a puritan Governor of Mexico, he had better omit the customary annual proclamation of a fast. For the [Mexicans] would most surely turn it into a great festival.

Thus ended the Holy Days. The stage passengers from Vera Cruz on these two days had a very practical lesson as to ecclesiastical power in this country, being compelled to walk in to the stage house from the city gates or to remain and take their chances of stealing into the city at night. A number of Americans were of the number and those walking in must have suffered terribly.

The *Tehuantepec Treaty* meets with decided opposition [in the Mexican Congress] and they say there is no chance of its passing.[29] If you have time and patience, can you not read my letter to the girls. They wish to know what I write but will be afraid to ask you. Kisses and all a mother's love to my darling boy and my little Angy.

Helen

My own dearest Ella: Fort Brown, Texas

April 20. Oh, my dearest sweetest Ella, I wish I could tell you, my sweet wife, how much I love you. When you come back I will love and cherish you more than ever, and will gladly devote my whole life to your happiness. I have such love and admiration for you, my own dear Ella, that my head is almost turned. Your undeserved expressions of love and endearment in your two letters made me the happiest of beings. To be really loved by such a pure, sweet angel as my Ella seems to me almost incredible. Oh that I was worthy of such love.

I wrote to Mr Jarvis four days since what I now repeat. The trial will be put off to the next court in six months so stay just as long as your health

29. The Tehuantepec Isthmus is the narrowest part of Mexico between the Gulf and the Pacific. In treaty negotiations at the end of the Mexican War, the United States attempted to claim the right of free passage for American citizens and merchandise across the Isthmus. The Mexicans rejected this claim and it was not made part of the Treaty of Guadalupe Hidalgo. During this time, however, New York financier Peter A. Hargous obtained exclusive transportation rights, called the Tehuantepec Concession, across the isthmus with the income from such rights for fifty years. The U.S. State Department sent an envoy to Mexico to negotiate a new treaty, but he was unsuccessful. Hargous surveyed the isthmus with the intention of building a railway. The Mexican senate, however, opposed the potential inhabitation of the area by hordes of U.S. citizens, and the concession was declared null and void in May 1851 (Covarrubias, *Mexico South*, 167); see HBC to EWB, Apr. 26, 1851, below.

is benefited. Everything goes on finely at home and the children and girls are doing well and are happy.

Remember, dearest Ella, as you love me, not to let the expense have the least consideration with you. My prospects have brightened even since you left and any amount you can possibly spend will be promptly met. I shall have no pleasure in laboring to make money, unless you will spend some of it in the way I wish and this is one of the ways.

Colonel Cooper, Acting Inspector General, has been with me about a week but will leave Wednesday for Corpus Christi. Colonel Cooper is a Robert [E.] Lee, and I have I think made my usually good impression.[30]

The children send love and kisses and the girls wish to be remembered. [Alfred] Bennett is well and often asks about Ann.

Ever your affectionate
William

My dear Mother, Mexico City

April 23. I am rather unwell today. The only ill turns I have had in Mexico have been caused by those murderous Mexican dinners. Do not think I speak in any disparagement of their cookery, which I believe an epicure would think delicious. I merely refer to its unfitness for myself.

Two or three evenings since, I dined by invitation with Mrs Hargraves. She called for me to ride with her on the *Paseo* (the fashionable drive), at five in the evening. On our return at dark, we found the company assembled for dinner. Mr Black, the American consul, Doctor ———, a French physician, and two or three Spanish Gentleman. About seven, Mr Hargraves offered me his arm to the dinner table. Mr Hargraves is a very pleasant man and likes to entertain company seemingly as well as you do. He has by no means, however, William's personal graces to set off his establishment. He is perhaps the richest foreigner, certainly the richest American in Mexico, lives in very handsome style, and adopts the Mexican fashion of dining.

The table was set with very richly flowered French China plate, with very wide borders of deep blue and gold, and rich cut glass. After all were

30. Robert E. Lee was a close personal friend of the Chapmans. This friendship developed from 1841 to 1846. During that time Lee had served at Fort Hamilton, one of the army forts in the New York Harbor area, while the Chapmans were at nearby Fort Columbus. Lee had also served with Chapman on General John E. Wool's staff prior to Buena Vista.

seated, soup was given by the waiters and on this being removed, course after course was brought, already carved, and passed by the waiters, each person helping himself.

At each dish, the plate is changed and though I did not count them, I think ten or a dozen plates were put before me. The last courses were turkey and ham and, to my great joy, the dessert came at last, no better for me, except as it showed the dinner to be drawing to a close.

I minced and picked as sparingly as possible, among frozen custards, ices, fruits of all kinds, candied sweets and all the mysteries of French confections, until, at length, I was delighted by a proposal from Mrs Hargraves, that we should remove to the drawing room for coffee. Their wines were claret and champagne. I believe the heavier wines are not considered very safe in this climate. My last ordeal was the coffee, which I took, hoping that one poison would aid the digestion of the dozen already swallowed. I did not feel well though I managed to, under the influence of excitement, appear lively and pleased. At ten, I excused myself, on the ground that my Irish servant was afraid to be left alone at night.

I went down the stairs and was delighted to find their luxurious carriage close with its soft cushions, ready to carry us back to the Hotel. In this too, they follow the Mexican fashion of keeping their horses harnessed to the coach and standing ready in the courtyard for immediate use. Mr Hargraves is exceedingly liberal in all his family expenditures, and without any ostentatious display of wealth, the establishment is on a handsome and liberal scale. Mrs Hargraves is a Philadelphian, young, agreeable and very handsome, two years married, and has one child for whom she has an Indian wet nurse.

Indian mothers are famous for their passionate love of their own children and Mrs Hargraves told me many anecdotes of this woman's devotion to her foster child. Among others, she mentioned her delight when the child gave any indications of a passionate revengeful nature. Mrs Hargraves seemed amused but I should have some fears that he might imbibe some rather questionable moral traits from his Indian mother. Mr Gallagher and Mrs Hargraves both have traveled extensively in California. He is preparing to return there with his family. He speaks very highly both of the mineral and *Agricultural* resources of the state and expressed himself favorably as to the climate. Mr Gallagher confirms by his own observation what seemed to be the extravagant newspaper accounts of vegetable produce in California.

Some other returning Californians, now in the city, give similar accounts. These poor fellows do really run the gauntlet in going to and returning from the El Dorado. By every route, disease or danger seem to meet them in some form. Of a party who arrived here about ten days since, one on the route from Acapulco to this place was dangerously bitten by one of the poisonous reptiles of the country, and another a harmless inoffensive man was stabbed in broad daylight under the Portales in the very heart of the city. The knife entered his side very near the heart, and for the first night, he was considered in a very dangerous condition, but is now recovering. His only crime that I can hear was in being a Californian. The Mexicans are naturally very sore on the subject of California.

April 26. I have given you the impression that Mexico produces on a stranger. I know not whether instinct, or the experience of history, teaches us that a nation precisely in this condition must soon experience change. However, the feeling is universal and all calm observers who at this moment survey Mexico as she is feel that her hour is nigh.

They themselves feel all the terrors of a mighty overshadowing power. The Mexicans are fearful of taking a single step, lest it may precipitate the progress of the United States. Afraid to venture on any enlightened policy in their Custom House regulations, the country is exhausted by smuggling, there is no money to carry on the Government or to pay the troops. They seem determined on one point, to give the Americans no possible footing in any territory remaining, and, therefore, the *Tehauntepec Treaty*, it is said, stands no chance whatever. It meets with most determined opposition in the Senate. Weak, timid and distrustful, they know not what to do and probably some stronger power is again to decide their destiny.[31] It is said the Mexican Minister is returning from Washington with very unfavorable impressions of the state of public feeling in the United States with regard to Mexico, and with the idea that General Taylor's death was a great misfortune to his country. I give you this political gossip as I hear it in conversations of Mr Smith, the American Secretary of Legation, a very thoughtful sensible man and Mr Forstall, the agent of Baring & Brothers, a very keen, sagacious man and most probably from his connections with a great English house, deep in the financial secrets of this unfortunate country.

31. This proved to be a prophetic observation. Arista's government was no stronger than others in the 1850s, enabling the French to establish Emperor Maximillian in power in the 1860s.

There is said to be a strong personal feeling against Americans, natural enough certainly, and it is amusing with what a mingled feeling of hate, dread, and holy horror, they regard the Californians.

In the *Portales*, on open porches, surrounding the grand square of the city, all the domestic toys and small wares of Indian and Mexican industry are exhibited. You have heard of their skill in modeling either in clay or wax, and here, among an infinite variety of specimens, you see caricatures of returning Californians. We have purchased two or three as specimens and if they ever get safely to the North, I feel assured they will amuse you greatly. They invariably give them the fair hair, the fine skin and blue eyes of our Saxon ancestry, dress them in a very belligerent kind of box coat, pantaloons pulled up. and boots covered with dust. A very scrunched up broad business hat, a very devil-may-care expression and attitude, always raising a glass of brandy or whiskey to their lips and with a belt or sash stuck full of bowie knives, pistols, dirks, etc. They are invariably armed to the very teeth, and the imitation is so capital that we, of the dreaded race, at once recognize our own countrymen. I believe I mentioned that one of the returning Californians very narrowly escaped assassination recently in these same *Portales*. At the same time, it is well known that they are perfectly safe from highway robbers. The very way they are represented stuck all over with knives and firearms shows in what dreaded estimation they are held.

With much love to all,

My dearest William, Mexico City

April 26. I write to assure you that I am not sick. There is something naturally irritating in the air of these regions and, of course, these qualities are increased at night. They say a medical man is unfit for enlightened practice here before the expiration of a year's residence and one must remain here awhile to know how to live properly. We are to make a party with Mr and Mrs Smith, Mr Forstall and others tomorrow to see "El Desiertors," the site of an abandoned monastery.[32] All my knowledge of

32. El Desierto de los Leones describes the ruins of a Carmelite monastery on the route to Toluca, about seventeen miles outside Mexico City. The monastery was built by Fray Andres de San Miguel, and the cornerstone was laid on January 21, 1606. It is noted for its acoustical properties. See Howard T. Fisher and Marion Hall Fisher (eds.), *Life in Mexico: The Letters of Fanny Calderon de la Barca* (Garden City, N.Y.: Doubleday & Company, Inc., 1966), 359–362, 548.

political affairs, I gain from the connection of Mrs Smith and Mrs. Forstall, two as good judges perhaps as can be found among the foreigners of the city.

I cannot close my letter without a line in addition. I feel the same uncertainty that I did on leaving home though there is stronger reason, of course, to know there is something at least unusual. I still think it only the natural result of disordered health, but I fear to exert myself much less it might possibly prove otherwise.[33] Mr Jarvis, of course, cannot understand the reasons for my conduct and must at times be somewhat puzzled. You may rest assured I will do the best I can.

When once again with you, all my cares and troubles will be at an end. I never went away from you before except for a short time and I never before realized how great was my dependence sheltered on your breast and with your fond arms about me, I should have no thought or wish beside you.

If Jane thinks of anything wanting for the children, let me know in the letter awaiting me [in New Orleans]. I hope you continue to write. It is so delightful to get a line from home. Love to all. Love and kisses to my darling boy and my little Angy. Ann sends love to Alfred and is guilty of such bad taste as to think Brownsville better than Mexico [City].

Ever your affectionate,
Helen

Willie wrote this letter to his mother.

My dear Mother, April 30, 1851

The *Corvette* went away yesterday, I stayed from school yesterday to play with Fred. I am going down to the Brasos tomorrow. When I get down to the Brasos, I am going on that excursion to the three islands. I believe Captain King and Judge Crane are going with us. I am very impatient to get down. I am talking about it constantly. Henry Phelps has gone away from here. Judge Moses sends his respects to you. I think we shall have a good deal of fun. Angy and Jane and Mary and myself are all well and have been so ever since you left. Mother, we shall love you more than ever when you come home. Jane and Henderson[34] took up the awning today in the

33. Chapman believed she might be pregnant, which, in fact, she was.

34. John Henderson was one of the watchmen in Chapman's employ. At this time, Chapman

bedroom. It will make it much cooler. I have nobody to play with now but Fred and so I am very glad to get down to the Brasos.

Willie

| William's letter continued on the same sheet.

My dearest Ella,

We go to the Brasos this morning to remain ten days. All are well. I have nothing this time, my sweet wife, to write about. There have been no mails since I last wrote. The children send love and kisses, the girls desire to be remembered.

My kind regards to the Captain.

Your affectionate,
William

My Dear Mother, Mexico City

May 1, 1851. I do not remember that I have told you much of the *Alameda*, or fashionable drives of the city. Like all Spanish works in this country, they are on a grand scale. The *Alameda*,[35] a public [park], is densely planted with forest trees, laid out in broad walks, decorated with large fountains, roses, stone benches, and surrounded by a carriage road. It is nearly in the heart of the city. Here in the morning, you see a few ladies walking and a great many gentlemen on horseback.

Passing out of the city through the *Alameda*, you arrive at the *Paseo Nuevo*,[36] the favorite drive of the fashionable and used during the whole year

was responsible for the government depots at Fort Brown, Brazos Santiago, and Point Isabel. The payroll sheets which survive from October 1851 indicate that he employed ninety-two workmen, although it is not clear whether they include all of those employed at the three depots. Of the ninety-two, two were clerks and one was a storekeeper (of forage for the horses); there were two wagonmasters, two wheelwrights, two blacksmiths, two strikers in the blacksmith shop, one saddler, seven watchmen, two hostlers, four laborers, two cartmen, and sixty-five teamsters. Only three could sign their names, the remainder marked an X to signify receipt of their pay (Quartermaster Payroll Roster, Oct. 1851, Fort Brown, Texas, CC).

35. Alameda Gardens was the site of the Aztec market at the time of the conquest. In 1592 the park was planted with poplars (*alamos*) and given the name Alameda.

36. Paseo Nuevo was the Tacubaya Causeway. An aqueduct ran down the center with a carriage road on either side. It is the present-day Avenue Chapultepec.

except at the season of Lent when for some religious idea, they confine their drives to the *Paseo de las Vigras*.[37] It is equally attractive, in some respects more so, and I can see no penance in such an exchange. The entrance to the *Paseo Nuevo* commands a finer view of *Chapultepec*, passing the *Gate of Belen* where General Scott entered the city. The Aqueduct with its solid stone masonry is a beautiful part of *Paseo Nuevo*.

There are seven or eight roads extending from various points in the city far into the surrounding country. They are perfectly straight, broad avenues, and lined on both sides with beautiful trees. Some of them are the original causeways of the great Indian city.

The rides of the Mexican ladies are confined principally to these two Paseos, with occasional excursions to *Chapultepec*.The recent military association of the *Fortress of Chapultepec* was of great personal interest to me.[38]

We wound around the hill in the carriage to the very summit and looked down on the rocky precipitous sides up which the American Army so desperately and bravely charged. I was glad to gain the top of the fortress and forget, in the beautiful valley scene before me, that time of anxiety and suffering. There is a beautiful flower garden on the roof and the buildings still bear marks of an attack. There is a military school with a very polite intelligent commandant, but the barracks seem rather ruinous and it has by no means the well-kept appearance of our military posts. But the spot itself is surpassingly beautiful.

On returning, we drove round the base of the hill and, passing out in another direction, we took the road to *Molino del Rey*[39] and afterwards to *Tacubaya*.[40]

At this place, *Molino del Rey*, the Americans approached over an open plain, exposed to a galling fire from the Mexicans and suffering great loss. Here, poor Daniels in the prime of his youth received his death wound.[41]

37. This is present-day Pino Saurez Avenue.

38. The battle of Chapultepec was fought on Sept. 14, 1847. The word *chapultepec* means grasshopper. There was a military academy atop Chapultepec Hill and at the base of the hill was a stand of cypresses said to have belonged to Montezuma. Both are located in present-day Chapultepec Park.

39. The battle of El Molino del Rey was fought on Sept. 8, 1847.

40. Tacubaya is the historic suburb in the southwest of Mexico City which was once the property of Cortez.

41. This is a reference to Charles B. Daniels. See Appendix A.

I have gazed on the wild scenery of *Contreras*,[42] have traced the path of the conquering Army to *Churubusco*,[43] *Molino del Rey* and up the lofty heights of *Chapultepec*. I can claim the distinction of having seen every spot distinguished by our arms from *Palo Alto* to the last great battle of the valley with the exception of *Monterey* and *Buena Vista*.

At Contreras, I realized more forcibly than anywhere else, the melancholy association of the spot. At *Chapultepec*, all is peaceful, at *Molino del Rey* and *Churubusco* the pursuits of ordinary life seem to divert one's attention but here [at Contreras], all is stern, still and solitary. The ground in many places is wild and broken, covered with bits of blue cloth, pieces of leather, fragments of mess furniture, the bleached bones of horses and the usual relics of a battlefield. In one part of the field on a conspicuous mound is seen a stack of human bones surmounted by a skull.

Viewing these scenes of victories, this march through a country which Nature seems to have fortified almost beyond the attacks of human skill, it seemed impossible to repress a feeling of pride in the daring courage of our Army. Opposed to war as I am and shrinking from its horrors, I felt for a moment as they say a soldier's wife should feel.[44]

Going over the whole war from Vera Cruz to the Capital, looking at the nature of the ground and the dense population through which General Scott's army passed we must arrive at one of two conclusions; either that our troops were gifted with uncommon skill and almost superhuman bravery, or that the Mexicans were [inept] and the people at large wholly uninterested in the struggle. There are [mountain] passes so strongly fortified by nature, that it would seem as if a very few, inspired with the enthusiasm of the old Greeks, might have successfully opposed the passage of ten thousand. I believe there is that invincible strength of will among American troops, that would have carried them through the most determined opposition, but if they had only been met by men who fought as we fought in the Revolution, it is frightful to think with what terrible carnage they would have forced their way to the gates of Mexico [City].

Helen

| Willie Chapman dated this letter May 4, 1851.

42. The battle of the Hill of Contreras was fought on August 19, 1847.
43. The battle of Churubusco was fought on August 20, 1847.
44. HBC to Henry Coppee, May 18, 1851, CC.

My Dear Grandmother, Brasos Santiago, Texas

Lieutenant Brewerton arrived here last Thursday with his wife. After he had left that afternoon we went on a fishing excursion. We had to carry some provisions to the soldiers at Point Isabel so we went to Point Isabel first. We then sailed over to a point off the mainland. It was pretty dark when we got there. I and Captain Anderson and Peter[45] went on shore to cook supper. We left Father and Fred in the boat.[46]

Our supper consisted of stewed oysters and coffee and hard bread and soft and a cold beef slab which we had brought with us. We then went to bed on the deck of the drum and slept sound till morning. We then let our anchor go and went to fishing. We caught first some catfish and I caught a Redfish and Peter caught a trout. We then had breakfast. We cooked the catfish for breakfast. We then sailed for the three islands, but the drum got aground. We then came back to the place where we breakfasted. Father and Fred stayed in the boat.

I and Captain Anderson and Peter went on shore, cooked supper and then I and Captain Anderson went hunting. I killed one snipe and Captain plenty. When we got back, I saw Peter and Fred both on shore. Peter said that Father had caught a Redfish. He caught another just as he was leaving the boat. We put up the tent and had supper. We made bonfire. We cooked my Redfish for supper. We then went to bed. We got up in the morning early and went aboard the drum with Fred to catch some fish. We then sent back Fred to Peter. While Peter and Fred were fixing up the things, I caught another Redfish. Peter and Fred then came with the things. We then set sail for Brasos and arrived quarter past one. I gave my Redfish to a Mrs Roberson. Angy and Mary and Jane are well.

Your affectionate Grandson,
Willie

| William added a postscript.

45. Peter (last name unknown) was probably a free black house servant. He is mentioned several times, but no particulars are ever given. He was murdered in July 1852 and his murderer was bound over for trial in Brownsville (New Orleans *Daily Delta*, Aug. 31, 1852).* See HBC to WWC, Aug. 8, 1852, below.

46. This is the first mention of Fred, who worked for William Chapman and later courted Jane Anderson. A widower, he had a son named Dick.

This is Willie's composition without any aid. He says that it is such a long letter that it ought to go in a separate envelope.

W. W. C.

My dearest Ella — Brasos Santiago, Texas

May 4. How happy it makes me to hear that your health has improved: if it could only be permanent, I should be the happiest of men. I wish in your next you would clear up certain doubts we had just before you left.[47]

Have no anxiety about the children. Angy and Willie ask of you daily, but seem contented. The whole family is here, well and happy. The girls appear to like my government and I have not scolded either of them yet. They are doing fine under my judicious management. You do not know how well I can do when I try and I feel that the responsibility rests on me.

The *Yacht* brought a letter from Mother postmarked March 31st. Your father was still confined to the house; he was better, though it was uncertain how his sickness might turn. She was well, and as she said nothing about grandmother I presume she is again about. Not knowing how long your father might be sick and unable to go the office, and thinking your mother's means might be exhausted by so much sickness, I sent her today $200.00. I told her in previous letter that she must keep constantly a servant.

There is no news in Brownsville, except that Miss Chamberlain has kicked Stansbury and the younger Miss Chamberlain danced like sixty at Mrs Fry's a few evenings since. The old woman made a great fuss and frightened all who came near her. The old man was absent at Galveston.[48] We have organized an Episcopal Church at Brownsville.

Willie and Angy send love and kisses to "Dear Mother."

Ever your most affectionate,
William

47. This implies that Helen had an inkling of her pregnancy in March.

48. Henrietta Chamberlain had apparently rejected the advances of R. N. Stansbury. On July 10, 1851, William Chapman wrote to Helen, "The engagement of Stansbury and Miss Chamberlain is broken off *forever*." The "old man" is probably Hiram Chamberlain at fifty-four, and, if that is the case, the old woman would have probably been his thirty-five-year-old wife, Anna. Mrs. Fry is most likely Francis Fry, the twenty-six-year-old wife of Captain Budd H. Fry, who later became deputy county clerk of Cameron County (*King Ranch*, I, 127).

Samuel Jarvis expressed some of his frustration with the Mexican bureaucracy in this letter of May 6, 1851.

Dear Major, Mexico City

I have had most vexatious delays in searching for papers, especially in the Treasury Dept. There have been three different secretaries since my arrival and all of them have, as you may suppose, sufficient work on their hands to prevent them from doing much for me.

In the Spanish Archives, there is a pile of papers as big as a house where they are now engaged looking up documents though with what success I cannot tell as yet.

Your long "Harry Love" report of the Rio Grande has just been published here in the Mexican Papers, a copy of which you will receive. It was translated by General Almonte, with marginal notes and he speaks very well of it.[49]

Remember me to all inquiring friends,

Samuel M. Jarvis

My dearest William, Mexico City

May 10. To live in Mexico even as quietly as I do at present, taking a stroll in the morning, or lounging on the balcony of an evening, without receiving some impression would certainly show a dull nature. There is a picturesqueness about the street life here, every day you are attracted by some object you never noticed before. Sometimes you see a huge moving mass of hens and chickens swinging and struggling from some central point, on looking closer you see the nearly buried head of a poor burro. A sofa or bedstead filled with light wares [is] apparently self-projected through the crowded streets, a closer inspection shows a Cargodor or street porter bent nearly double under this load. It is incredible what heavy weights these men carry. It is said that really frightful burdens are placed upon Indians in the mines, even as great as six hundred pounds. "They cannot live long," I remarked.

49. The report was published in El Universal. Helen Chapman sent William her translation of an editorial, printed in the same newspaper on March 12, 1851, expressing alarm over predicted additional incursions into Mexican territory by Americans. Publication of the Harry Love report must have stiffened resistance to the proposed Tehauntepec railroad.

"No, they die off very fast," was the reply.

What would you think of a short stubby Indian girl trotting in from the country in her gay red petticoats, her girdle closely hung all round with live stock, hens, chickens and turkeys looking at a distance like a feathered tunic? On another woman, you will see suspended from her back, a huge sack of fruits or vegetables and above that a baby, its little legs astride and riding very securely on its verdant seat. Through the center of the streets there is a line of paving stones. These are removed, it seems to me, almost daily and standing in these trenches, waist deep, you see a long line of prisoners with a guard of soldiers employed in removing from thence black offensive filth.

While walking this morning, I noticed on the side walk some beautiful specimens of knit lace of different widths for sale. I could scarcely credit my senses, on learning that it was the work of one of these same savage looking street cleaners. It is a very common employment of the soldiers, and you see them knitting a fabric around the Guard house that would seem to require the delicate fingers of a woman unused to rough labor.

We live on La Calle de San Francisco, one of the finest in the city, and I am never tired of gazing down onto the crowded thoroughfare below. Decidedly the finest looking men I see in the streets are the Priests. They look taller to me, perhaps in consequence of their long cloaks, and have a far more intellectual look than any other persons I meet.

The last time I was at Mrs Hargraves', I was introduced to a priest who was a friend of the family and I had conversed with him for some time. On the crown of his head a spot was shaved about as large as a half dollar. Otherwise the hair is worn, after the fashion of laymen.

I must not forget to tell you some "table talk" at Mrs Hargraves the same evening I met the Priest. Mr Jarvis had left me there to transact some business and being detained until their dinner hour, they insisted on my going with them to the table though I had already dined. They are a very easy pleasant family and the talk was very animated. A mail had just been received from the United States giving the very welcome intelligence that Governor Letcher would soon return to resume his duties as Minister and there was much speculation as to whether or not he would bring Mrs Letcher.[50] There were various opinions but all were agreed in thinking that the old Governor would be obliged, in case Mrs Letcher did come, to

50. Robert Perkins Letcher, former governor of Kentucky (1840–1844) and staunch Whig, served as minister to Mexico from 1849 to 1852. His reputation was that of a humorous,

change many of his old habits. For instance, he must dress less carelessly, shave more frequently, (you see all wives are alike) and above all would have to give up playing cards on Sunday. In the midst of their comments, Mrs Hargraves exclaimed, "Well! I do not think it right to play cards on Sunday! Do you, Senor?" turning to the Reverend Father.

The Priest very calmly and quietly replied, "I think it indifferent. If it be right on any day, I think it would be right on Sunday."

If I should write this to Mother, I can conceive how some of my good Puritan friends in New England would exclaim, "Oh! The morals of Roman Catholic Priests!" But as I wish always to be just, I should certainly tell them the publicly expressed sentiments of a Baptist clergyman [Rev. G. G. Goss, from the United States] who is boarding with us, at the same Hotel. He was a Chaplain during the war, and is here to negotiate for the purchase of a burying ground for the U.S. Government.

He asked me one day at the dinner table if I had seen a bull fight and remarked, that during the occupation he wished to see one, but did not think it proper to attend on Sunday. He added that for other visitors in the city and under other circumstances he would not think it wrong to witness the scene on that day, but he thought it would hardly do to leave his duties for that purpose. [This example] only shows how a man's opinions are affected by latitudes and teaches us the sublime and difficult lesson—*Charity.*

Helen

My dearest William, Mexico City

May 14. In reply to your letter, when I do not write expressions of the tenderest, most devoted affection believe me, my own best and dearest, that I am constantly saying them in my heart. You deserve far more even that a woman's best love can render and among all my other blessings I consider this the richest that God has given me such a husband. Ann is well. Mr Jarvis has a bad cold.[51] I am very tired or I would add more. Love to all. God bless you, my own dearest love.

Helen

amusing man, effective as a speaker, known for his wit and anecdotes (*Dictionary of American Biography,* ed. Dumas Malone [New York: Charles Scribner's Sons, 1935] , XI, 193).

51. Jarvis's efforts continued to meet with frustration, although he learned that a Mexican treasury official had built a warehouse on Brazos Island in 1826. He did not find a copy of the

My dear darling Willie, Mexico City

May 14. I cannot write you such a good letter as I wished, because all day yesterday I had company, and today I am not very well.

I must tell you about a young gentleman from California, who took up so much of the time I intended to spend in writing to you. You know you have often said, "What is the use of learning Spanish?" I presume he could tell you very feelingly. He came on horseback from Acapulco, and scarcely knew Spanish enough to get eggs or chocolate on the road. You would have laughed to see him at the hotel.

He had with him only four shirts and Annie found him one day at the kitchen door trying to make the old washer woman understand that he wanted a shirt to put on at three o'clock. But this was altogether too much for his stock of Spanish. Instead of saying "Quiers," (I wish), he kept repeating, "you- quiere." The old woman did not well see what she wanted of a shirt at three o'clock, but she kept saying, "Si. Si. Senor," and so they went on till Ann was obliged to tell her what he wanted. Think of Ann turning interpreter! That will make Jane and Mary laugh I think.

Another time, he had been buying some wax figures from an old woman, and he wished to tell her that she must pack them that day, because he was going to Vera Cruz in the morning. But he said," You-vamos a Vera Cruz, I." The old lady told him that she was too old but she would send her daughter. Then Ann told him that he had been inviting the old woman to go with him to Vera Cruz in the morning.

So you see there is no end to the blunders of people in a foreign country who do not understand the language of the people. Your father says, "The children are happy and the girls are doing well." What delightful news!

Your affectionate,
Mother

My dearest William, Mexico City

May 16. The stage has just arrived from Vera Cruz, bringing a load of Americans. Two ladies are among the number. They look as we did [when we arrived], covered with dust and dirt, and it is amusing to see their brisk lively manner contrasting so strongly with the movement of the

Grant of Padre Balli, but he did obtain copies of the laws and other papers needed (SMJ to WWC, May 14, 1851, and SMJ to WWC, May 25, 1851, CC).

Mexicans. One, a large strong looking man passing from his room along one gallery called out to his friend on another, "Well, I think the first thing we had better do is to start off, and try to buy a chart of this house."

I sympathized with him for on my first arrival, I thought I should never be able to find my way about this labyrinth of courts.

9 o'clock. Mr and Mrs Smith have been spending the evenings here, and have but this moment left. From all I can learn, I suspect Colonel Letcher is about as unfit for the station of Foreign Minister as any man can well be; and if all scandal be true, there were some very amusing and farcical scenes connected with the formation of the Treaty of Guadalupe Hidalgo.

An Express arrived this morning with some news from Mazatlan, the precise nature of which is not very well known. It is supposed to relate to a threatened descent of Californians on Mazatlan or Sonora. An American whose name I forget, was with the President this morning after the arrival of the Express. It is said Arista exclaimed, "Damn the Fellows! Did you ever hear anything like it?"

May 17. I begin to be very impatient to see home once more. Mr Jarvis is not very well. The business moreover worries him and I think he is afraid he may accomplish nothing. I do not know what you would do if you saw how these lazy Mexicans are to deal with. Mr Jarvis is worried; Mr Smith, awfully fretted; and Captain Glover, storming with fury and impatience. They say the waiters at his hotel run when they see him coming and fly about to wait on him as if they expected a cane every minute over their ears. I believe you would be taken up within a week for assault and battery upon the peaceful (very peaceful) citizens of the Republic.

There are some Americans here just arrived, among others Colonel Ramsay and family.

I have scarcely been out of the house for a week. There is no want of exercise and fresh air, however, in wandering over the hotel.

Helen

| Helen enclosed a note to Willie.

My dear Willie,

May 17. Remembering your fondness for Chocolate, I send you some of the best in Mexico. One cake would make you and Angy a breakfast, but I presume you will wish to give Jane and Mary a treat sometimes.

I am very impatient to see you, my dear boy. My health is very good and when you see me looking so much better I think you will be very glad I came.

I send you two soldiers because I could not find anything else. If you do not want them, you can give them away. Tell Jane that Angy's doll is not much of a beauty but about as handsome as the Mexicans make them. I expect Angy will say "it is *muy feo.*" (very ugly)

God bless you all,

Your loving Mother

William Chapman sent this letter to New Orleans, so Helen did not receive it until her arrival there on the return trip.

My dearest Ella, Brasos Santiago, Texas

May 20. At the request of Mother, contained in her letter which I enclose, I convey to you now the sad intelligence of a death in your family. Your father died on the 4th of April without pain or a struggle. He never recovered from the sickness which Mother wrote you about before you left. During his sickness he said he had no wish to live that he might become a burden to his friends. He spoke of you and me with great affection.

Do not grieve too much, my dearest Ella, at these tidings. Your father was quite old and even with a stronger constitution he could not have lived many years longer. Do not let your health suffer by dwelling too much on this event.

How happy shall I be, my sweetest Ella, when I can again fold you to my breast and kiss away all your troubles. Oh! Ella, I love you more and more every day, and I am sometimes almost confused when I think, (and that is very often), how much I love you. God protect and bless you will be the prayer of your very affectionate husband.

William

My dearest William, Mexico City

May 21. Delightful as has been the regular appearance of your bulletins of good tidings, each has thrown me into a perplexity for I was wholly in doubt as to the best course for me to pursue. Without any reference to my own feelings, I wished to do what was right and best but it seemed almost impossible to come to a decision. If I remain here, admitting that our hopes are not groundless, it must be at least until January and I have no experience of a winter in this peculiar climate.

Mr Smith thinks it is too cold to pursue any occupation whatever. They called it their warm season when we arrived, yet in these thick stone walls, mornings and evenings, I felt excessively chilly and was glad to get into the sunshine. It would be a very cheerless place it seems to me for sickness, then too there would be a foreign physician, speaking a different language and unacquainted with my constitution. The possibility that I might have to depend on a Mexican nurse and above all the opinion prevalent here that it is a very trying climate to infants of foreign parents. If they survive infancy, they are said to be fine healthy children, but the ordeal is considered trying. Allowing it to be as we hope, if I succeed in avoiding an accident until Mr Jarvis is ready, I think the journey will be of benefit rather than otherwise. In any case, the danger is always greatest in the first three months and I shall have passed that period before starting.

It seems necessary to come to some decision on the subject and to acquaint you with it but I have dreaded to make any allusion to a subject upon which you are excessively anxious and I cannot bear that you should form hopes which may be disappointed either by discovering it to be the consequences of ill health or by the same accident that has previously followed such a situation.[52] According to all ordinary rules I have reason to think it is so, but from my carelessness and from the conviction that such an event would never again happen, I am wholly unable to tell how long it has been the case. I believe I have come to this decision, independently (as I wished) of my feelings, but I cannot deny that I am becoming exceedingly impatient to find myself once more in my own dear happy home.

I am sure, my dearest husband, that we love each other too much to bear a long separation patiently. Unless for very urgent reasons, nothing could make me feel contented remaining here, but the feeling that I might be insuring to you a great future happiness.

I have denied myself a great deal of sight seeing because I was so fearful of doing an improvidence. Dearest Willie, if all things should go right I may be able to make you a present equal to the silver tea set and the idea that I can give you anything in return for all you have lavished on me makes me inconceivably happy. Do not let Mother know anything of this until I am safe at home with you. She has anxieties enough now probably.

52. Chapman can only be referring to earlier miscarriages here.

I often wonder if any other woman has such a husband and boy. Since I came away I find that little Angy comes in for a very good share of my love. She does not hold a place quite equal to Willie. Still she seems like our own. Kisses to the children and kind remembrances to the girls,

May 25. Everything looks promising for our hopes and my health continues excellent. Perhaps this delay is providential though it is certainly hard to bear. I will go by the next boat if Mr Jarvis is not ready. Miss Bacon is doing nothing as yet and I fear has made a great mistake [in coming to Mexico City]. Love to all. Tell my darling Willie that I can scarcely control my impatience to be with him again. Kiss little Angy and give kind remembrances to the girls. God bless you all. My heart is with you always.

May 28. I hope we shall leave by the next steamer though it will hurry us considerably or rather Mr Jarvis.

He is feeble and somewhat nervous and irritable and, in short, though he may be very much like men in general, he is very unlike, my own dear, cheerful, energetic husband. If you get this in time, I wish you to put me in possession of funds independently of Mr Jarvis. I mean, for purchases in New Orleans. I do not intend to spend any large amount, but I have shopping to do for Jane and Mary. Mr Jarvis thinks you will look darkly at the quantity of money already spent, but I do not think any has gone foolishly.

I wish you would speak yourself to Alfred Bennett and ask him about his prospect of being able to pay me. Ann has worn out nearly all her clothes and I must advance money on her wages when we reach New Orleans. He ought to be paying it now if ever and I think it would be better for both to let him see that you expect it. Ann is anxious that you should speak to Alfred as no one knows of the transaction. Write to me about what I can properly advance Ann. I think your letter will reach me in time. My health continues good. My clothes are getting shabby as well as Ann's and I hope I shall see no one in New Orleans. I have grown fleshy too and they are rather uncomfortable.

I begin to think of nothing but "home sweet home." Can it be possible you will receive me with as much delight as I shall meet you. I sometimes think I did wrong to separate myself so far from you and yet when I remember the very great change it has effected in my health I believe I acted for the best. If I can only get home safe!

Your loving,
Helen

My dear Mother, Mexico City

June 1, 1851. I have just returned from a pretty ceremony at the "*Colegio de las Ninas*" (a girls' school) in honor of the Virgin. The church was decorated in the gayest manner with flowers and a profusion of wax lights. Before the main altar, a carpeted staging was erected and at intervals to the sound of very lively music, and the singing of young girls in the choir, little girls from the ages of eight perhaps to twelve came on to this platform, with beautiful baskets of choice flowers as an offering to the Virgin. The children were all beautifully dressed in pure white with lace veils.

Mr Hill, one of the [Texas] prisoners taken when he was only fourteen years of age, and adopted as a protege by Santa Anna, called during the morning. He is very gentlemanly and intelligent and his whole history reflects a great credit upon Santa Anna and other Mexican officers.[53]

June 3. The women of Mexico are universally praised and the men are invariably condemned for their conduct in domestic relations. The wife of General Arista, the President, they say is shut up in a convent; whether for her own transgressions or her husband's convenience, I do not know. In his own official residence, the palace, he keeps his mistress, the wife of another man. Those who understand Mexican society best say that if the women are guilty of levity, the conduct of their husbands is such as goes far to palliate their faults.

Helen

My dearest Ella, Fort Brown, Texas

June 4. Your sweet letter of May 21st was received yesterday and made me very happy.

[When] we expect you at the Brasos, we will go down to receive you with our arms and warm hearts. Willie says he will have a bonfire when you arrive. I have provisioned him some tar for that purpose.

Willie, Angy, and the girls are well and almost beside themselves for joy, (in which I heartily join), at the near prospect of seeing the sweet, bright star of our happy home. I am glad you have decided to come home. Come back, dearest Ella, home is not home without you.

53. This is a reference to John Christopher Columbus Hill of Columbus, Georgia. He was a member of the Mier Expedition in late December 1842 and was one of the Texans taken prisoner. See Appendix A.

I saw Bennett today: he is well and grinning in the hopes of seeing Ann by the 4th of July. Love to Mr Jarvis and regards to Ann.

Ever your affectionate,
William

My dearest William, Mexico City

June 7. We had made all our arrangements for leaving on Monday but some vexatious difficulty has arisen respecting the copy of a paper that Mr Jarvis considers important so I am afraid to say when we will go. Soon I hope, for with all the pleasure of this delightful journey, there is still no place like home sweet home.

Mr Jarvis is terribly impatient and disgusted. It is well you are not here for you would either get a brain fever from irritation or be imprisoned for contemptuous and belligerent treatment of these lazy officials with their eternal "mananas" and "poco tiempos."

I shall write the last letter I hope on Wednesday, June 11th. Love and kisses to Willie and Angy. Send remembrances to the girls and to all friends. For yourself love, that in such an old married woman would seem to some almost foolish in its fondness, but it is not possible to love such a husband too much.

Ever your affectionate,
Helen

My dearest Ella, Fort Brown, Texas

June 10. I sent Henderson over to Matamoras at 3 o'clock when the mail from Mexico arrives and he returned saying there was no letter for me. I was exceedingly anxious and apprehensive that you were sick or something had happened to you. I, however, tried not to think of it and went to ride in the carriage at 6 o'clock with Angy and Willie. Judge my relief and extreme happiness when on my return I was handed your dear letter. It had been put in the wrong pigeon hole in Matamoras, but was afterwards discovered and brought over by Mr Stillman's clerk. I read your beautiful letter to Mr and Mrs Stillman and to Captain Phelps. They seemed much pleased. The gratification your elegant, incomparable letters have given me, more than compensates for all the expenses of the journey. Mother says, "Your kindness in sending Helen's letters has furnished not only a treat for myself, but many of our friends. I assure you they are much admired."

I have had a talk with Alfred this morning and he says that he has no money, but that Mr Scarborough owes him $80.[54] He has gone out to try and get a part of it, but has little hopes of succeeding at this time as Mr Scarborough is sick.

Perhaps you had better let Ann have all of her wages due, say $40. With her energy and perseverance, she will make Alfred pay you gradually. I wrote to New Orleans and found it was impossible to get employment for Alfred there.

I enclose you an order on Messrs H. S. Stone & Co., 57 & 59 Common Street, New Orleans for what money you want. Get whatever you wish, my dearest Ella. I do not feel poor even if Mr Jarvis does for me. You will see on the list that I requested Mr Stone to show you some claret wine. I find that I am sometimes compelled to have claret on the table and I thought I had better pay a fair price in New Orleans, than an extravagant one in Brownsville for the same article. I hope you will not be displeased with me, my sweet Ella, for this for I thought I could scarcely avoid it without appearing mean.

Oh, I am so happy that you are getting fleshy and are coming home so soon. I often wonder how I have got along without you. Yet I am so glad you went away. If your health should not be better hereafter, at least, My sweet Ella, you have had three months of happiness and freedom from pain. Oh, my dearest Ella, if I ever loved you, I love you now with my whole heart and I hope I shall render myself more worthy of your pure love.

William

Jarvis hurled some final insults at the Mexican bureaucracy, dated June 11, 1851.

Dear Major, Mexico City

I have this day drawn on you in favor of Bates, Jamieson & Co. for fifteen hundred dollars. This amount includes all our expenses, past and

54. Mr. E. B. Scarborough was the editor of the *Rio Grande Sentinel*, the Brownsville newspaper. See Appendix B, March 12, 1850.

prospective, to New Orleans and includes a pretty large amount of purchases including some silver plates.

For the past 10 days, I have been endeavoring to procure a copy from the Minister of State of a certain paper listing grants of land given by the Mexican government up to the year, 1838. They declined giving it on the ground of my not having the right to ask for it and for fear of its prejudicing the rights of Mexican land holders in Texas. These are some of the disgusts one is obliged to endure in business connected with this government, their suspicions and jealousies are only equalled by their procrastination, and indolence.

Arista, the president, hearing I was to leave, sent for me a few days since to take leave. He was polite and kind in his messages to you and wished me to mention to you his desire that our officers would do all in their powers to abate the disturbances on the frontier, such as the invasion by armed parties from our side.

Mrs Chapman is now rather anxious to get away, both on account of the family and the arrival of that most excruciating bore, Miss Bacon. What induced her to come here, I don't know, but here she is, quartered in the same house and kindly bestows her leisure time for Mrs Chapman's benefit. We are heartily sick of her and shall leave the moment I can get my business through with and go to Jalapa, there to await the Steamer. Miss Bacon evidently counted extensively on our patronage and introduction to society here in which she made a great mistake. You will see her back yet in Brownsville and I am anxious to get away before she finds out her mistake. She may wish to return with us to which I most decidedly shall object.

With my kindest regards to all, I remain,

Samuel M. Jarvis

My dear Mother[-in-law], Brasos Santiago, Texas

June 11th. A letter from Helen dated May 28 [said she] expected to leave the City of Mexico in three or four days to meet the steamship, *Alabama*, at Vera Cruz. I expect to see her safely home before the 1st of July. She writes that her health is good and that she is getting *fleshy*. Just think of it. She is in not only fine spirits, but is also inconceivably happy.

Willie is well and sends love. My love to Aunt Betsey and all.

W. W. Chapman

My dearest William, Mexico City

June 15th. We start tomorrow morning for *home dear home* to be in readiness for the *Alabama* which, it is supposed, will leave on the 24th of June.

We are all well and eager for the meeting with those we love. Kisses to the children and love to all.

Helen

My dear Mother, Puebla, Mexico

June 18. I arrived here on the evening of the 16th completely worn out. My last day in Mexico was a very fatiguing one and the night still more so.

I had a room full of company and some of my good friends were so inconsiderate as to keep me up until after twelve; though knowing I must rise at three in the morning. Before I could undress and finish my packing it was after one so that I had not two hours of sleep.

Mrs Ramsey and myself had been invited that evening to the [National] Palace to hear the music of three fine military bands. About nine o'clock after some had left, we excused ourselves to the others and went, unwilling to lose the opportunity. It was a very pleasant closing scene and one that will long leave a very agreeable impression. The Plaza of Mexico bounded on two sides by lofty buildings, with their arched portals, on the third by the Palace and on the fourth by the Cathedral—large and nobly designed is a grand sight by moonlight—far surpassing the view of any public square in the United States.

On this night the effect was greatly heightened by the presence of three fine brass bands in their showy uniforms before the Palace, clearly seen by a brilliant torchlight. [With] the crowds of people and the fine music, there was an old world grandeur never seen at home.

The reception room of the Palace is large, lofty—well, but not richly furnished. At one extremity, I noticed a full-length portrait of the Emperor Iturbide, a common, heavy, homely looking man. I have often met his two sons in the street—one rather a fine looking but very dissipated young man,—the other more estimable in character, but almost without exception the most miserable, insignificant-looking man I have ever seen.

Wearied out as I was, on my return I ascended to the roof of our hotel to take a last look at the silent city so peacefully slumbering in the calm moonlight. The summer moon shone down on thousands of the humble and helpless, the guilty and the wretched. I may never in all human probability see Mexico [City] again.

I was in some respects less able to bear fatigue than on my journey up and when I arrived in Puebla about four in the evening, I was completely exhausted. All day yesterday I lay on the bed. This morning I rose early and we started for Cholula six miles distant. We procured our carriage from an Englishman who for the sake of speaking his own language, very gladly I believe, accompanied us. It was market day and the whole road was crowded with Cholulan Indians.

On our way, we met an English merchant, Mr Smith, in his carriage proceeding to the city. We were entire strangers but the circumstance of being foreigners and speaking the same language seemed to be a sufficient claim upon his hospitality and he sent back orders that breakfast should be prepared for us at his "Hacienda" (or Estate.) It lies on the outskirts of the old city of Cholula, and is a very comfortable bachelor residence. The housekeeper, a nice respectable looking Mexican, seemed to have a multitude of attendants; and probably like most other foreigners this English merchant has the privileges without the restraints of marriage.

After a good breakfast, we proceeded to the so-called pyramid though all trace of its pyramidal appearance has completely vanished.[55] It rises from the level highly cultivated plain, a steep wooded hill; crowned at its summit with a neat and tasteful church. A traveler would never suspect its artificial construction, and so completely in the progress of time, has it been covered by trees and a luxuriant undergrowth that it is only by close examination of portions where it has been cut away, that the conviction comes upon you that it is really a stupendous work of human labor. The sunburned brick or adobe of which it is composed is clay colored, and does not differ in appearance from common earth. There is a cave extending far into the mountain and as far as you proceed, you find the same evidence of artificial formation.

Helen

My dear Mrs Smith,[56] Jalapa, Mexico

June 21. I cannot lose this opportunity of writing a few lines especially as I know your kind interest in my safe return may lead you to exaggerate

55. Although Chapman was apparently unaware of it, the Tepanapa Pyramid in Cholula, with a base length of 402 meters and a height of 70 meters, is the largest such structure on earth.

56. The following two letters survive in draft form. The originals were sent to Mrs.

our unfortunate meeting with the robbers. I am happy to tell you, however, that aside from the inconvenience and loss I have not been in any way a sufferer. I bore it all very cooly and philosophically and would not allow myself to fall into any nervous and lady-like tremors. My Texas training, you see, has been of use to me.

As you must once more, at least, pass over this route, you may have some anxiety to know how these gentlemen of the road treat their lady passengers.

A little after four in the morning not very far from Puebla, I was aroused from a state of drowsy half consciousness by hearing Mr Jarvis exclaim, "Here come the robbers," and, on looking up, I saw two well mounted horsemen one at each window holding toward us a loaded pistol. We were alone in the carriage and I instantly said to Mr Jarvis, "Make no resistance. It would be utterly useless." He was himself conscious that if he fired at one robber, the other would instantly have fired his pistol into the carriage.

Mr Jarvis at first was the only one motioned to leave, but with an impatient command and still farther projecting their pistols into the window, they signified that we also should leave the carriage. We did so, Ann shaking with terror and just ready to bust into an Irish howl. Mr Jarvis was first searched and they found about twenty or twenty-five dollars. One of them then approached me and demanded my money. I answered that I had none, but the word of a lady it seems was not sufficient, and he immediately commenced rather a rude search from my neck to my waist without, however, unfastening my dress. The same ceremony was performed with Ann, but less thoroughly. We were then allowed to stand aside while the carriage was searched. That being accomplished, Ann and I were allowed to reseat ourselves and they commenced the plunder of our baggage.

I think they took everything nearly from Mr Jarvis's trunk except two shirts. From mine, they took everything which they believed could be useful to themselves or their ladies. They threw out things in every direction on the ground and after making their selections mounted their horses and rode off at full gallop. While the driver of the coach sat perfectly neutral, motionless as a statue, his assistant was very usefully employed in taking down the trunks and packing the plunder upon the horses.

Some American lady in Mexico [City] told me that she rather wished

Buckingham Smith, the former Julia G. Gardner of Concord, New Hampshire, and John Hill (see Appendix A).

to have an adventure with the robbers. Lest you might possibly have the same romantic fancy, let me assure you that to be forced from a coach on a solitary road in that cold and uncertain light and to stand still while such a ruffian passing his arms though the bridle of his restive horse with one hand which holds a pistol to your breast and with the other hand places his rough grasp upon your person is by no means a position to be desired. I knew their object was plunder merely and my only fear was that with the rearing and plunging of his horse and his own fierce hurry to get off before daylight, the pistol might be discharged accidentally. On our arrival at Perote, we examined our trunks and tried to reduce the refuse into some order.

They overlooked or did not know of a compartment in the top of the trunks and thus a few necessary articles were secured. All my dresses (they were not very numerous fortunately) were taken with the exception of a gingham and a white dress. My Mexican bonnet to which they are heartily welcome, even a Mantilla crepe shawl, threaded lace veil, and some very fine linen undergarments, had all disappeared with other things of less account. Strangely enough in the general search, my watch chain was overlooked, while poor Mr Hill's daguerreotypes were seized upon as jewel cases. After all is said and done, however, we have the satisfaction of thinking that they might have done much worse. They did not discover the gold Mr Jarvis wore about his person or silver plates to the value of $125.

At this moment at four o'clock p.m., the rain is pouring in torrents. All the mornings, it is cloudy and all the evenings, it rains. A great many Americans are waiting passage in the *Alabama* which is advertised to sail the 26th. Among them, Prince, the gardener from Flushing on his return from California with great additions to his floral collection. The hotel and tables are delightful, but I am too much an invalid to enjoy them or even the scenery of this most lovely spot. I do not see that it is any more beautiful here in the summer, for in Jalapa there seems to be a perpetual spring.

Yours very truly,
Helen B. Chapman

My dear Mr Hill, Jalapa, Mexico

I regret exceedingly to inform you that in the robbery of our baggage on Thursday morning last, a short distance this side of Puebla both of the daguerreotypes designed for your mother and sister were among the pillaged articles. I lamented their loss much more than I should have done other articles of much greater monied value, because I knew they would have afforded such extreme pleasure to your friends.

The robbers probably, without waiting to examine them, mistook them for jewel cases and it is beyond measure annoying that they could have been thus sacrificed.

The mineralogical specimens and other articles you so kindly gave me were allowed to remain.

When writing to you mother I will mention this unfortunate circumstance as the reason for not forwarding your promised gifts. We leave in two or three hours from Vera Cruz. With my best wishes and regrets, believe me dear sir,

Yours very truly,
Helen B. Chapman

My dearest Helen, Brasos Santiago, Texas

June 27. We (the whole family) came here last Sunday certainly expecting you that day in the *Fanny.* And oh, we were so disappointed on hearing that you were not on board. Willie could scarcely keep from crying, and for my part, my own sweet one, I have not been so unhappy for years and remained so until the following Tuesday when I got your letters of June 11th which explained all. I was then glad that you remained, for every day's delay in Mexico I know benefits you. Oh Ella, dearest Ella, how glad I shall be to see you again.

General Whiting and Colonel Tompkins have been here on a tour of inspection and expressed themselves much pleased with everything. I believe I told you that the Inspector General had been here before.

Captain Arnet says he must bring you to the Brasos in the *Major Barbour* which he still commands, but I think you will find the *Fanny* more comfortable, and you will be less liable to extreme seasickness, which should be avoided in *certain conditions.*

Willie and Angy and the girls are perfectly well and more happy since they have recovered from their great disappointment.

Your ever affectionate,
William

11.
A NEW CHAPMAN

July 1851 through March 1852

When Helen Chapman returned to her "circle of loving hearts" in July 1851, her joy knew no limits, according to her letters to her mother.[1] Yet, as the birth of her second child neared, her awareness of mortality again took the upper hand. Perhaps the demands of a new family member account for the scarcity of correspondence in late 1851 and early 1852, although Chapman continued to solicit financial help for her needy acquaintances.

The Chapmans and their Brownsville neighbors were affected by the Merchants War, which boiled up south of the Rio Grande in the fall of 1851. José Maria Canales had published El Plan de la Loba in September, calling for a variety of reforms, such as tariff reductions and fugitive slave laws. José Maria Jesus Carvajal raised a thousand-man army which included several hundred Texans sympathetic to the economic changes specified in the plan. In late September the troops took Camargo and headed east. A month later they reached Matamoras, and the "rattle of musketry and the roar of cannon" could be heard from Fort Brown. Civilians fleeing the conflict crowded into the town. Carvajal's forces faded temporarily toward the west in November.[2]

That same month, the lawsuit filed by Leonard Dobbins over the government's use of land at Brazos Santiago was dismissed. The documents Captain Jarvis struggled so valiantly to locate in

1. HBC to EWB, Aug. 1, 1851, below.

2. The Plan de la Loba, first pronounced at the Camp of the Loba, was signed by J. M. Canalez and others. It was published in the Matamoros *Bien Publico*, quoted in the Brownsville *Rio Bravo* of Sept. 24, 1851, and further quoted in the New Orleans *Daily Delta*, Sept. 30, 1851 (John Salmon Ford, *Rip Ford's Texas*, ed. Stephen B. Oates [Austin: University of Texas Press, 1987], 196; *Handbook of Texas*, II, 176; HBC to EWB, Oct. 21 and 22, 1851, below).

Mexico city proved irrelevant when the government buildings were removed from the contested land.[3]

My dearest Ella, Fort Brown, Texas

July 10, 1851. I would not advise you to remain long in New Orleans. I never shall want for anything if I can only get you back. The little and big hearts about the house, in our home, are all beating for you and you only; they will be in constant and increasing excitement until you come, my sweet one.

As for local gossip, Mr Garey and Margaret Vernon are to be married tomorrow night.[4] Mr Grimsted and Parson Craven's wife's sister are soon to follow in their steps. The engagement between Stansbury and Miss Chamberlain is broken off *forever.* Denman is married. Mrs Brewerton, Mrs Vielé and Mrs Holabird are all at Ringgold Barracks.[5] Colonel Wilson has joined them there. Major Porter was beastly drunk in the street last night and arm and arm with Williams, our ambulance driver, who was also very drunk. Mr Garesché will probably be tried here, instead of New Orleans.[6]

Mr Mather arrived on the *Fanny* two days since. He called yesterday morning and delivered your letters and packages from Mexico. The latter made the children happy and the girls laugh. This morning we had some delicious chocolate made from 3 cakes of what you sent. I called on Mr Mather last evening and had a long talk with about you and Mexico. He says that when you try to go away from Mexico City that Mrs Hargous,[7] Mrs Smith and Miss White will lay an embargo on you: that you have completely won their hearts and everybody else's. He says if you write as well as you talk that a better letter writer never wrote from Mexico. He said much else that made me very happy. I love to hear my sweet Ella praised. It verifies my own good taste.

The children send love and kisses.

William

3. Basse & Horde (Attorneys) to WWC, Nov. 11, 1852, CC.

4. John E. Garey was a Brownsville auctioneer and commission merchant.

5. Brewerton's husband was First Lieutenant George Douglas Brewerton; Teresa Griffin Vielé was married to Lieutenant Egbert Ludovickus Vielé, and Mary T. Grant Holabird, of Amenia, New York, was the wife of Samuel Beckley Holabird.

6. Lieutenant J. P. Garesché's alleged offense is unknown, but he must have been acquitted, as he was still serving as acting assistant quartermaster at Fort Brown in 1855.

7. This spelling suggests that Helen befriended Peter Hargous and his wife while in Mexico City.

My dearest Ella Brasos Santiago, Texas

July 17. We came down here from Fort Brown, (the whole family), on Saturday the 12th instant with some slight hope that you would be here the next day on the *Fanny.* Willie was much disappointed though I told him beforehand that there was only a possibility of your coming.

The *Fanny* will leave New Orleans again on Thursday, the 24th, and be here on Sunday, the 27th. By her I shall expect you and if you do not come or I do not hear that you are well, I shall be miserable. The *Fanny* is now the only boat that runs to the Brasos so that if you do not come on Sunday, the 27th, we shall have to wait two weeks longer.

Oh, my dear sweet Ella, how I want to see you and how much more I love you than I ever have before. Come home, dearest Ella. Home is not home without the star that brightens and gladdens everything. So long as I knew you were in Mexico and your health improving, I was contented and bore the separation bravely for me, but now that your have turned your face homeward, I am childishly impatient to see my own dear little wife.

The children are well, perfectly well and send love and kisses. They are both talking of your constantly.

Your ever loving,
William

My dear Mother, New Orleans

July 23. I arrived here last Saturday on the Schooner *Robert Spadden* from Vera Cruz and immediately drove to Colonel Hunt's office to procure my letters. This was the first intimation of my dear father's death. You did well to wish that I might hear of it on the way and I tell you frankly that I am so completely worn out and exhausted in body and mind that I cannot bring myself to realize it. My emotions seem paralyzed. I have gone through enough to kill any woman in my condition it would seem. For contrary to all expectations, I must tell you that I am again to become a mother.

On the way down from Mexico City before daylight, we were robbed and a Mexican ruffian held a pistol to my breast while searching me. We were detained at Vera Cruz a fortnight in the very height of the sickly season and then at last took passage on a miserable little schooner where for eleven days I was obliged to sleep on the hard floor of the deck. Coming up we had a fearful tragedy and a young man with whom not five minutes before I had been earnestly conversing fell overboard and was launched into eternity. I will write you particulars of all when I reach that blessed haven of rest, my own house. Everybody has deserted New Orleans and I have seen no old friends.

You are so unfamiliar with the kinds of excitement I have passed through that you cannot realize my difficulty in bringing before my mind the sad truth that the object of so much love and charity has at length gone to his rest. It will be only when I go home and miss the placid, thoughtful, earnest face that exercised such a powerful spell over my childish heart.

I have always felt perfectly convinced that there must have been great elements in a character that still preserved the respect and heart-felt devotion of those who knew him best. God be thanked that the sunset of such a life was calm, honorable and peaceful, leaving behind a soothing twilight of hope and consolation.

I am sorry to give you such intelligence of myself because I know it will increase your anxieties, but that Being who has carried me safely through extreme sickness and various perils will watch over me when my hour of trial comes. I would like you to look over my bundle of Willie's baby clothing, whiten it as well as you can, and I will send for it. I would like it all sent.

Helen

My dear Mother, Brasos Santiago, Texas

Aug. 1, 1851. I know you will be relieved to hear that I am safe at home at last, but I do not think you can conceive my joy in feeling that the last stage of that toilsome and painful journey is accomplished, that I am welcomed to an unbroken circle of loving hearts and that all is well.

We left New Orleans on Thursday last and should have arrived here on Sunday noon, but we had a very stormy bad passage and did not succeed in making this port until Tuesday noon. They were consequently in much anxiety for our safety and very happily relieved when we made our appearance.

I was unwell in New Orleans, but in my hurry while doing some shopping for myself I purchased two dresses for you and sent them by Mr Morris.

Willie is well. He seems to be growing fast. Angy is healthy, good humored and "as brown as a berry." It was almost worth the trial of separation to be so warmly welcomed home. Such a loving husband, such good affectionate children and such attached faithful servants seldom fall to the lot of any woman. We have indeed a happy home.

Aug. 7. I wrote you so much and yet so little from New Orleans that I know you are in a fever of anxiety. I began to write an account of the robbery but I fear it will not be finished by this mail. I ought to have told you that I was not frightened. Indeed I am astonished at the nerve and courage I have acquired within a few years. I seem to fear nothing. Vomits and storms at sea were all met with the same coolness and I remember on the first moment of seeing the robbers at the windows, I thought at once I must not endanger my child's life by any foolish turn.

Of course, I need not tell you that when I left home I had no idea of my situation. I supposed it was the lack of regularity that I had noticed before and Dr Jarvis was altogether inclined to disbelieve it. The usually fatal [first] three months was passed in the City of Mexico and probably it is to this rather strange remedy that I owe my present condition. I think I may expect my confinement about the early part of November. My health is good.

It is raining and I am really too languid to write more. God bless you, my dear Mother. Love to all the family,

Aug. 9. I have time again only for a line to let you know I am well. The boat brought us company and we have visitors that leave by the Steamer this morning.

Willie is very well and full of going north next spring. He is still too young to understand how fruitless it is to make plans months ahead. When you get time and composure of mind, will you ascertain and inform me what is the ordinary progress of boys of twelve. What studies they pursue, and how far advanced in each. He is very desirous of not seeming backward, and if I come out of my ordeal with any degree of health, I can advance him considerably. I have no desire that he should be forward. We have had enough of precocity in the family.

Townsend goes to California in the fall. The Major begins to talk of change again and rather looks to El Dorado.

They have come for my letter.

Helen

My dear Mrs Hill,[8] Brasos Santiago, Texas

During a visit of between two and three months in the City of Mexico, I made the acquaintance of your son, and promised him that, on my return to Texas, I would send to you two Daguerreotype likenesses of himself, the enclosed letter to his brother, and a letter conveying such intelligence of his character and prospects as I knew would give you much pleasure. Most unfortunately, while on our passage from Puebla to Perote, we were attacked by robbers, our trunks plundered and among many valuable articles, both miniatures were carried off probably under the impression that they were jewel cases.

I wrote from Jalapa informing him of this misfortune. I feel certain, however, that what I have to say of his gentlemanly deportment, his studious habits, and the high estimation in which his character is held by both Mexicans and foreigners will almost compensate for this disappointment.

Soon after my arrival in Mexico, I often heard him mentioned as a protege of Santa Anna from the circumstance of being made a prisoner at such a tender age. I had some curiosity to make his acquaintance. An opportunity was soon afforded me and on hearing that I had come from Texas, he seemed delighted to see me.

I twice visited with him at *The Mineria*, a noble institution where apparently he has every opportunity of receiving a thorough and complete education. I know how anxiously you must have passed days and sleepless nights for this long, lost child and how deeply every little circumstance connected with his life, character and personal appearance would interest you now. He is about of middle height, handsomely and very neatly dressed, quiet, modest and gentlemanly in his manner, ambitious to excel in his studies and merit the confidence of those who have so generously supplied his wants. I made inquiries as to his character and habits and am happy to assure you that I believe his habits perfectly good and his moral character irreproachable.

He speaks with the utmost affection of his family and eagerly looks forward to the time when he may be allowed to visit the scenes of his childhood.

8. Elizabeth Hill, of Yellow Prairie, Texas, was the mother of John Hill. She replied on November 23, 1851, saying that she had married Alexander Thomson in May 1850 and was living in Caldwell, Burleson County.

His life thus far has been a strange romantic history and it would have seemed that a boy thus thrown among strangers in a foreign country, and such a country as Mexico, would almost inevitably have been ruined, but God seems to have watched over the little Texas prisoner from the first hour of his capture to the present hour and it gives me the warmest pleasure to assure you that when that long expected meeting arrives you will clasp in your arms a son of whom you have every reason to be proud and who I fervently hope and trust will be a blessing in your declining age.

With kindest wishes for your speedy reunion and his future prosperity, I remain,

Very truly yours,
Helen B. Chapman

Helen Chapman wrote to Mr. Fairchild, secretary of the *Christian Union*, on August 14, 1851, in reply to his inquiries.

Mr Fairchild, Brasos Santiago, Texas

Your letter of July 15, 1851 was duly received. I am certainly interested in the success of your mission and will gladly give any information in my power.

With reference to your question as to the Baptist Mission, I have to state that so far as I am aware Mr Monsaloatge has no connection with it, and indeed if it be a mission, it is without influence so far as the Mexican population is concerned. It has no organized church, no house of worship, and no stated preaching. Mr Wombwell teaches an English school, but this mission, as now organized, cannot substitute for the one your society has established in the valley of the Rio Grande.

It is possible that a desirable union might be effected between the two missions by uniting in the same building a free English and Spanish school. This is a mere suggestion and I know not if it would be expedient or practicable.

Mr Monsaloatge has at present eleven scholars at $1.00 per month and it is found to be very difficult to collect even that sum. I doubt if Mr Wombwell has a larger number. Miss Chamberlain has but two or three scholars[9] and the only other school has been abandoned for want of

9. Hiram Chamberlain had founded the Rio Grande Female Institute, where his daughter Henrietta taught.

encouragement. Mr Monsaloatge mentioned that if he might establish a free school he could collect a hundred scholars and that he should be delighted to do so if he could be assured a moderate income.[10]

Indeed, my dear sir, it is impossible to give you any idea of the wretched poverty of this population. They really cannot afford to pay more than a trifling sum for the education of their children and the greater portion are not capable of making any sacrifice. The consequence is that in a population of two or three thousand, the children are growing up wild in the streets in ignorance and this must continue unless help comes from abroad. There is, at present, no state provision for education.

It is useless to speak of evils for which in the nature of things there is no remedy, but to urge upon missionary societies the necessity of endowing their missions more liberally is indispensable to their success so long as the public will not meet these demands by increased generosity. Missionaries should not be slavishly dependent for the very bread they eat upon a people who in their contributions are governed solely by caprice and who do not hesitate at once to withdraw all support from a man who does not please the population well. It is expecting too much of human nature to suppose that a missionary under such circumstances can do his whole duty. To all those who will reflect upon the character of such a population, it must be self-evident. I shall be greatly disappointed if the trifling sum of 1000 dollars cannot be raised for a school building where its importance is so manifest. If this could be accomplished and your society could continue to Mr Monsaloatge his annual income, there would be a prospect that the Mexican children at least might be withdrawn from this hopeless degradation.

With reference to your inquiry as to the acceptability of clothing, bedding, and books, almost anything would be highly useful. We are at present at Brasos Santiago and Mr Chapman has had no opportunity of communicating with Mrs Monsaloatge as to her wants. She is a very delicate woman, nursing a feeble infant and doing all her own work. The wardrobe of both is very deficient, and if there is any disposition among benevolent ladies in New York to cheer [her] heart with presents of this kind, they might, with little expense, do much good.

For women's wear from November to April, calicos, ginghams, and mousseline de laines are most useful; during the remaining hot months,

10. In August, Learned of New London, Connecticut, sent Helen Chapman $60 in response to her appeal published in the *Christian Union* (HBC to EWB, October 7, 1851, below).

cheap thin muslins. During the winter, flannel underclothing is highly necessary for those who like Mrs Monsaloatge are threatened with pulmonary disease and it is not probable she has the means of procuring it. Any article of infant's clothing or the lighter kind of goods for men's wear would be highly acceptable. Broad cloth is not much needed, but alpacas [and] merinos are most worn by men. Bedding or pieces of cotton are always highly acceptable in such places.

I believe I have answered [your] questions as fully as I am able. Any assistance I can render the mission will be gladly afforded, and with fervent wishes for the success for your very important operations here as well as elsewhere,

I remain,
Helen B. Chapman

My dear Mother, Fort Brown, Texas

Sept. 25, 1851. As usual, you are the person to be neglected. I could not bear to delay a letter to [Welles] any longer so I have written him this morning and that leaves me only fifteen minutes for you. I have really been too much hurried since my return to write a line. I have a mass of correspondence on my hands that seems to be constantly accumulating.

I have some reason to think my confinement may take place earlier than I had supposed and I dare not depend wholly on the arrival of the bundle of baby clothes from you.

Oct. 5, 1851. I commence this letter before the arrival of the boat with some hope that I shall be able to fill a sheet.

I am very well and have need to be so, for I find plenty to do. The servants did wonderfully well when I was gone. Still I found both the children in need of clothes, the Major's needing a general repairing of many things, for myself to repair the wreck made by the robbery and some household sewing.

You might think perhaps that in such a wild place as Texas, I might get along very easily and with very little but the Major's ideas of living are on a grand scale. The children must be neatly and becomingly dressed. We never, or scarcely, sit down to a tea table alone. He must have a nice fresh shirt every morning and wears nothing but white pantaloons and white vests. Our washings are enormous but I am fortunate in having an Irish girl who washes beautifully. My other girl is a great help to me in sewing and if I wish to send out work, there is a widow here who sews beautifully.

The Major cannot bear to see me sew and nothing irritates him so much or would set him against helping any poor relation as much as suggesting the necessity of doing so on the grounds of economy.

In every family there is a household god, almost always unhappily an earthly idol and the character of every child to the latest day of its existence is influenced by the nature of this worship. With some it is *wealth*, with some *position*, with some *show*, in our family it is *comfort*. The free and constant use of the best, an abundance of easy chairs and sofas, a profusion of agreeable books, a systematic keeping out of sight and mind everything annoying and disagreeable, no talking of troubles and every anxious thought of my own heart is never even allowed to cast its shadow upon my face.

Children, servants, and all seem to act constantly on the principle that the Major is never to be annoyed, never to be troubled with any domestic wants. In his own house, he lives as in a hotel. Money is freely supplied for all this and such conveniences are furnished as to render all this system of living easy and pleasant. I could give a happy home and a most comfortable support to any friend who could relieve me in these cares, but I know of no earthly being except yourself who has sufficient tact to preserve this peculiar domestic condition.

The servants are delighted at my situation and have really made almost incredible efforts to put the house in readiness and get everything in order. They all show a tenderness and gentleness, a disposition to relieve me in every possible way that really excites my gratitude.

Part of the family is now at the Brazos. The Major, Willie, Mary, and Mr Whiting who has just heard of the death of his father, General Whiting at St Louis. I think I have mentioned this unfortunate young man before.

On the day his father died suddenly and without warning, poor Henry was attacked for the second time at least with "delirium tremens." For three days we supposed he would not survive, but he has again overcome the shock and has gone down to the Brazos, pale, emaciated, trembling and with all those fatal marks of debility so familiar to my memory. He is one whom everyone pities, whom no one has the heart to condemn, most carefully educated, well principled, lovely and amiable in character. From his mother's family, the Macombs, he inherits a thirst for that poison that seems to defy all control. How my heart aches for him!

Oct. 7. Two or three mails since, I received a letter that really gave me pleasure. Before I went to Mexico City, I wrote a private letter to Dr Baird urging the necessity of extending the facilities for the Mexican mission here in Brownsville and desiring his influence in procuring a subscription for a thousand dollars to build a school house. The letter was received, opened by the secretary of the *Christian Union* (Dr Baird being in Europe), and published in that journal with very high commendation and was so favorably received that one gentleman in New York offered a hundred dollars. The letter I mention was from New London signed Ebenezer Learned saying that he had read with much interest a letter from me to Dr Baird in the *Christian Union* setting forth in strong clear light the wants of the mission and that he and two or three friends wished to place at my sole disposal the sum of sixty dollars which he enclosed in the form of a draft. The letter was very handsome and as it was the first money I had ever earned from strangers by my pen, I was really gratified. We have since received a letter from Mr Fairchild, the secretary of the *Christian Union*, and I hope something will be accomplished.

Mr Monsaloatge has one child and will probably soon have another. I always write in such a hurry that I never have time to write about little Angy. I was fearful this new position of affairs might affect her interests unfavorably but the Major fortunately takes precisely the view I could have desired. He thinks that her adoption has brought this unexpected blessing upon the family and I find others regard it in the same light.

She is a very bright child and we both are fond of her. The greatest objection to her personal appearance will be her complexion, so dark as to give her a decidedly foreign appearance.

There are revolutionary moments up the river and General Avalos is preparing Matamoras for a state of siege.[11] Business is very much depressed and everything in this country is distressed and melancholy.

I have my whole house in order; every hole and closet is clean and arranged. How I wish you could be with me. Love and a fervent, God Bless You, to each and all.

Oct. 21. There is no steamer in the harbor, but I can scarcely expect to have many more days at present for writing letters, so I will try to have one ready for the mail whenever it may leave.

11. Carvajal's forces captured the garrison at Reynosa on Oct. 6, 1851. Anticipating his advance, Avalos sent out a frantic appeal for reinforcements at Matamoras to the military commandants at Victoria, Mexico City, and Tampico (New Orleans *Daily Delta*, Oct. 14, 1851).

We are in the midst of gloomy times, but I doubt if we realize it as you would do at home. Somehow, in a frontier life, we become so accustomed to strange events, to unpleasant excitements and tragic occurrences, that we become, in a measure, hardened. If I had always lived in Westfield, I think I could not as I do now sit calmly and write while cannon is thundering on the opposite side of the river advising me but too plainly that at this very moment Matamoras is suffering the horrors of civil war. The day is beautiful, the air still, the sky cloudless, yet those fatal shots seem to poison the whole atmosphere.

Yesterday, Carvajal took possession of Fort Parades and in the evening we rode down to Freeport, the American town directly opposite.[12] The whole road was lined with Mexicans, the greater part women and children removing from the besieged city. Brownsville is crowded to overflowing and I suppose great numbers are without shelter. But the climate most fortunately is genial, and a night out-of-doors is not at present a very terrible thing.

As vultures crowd about carrion, so the slightest note of war seems to bring together everything vile and wretched. For a week or fortnight past, Brownsville has been filled with wild, strange looking beings, many of whom, probably in spite of all the vigilance of troops from the garrison, have effected a passage to the other side. Cannon is stationed at the ferry opposite Fort Paredes, and the U.S. Steamer *Corvette* has mounted guns and passes up and down the river to intercept armed parties.

But with such a river being fordable at any point, it is impossible to prevent sympathizers from crossing. Brownsville is in a great state of excitement, and, indeed, the frontier is in a most unhappy condition.

The Major is getting tired of this station and talks of applying for another. My life is such a busy one I have no time to think in what kind of a place I do live. We are expecting General Persifor Smith by every boat. I hope he will not come until I get well, for there will have to be a great fuss for the General.

Oct. 22. All day yesterday we heard the rattle of musketry and the roar of cannon. Last evening, riding through Brownsville, we saw, as usual, crowds of Mexicans and the whole American population in a state of most intense excitement. All business was suspended, and the highest houses were covered with people witnessing the battle.

12. With his 1,100 troops, including 400 Texans, Carvajal set up his headquarters October 20 on the western edge of Matamoras, at Fort Paredes. The siege of the city began on October 21 and lasted until October 30 (New Orleans *Daily Delta*, Oct. 21 and Nov. 4, 1851).

We hear this morning that but two Americans were killed, one a Mr Culou, a very respectable man not long married.[13] One of our old teamsters is badly wounded. Several Mexicans of some note are killed or wounded. Man is a strange animal and at the first note of war we seem to recognize the brutal propensities much more than those which are supposed to elevate him above other animals. This Mr Culou was a young man, a good citizen, mild and inoffensive in character, married and it would seem one of the last to show such traits as he exhibited yesterday. Since the fighting commenced, he has seemed frenzied with excitement. He rushed over to Matamoras and early in the engagement killed a man with his own weapon. The most remarkable part of his conduct is this, he insisted on going to gaze upon the man he had sent to instant death. Not long after he was shot through the body and he died instantly. Last night his body was brought home to his wife, a young, feeble, sickly woman about to become a mother. This is life on a frontier, where passions are unrestrained by the strong arm of the law.

One hundred and fifty Mexican troops arrived yesterday from Vera Cruz, but it is not safe for such a small body to march up to Matamoras and they have no river transportation. To convey them in our steamers it is believed would be a violation of our neutrality laws. For such slight measures as our own regular troops are compelled to take to prevent the passage of armed parties, the towns people have become hostile in feeling and the position of the Regular Army here is by no means pleasant. As of this hour. 12:00 a.m., hostilities seem to be suspended. God grant they may come to some accommodation.

> The letter is unsigned, and the following paragraph is in William's handwriting.

My dear Mother[-in-law], Fort Brown, Texas

Oct. 29. For reasons which I will name in my own note, Helen desires me to finish her letter. The battle of Matamoras is still going on: which party will win it, no one can tell and we don't care. We, however, exceedingly regret that any Americans have joined them, at least at this time.[14] We are

13. A Mr. P. Culver was mentioned in the New Orleans *Daily Delta* of November19, 1851.

14. The U.S. government maintained its neutrality in this conflict, much to the disappointment of many Texans, as well as Mexicans.

entirely out of danger here though we see much of the suffering of war. Brownsville is crowded with women and children destitute of shelter and food.

Childbirth was a potentially fatal ordeal for Chapman. In the days immediately preceding her confinement, she wrote a special prayer as well as separate letters to her son, husband, and mother to be opened in the event of her death.[15] On October 23, 1851, Helen Ellsworth Blair Chapman gave birth to her daughter and namesake, Helen Blair Chapman, at Fort Brown. The letters fortunately remained unopened and unread.

A beautiful, still Sabbath morning and I am alone. There seems to be a stillness in these Southern latitudes I never knew at the North, or it may be I have a more intense appreciation of what the very young shrink from with dread: rest, repose, silence, and the power to commune with my own heart and be still.

The wind scarcely ruffles the orange trees and vine leaves around the door but human hearts at this moment are beating angrily and fiercely. A cloud of civil war is darkening the atmosphere and helpless women and innocent children grow faint with fear. In Matamoras they are now expecting an attack from the revolutionary troops of Carvajal and I listen every moment expecting to hear the sounds of conflict breaking the delightful stillness of this heavenly morning. There are many grievances that need redress, but this is a fearful remedy.

Thank God that in my own heart there is serenity, peace, submission to God's will, a willingness to live or die as his wisdom shall determine. The family are all at church and I have time to think of the trial that is near at hand. Will there be joy in the household for the safe deliverance of another spirit into the circle of its love or will there be a mingling of joy and grief [for] birth and death. It is well we do not know. I am resigned.

I gaze around me on a family so devoted, a husband so loving and affectionate, a boy so good, so tender, so obedient and so devoted, on the little child of our adoption, on servants so faithful, so eager to save me

15. The prayer was probably written on October 19, 1851. Helen's letter to her mother is not reproduced here (HBC to EWB, Oct. 22, 1851, CC). Its tone is very similar to the others, but Chapman hints that her mother would be involved in Willie's care should she die in childbirth.

all care and vexation and [to refuse] to admit the possibility of my removal.

Oh! If it must be that I shall leave them, grant them, merciful Father, the consolations of thy spirit, be a father to my motherless ones, be the strength and support of my beloved husband, lead him to find comfort and hope in the assurance of a future reunion and may he, in new ties upon Earth, find consolation for those already riven.

Bless my sorrow stricken mother. If her earthly support is withdrawn, oh, give her the sustenance of a Heavenly Arm. She is a widow and thou the widow's God and friend. Prepare me for whatever thy wisdom has appointed for the training of an immortal spirit. My only plea before thee is that I do believe in the lord Jesus Christ. In the shining robe of his righteousness, in the boundless embrace of a love that encircled the penitent Magdalene and a thief upon the cross, I would hide the poverty of my own spirit and would venture to appear before thee. For His sake, do hear and accept my prayer.

My Beloved Boy,

Oct. 20. It is a trying and difficult task to address you as I do now with the impression that these pages may be read by you when I have been borne away from your sight to the grave. If such a trouble must cast its shadow over your young life, may he whose wisdom ordains it give you strength to bear.

I know to a child so devoted the last words of a dying mother would have almost the force of a revelation from God and, therefore, I tremble lest in my human frailty if I attempt to give counsel in your future life, I may unconsciously lead you astray.

I cannot do wrong in urging you to make the Bible the guide for your life, to study the precepts of Jesus Christ. You will be told that you must receive every precept of the Saviour with allowance, that any approach to a literal fulfillment of those sacred commands would completely destroy your success in life. Beware of such advice. Let not success in the world be your object. Remember that what the world calls success is, at best, but a doubtful good. It cannot bring happiness. It cannot give even peace.

Force yourself on the threshold of life to think. Ask yourself these great questions. From whence comes this mysterious double nature of body and spirit? Where will it go in a few short years when I, like [everyone], shall descend into the grave. Does my soul with its rich wealth of affections, its unsatisfied yearnings for good, end all its strugglings in the same grave where the body returns to death?

The young do not love these thoughts. It is easier and pleasanter to cast them behind you. They cast a shadow over the brilliant sunshine of your youthful life, but if you give them your attention, if you receive into your soul the conviction that you have an immortal nature, you will so model your life as to make the summer of your manhood rich and glorious, its decline honorable and blessed of God and man.

Oh! How gladly would I be to strengthen and console you when crisis approaches, when you leave the shelter of a loving home and go forth to the battle of life. Go forth into the world [armed], not with good habits alone, but with principles. Decide always in God's strength upon the rules of human action. You know not how great a thing I ask of you, how in this struggle for truth you will be assailed by foes without and by foes within, how the fiery passions of youth will urge you to rebellion. [It is my hope] you will see that the great business of life is to discipline the spirit—to save the soul.

"What shall it profit a man if he gains the whole world and lose his own soul or what shall a man give in exchange for his soul." If this belief in the undying nature of your spirit once becomes a practical belief, all that concerns this life solely will at once sink into its relative importance. You will not be unduly elevated by the applause or depressed by the censure of your fellow men. You will not be too anxious about worldly wealth because you will bear constantly in mind that as you entered the world so will you leave it, carrying nothing.

You will consider honesty [to have value] far above worldly gains, because you will know that poverty can only distress your body but that dishonor will forever stain your soul. For the same reasons, in your care to guard this immortal treasure you will beware of anger, hatred, malice and uncharitableness as fatal and deadly evils. This, my beloved child, is the great battle of life. In your own strength, all this would be impossible. Before you go forth to conflict you can furnish yourself with armor, helmet and breastplate, with the weapons of faith, hope and prayer from the treasury of God's love. Pray always at school, at play, in social joy, in the serious business of life. Let a prayer for strength, for guidance, for wisdom be constantly ascending on high.

Let all your aims and motives be great, let your ambition be of no mean personal nature, look beyond the applause of men to the approbation of God and your own conscience. Model your views of right and wrong not by the loose maxims of the world, but by the sublime precepts of Jesus Christ.

Study early and carefully your duties as the citizen of a great and influential republic. Let your vote be a solemn act of duty and remember that no man has a right to live unto himself. Preserve your health by temperance and regularity and cultivate your talents assiduously as duties that cannot be put aside without grievous sin.

Remember that you have no right to keep yourself aloof from active participation in the affairs of life either from a love of ease or from a sensitiveness that would shrink from observation. You are to bear cheerfully and manfully your share of its burdens according to your measure of talent and wealth. You are to put your strength to every great work of human benevolence. On every great agitating question of public duty you have no right to be neutral because the great work of human progress is God's work. Try to come to a decision on these subjects bringing to bear the whole strength of a disciplined intellect and measuring them by the great principles of right and wrong.

In a republic like ours, no boy can form a conjecture of his future position. You may chose the quiet and shaded walks of life and when you least expect or desire it, you may be called forth into a prominent and distinguished position. I am inclined to be of the opinion of General Taylor that no citizen has a right to seek or refuse civil honors.

It would be my wish to see you pass through life in the safer and happier course of a private citizen, but if you should be called to a higher sphere of action, remember that your very position reduces your power of consulting your own interests. You are the servant of the people. You are not to seek your own advantage or your own popularity but the greatest good of the greatest number. You are to watch and pray that you may be saved from the dangers of a selfish ambition. I honestly tell you, my dearest child, that I would rather see you to the grave in your youth than to see you live holding the world's honors while selfishly sacrificing the high interests of your fellow men in order to advance your own selfish views of aggrandizement.

One thing more, men of the world will tell you never receive an insult, if a man call you liar or scoundrel or say an insulting thing strike him in the face or knock him down. My dear child, I have had much experience of life.

I have seen the refinement of cities and the coarse roughness of frontier life and I firmly believe if you model your whole conduct on such principles as I have given you such undignified and disgraceful scenes can never occur. It scarcely ever happens to a man of elevated dignified character. A man who never stains his life with a falsehood, who bears about him the indescribable air of a man occupied with great thoughts is never called upon to assert his dignity. There is something so commanding about the whole aspect of such a man that no one ever dares to assail him with rudeness. Even if it should occur, the look of silent contempt with which such a man would regard such ruffianism, I am inclined to think would be more powerful that the ordinary and vulgar ways of resenting insults.

And now my darling child, I must bring this long letter to a close. My counsels are full of imperfections. This is not intended for your guidance now. You are too young to understand all of what I have written now but I hope it would comfort you to know that though my voice must be forever mute, I had left behind this memorial of my love.

It may be that God will grant your earnest wish [to] have a little sister or brother. One that you can call in truth "my own brother," or "my own sister." If this blessing is sent from Heaven, do not let it make you indifferent to our poor little Angy. Remember that by her father's poverty, she is forever divorced from the love of kindred and that in adopting her we promised not only a home, food and clothing, but the love of a father, a mother and a brother. Try to forget that she is not one of us and do not let her little nature droop for want of affection. In a mother's prayer you know not how much love is gathered. May God forever bless you, my beloved child.

Mother

My beloved Husband,

Oct. 21. I know that if it should be determined that my spirit must pass away in the approaching struggle it would be a consolation to find some memorial of my love, some last words of hope and consolation. As I have often told you I am oppressed with no presentiments of evil. I rejoice, for your sake especially, that a new bond of love may be given us; and I have no more reason than others to dread a fatal termination of this long desired event. Still I believe that, as she approaches them a second time, every woman who has suffered those mysterious agonies must feel that it is a struggle between life and death and must realize, more than at other moments, the uncertainty of her earthly existence.

With all my present infirmity, your love and kindness has made my life too sweet and pleasant to make me wish to die. I would live for my children, I would live to repay all your devotions in some slight measure, by my sympathy, my tenderness and love. It grieves me to think that if I must pass away, no one on earth can appreciate your noble nature as thirteen years of intimate communion has enabled me to do. No one like me can appreciate the almost womanly tenderness of your nature, its warm gushing benevolence and deep affections. Oh! how fervently I pray that if I may no longer be spared to give you a happy home, some gentle true-hearted woman may be found to supply my place. You have so little harshness of spirit to contend with this harsh world that you, more than other men, need the warm sympathies and consolation of home and if you should suffer a widowed heart, do not nourish your grief as something due to my memory. Time, the great consoler, will bring to you, as to all others, his healing power and when you find yourself looking on other women with interest and your mind becomes reconciled to the thought of forming a new home, do not reproach yourself with want of devotion to my memory, but remember that if in the spirit world it be possible to know what is passing on the Earth, it would add to my joy, even in Heaven, to know that you were no longer desolate, that your mourning had passed and that you were again responding to the sweet influences of love and joy.

You know I have always felt that the living should never be sacrificed to the dead. We are never left wholly desolate. If ties are broken, other ties still remain.

If my spirit should pass away, at the same moment the wail of a feeble infant, the appealing cry of our child, our newly given blessing, may arouse you from the bitter sorrow. Our gentle hearted boy will need all the fondness of parental love to keep his little heart from breaking, the little motherless child of your adoption will appeal to you for care and affection and you cannot give way to a selfish and solitary grief. For my sake, my own dearest Love, meet it with manly resignation, turn your thoughts away from the grave to my new spirit home. Do not let my death hang like a gloomy cloud over your life. You say that I have richly blessed your existence, do not let me have the bitterness of knowing that my loss would render you a perpetual mourner.

Seek, by travel, by change of scene, by intercourse with your fellow men and, above all, by prayer, to attain calmness and even cheerfulness. I know that, in your tenderness, our children would find an almost maternal care. I know that, for my sake and even for her own, you will continue to cherish and comfort my poor mother and I regard the possibility of leaving this world with not a single anxious care for those I love. My most anxious thought is for you, my dearest William. Oh! can it be possible that I shall be lying cold in the grave when you return to a desolate home from a conflict with a world that so often abuses your generous and confiding nature. God grant that I may be wrong, yet I cannot but feel that even if you find consolation in new ties, no one like me will know how to soothe your wounded heart, to restore your broken confidence and refresh your spirit for another day of vexation and conflict. Oh! How gladly, if it were possible beyond the grave, my love would encircle you with blessings.

One source of pure joy will be to watch you continue your wide sphere of usefulness. Continue to bless others and blessing will surely come to your own soul. Oh! With what fervency of affection, I pray God to bless you,

Your loving and affectionate,
Ella

Dear Mother[-in-law], Fort Brown, Texas

Oct. 29. I have the pleasure of informing you that we have a daughter, which was born on the 23rd instant. She was at once named Helen Blair Chapman after the most perfect woman and mother I ever knew. Both Helens are doing finely, and you need not have the least anxiety. The little girl is a perfect beauty, with very dark if not black eyes, high Blair forehead and unfortunately the *long* Chapman head. I send you a specimen of her dark brown hair. She is very good and only cries at meal times, and then without any reason, for she has an abundance of nourishment. I am sitting near Helen and she is the picture of contentment and happiness. She desires me to say that her confinement was short and painful, but attended with no such bad consequences as the first. Willie is perfectly delighted and has said a thousand times, "This is my little sister," "I am now not an only child," "Now I have someone to call me brother," etc., etc.

Angy hardly knows what to make of it, and asks if Willie will love her as much as he does little Helen. I will write you again next mail, which will be in two weeks.

Helen and Willie join me in much love to all.

Yours affectionately,
W. W. Chapman

My dear Helen, Westfield, Massachusetts

Nov. 16, 1851. I cannot describe the rejoicing that filled all our hearts when the Major's kind letter was opened and we knew that you were the loving mother of a living child and that the child is a daughter adds, if possible, to our pleasure. All your friends here expressed a great deal of pleasure at the event.

I rejoice on the Major's account even more than on yours. His large heart and strong affections ought to have objects very near to lavish them upon. Willie and Angy will love the little thing so well they will be contented to be put aside a little. I begin to think I shall love her as well as Willie, though I am in some doubt about it. I shall never probably have the care of her I have had of Willie.

I hope she will grow up like her mother. I can ask nothing better for her. If she inherits the beauty of her father's side of the house so much the better. To see Willie like his father and Helen like her mother would be the extent of my ambition.

With all your other writing, I will be contented with short notes merely to say how you are. How eventful has this year been for me, ties broken and new ones formed.

Mother

My dear Mother, Fort Brown, Texas

Nov. 18. I can write but a very few lines, but I [wanted] you to see my hand-writing again. I am doing very well but am still weak. Next week I shall go to the Brazos and the salt air, I doubt not, will restore my vigor. The baby is thriving, well formed without blemish or defect of any kind apparently. If it lives, my vocation is fixed for some time to come. Willie is delighted and happy and Angy, poor little thing, is happy in her ignorance that it may seriously interfere with her happiness. By the next mail, I hope I can write more. How thankful I ought to be for my mercies.

God bless you all
Helen

My dear Mother, Brazos Santiago, Texas

Nov. 30. We came down here three days since for the benefit of my health. I can give you a specimen of Texas traveling. Before we left home,

I had only rode out in the sunny part of the day, the baby had never been out of the house. It was just after a Norther and there was a strong south wind blowing.[16]* On arriving at a piece of water [Boca Chica] that forms the island of Brazos, we found it impossible to cross except by a small boat and we were between five and six miles from home.

Our family consisted of the Major and myself, three children and three servants. We were in two carriages and there was a covered wagon with baggage. The only alternative was to go over to the mouth of the river six miles and spend the night, or go across in the little boat leaving the carriages and wagons behind and getting home as we could on drays.

We decided on the last plan and remained at a little board hut while men were sent home [to Brazos Santiago] for the drays. The girls, stout Irish girls, determined to start with the baby on foot and walked the whole distance transporting our little treasure without harm or suffering.

It was dark when the drays returned to the crossing, bringing a bed and blankets for my protection and after nine in the evening when I arrived safely at the house. Notwithstanding all this exposure, I am better here than I was above.

The baby is called very pretty and I believe is a pretty child, with small delicate little features and a kind of symmetry about them rarely seen in young children. She is fretful, however, and I am as foolish with her as I was with Willie. Every cry goes through my heart.

The poor child was ushered into the world with roaring of cannon and the rattle of musketry. All that day of her birth, the battle was raging in Matamoras and war has come nearer to my sight than ever before. Some of the wounded have died of lockjaw or bleeding and in Brownsville, we see them limping or with their arms in slings. The end is not yet, and this frontier is no place for those who love peace and quietness.[17]

Mr [Buckingham] Smith, the old U.S. Secretary of Legation, whom I so often mentioned in my letters from Mexico has been here and remained with us two days.

16. During the norther on November 25 "all the small vessels in the harbor" at Brazos Santiago were damaged. The *Fanny*, en route to New Orleans, barely survived the storm, and the *Grampus* was dragged from its moorings (New Orleans *Daily Delta*, Dec. 6, 1851).

17. Carvajal ordered his troops to withdraw from Matamoras on October 30. Although there were several subsequent battles, the revolution faded (Lea, *The King Ranch*, I, 82, 86; New Orleans *Daily Delta*, Oct. 14, 1851, quoting the Brownsville *Rio Bravo*, and a later extract from the Brownsville *Rio Bravo* of Nov. 5, 1851, quoted in New Orleans *Daily Delta*, Nov. 19, 1851).

The Major and Willie send their love. Angy often asks which is the pleasantest place, Westfield or Heaven, and in her own mind is very much disposed to give Westfield the preference.

Dec. 26, 1851. Your letter of congratulations was received. With one foot on the rocker of the baby's crib, I am making the attempt to write a few lines. As for myself, I can scarcely realize that I am the living mother of a living child and though I had no presentiments of evil, I thought it possible there might not be sufficient energy in those organs to produce unassisted delivery. I feared it might be necessary to use instruments, my nervous energy has been so impaired, but, thanks to a merciful Providence, all has gone well.

Dr Jarvis was nominally in attendance but really during my labor and even at the moment of delivery no one was with me but Aunt Phyllis, an old mulatto woman who moved here from Hartford nearly twenty years ago and is not even a professed midwife though in this country she often officiates in that capacity. Dr Jarvis, supposing that nothing would take place for some time, was quietly waiting in his own room in the same building.

This child has commenced with being very exacting. I would, with delight, let her lie quietly on the bed, but she never gives me a chance. She seems to be perfectly healthy and yet there is a nervousness about her. Every evening she has a periodical fit of crying. She is improving, however, and I have great hopes that she will require less attention after she is three months old. She is fair, plump and has the same muscular strength Willie possessed.

As for myself I feel sometimes like "the old woman who lived in a shoe." Willie thinks no one but me can attend to his lessons. Angy must look at pictures and ask ten thousand questions and the baby must have her full share of attention. My cook was married last week, but I have made an arrangement even more to my satisfaction. Mary [Nugent] was a good worker but rather coarse and rough. Jane [Anderson] goes into the kitchen and I have Mrs [Eliza] Foley, a very respectable widow woman from New York to be nurse. She came out with Mrs Vielé, a young married lady, but was treated so rudely that she left her.[18] She lived several years with Mrs

18. Theresa Vielé viewed the departure of Eliza Foley differently: "The abigail I had taken with me received an offer of marriage while in Brownsville, which (being over thirty-five) she accepted with alacrity, preferring a permanent situation at the head of the establishment of a sentimental blacksmith, to one less certain" (Vielé, *Following the Drum,* 131).

and Dr Francis in New York and is an excellent seamstress, understands dressmaking and has a very gently kind manner with the children. From neither Jane or Mrs Foley will they learn anything bad or vulgar.

The Major and Willie are at Fort Brown. I shall stay here a month longer at least. My health has so much improved. I think from something he said last week that he will send you some money before long. I have been troubling myself considerably about a gravestone for Father. The Major's mother's expenses are great and he is not making any money at present. I do not like to mention it and yet it is something I do not like to see neglected.

Feb. 17, 1852. I intended by this mail to send you one of my old fashioned letters; but I have again delayed till the last minute. Yesterday immediately after dinner, I had a visit from the Poetess of the Rio Grande and she did not take her departure till this morning before dinner. She wrote to me begging for my influence to procure some favor for her husband and in my sympathy, I invited her to come and see me and have heard so much of "sympathy, communication of spirit, meeting at last a kindred soul," and all that canting nonsense that I have almost lost my pity and my patience. She is a little, homely, withered, spectacled old woman and sends forth her productions to the world over the romantic signature of *Cora Hargrave*. You will see at once from the enclosed that "Cora" or Mrs Bangs is a little deficient in common sense, and if I am low in the humor and can get time, I will tell you more of her sayings and doings.[19]

I am alone again. Willie having gone up to Brownsville with his father.

Jane, my treasure of a servant, returned by the last steamer and I shall now have more leisure. We have had a good deal of Mexican company lately, General Uraga and staff officers from the War Steamer, and Captain Makier, aid to General Arista.[20] Mexico is in a distracted condition and these gentlemen themselves say a crisis is rapidly approaching. The Regular [U.S.] Army here is too small to offer the slightest check to the

19. In a letter thanking the Chapmans for their hospitality, Caroline Bangs enclosed a poem which concludes, "The rain is o'er,—The sun peeps forth; / The rainbow spreads from pole to pole; / Thus tears by gratitude drawn forth, / Doth spread a rainbow over the soul." Caroline Bangs sought William Chapman's support for her husband, Samuel Bangs, for the position of lighthouse keeper at Point Isabel (Caroline H. Bangs to HBC, Feb. 14, 1852, CC). See Appendix A.

20. The Mexican army officers mentioned here were at the Brazos in response to the Merchants War. General Jose L. Uraga was in Matamoras on November 22 (New Orleans *Daily Delta*, Dec. 6, 1851).

sympathizing movements on this side of the river and altogether our situation is not a pleasant one.

I cannot tell you of my troubles while they are pushing upon me for I always say to myself, Mother has cares enough of her own, but when the storm has passed over I feel like telling them. I have no time to enter into particulars, but I can only say that I have been harassed to death by the unfortunate relations subsisting between the Major and Captain John Phelps, the son of the ex-senator from Vermont. Captain Phelps is a man in some respects of remarkable talents and with many excellent traits of heart, but he is also eccentric, visionary and strange.[21]

He has been very friendly until this winter but for the last three or four months, though professing the highest admiration and respect for me, he has really persecuted the Major and has made statements that would seriously affect his reputation. The Major has been half crazy and between my exertions to keep them from open quarrels and prevent a court-martial, I have suffered more mental anxiety than you can conceive. At last, he put a statement in writing that could be proved at once as a falsehood and dismiss him from the service. The Major was furious and insisted on a court-martial and I was in great distress for the suspicion long since awakened had grown to a certainty in my mind that he was the victim of a partial insanity. They were both New England men and my heart ached for the Captain and his family yet I could convince no one.

But all at once he seemed to awaken to a sense of what he had done, tore up every trace of his folly and seemed completely overwhelmed with misery at what he had done. The impression now is general that he is laboring under monomania, and with every one there remains a profound impression of pity. He has a noble intellectual forehead and though not so old as the Major, his face is ploughed with furrows. The Doctor ascribes his condition to *hard drinking*. Captain Phelps told the officers that he was a mere wreck in mind and body. You had better not let any one know of this for it might reach his father.

I have told you of poor Henry Whiting who drinks too much. Young Patrick Calhoun, the son of the great statesman, was here at the time my baby was born and is going fast on the same path of ruin. [Welles]'s career of privation and hardship in the far West has proved less fatal after all than

21. The nature of Phelps's dispute with Chapman is not known. Chapman, as quartermaster, answered to General Jesup rather than the post commander.

that of those who have been favored with all the prestige of rank, influence, wealth, and parental care.

Angy is fast learning her letters and is learning to sew very prettily. She is a very interesting child and I love her well enough to make her happy.

Yours affectionately
Helen

P.S. My sweet baby is growing and thriving. Her fretfulness has vanished and in my intense enjoyment of her babyhood, I forget all my cares.

Chapman recalled events of March 1852 in a letter to her mother dated August 16, 1853.

My dear Mother, Corpus Christi, Texas

I was riding with Dr Jarvis in his new carriage and on entering Santa Rita, a little Mexican village on the American side of the river, he asked if I would not like to stop and see an old American lady living there.[22] I said, "Yes," and he drew up before one of the huts or Hacales as they are termed. The village is composed of about twelve of these adobe huts, and a little Roman Catholic chapel of precisely the same construction, only surmounted by a rude cross. On an island [in the Rio Grande] near this little settlement are the remains of a gentleman's establishment, a large frame house, going to decay. The place had been owned by a Judge or General Stryker and, at the time of my visit, was still occupied by his widow who, after his decease, married a great, swaggering, drinking, do-nothing sort of Texan. The estate was embarrassed at the time of Stryker's death, the title disputed, and so the property all went to waste.

We rapped at the rough, heavy door of the hut and it was opened immediately by an aged woman, very poorly dressed, but remarkably neat. At the first sight, she struck me instantly as being wonderfully like our friend, Mrs Amos Fowler, the same keen, rather sharp, but handsome,

22. The "old American lady" was Martha Brennen. Santa Rita, the original county seat of Cameron County, was about six miles upriver from Brownsville. John Stryker received the original land grant from Mexico in 1834. When Martha Brennen's death was announced twenty-one years later, she was said to be the oldest resident on the Rio Grande *(Galveston Daily News*, Mar. 22, 1873).

features, full of the same kind of character, energetic, active but not meditative.[23] She addressed us with perfect ease and with a language and manner not often seen in old Texas settlers.

She invited us into the only room, which was exceedingly neat, but a very curious study to me. It had no floor, but the ground had been trodden to a smooth, uneven surface and it was carefully swept. In the corner stood a very tidy bed, and on a line with it, a very old, but once handsome, sofa, over it a shelf of books and in another place, I believe, there was a small mahogany table. There was also a Yucatan chair, mahogany with yellow leather bottom which she handed to me.

She was very cheerful, talked intelligently and even gracefully, made no apologies and seemed to feel no embarrassment whatever. The place was tolerable enough at that season of the year, but as I drew my feet up to the rungs of my chair, the cold earth chilly to me even then, I thought what a desolate, wretched, winter dwelling for a woman nearly seventy-three years of age who had unmistakably been accustomed to the comforts and even elegancies of life, no floor, no chimney, not even a mat for carpet.

The doctor is rather rough and, though a very just man, not very benevolent, but it seemed to strike him also that it was a very dreary place for such a woman and he said, "Why don't you get a chimney built here, Mrs Brennen. I don't think it would cost more than five dollars?

I think I never shall be able to describe in what a smiling, peaceful sort of way she said, "But Doctor, we don't very often see a gold piece in this part of the world."

She immediately changed the subject to something not personal, instead of going off into a lamentation about her sorrows, poverty and reverses as almost any other old woman would have done. She not only excited my sympathy, but she offered me a curious study and I determined to see and hear more of her.

On questioning old Aunt Phyllis who knows everybody, I learned that she [Martha Brennen] settled in Matamoras with her husband and three children more than twenty years ago. They made their way through Texas with trouble and difficulty, losing nearly everything they possessed on their journey.

They kept a boarding house in Matamoras for the best foreign residents and she was universally respected as an ambitious, energetic and

23. Mrs. Amos Fowler was a Westfield acquaintance.

very industrious woman. Her husband died first, then her son, in New Orleans of Yellow Fever, then the last and worst blow of all, both her daughters, one a young woman over twenty, the other a young girl of ten or twelve, died within twenty-four hours of each other in the first visitation of Cholera. In those days it was all terror and consternation in the presence of that terrible destroyer and she ran distractedly between the bedsides of the two sufferers, powerless to soothe or save.

For three years after that period, she was supposed to be deranged and it is said that she would go to the graves of her children at night and tear the earth with her hands to find her way to the coffins. She does not herself think that she lost her reason during that time, but told me, in our after acquaintance, that she was useless, despairing and wholly unsubmissive.

After this, she returned to the daily duties of life and for some time kept house for an American gentleman who afterward went to the City of Mexico, leaving her there in Matamoras a lonely woman to find another home. She established a little home for herself, but shortly after, General Stryker made her great promises if she would go and spend the rest of her days with his wife who was then near her confinement. He was considered very rich and she was persuaded against her better judgment. Very soon came the crash, General Stryker died, her old patrons in Matamoras were scattered all over the world perhaps, so she took refuge in one of those little uninhabited huts, too old to go about seeking employment and no one providing it for her. I asked Phyllis if she had ever done anything to alienate sympathy? No, her conduct had been blameless, she was only completely forgotten and in western life, if you disappear for a short time, that is your inevitable fate. I had lived within eight miles of her for three years and knew nothing of her existence.

At the time I made her acquaintance, she was sixty-eight, very much wrinkled and looking considerably older. She was, however, in remarkable health and capable of much labor. What could be done for her? I talked about her, but what to do. It is very hard to beg for her. In the first place, I had begged a great deal already and again, though I can write a begging letter, I blush and stammer and act as if I were doing a dishonorable rather than an honorable thing. Then too I felt her to be a person who should be aided in a very delicate way. Or if I were only rich, what exquisite enjoyment I could picture myself, not in supporting her in idleness, which would not gratify her, but in giving her opportunity to exercise her own energies.

The next time I went, I took Phyllis directing her to see Mrs Brennan alone, and try to discover her situation. As I suspected she was nearly destitute of clothing and though, perhaps not suffering actually from hunger, rarely tasting tea or living as civilized people are accustomed to live.[24]

Helen

24. Helen continued her interest in Martha Brennen's welfare. In January 1853, she sent a letter to President Millard Fillmore presenting a claim on behalf of Brennen for damages sustained to her cotton crop during the Mexican War. Although Senator Butler from South Carolina, Brennen's home state, presented a bill for relief to Congress, this effort was ultimately unsuccessful (WWC to HBC, Feb. 13, 1853, CC).

12.

AN END AND A BEGINNING

April through November 1852

More changes floated on the spring breeze for the Chapmans in 1852. By military standards William had been at Fort Brown well beyond the typical tour of duty. The military depot at Brazos Santiago was broken up, and many of his friends were moving to other assignments. Apparently William alternately considered resigning from the army and accepting a new post. In May he received word of his transfer to San Antonio. In a private letter, he requested a post on the seacoast, pleading that Helen's health required it.[1] When William took up his duties in Corpus Christi in June, the family remained in Point Isabel while he assessed the new location.

From her newly purchased cottage at Point Isabel, Helen Chapman was untouched by raiding Indians and Mexicans who struck near Brownsville in June. Nevertheless, a local newsman reported that enough "horrid accounts" abounded to fill a daily newspaper in the town.[2*]

Soon after William Chapman arrived in Corpus Christi, he could write, "My first impressions of the place are favorable."[3] His chamber-of-commerce boosterism never let up until Helen, nearly one-year-old Ella, Mrs. Foley, and Jane Anderson joined him in October. The Brownsville chapter of their lives had closed. Yet Helen found the change to be refreshing and was enchanted by the beauty of the new scenery.

1. WWC to Colonel D. D. Tompkins, May 29, 1852, CC.
2. New Orleans *Daily Delta*, June 22, 1852.
3. WWC to HBC, Aug. 9, 1852, below.

My dear Mother, Brazos Santiago, Texas

April 2, 1852. I came down here a week since. I am here alone with Mrs Foley and the baby. The baby is a sweet lovely little creature, blooming and healthy as possible. You will feel anxious I know about Willie and will fear that his health, morals and manners may suffer from these frequent separations, but they say he is very conscientious about doing in my absence everything that he would not in my presence.[4]

Jane is with him, a real Christian in thought and deed. His father attends to him personally a great deal and he has but one playmate, Colonel Nauman's son, a fine well bred boy.

The Major went out to the sheepfarm a fortnight or so since and seems delighted with his prospects in the wool business. He is full of hope too about the silver mine and altogether is in high spirits.[5] I still think the chances equal that it may give him a fortune or sink the little he now has.

Sometimes the Major talks of remaining here and resigning. His sheep business would nearly support him. I have made up my mind that it is my duty not to oppose him. Before ten years have passed the whole of the civilized world may be convulsed with war and his life is too valuable for the chances of a battlefield. Other men of far less usefulness in civil life could fill his place just as well.

Angy is well. She is one of the best children in the world and makes but very little trouble. Her father has another baby. Two in thirteen months!

I think if I had not three children I would try to get home this summer but I have not courage to move with so many. Love to all.

Helen

My dear Mother, Fort Brown, Texas

April 15. I have time but for a line before the mail closes. The Major is still up the river. The children are all well. I had company yesterday and have company again today at dinner. Dr and Mrs Prevost have returned. Mrs Prevost [is] very much Americanized in appearance and improved.

We [soon] lose Dr Jarvis who is ordered to San Antonio. He is in and out like one of the family, a man of sterling integrity, sound sense, and

4. This was probably not what Helen intended to say, but it may have been true.

5. William had invested in both these enterprises with Charles Stillman.

cultivated intellect. I rely on him not only as a physician but as a firm friend in emergencies and no one here can ever supply his place to me.

The baby is very well, very pretty in our eyes, and very playful.

April 28. The Major has gone up to the silver mine to be absent a month. He has high hopes but I am still faithless.

I am fortunate, however, in having such a nurse as Mrs Foley. The baby sleeps in her crib, the nurse in a little bed by her side. She goes to sleep regularly at eight in the evening and does not wake until two in the morning. She is then brought to me, nursed, and afterwards removed to her crib when she sleeps soundly till between four and five in the morning. For the last four months, we have not been up with her a single night. She is wonderfully healthy and never seems in the least affected by my turns of asthma.

Mrs Foley's matrimonial project is at an end (her love having gone to California.)[6]

I wish you would get some nice person in Westfield to make for me two very pretty white sun bonnets. I want them pretty enough for any occasion in Texas.

Love to Grandmamma and all.

My dearest Ella, Ringgold Barracks, Texas

May 4, 1852. I have been so long on the way that I thought a letter from me would not be unacceptable, more particularly as I have picked up a little news that will interest you. We arrived here this morning, having been nine days on the River. We leave tomorrow morning for Roma [Texas] and the next day for the mine.[7] I saw all the officers of the court[-martial] this morning and then went to Camargo, Mexico, where we dined with the commanding officer.

Dr [Ebenezer] Swift is married and has gone to his new post in the woods with his bride. While on his way, passing some post, the commanding officer of it ordered him to go back to some point and attend a soldier who had been wounded in a quarrel with another soldier. He refused to go.

6. This may be the Brownsville blacksmith whom Theresa Viele mentioned as the cause of Mrs. Foley's leaving her employment.

7. As well as may be determined, the silver mine was in the Mexican state of Nuevo Leon near a tributary of the Rio Salado which enters the Rio Grande between Laredo and Camargo (Graf, "Economic History of the Lower Rio Grande," 60).

The commanding officer then sent the wounded man to his own surgeon: the wounded man died in two days. Charges have been preferred against Dr Swift and General Smith says he shall be tried.

All the members of the court are here and Majors Paul, Garnett, Brewerton, and Doctors Campbell and Stiner are ordered to be tried.[8] Doctor Stiner for writing a disrespectful letter.

Mrs Mumford is still in San Antonio. Denman says that little Tommy is a beautiful boy. Mrs Doctor Brown has duplicate infants, one on each arm at the same time. What would you do in this fix, Ella? Tell Mrs Stillman that Don Carlos is prime.[9] I am as hearty as a buck, but if thinking of my angel wife and sweet children will make one grow thin, I shall lose some flesh before I return. A belief in the certainty of this fact might not make you as hopeful as the knowledge that you are constantly in my thoughts.

Love and kisses for Willie, Angy and Helen Blair.

Ever your affectionate,
William

My dear Captain,[10] Brazos Santiago, Texas

May 5. The Major says he promised for me that I would answer your letter by the next mail. I had some hesitation in writing again for it would seem like involving you in a correspondence for which very likely you have no time and where the advantage would all be on our side. In our banishment to this poor forlorn little corner of the Union, we certainly ought to be very modest in the matter of correspondence. As for me, for the greater part of the year I am actually forced to live on Brazos Island because I cannot breathe in peace at Fort Brown.

I have lived here sometimes for days and weeks in a profound solitude wandering on the sea beach and listening to that eternal surging of the waves. In this enforced solitude I have become I believe a wiser and, I trust, a better woman. The thought*less* gaiety of those old times we had at Buffalo

8. Majors Paul and Garnett were ordered by General Harney to capture Carvajal. Although they each approached Carvajal's camp, neither executed Harney's order and were charged with disobeying orders (New Orleans *Daily True Delta*, Mar. 5, 1852).

9. He is referring to Charles Stillman.

10. Captain William B. Blair, to whom this letter was addressed, was an old friend but not related to Helen Chapman. She had written them in November 1851 on the death of their child. The main purpose of this letter was to provide an introduction for Dr. Jarvis, who was being transferred to San Antonio, where the Blairs were stationed.

and Governor's Island is remembered as some enchanting dream and though I would not again, any more than you, wish to live over those days of careless enjoyment, I fear I am sometimes guilty of wishing to be not to quite so thoughtful as I am now.

My own lot is full of blessings and I cannot point to any overhanging cloud of sorrow. My brother has passed through that perilous time of life in which men are either wrecked forever or disciplined into usefulness. My father's later life was honored and peaceful and more than a year since he died serenely and without a struggle.

But for the last four or five years, I have seen altogether a new phase of life. I have witnessed the wildest, most disgusting dissolution. I have witnessed all around me violence, immoral recklessness, all the worst features of one of the very worst frontiers. Unoccupied by any private grief, the cry of human suffering is unceasingly sounding on my ear and the question is forever recurring, what can I do to make it less? But I sometimes look back with a sigh to those days when I could give myself up so unreservedly to the joy of the present moment.

But most certainly if I go on in this vein, I shall lose all chance of ever receiving another letter. You must allow me [the] excuse that I am completely alone with only my nurse and baby, the rest of the family being at Fort Brown. There is not a sound save the roaring of the wind and the dashing of the waves, not a sight to break the memory of the sea and sky.

The *Yacht* went to sea this morning and as [it] disappeared I looked around on an almost unbroken solitude. The Brazos is in effect broken up. The steamers sold, the workmen all discharged. It seems now to be good for nothing but as a breathing place for me and as ladies are now so perseveringly edging themselves into every profession, I think it would be well for the President to commission me and station me for life at Brazos Island.

In all our long residence here we have been the only stationary people. We have a very pleasant command at present but they are about breaking to return to their summer quarters at Pascagoula. I shall miss Mrs Nauman exceedingly. She is a most estimable woman and the intelligence and good behavior of their children reflects great credit both on her and the Colonel [George Nauman].

A ridiculous little miniature Mexican fleet is lying off the mouth of the river consisting of one steamer and two little schooners. For what purposes, nobody knows. Poor unfortunate Mexico. She is so threadbare, utterly unable to keep up a decent appearance among the nations of the earth that I think it would be better to give up the attempt. The revolutionists have so completely failed that it would seem that there is no chance of renewing the struggle but many think the end is not yet.[11]

The Comanche came down from Camp Ringgold yesterday and I understand General Harney is at our house in Fort Brown. Lieutenant and Mrs Vielé went out in the *Yacht* this morning. About a fortnight ago before leaving Camp Ringgold, they lost their child, a fine beautiful boy six months old.

There is so much consolation in the death of children that I have always felt I could be easily comforted in such affliction but now when my baby looks up into my face with its glad smile I feel what a heart-breaking thing it would be to have such a source of joy and gladness removed from my sight forever. I sympathize most deeply in your sorrow for I know it is greater to you than to most men, but I pity your poor wife far more. May God comfort her and save her from such sorrow again.

Dr Jarvis is ordered to San Antonio. He is one of the most delightful men in conversation I ever knew. He is always interesting, never wearisome and I really do not know what we shall do without him. The doctor talks much better than I can write. I shall leave it to him to tell you all the garrison news. Although very much disposed to sit down and cry over his departure, I am unselfish enough to congratulate you over the accession of a very pleasant member to your already large military society in San Antonio. He is one of the best conversationists (if there is such a word) that I ever knew. Other men talk as well perhaps but talking is a very different thing from conversing. He talks with you, not to you.

We have a dear little friend perhaps in your neighborhood, Mrs Mumford, a niece of Mrs Staniford. She is a very lovely woman and so good it seems strange why she should be so severely and sorely tried. She is one of those naturally gentle amiable characters who do not seem to need the discipline of suffering as those of a different stamp. I know that your wife is a gentle true-hearted woman. Mrs Mumford is very sensitive about kindness and notice of her, far worse than fatherless, boy and I know you would both be delighted to gratify her in a feeling so natural.

11. Carvajal had attacked unsuccessfully at Cerralvo in late 1851 and at Camargo in Feb. 1852. His efforts to recruit soldiers since that time had been ineffective (Ford, *Rip Ford's Texas*, 204).

I have resolutely restricted myself to one sheet so lest I might find my pen galloping off on a new sheet, I will say adios at once. Much love to Mrs Blair and a kiss for the little girl.

Helen Chapman

My dearest William, Fort Brown, Texas

May 18. I am sorry this mail carries you so much annoyance, however, I feared to delay [sending] it lest it might derange your plans.[12] I understand that Mrs Van Vliet and Mrs Dr Moore and sister and very possibly Captain Van Vliet had made some exertions to procure the station.[13] You must not feel embarrassed on my account and the children in any arrangement you find it necessary to make for we can easily take care of ourselves. I am doing nothing until I see you. I know not what I ought to do. I shall make all necessary traveling arrangements and when you come we can easily pack up or sell off as may be advisable.

Willie sends much love. The baby grows sweeter every day. She is very playful and when you once more hold the sweet little darling in your arms you will say that the Quartermaster's department "May go to the dickens."

I hope you will get down in time to see Dr Prevost. His wife is very much improved and really looks pretty. God bless you, my own dearest love prays ever,

Your affectionate,
Helen

My dear Mother, Point Isabel, Texas

June 4, 1851. I have no time to enter into details and can only tell you briefly our arrangements. The Major has been ordered to Corpus Christi a hundred [and sixty] miles up the coast and has decided to leave me at Point Isabel. He has bought me a nice little cottage with four rooms on the ground floor and two upper rooms, and a kitchen. I keep my horses and carriage, two women servants and a man servant. This seems to me woefully extravagant but the Major will have it so. He feels rich in anticipation of the mine.

12. William Chapman had perhaps heard of his reassignment by this time.

13. Captain Stewart Van Vliet had apparently made an effort to win assignment to Fort Brown. See WWC to HBC, July 5, 1852, below.

We delayed our arrangement until the *Yacht* arrived bringing your letter of May 22. If I had heard you were worse I should have gone to the North immediately but it was so encouraging that I have given up any idea of an effort for which I really feel at present unequal, setting aside all considerations of expense. Our present plan is to send Willie to you next month with Mr Jarvis.

The Major can visit me once in about two months. This place is directly on the coast and suits me even better than the Brazos.[14]

June 8. I have been over to look at our new house [at Point Isabel] and I like it very much. It can be made very pretty and convenient without much expense. The Major is very much attached to this country and I think it doubtful if we ever leave it [permanently]. So long as we can be in the neighborhood, he will not resign but if he should be ordered to any great distance that will probably be the result.

My attachment is altogether of a different kind. There could scarcely be found a spot less suited to my natural tastes. Flat, insipid, hot and, worse than all to me, a slave state! I have a great relish for the refinements and elegancies of life and yet I am really not only resigned but contented to spend my days here. I know I can be useful far more apparently [here] than in an older community and there is really an exquisite gratification in feeling that you are working with those whose labor it is to "make the wilderness bud and blossom as the rose."

Rough unsightly and unpromising as everything now seems, I love to look forward to a time long after I am in my grave when the bright fragrant flower of civilization shall everywhere meet the eye.

Love to Grandmamma and all. Willie sends love.

Helen

P.S. The Major insists on my writing how he has arranged my establishment. As soon as I get settled, I shall put it on a more economical footing.

June 30. I have been worried and harassed in various ways this summer, nursing the baby, [and] the overpowering lassitude of the summer climate.

This breaking up of the family saddens me. The Major will take charge of the [army] depot at Corpus Christi. I remain here and Willie goes north with Mr Jarvis the 14th of July. With God's blessing you will see them either

14. Chapman must have meant that the place was directly on the mainland instead of the coast. Padre Island acts as a barrier between the city and the Gulf.

the last week of July or the first week of August. It is a comfort to think that it will be better for him and I hope it will give you a new lease on life. He is a dear little fellow, not very learned, but loving, true hearted and intelligent.

Poor little Angy spends the summer and perhaps the next ten months at Mrs Fry's.[15] Mrs Fry is a *young* lady though like others quite an *old* married woman. She has no children and is very fond of Angy. The Major makes the arrangement on account of my health and I do not think it wise to object. When I get strength and resolution, I must write a long letter about the poor child.

I am inclined to agree that rest will do me good. The baby is as little trouble as a baby can be. Mrs Foley is an excellent nurse and takes the whole care of her nights. She sleeps in her crib and is brought to me only twice to be nursed. When the baby is weaned, I shall be very comfortable.

It scarcely seems as if she could be my child. She is a gay, bounding, happy little creature. The milk always seems to agree with her and to all appearance she could not be a healthier child. God be praised.

When Willie is fitted out for Westfield, the Major for Corpus Christi, the furniture unpacked and the house put in order, I hope I shall have more time to write.

The frontier is in a dreadful state and within five years there will either be war or a strong military force all along the river. No other lady than myself would dare travel alone with servants as I do and I begin to think myself it is almost too daring. If anything calls me up the river [to Brownsville] after the Major's departure, I shall take the public stage.

God Bless you all,
your loving,
Helen

My dearest Ella, Brownsville, Texas

July 5, 1852. Your letter was received this afternoon, while I was talking with Mr Monsaloatge. I told him all you desired me to say and what we would do for Angy. He said he did not know what to say about giving her

15. Frances Fry, age twenty-six, was born in South Carolina. Her husband, Budd H. Fry, originally from Virginia, was forty-seven. A former boat captain, he was serving as clerk of court in Brownsville in 1852 (United States Seventh Census [1850], Counties of Cameron, Starr and Webb, Texas, Schedule I, Free Inhabitants; Lea, *King Ranch,* I, 127).

to Mrs Fry. He would be willing that we should give her to any person away from Brownsville, but he was afraid it might not look well to give her to Mrs Fry while he remained here. I answered him by saying that, on the contrary, persons would praise him for providing so well for Angy, when it was known he was poor, had two other children, and the prospect of more. He did not seem to know who Mrs Fry was and I took him around to her house and introduced him. On leaving the house he asked me the occupation of Captain Fry. I told him to think over the matter and give me an answer tomorrow.

Captain Van Vliet will take some house temporarily and after the 20th of July take ours [at Fort Brown]. Captain Van Vliet wishes a nurse for their 11 weeks old child.

The roads were very bad yesterday and we were nine hours coming up to Brownsville. You had better not come up until Monday, and it will take until then for the roads to improve much, besides I want you to stay up here over Thursday. All the ladies are to [put on] a Fair on Thursday night for the purpose of raising $200.00 toward the support of the Methodist Mission. Mrs Fry is to be post mistress on the occasion. Can't you for the good of the church write some letters (poetic) as in days long gone by for particular characters to read, say Mr and Mrs Stillman, Mrs Fry, Henry Whiting, Judge Gurnised, Mr Patterson, Sam Jarvis, and Judge Bigelow.

Mr Hopkins is to be clerk at Fort Brown and Judge [Benjamin] Moses at Brazos. Mr Leach is to occupy our house at the Brazos. Mr Stillman goes out to the sheep ranch tomorrow with several gentlemen. The children and Mrs Foley are well.

I have had a very pleasant day and have called on four ladies. The ladies express great delight that you are to remain in the valley of the Rio Grande.

You cannot imagine how unhappy I am that my absence from Point Isabel deprived me of the pleasure of riding with Mrs Bangs, the charming Cora! Please communicate to her my sincere regrets in the most suitable terms and say to her with a very affectionate smile that happiness is yet in store for this poor mortal. We find so few friends in this cold and weary world of congenial tastes, feelings and separations, that we should seek their society as much as possible in our lives. Good Night Sweet Ella.

July 9. Mr Monsaloatge has just been here, and consents to give Angy to Mrs Fry. He says if his wife was not the very devil, (to use my expressive language), he would like to take her home, that he had rather part with his other two children than Angy, that his wife will not allow him to have a servant or even a little girl to assist in the house, that he has to do everything and that he leads a sorrowful life. I told him that he should be master at home, he said he could in any other country but this. There ought to be no law human or divine that forces such people to live together. I am ashamed of my complaining when I see such real actual trouble.

Ever your very devoted,
William

My dear Mother, Point Isabel, Texas

July 14. Willie is just on the point of departure and my courage almost fails me at the last. God give me faith and trust for I never needed it more. I think if he was going by land I should feel it less, but to see him going forth on the treacherous ocean is heartrending.

He is pretty well provided with clothes and I think will not be much trouble, but a great comfort. God knows he is so to me. The Major leaves in a few days for Corpus Christi. My head aches and my heart aches. Heaven bless you all, my dearest Mother. In great Haste,

Yours as ever,
Helen

Dr. Nathan S. Jarvis wrote from his new post at San Antonio on July 21, 1852.

Dear Major, San Antonio, Texas

I have never learned how you like your change [to the new post in Corpus Christi], but presume that you are pleased with it and in the present condition of things on the Rio Grande, I deem it in every respect preferable to a residence at Fort Brown. The last letter I received from there was Sam [Jarvis]'s dated the 14th of last month about the express sent by the citizens of Brownsville for military aid.[16*]

A party of Comanches that were here on a visit a short time since on their return robbed the inhabitants of Fredericksburg and they have even threatened to go to war. I should not be surprised if we have another Indian war. A fatal mistake or omission was made by our Government in the terms

16. This was mentioned in the New Orleans *Daily Delta*, June 22, 1852.

of annexation that no land was reserved for the Indians. The consequence is that the poor devils have not food or ground of their own although they are the rightful and original possessors of the soil. The Texans boldly run their lines and locate their headrights wherever they find them settled down and drive them from places where they were born and have spent their days. They are now driven to the barren and sterile region of country where nothing will grow and where not a particle of game of any description is found. They have fled to the lower country which will result in death if caught by our troops or the Texans. Starvation or death seems to be their lot and destiny.

Among the innumerable sins and abominations growing out of the Annexation of Texas, this may be considered one of the most flagrant violations of the rights of the poor Indians. I speak now of the Indians residing in what is called North State of Texas.[17] The Comanches, being a roving and predatory savage like the Bedouin Arab, has no fixed abode and cultivates neither corn or any other description of grain or vegetable. His hand is raised against every man and he becomes the enemy of all and consequently can expect mercy from none.

I see Mrs Mumford occasionally. She spoke to me the other day respecting Captain Mumford. I told her frankly what I had heard respecting his conduct and that she could hardly entertain a hope of him ever returning. She told me she had received a letter from him very unsatisfactory in its tone and character to what she fondly expected and that she had now abandoned nearly every hope for his return. I have heard since from someone that it is his intention to apply for a divorce. She has not said anything to me on the subject.

Among former citizens of Brownsville here are Rube Clements [who] goes by the sobriquet of "Whiskey Straight" from the fact of his always taking his favorite liquor undiluted or unpolluted with water. He had a report the other day that Brownsville had been taken and burned by the Mexicans. This story, like all other Texan stories, attracted no attention and consequently no belief. The "Father of lies" must have formerly made this country his favorite abode judging by the character of his children in that particular weakness residing in Texas. Lying, like Faithful's learning, comes by nature.

17. By mentioning the "North State of Texas," Jarvis was probably obliquely referring to Mexico as the "South State of Texas."

Give my kindest regards to Mrs Chapman and believe me truly and ever,

Yours,
N. S. Jarvis

[I hear] that you have bought a house and that Mrs Chapman will reside at Pt Isabel. How is this? Mrs Chapman cannot possibly prefer that place to Corpus Christi which is immeasurably superior to it in every respect as a residence.

N. S. J.

Helen Chapman wrote to Ebenezer Learned, who had contributed toward Ramon Monsaloatge's school, on August 5, 1852,[18] expressing her prescient view of the "dreary hate" existing between the former American and Mexican populations in the new state of Texas.

Dear Mr Learned, Point Isabel, Texas

I [write to] inform you that our residence is removed to another portion of the Texas coast and that for the present all hope of establishing a school for the Mexicans on the Rio Grande seems to be at an end.

I have by no means, however, abandoned the idea. I am more than ever persuaded that it is absolutely necessary to [educate Mexicans] for their new position in our republic.

It seems to me that this question of their [education] would be a proper subject for national legislation. Particularly from our treaty stipulations, they are entitled to all the rights of freemen. Unacquainted with our language, they come to the polls and give out their vote as utterly unconscious of what they are doing as if they were driven cattle. The scenes on election day are disgraceful beyond any power to describe. The laws of Texas as I understand [them] would greatly restrain the privilege of voting among Mexicans requiring as they do a long residence in the state. But where perjury is a crime of daily and hourly occurrence, it is evident that no check can be placed on their liberty, and, at any time, the meanest bribe of a glass of liquor can procure any number of votes.

18. See HBC to EWB, Oct. 7, 1851, above.

But [bribery or election fraud] is not the greatest evil to be feared. Aside from the great truth that they [Mexicans] actually belong to the human family and have a right to our aid by virtue of that, there are important social and political reasons for elevating them as quick as possible.

The old and deadly feud between Mexicans and Texans will exist so long as the imperfect civilization continues or so long as they can remain in the position of oppressor and oppressed. You can scarcely make an old Texan regard a Mexican as anything but a wild beast. He may be generous, just and true in all his relations with his own class and yet he will use Mexicans as beasts of burden without any thought of mercy.

Then too, the Mexicans, even in vices, are so unlike ourselves that there can be no natural sympathy. They are Asiatic in character, cunning, secret, cautious, stabbing in the dark, treacherous and in a new country like this where one is unprotected by any well organized police, they drive one to desperation by their petty system of crimes. This [Mexican] character is altogether at variance with that of the western settlers. [On the other hand, a Texan] may commit more crimes in one day than a poor Mexican will in a year, but he does it openly and unblushingly in the light of day. His great faults are almost always redeemed by some great virtue. [A Texan] considers cowardice and treachery the two most detestable vices of Mexican character and there is no hope of preserving peace between the two nations under such circumstances except by bringing both classes as much as possible under the humanizing and peace-making influences of Christian civilization.

In California, it is evident that the Chinese population are thus creating the same disturbing influence. They are a quiet, industrious sort of people. You can point to nothing very bad and you see no apparent reason for this deep seated hostility among the white settlers. The difficulty is in the race. The European races all seem to mix and harmonize easily with our own, but from the Chinese and Mexicans our own settlers stand aloof and regard them with distrust and aversion.

And especially in Texas added to these natural causes, there are men still living who were eye witnesses to those terrible massacres exceeding in savage vindictive hate and wanton destruction of life anything conceivable in modern warfare. Until the fearful scenes at San Jacinto, Goliad and the Alamo fade away into the dimness of legendary story, it is vain to hope that this dreary hate may be subdued between men who are now living side by side as citizens of a common republic.

Who can hope that with such elements the wisest efforts of statesmanship can long avert another war [with Mexico] followed by another absorption of territory burdened with a population so unfortunately incapable of assimilation. But the consciousness of your sympathy with my wishes has led me further than I intended and I have only time to state that I remain,

Truly yours,
Helen B. Chapman

My dearest William, Point Isabel, Texas

Aug. 8. According to promise, I am at the writing desk this afternoon. Things are going on very smoothly in the family and we do somehow manage to exist without you.

The day after you left, however, we were convinced by sad experience that a man is a very necessary part of an establishment. The Drayman was too busy to do anything but find the cow and that is no slight service for she makes almost daily visits to Mr Holly's. Governor Henderson did not make his appearance.[19] We wanted water and a dozen things we knew not how to get. I was inquiring of Mr Caldwell about the man Hartman mentioned when Henderson made his appearance.[20]

The blinds were all hung, the hooks put on, a shutter put in the store room and everything completed on Thursday.

The carpenters, I think, did pretty well at last and I am almost sorry we engaged Moore. They can barely pick up a living here and both are married men. Mooney, the carpenter who had delirium tremens, went north on the *Scull*. He seems completely sobered and very much frightened at his condition.

The trial of Peter's murderer comes off on Wednesday, it is said.[21]* They will attempt to show that Peter was himself a man of violence, stained with crime and a shedder of man's blood. I do not see how this can affect

19. This was John Henderson, a handyman employed by the Chapmans, who was nicknamed after the first state governor of Texas, James Pinckney Henderson.

20. H. N. Caldwell of Point Isabel worked for a steamship company.

21. The houseboy Peter, who had lived with the Chapmans for at least two years, was killed in early August 1852. According to the newspaper report, Peter "committed some indecencies" in the house of a man named Thibault. When he repeated his acts, Thibault pushed him, and Peter fell, breaking his neck (New Orleans *Daily Delta*, Aug. 31, 1852). Thibault was spelled Tebow in the 1850 census.

the question [of guilt or innocence], but it may very likely have its weight in a Texas court.

I told the carpenter about the railing [for Peter's grave] and they said they had one already, intended for Mr Heddricks, I think. The carpenters went to Captain King[22] and as I understand, he wishes them to delay for a few days and desired them to make a very cheap one as there would not be money sufficient for anything expensive, that there were debts, one a bread bill from the Brazos baker for twenty five dollars. I told the carpenter it was probably a liquor bill and the baker had no business to trust him to that amount. Poor Peter! I fear he will not have even a decent grave.

I hear nothing certain but from such rumors as do come down the river, I think Brownsville must be in a wretched condition and I am glad you are out of it. Henderson repeats a report that the life of McDonough, the carpenter, has been threatened, that a mob had collected around his house with such threats of violence that his wife had become so frightened she had gone to Matamoras. Their excitement against him has some connection with the market, he knows not how.[23] I understand they intend to contest the elections in Brownsville. The role of the county has, in reality, very much diminished whereas the number of votes given in on this election, I understand, was greater than ever before.[24]*

Very kind regards to Mr Patterson.[25] The Kings are very sorry at parting with him and I fancied Miss Irene blushed a little when she was telling *how very sorry Ma* was in parting with Mr Patterson.

Jane and Mrs Foley went to the bath house this morning, and the baby and I had a fine sleep together on the bed. She continues very well and is a great comfort. How sorry I am you must lose so many of her pretty ways.

22. This is Captain Thomas B. King of Point Isabel.

23. A building for a market in Brownsville was under construction at this time.

24. A Brownsville correspondent wrote that the ballot box, "accompanied by judges and clerks," traveled to voters up and down the Rio Grande for the August election. The river was so "confounded crooked" that they might have accidentally gotten some votes in Mexico, not being certain which side they were on (New Orleans *Daily Delta*, Sept. 8, 1852).

25. William S. Patterson was employed as a clerk in Chapman's office at a salary of $100 per month. He had achieved notoriety only once before when he was jailed in Matamoras in 1848 for a debt. The captain of the guard was ordered to take the prisoners, mostly military personnel, to police the city plaza. Patterson refused and was bound, gagged, and exposed to public display in the Plaza. The event became known as the "Bucking of Billy Patterson" (*American Flag*, Jan. 19, 1848). Samuel M. Jarvis was Chapman's other clerk.

The baby sends a kiss to Papa. The mother sends love and kisses without measure.

Your affectionate,
Helen

Willie Chapman gave his mother the news of his trip on August 8, 1852.

My dear Mother, Westfield, Massachusetts

We arrived in New York on the 30th of July. Mr Jarvis went to his brother's office and I went with him. There was no room in the Hotels so we stayed at his brother's house. I was some seasick. We got to New York on Friday and left it on Monday in the morning. I arrived at Westfield at 3 o'clock. Aunt Betsey when she came to the door knew me. I went blackberrying the day after I got home with Uncle Charles. We got the pail nearly full. I have been whootle berrying too. Fanny Pelletreau got here one or two days after I came. I am well. How is Jane and Mrs Foley. Kisses to the baby.

Willie

A letter from Emily Blair accompanied Willie's.

My dear Helen,

Willie is the same dear little creature as ever, perfectly well and contented.

He tries to say Grandma, but Aunt Emma slips out every time. Dear little creature, the very first thing he did after he came in and kissed me was to ask, "Where is Grandmama."[26] He looked very much shocked when I told him she was dead, was just ready to cry out when the boys came rushing up to see him and directed him from it. We [planned] to put him in her chambers to sleep the first night with no thought of his feeling bad, but he

26. See Chapter 4, n.18. Ann Ellsworth Welles, Willie's great-grandmother, died on July 17, 1852. Helen Chapman received details of her last illness and funeral arrangements. The funeral cost a total of $17.00 (Elizabeth Welles Pelletreau to HBC, July 20, 1852, CC).

inquired if his grandmama had died upon that bed. He said the chamber seemed so lonesome and he thought of his grandmama dying.

Toward [bedtime], he proposed sleeping in the north bedroom. The bed was very small but he got in and did very well. I told him we would bring the sofa out and he might lie in the dining room but no, he should feel just as bad if someone had died on it. The next day I put up a wide bedstead in the north bedroom, and he seems very well contented [there]. The school begins in about a fortnight and I have no doubt he will do well. He eats with good appetite and never gets tired of berries and milk. I wish most earnestly to do him good and keep him in a good way.

The other day, I forget what gave occasion for it, I said, "You must be moderate in it, Willie. You know moderation in everything marks a gentleman."

"I did not know it," said he, "but, I'll learn it." He either has a wonderful instinct of propriety or you drilled him not to talk of home and you folks.

Mother

My dearest Ella, Corpus Christi, Texas

Aug. 9. The first mail for Point Isabel does not leave here until Thursday but I have just heard that a Mexican will leave here for Brazos via Padre Island today.

We left the Brazos at 4 o'clock on the 4th and arrived at the Corpus Christi bar at 11 o'clock the next morning. A lighter came along side [the ship] and took us inside the bar to St. Joseph's Island where we remained all night. The next day we came to this place 30 miles from St. Joseph's Island.

Fred and Dick are well.[27] Fred will leave here today for the Brazos via New Orleans. There are two good schools here and I shall send Dick to one of them as I have nothing for him to do except for a short time in the morning. I took him with me to Sunday School, which consists of about 40 scholars. Afterwards we went to church, the first preaching they have ever had in Corpus Christi.

27. See Chapter 10, n.43. Fred could not find work at Point Isabel and went with William Chapman to Corpus Christi, but could not find any employment. Subsequently Fred left Dick with William Chapman and went to New Orleans, where he found work on a Gulf steamer (HBC to Willie, Sept. 7, 1852, below).

We board at the Capital Hotel. I pay $25 for myself and $10 for Master Dick. We have two rooms in the second story of a stone building for our office. I sleep in one and Mr Patterson in the other. There is plenty of breeze.

The site of Corpus Christi is really beautiful, and there are some pretty residences here, the prettiest one with dormer windows and which was occupied by Colonel Abercrombie. I have the refusal of it at any time at a rent which will be covered by my commutation. It has a nice yard in front walled with shrubbery and a large garden in the rear. It is on the ridge about as far from the water as [our] cottage is at Point Isabel and overlooks a beautiful bay 20 miles across. The place is very healthy and the drives and back country beautiful. My first impressions of the place are favorable. I have already entered upon my duties and think they will be agreeable.

Ever your affectionate,
William

My dear darling child, Point Isabel, Texas

Aug. 11. The *Yacht* goes this evening and though I have delayed writing until nearly the last hour, I will try to give you some idea of home [at Point Isabel]. There is an outside appearance of order in the house, though there is yet a great deal to be done. I hope in a month's time we shall be quietly settled.

A gloomy place it would indeed be but for our sweet little baby, our darling little Helen. I think she is losing her beauty somewhat and is growing stouter and more robust. Her two little teeth stand out very conspicuously between her laughing little ruby lips and she understands their uses perfectly as your face would testify if you were here. Aunty Foley and Mother get the full benefit of their sharp little points. She is very stupid about creeping, but shows great inclination to walk and stand. If we put her on the floor and she can find anything to hold by, she is on her feet at once. She can take the combs out of my hair and then uses them in hammering my face without mercy.

Your father left on the *Major Barbour* just a week since. There was a very strong southerly wind blowing and they expected to go over the bar in twelve or at most twenty hours. [Governor] Henderson is with me and is altogether the best man I could have had staying here. Peter had got drinking quite badly and I could not bear to be left in such a lonely lawless place with a man who is not steady.[28] Poor Henderson is not very smart but he is faithful and always at home. He amuses himself every evening with his fiddle. Henderson is rubbing up some of the furniture today.

Dick went off with your father and if he does not do well on land he is to be sent off to sea. Poor Boy! He has not behaved well of late and it seems impossible for us to effect any reformation. But all things are possible with God and therefore, my darling child, we can pray with hope and faith that he will renew his heart and put a right spirit within him.

Jane sends a great deal of love and wishes me to tell you that she shall try to hold out in Texas until the next spring so as to go North and see you. They, none of them, ever speak of you without saying "Poor little Willie" and until you went away I believe they did not realize how much they loved you.

You would have been very solitary had you stayed here. There is no amusement of any kind here. I need not tell you, my darling child, that I miss you every day and every hour. Still if I can but feel that it is for your happiness and your good, it will not be a painful separation. If I were staying here for my own ease and comfort, I should feel differently about this separation from your father, but I do it in compliance with his wishes and for reasons that he considers important. So I am content. May God bless and keep you, my own darling.

Your loving,
Mother

My dearest Ella, Corpus Christi, Texas

Aug. 12. Yesterday I called on Mrs Captain Britton, Mrs Colonel Kinney, Mrs Ohler and Mrs Major Browder, all very pretty and intelligent ladies, a little better than anything at Point Isabel.[29] This evening I am to call on Mrs. Mann, said to be a very pleasant lady. There are two day schools and a Sunday school in the place but no church. A fine chance to establish an Episcopal one and perhaps Mrs Chapman will have that honor yet.

28. The existing letters do not indicate that Helen ever mentioned Peter's murder to Willie.

29. See Appendix A for H. L. Kinney and Forbes Britton. Ohler was an early land speculator in Corpus Christi. He and his family soon moved to Indianola.

Corpus Christi is far more desirable than the Rio Grande, and if I had no [business] interests there, I would turn my back on it forever. Don't say so, I shall make no investments here for I have no means at present, being close reefed in money matters. Several officers have made investments here and others intend doing so. The air is charming.

Fred left for New Orleans the day before yesterday. His son Dick had a good crying spell and I gave him my fish line and after catching a larger fish than he ever caught before, he seemed quite reconciled and contented. I do not know whether he is more fond of horses or the sea.

Kisses to little Ella and kind regards to the girls.

Aug. 14. I continue to like Corpus Christi very well and it is perhaps as good as any post that I could get with my present rank. Doctor Jarvis [writes and] expresses surprise that I have purchased a house and located you at Point Isabel and says that "Corpus Christi is immeasurably superior in ever respect."

Bob Granger from Llano, Texas [writes], "I hear you have been ordered to Corpus, a pleasant change I should think from the Brazos or Brownsville. I prefer it to all Southern stations. It is certainly the most beautiful spot on the Gulf coast or near it that I have seen, healthy too, and offering everything good that comes out of the sea. We in the 'mountains' envy you greatly. We hold, however, that you would be better pleased with our society which we flatter ourselves is 'dem fine.'"

We now have here Colonel and Mrs Bainbridge, Captains King, Caldwell and Carpenter, Miss Carpenter, Lieutenant and Mrs Johnson, Dr Anderson and Lieutenants Reynolds and Underwood. Denman and wife and Holabird and wife will be here in four or five days and Mother and Mrs Granger about the first of October.

We are building of stone and will have up buildings that will shelter us during winter by the 1st of October and hope to have the officer's quarters completed by the first of March.

Corpus Christi is a drier climate that the Brazos and if I were satisfied that the Northers were not more severe I should regret exceedingly that I did not bring you. All money considerations or interests sink into insignificance in comparison to the deprivation of your *Heavenly* society. Oh, Ella! I do think you are the purest, most angelic, the most perfect being I ever knew or heard of. If I can only be with you and our darling pure boy and sweet little Ella it is, at times, all I desire.

Kisses to the baby and kind regards to Jane and Mrs Foley. Who have you got for a man servant? If you are hard pushed, Peter Rouche has kindly offered to lend a hand.[30]

William

My dearest William, Point Isabel, Texas

Sunday, Aug. 15. Your unexpected letter of August 9 delighted us exceedingly, because you were so evidently pleased with your new duties. It was handed to me in Mrs Hill's dining room, at the close of a religious service held for the first time by Mr Passmore.[31] He came down on Wednesday morning and remained until Friday afternoon. He seemed very much pleased with his visit. He visited all the families here [at Point Isabel] and was very pleasantly received. Mr Passmore says the baby is the prettiest he has seen in Texas, rather a dangerous speech for a clergyman.

Friday morning, shortly before dinner, a strange gentleman called, and introduced himself as Major Garnett from Camp Ringgold. I happened to be in the parlor with Mr Passmore, and we had quite a long agreeable conversation. I invited him to dine with us, but he declined on account of his health, the recovery of which is his object in coming to Point Isabel. He seemed to regret very much that you had left. He is very much of a gentleman and I should be very happy to do anything for his comforts. Major Garnett thinks Corpus Christi the best port in Texas and says he would be willing to be stationed there the rest of his life.

You have replied to Mrs Mumford that we do not require Mrs Staniford's servants.[32]

30. Peter Rouche, originally from Mexico, was a forty-seven-year-old laborer who worked for the army in Brownsville (United States Seventh Census [1850], Counties of Cameron, Starr, and Webb, Texas, Population Schedules).

31. Reverend William Passmore organized the Episcopal Church of the Advent in Brownsville in April 1851 and raised funds for its building. William Chapman was one of nine vestrymen. Passmore had twenty-one calls from churches in eight different dioceses from Pennsylvania to Texas. The church building was completed in 1854 and stood on the corner of Washington and tenth streets in Brownsville (W. H. Chatfield, *The Twin Cities of the Border* [New Orleans: E. P. Brandao, 1893], 8, 9).

32. Jennie Mumford had written to offer the Chapmans the use of several of her aunt Jane Staniford's personal slaves during the time they were planning to travel to the North (Jennie Mumford to WWC, July 28, 1852, CC).

I have been so troubled about water that though very reluctant to incur additional expense, I concluded to get a well of my own. I can get a well made for ten dollars and a barrel with a rope for five dollars. The drayman would not hold to the bargain made with you, but insisted on charging 50 cents for every load of water, carrying only three barrels at a time. If Judge Moses sends a barrel of water from the Brazos, I have to pay twenty-five cents for getting it from the wharf. You are so desirous that the grass shall not suffer that I thought it would cost more in the end to pay so much drayage than to have one of my own. Henderson himself proposes drawing it on horseback *a la Mexico*.

We are still about the everlasting business of "putting to rights" and brushing up old furniture. The new blinds are a great improvement. I busy myself through the day and in the evening either ride or walk, often the last.

The baby is constantly trying to stand on her feet and needs watching more than ever. Jane sends love to Dick, though in no very great excess, I fancy. [Jane and Mrs Foley] both thought it would have been better than any comedy to see the expression of his face when he was following you about to the Church and Sunday school.

Helen

My dearest Ella, Corpus Christi, Texas

Aug. 19. Your first letter of August 8th was received the day before yesterday and I was glad to hear that you were getting on so well at home without me and that the governor had been inaugurated.[33]

I would tell Captain King to pay no bread bills as Mr Patterson says Peter could not have had any. I have the baker's receipts in the bread book for all I ever got and just before I left I made a final settlement and got his receipt. Mr Patterson says that Peter cannot owe possibly more than $40. Captain King found $143 on Peter.

Let the carpenters put up a nice railing on the house and I will pay any balance if Captain King has not enough money.

Dick tried to plead off from going to school but I took him there and now he goes regularly. The mail closes at 10 o'clock. Love to little Ella,

William

33. This is a humorous reference to John Henderson, the handyman.

My dear sweet boy, Point Isabel, Texas

Aug. 23. The *Yacht* came in yesterday bringing the news of your safe arrival. I am sorry you could not have seen poor dear Grandmamma once more in this world, but she has gone where there is no more pain and no more sorrow.

I would like to hear something of your first impressions. Did Westfield seem as pleasant as you expected? Did the old elms look as large and green and the old house as pleasant as your memory and fancy had pictured them? Did the blackberry field excite any such burst of enthusiasm as when a "wee toddlin" thing, you cried out "The berries, the berries!" or did you survey it with the moderation Aunt Emmy preaches.

Your father is delighted with Corpus Christi and may possibly wish us to go there this winter. He misses the baby very much and on his own account I regret that he has made this arrangement.

Fred could do nothing in Corpus Christi. The lighting business is overdone. We are looking for him here any day from New Orleans. Jane is rather low spirited. It is lonely here for her and she misses you very much. In the evenings, she and Mrs Foley sit in the little dining room behind the green screen and often their whole talk is of you, your sayings and doings.

Dick is doing very well so far with the Major. Peter Rouche is here and is going over to Corpus Christi day after tomorrow. The Point Isabel Light House is finished, but will not be in operation for two months. Mrs Foley, Jane and Henderson send love.

Mother

My dearest William, Point Isabel, Texas

Aug. 25. The mosquitoes are almost beyond endurance and here at the writing desk with all the doors and windows open, I am nearly distracted with them.

I hear that Mr and Mrs Fry are going away and that Mrs Fry was going to give up the charge of Angy. I do not know if the information is correct, but I think it very possible. If this be so I shall regret it on your account, much more than my own. I dislike to see you additionally burdened while you have so much upon your hands. But on the other hand, I almost feel the need of a child in the house. The baby is perfectly delighted when any little folks come in and it is very awkward for Mrs Foley and I to be following her in her perpetual motions. If Angy does return, she may be a source of great blessing to us.[34]

Your Affectionate,
Helen

My dearest Ella, Corpus Christi, Texas

Aug. 26. I went to church the next day after I got here, a perfect stranger to all and was taken for a new Methodist minister. Yet they could not exactly reconcile the "Handsome and gracefully trimmed moustache and whiskers" with my evident calling.

Mr Stillman does not object to my selling some of my mine stock and I have offered Captain Jarvis one fourth of my interest on the same terms that Colonel Reynolds will sell for.[35] Colonel Reynolds asks $10,000 for the same amount and sold some in Monterey at that rate. I hope I shall get the same.

Mr Stillman will go up to the mine with Captain Jarvis about the 15th of October and will probably remain two months. He is greatly encouraged about the mine. But he is so completely disgusted and annoyed about the election [in Brownsville] and the conduct since that party that he has concluded to close his business in Brownsville, and has offered his store for one half of what it cost him. His "Boys" will probably carry on his business and he will aid them. All the last lot of pistols are sold and more ordered.[36]

I have also written to Mrs Mumford, saying that we did not need the servants. I hope she will come here to live.

Mr Patterson does not like Corpus Christi as well as I do, but he says he likes it well enough. I really begin to think that he has left his heart at Point Isabel. Mr Patterson [said] the other day that he believed he would get married and have a little ranch. He has been very sober and quiet ever since he came here.

Well, Dick has voluntarily turned farmer and has commenced today on a beautiful farm 18 miles from Corpus Christi on the Nueces River. Colonel

34. At this point Angy had been living with Mrs. Fry for at least two months, perhaps longer, possibly in anticipation of a reassignment to a new station (HBC to EWB, June 30, 1852).

35. See Chapter 10, n.3. This is a reference to the capital stock of the Santa Rita Silver Mining Company, which owned the Jesus Maria Vallechille silver mine.

36. Charles Stillman and William Chapman bought revolvers from Samuel Colt and imported them in large quantities into South Texas (Charles Stillman to WWC, July 20, 1859, CC).

Parkerson, an excellent, kind-hearted, cultivated and very refined gentleman came down from his place and stopped at the same hotel where I board. He happened to hear me say one day that I wished Dick would take a notion to farming. This morning he saw Dick and got Dick to say he would see about it. Mr Patterson and I advised Dick to accept the offer of Colonel Parkerson which was that he would clothe him well, teach him to read and write, treat him kindly, make him a farmer, and when he was 21 years of age to give him a good farm of 100 acres, and 10 cows and calves. Dick made only one condition which was that he should not be bound. Colonel Parkerson did not desire it and said if he could not keep him by kindness he did not wish him to stay. So Dick packed up the old green box with the rusty padlock and started with the Colonel for his new home at 2 o'clock today. He has behaved perfectly well (except one little fib) since he came here, and I really felt sorry to part with him. I gave him some fish lines and hooks, a powder horn, some steel pens, a lot of paper and some pocket money, and a black hat and he bid Mr Patterson and myself good-bye in a very graceful and feeling manner. I also gave him a handsome riding whip after I heard the Colonel had purchased a saddle for him.

Well now, Dear Ella, what do you think about coming to Corpus Christi? The reasons which I gave for your remaining at Point Isabel do not appear quite so strong now. I think that this is a drier climate than the Brazos and perhaps would suit you as well. I am offered a pretty cottage on the hill. Or we can have rooms near the water. It is a very quiet place with no dust and scarcely any Mexicans. The gentleman who owns our cottage has expended $500 for the shrubbery in the front yard. He has 40 sweet orange trees (small). I think that Mr Caldwell would take the house [at Point Isabel]. If you wish to come, these strong arms will be ready to receive you.

I shall endeavor to come to Point Isabel about the 1st of November. Regards to the household and kisses for the baby.

William

| Willie Chapman also heard from his father.

My dear Willie, Corpus Christi, Texas

Aug. 29. I enclose two letters from Mrs Bangs, the Poetess of the Valley of the Rio Grande whom you know. I send them, thinking that they will make "Aunt Emma" laugh hard. Mother has one more addressed to me from the same lady, still more high flown, or high *flung*. When you write to Mother request her to send it to Aunt Emma.

I like Corpus Christi very much: it is a beautiful city at the head of a bay 20 miles across. It is much prettier than Brownsville and has several neat cottages. We have a fine sea breeze here all the time. There is fine hunting and fishing, but I have been too busy to indulge in either yet. When I kill my first deer here I will tell you.[37]

I think of you very, very often. Your little dingy is anchored in front of my office window and the office is not more than 20 yards from the water. I have named your dingy "Anna Smith" and hereafter she will be known by no other name. I hope Miss Anna is as graceful and beautiful as her namesake, eh? Billy.[38]

Mother is well. Mr Passmore preached in Mrs Hill's dining room one day last week and he stayed at our house while he remained at Point Isabel. Would you not like to see "Blair Cottage" and its sweet inmates. I know of somebody else who would, guess? Mother says that little Ella has become more upright in her conduct. That is, she tries to stand up on her little feet, and falls down now and then.

Henderson has got a barrel with a rope hooked up to it and draws water for Mother with old Tom like the Mexicans.[39] The drayman promised me to draw three barrels of water on the dray for 25 cents, but after I left, he increased his price on Mother to 50 cents and, as the old lady can't bear impositions, and wished to be independent of "Mr Dick," the drayman, she got a new barrel for $5 and had a well dug for $10 more and put the Governor to work on her own hook. Great Woman that, is she not, Billy?

My dearest William, Point Isabel, Texas

Aug. 30. Mr Monsaloatge, to use your own very expressive phraseology, has been playing the devil generally about Angy. He came down on Saturday and handed me a letter in English of eight pages. The request contained in it was that I would write to Mrs Fry requesting her to give up Angy to him. The reason assigned was that I could no longer [have] her

37. WWC to WBC, Aug. 22, 1852, CC.
38. The identity of Anna Smith is not known. WWC to WBC, Aug. 22, 1852, CC.
39. Old Tom was a horse.

because in all my acts I was now governed by Miss Helen Chapman or words to that effect.

The tone of the letter was by no means pleasing but I read it through in his presence and, after folding it up, I said very calmly, without any feeling and with a manner that seemed to say I desired no conversation on the subject, that I would write immediately to Mrs Fry and would answer him also by letter. He rose immediately and, with the ordinary salutation, left. I did not see him again. Mr Passmore was at Point Isabel at the time and to him I wrote immediately, resigning all control over the poor child. Today, I mailed a letter to Mr Monsaloatge and, to prevent all misconstruction, I sent a copy to Mr Passmore having first read to him Mr Monsaloatge's letter. I have requested Mr Monsaloatge to address you in case he wishes to hold any further correspondence. I will send copies of his and my letters. He has been annoying Mrs Fry a good deal of late and if he writes to you, you had better not answer it until you receive these copies.[40]

Mr Caldwell goes up in the morning and I send this by him. I have just written a note to Mr Hillman [of the Santa Rita Mining Company]. We are getting on famously in the way of correspondence. My notes are half business and half friendly. From his replies, I judge he likes them very well and it is amusing to see him try to throw off his formality. He unbends before he gets to the end of a note, but so far it has been "Dear Sir," on my part, and "Madam," on his. He wrote quite a long account of the report from the silver mine which was just about as intelligible to me as so much Hebrew text would have been.

I am going to take a little ride and must close my letter. Kind regards to Mr Patterson. Goodnight and God bless you,

Helen

My dearest Ella, Corpus Christi, Texas

Sept. 2. Your letter of August 22 by mail was received yesterday.

If Mrs Fry has the least wish to give up Angy, I do not know that I shall regret it. Willie is away and she will be company for us. The expense never had much weight with me. It was the fear that your feeble health and the necessity of more perfect quiet would forbid it. If she is a good child, (and

40. Thus Angy returned to her father. Early the following year, the Monsaloatges left Brownsville, and Helen lamented, "I have lost sight of the dear child, forever perhaps" (HBC to EWB, Apr. 3, 1853, CC).

you can make anyone good but your husband), it will be an advantage to our darling to have her grow up with a child like Angy, stationed at out-of-the-way posts as we may be. Do not discourage her from coming back to us. From the circumstances under which we took her, if we do our duty by her, I feel that it will be attended with a blessing.

General [Persifor] Smith who is on leave in New Orleans is coming here tomorrow to see if he likes Corpus Christi with a view of bringing Mrs Smith here and perhaps changing his headquarters from San Antonio. Would it not be fine to have old Jarvis and Blair with us again. If Corpus Christi should agree with your health, you will like it far better than Point Isabel or Brownsville.

The site is really beautiful. The main town is on a bluff near the water and then comes a hill 150 feet high on the top of which and overlooking the bay and lower town are the fashionable cottages. Corpus Christi will gradually increase as the farming country in back of it fills up. People of means live in town and have farms in the country. Point Isabel can never be any larger.

In regard to your coming here, if you prefer to come here, I can find you a good house. The main reason for your remaining [in Point Isabel] is your own comfort, quiet retirement and happiness. Mr Stillman's decision to give up his business in Brownsville makes the [other] reasons which considerably influenced me to leave you [there] less strong. In fact, they are now of very little weight.

I shall, if possible, visit you about the time the *Major Barbour* will be at the Brazos, say about the middle of October. If you think of coming, Mr Caldwell will have the first refusal of the house.

Mrs Hatch, (a very sweet woman), and her baby are boarding in town while her husband is scouting towards the Rio Grande. Mrs Elliott with two children and five servants is keeping house. She is a spoiled child. I take them both to ride occasionally in the ambulance. The one is a devoted mother and the other don't care shucks for her babies.

You asked me how I liked the gentlemen and that I had said nothing about them. Well now, Ella, the less said about them to such a perfect being as you the better. They are not to my taste. Most of them live to eat, drink and make money, not to think or to think rightly. I have never taken "a drink" with any of them yet and never offered them anything, even wine, in my house. My temperance rather astonished them at first evidently, but now they seem to understand me. Lieutenant Field, who is still here is a fine young officer and he and Mr Patterson are about all my society, at least during the evenings. Gentlemen call at the office during the day, but before they leave I find that they wish to sell or borrow something.

On many accounts I love the Rio Grande still. There are two old men in this place who are good Methodists but they are persons of no refinement.

There are some good women here. Mrs Mann, I like very much. Mrs Kinney is fashionable. Mrs Browder is a fine woman, but having been here only two months has not yet become reconciled to leaving her family near the "Yazoo." Mrs Butler is good with 3 well behaved children. Mrs Dr Maloney, I have not yet seen. Mrs Ohler is like Mrs Falco [of Brownsville], but not so prudent. Mrs Dix, a good woman; her daughter, excellent, they say. I have not yet made their acquaintance. She looks as good as Aunt Betsey and is something like her. Widow Kinney, good. Mrs Captain Britton, good. Mrs Stewart, jealous of her husband. Widow Swift, good, I believe.

Our cottage has a garden attached and affords plenty of vegetables in the fall and winter and in the spring if there is any rain. There has been but little rain this season until I came here. Since then we have had three showers and the last two days, it has rained pretty hard.

There is a pretty drive along the beach of three miles to the reef. There are also pretty drives up the Nueces river. General Harney has purchased 10,000 acres of land within sight of the city and two building lots on the hill near our cottage.

William

My dear William, Point Isabel, Texas

Sept. 5. Yours of Aug 26 was received. I certainly did laugh a little over your letter and to this moment I am in some doubt whether you are serious or joking about wishing me to come to Corpus Christi. I have gone on the supposition, however, that you were serious so far as to talk with Mr Caldwell about renting the house. He seems inclined to do so and will write to you on the subject. He offers fifteen dollars per month, but wishes the privilege of holding it for two years. He says it is a low rent for the house, but is all he feels able to give for the present.

Rents have fallen in Brownsville very much of late I understand. Mrs Evans tells me the lighters have not made their expenses this summer. If there is any prospect that we shall soon live in this house again, I would prefer renting it to Mr Caldwell for fifteen that to almost any other in the country for thirty. I presume the pay is certain and they are of the class of tenants who improve rather than injure property.

The roof is put up between the hall and kitchen doors. The expense will be twenty five or thirty dollars, and I hesitated some time about getting it done, but I believe Mr Stillman's letter about the mine decided me. So you see what mischief it is doing already.

Mr Monsaloatge has really taken away Angy and she has been with him for more than a week. He says, "Seeing all that takes place in my presence, and not knowing what may take place in my absence, I now say and promise and swear, that I want to be Anjelita's father and take care of her while she lives"[41]

The Spanish jealousy of Mr Monsaloatge has been aroused or else he wishes an excuse for taking back his child. I do not know which. I have been very anxious throughout the whole affair to do right.[42] [He ends with] "Mrs Chapman, I am truly grateful for all you have done for my daughter and beseech you to receive kindly what has been said by a father sore in spirit. I beg you also to say to Mrs Fry to deliver Angelita to me as soon as it may be possible for her to do it, so that I may again accustom her to speak her mother tongue while I am in Brownsville."[43]

So little Angy has gone from us, may God watch over her! Our family is so reduced that I care not how we live now whether housekeeping or boarding, just which you think advisable. Willie is at the North, Dick is disposed of,—"A fool for luck," and Mrs Foley wishes to go to California in March if she can not get Col Parkerson to *adopt* her in Texas.[44] Jane, I presume, will stay and go North with us. So in view of all these circumstances, you can dispose of us as you like.

Mr Patterson wrote to George Moses [here] that he would like to change situations with him, whether seriously or jokingly, I do not know. If you think he has left his heart at Point Isabel, it must be in the keeping of Miss Irene. Really I am inclined to think that Mr Patterson could not

41. Chapman quotes from Ramon Monsaloatge (hereafter referred to as RM) to HBC, Aug. 26, 1852, CC.

42. HBC to EWB, Sept. 7, 1852, CC.

43. RM to HBC, Aug. 26, 1852, CC.

44. Apparently Eliza Foley was envious of young Dick who was apprenticed to Colonel Parkerson, as mentioned in WWC to HBC, Aug. 26, 1852, CC.

do better. Considering her advantages, she is rather a remarkable girl with good sense, good principles and a character of her own, far superior to her mother. The trouble is, I fear it would be marrying the family to marry Irene. If left a widow I know of no woman who would be, I think, more helpless than Mrs King, and if there is any truth in the [local] gossip, Capt King is in very deep water and cannot keep afloat much longer.

I had a talk with Judge Moses about the railing and he promised to talk with Capt King about it. Capt King said they were waiting for scantling. Judge Moses offered to furnish it but I see no signs as yet of its completion.

I wish so much you could see the baby. She creeps about the room in the most comical manner imaginable, on one foot and dragging the other leg after her. We say, "Clap hands for Papa." and she strikes her little hands together while her eyes are sparkling with merriment.

Helen

My dear child, Point Isabel, Texas

Sept. 7. Your father has changed his mind about our staying here and wishes us to go to Corpus Christi. We shall probably go before winter. Fred is here and he says it is a very pretty place, that is, for Texas.

Fred is at present [working] on the *Yacht* at $25 per month plus his board. I think he and Jane are engaged for he bought a pin for her not long ago and this time he brought her a very pretty ring from New Orleans and I do not think she would accept such presents if she did not mean to marry him. I trust she is too honorable to receive such gifts and then reject him.[45]

Mr Monsaloatge came down about ten days since and told me that he wished to have Angy again for his own child. He has grown suspicious and I think is afraid that Angeline will not be loved as well as Helen. Of course, I could not object and so the poor little child has gone. I hear that she is perfectly contented, though very unwilling to go with him at first and if I can only believe that it is well with her I shall be willing to have it so.

I am sorry you must miss seeing your little sister's pretty baby ways. She creeps all about the room but in a most comical manner, on one foot and dragging the other leg behind her. Like old Dame Hickett's wonderful

45. Jane Anderson did not marry Fred. She married James Renahan, a building contractor from Belfast, Ireland, in Corpus Christi in 1853. Helen described him as "a large, handsome Irishman, good humored and steady, I believe" (HBC to EWB, May 15, 1853, CC).

Cricket, she performs many astonishing tricks. We say, "Clap hands for papa and clap hands for Brother Willie," whereupon she strikes her little hands together in great glee. When we ask her to kiss us she goes through the motions with her little red lips in a very bewitching fashion.

The baby carriage is nearly a failure for she will not sit still in it. The first we know she is standing up and jumping. She is forever in motion, never quiet except when sleeping. Her eyes will be hazel; they are no longer blue. Oh! how you would love the sweet little creature if you were here.

We (the baby, Jane, Mrs Dervent and two or three others) went over with Fred in the *Drum* to Brazos Santiago yesterday. The old office looked natural but had a desolate, deserted look. I dined on board the *Yacht*. Captain Thompson inquired very particularly about you and praised your conduct while going over to New Orleans. He seems very fond of you.

I suppose by this time you have commenced going to school. Be calm, patient and hopeful and you must succeed.

My dearest William, Point Isabel, Texas

Sept. 9. Mr Caldwell has engaged the house and I will very gladly return with you the last of October.

I think it probable that Jane will be married this Fall. Fred brought her a ring from New Orleans. When you decide whether to rent a house or board, let me know about the rooms.

I dined with Captain Thompson on board the *Yacht* the day before yesterday. In great haste,

Helen

My own dearest Ella, Corpus Christi, Texas

Sept. 9. Your kind letter of August 30 was received the day before yesterday at sundown.

I felt annoyed that Mr Monsaloatge, after all our kindness to him, should treat you as he did. I liked your dignified course towards him very much. You have acted right towards him and Angy. I begin to think that he is a bad man and perhaps the sooner we dissolve all connection with him or his family the better. Whatever is right we will do still, and when I come to see you, we will decide definitely on this matter. In the meantime let it give you no further trouble or anxiety.

The *Major Barbour* will leave here this evening for New Orleans and Captain Arnet expects to be at the Brasos about the first of October. He is to write me as soon as he gets to New Orleans when he will probably leave for the Brazos. I shall try and be there about the time he is and then, dear Ella, if you prefer to come here, we can come on the *Major Barbour.* General Smith will be here tomorrow when I shall ask him for a 20 days leave.

I have engaged you a beautiful cottage, prettier than ours at Point Isabel, with considerable shrubbery in the yard and a large garden just planted in the rear. I think you will be even more quiet here than where you are and I can relieve you in the duties of housekeeping as I have plenty of time. I am going to be a much better husband and man in all respects than I have ever been before.

There is very little at this post to interest me without my family. The Rio Grande seems more like home and yet I would not care to go back unless there could be a commanding officer at Fort Brown who ranked me.

Since writing the above, I have received some flattering letters from Colonel Tompkins. He approves of all I have done, gives me all the mechanics, materials, supplies and funds I have asked for, and is quite complimentary in advance. He has, agreeably to my request, defined the extent of my duties and I feel much relieved for until now everything has been uncertain. I shall have enough to do and yet not too much.

Remember me to Mrs Foley and "Mrs Fred." Kisses for my darling one and much love to my Sweet Ella from the overflowing heart of your,

William

My dearest William, Point Isabel, Texas

Sept. 15. Wednesday is the great day of the week to me because Wednesday night brings your letter. It seems very desolate without you and I felt rejoiced that you had made arrangements to take us back with you. Indeed, My dearest William, we have lived so long together that I think neither of us can get on very well alone. So for the rest of our lives I think we had better arrange matters so as to live together.

I shall not be sorry that I remained here throughout the summer. We have perfected all necessary improvements to the house and if we ever wish to come back to the Rio Grande, we have a nice comfortable house ready for us. I should be very well contented to live at Point Isabel if circumstances should render it advisable. For a permanent residence, I should prefer living on the Gulf coast to a bay coast so far inland. At present, I would a thousand times rather live at Corpus Christi or with you, I care not where! We have pretty nearly chosen Texas for better or for worse and now the best thing we can do is to make the best of it. Don't you think so?

I like the Caldwells very much from what I have seen. Mr Caldwell will improve the place very much with cultivating shrubbery and flowers. Mr Caldwell has gone to superintend his sheep shearing. Just as he was starting last night, he told me that the Indians had been among your sheep but that they had been driven away. If it be so, I suppose you will hear about it from Mr Stillman. I am anxious to hear from Mrs Stillman, her confinement may be expected now at any moment.

I think Jane means to be married this fall though she has not told me positively if she will leave. I hear nothing more from Mr Monsaloatge.

Kind regards to Mr Patterson. I think if we keep house at Corpus Christi, you had better ask Mr Patterson to live with us. It will be better for him and we can set a better table.

Helen

My dearest Ella, Corpus Christi, Texas

Sept. 16. Unless you are committed to Mrs Caldwell at $15 dollars a month, *he* cannot have the house one cent less than $20. In my offhand way, I told him when I first purchased the house that I would be willing to rent it for fifteen or twenty dollars per month if you did not remain at Point Isabel, but since that time we have greatly improved the house and premises, and we have paid, or will pay when your excellent improvements are completed, at least $150 cash. He now pays Mr Langdon $10 per month for his small house not including the *amphibious* part and if he prefers to remain there instead of paying the exceedingly reasonable and low rent of $20, let him do so.

Captain Butler is just as good pay and if Mr Caldwell does not want the house at $20, send Henderson to Captain Butler or his son and offer it to him. Mr Caldwell has the refusal of it as per agreement. Give him my ultimatum and if he declines, offer it to Captain Butler and invite him to examine the house and premises.

Corpus Christi may not agree with you and you may have to return to Point Isabel next fall, so that I am indifferent whether I rent the house or not. Mr Caldwell can have the house at $20 per month for two years provided Mrs Chapman does not want it in one year or next fall and on no other terms unless you are in honor committed. $15 per month is only 12 percent on $1500. Oh, No! Mr Caldwell, however hard the times are, you cannot pull that game on my little wife. Right is right and the house may rot "solitary and alone" before I will suffer anything that is not right.

General Smith and Captain [George B.] McClellan of the Engineer Corps arrived here about a week since and leave today for San Antonio. Both have treated me with great respect, courtesy and consideration. It is pleasant to be with some new officers and get some new ideas and opinions.

I have got permission from General Smith to visit you in October. I shall leave here the 5th of October on Tuesday and be with you on Friday or Saturday night and remain 10 or 12 days.

I have engaged conditionally a pretty cottage with two parlors, two bed rooms, dining room, work house, kitchen, servants room below and three bedrooms above with a fire place in each parlor and one in one of the bed rooms above.

Since writing [the foregoing], General Smith has given me his last wishes about Corpus Christi. He wishes me to provide houses for him and staff by Christmas. He has told me which house to hire for him and he examined it today. It will not compare with yours. He mentioned the following as those who would come for certain: Colonel Johnson and family of the Topographical Engineers, Lieutenant Smith and wife of the Military Engineers, Major Deas and Family, Lieutenants Gibbs and Wood, and Captain McClellan.[46]

The General was very confidential and I know we shall like one another. If the headquarters are here, it will suit me. If I am of any account, I shall be appropriated and General Smith, you know, is a rising man. I believe there is a Providence in my coming here and must fall back on my old doctrine that "everything happens for the best."

The General approved of everything I submitted to him and yet he has a mind of his own. He is a treat. I was nicely dressed every day while he was here. Today the General has left and I shall take a rest and not shave.

46. Colonel Joseph E. Johnston, Lieutenants Martin Luther Smith, Alfred Gibbs, and Thomas J. Wood, and Captain George B. McClellan were all West Point graduates who later became generals in the Civil War. George Deas became a Lieutenant Colonel in the Confederate Army (Francis B. Heitman, *Historical Register and Dictionary of the United States Army, September 29, 1789 to March 2, 1903* [2 vols.; Washington, D.C.: Government Printing Office, 1903]).

Tell Judge Moses to be on the lookout to see when I arrive on the [southern] point of Padre Island on Friday or Saturday, the 8th or 9th of October, and to send a boat for me when he sees the ambulance.

Sept. 22. The change to this place will be an experiment and I pray it may result like the one to the City of Mexico. I am glad that you are pleased with the change for it will make me so happy to have my own sweet Ella with me.

You may have to return to Point Isabel if you find that this place does not agree with you and this you cannot decide definitely until the first of May next. Therefore if Mr Caldwell is not willing to give $20 per month for our cottage, I prefer it should remain vacant until that time. If we once fix the price at $15, we never can raise it and $15 will not keep it in repair and pay the legal interest on $1650 which the place has cost me at least. If you should decide next spring never to return to Point Isabel, I would prefer to sell the cottage at auction for what it will bring than to hold it and rent it for $15 per month.

Good grazing land can be purchased [nearby] at $1 per acre.

Tell Jane and Mrs Foley that I shall not love them if they leave you before next May and if they will remain until then I am willing to live on bread and cheese during washing days and ironing days and Sundays.

Now, dear Ella, having answered your letter, I have some pleasant news to tell you. Not about the mine or sheep or the improvement of the Rio Grande or churches, or schools or elections but about love and matrimony, more particularly the last as I am in some doubt about the first as the sequel will perhaps explain.

Last Sunday night about 8 o'clock Colonel Staniford and Mrs Mumford arrived here. Mrs Mumford said she wished to talk with me in private. Little did I know what was coming. We went into Colonel Kinney's library and talked till one o'clock. She had pretty much decided to apply for a divorce and wished to do it at Corpus Christi. After I told her of Captain Mumford's conduct at Matzalan, she no longer hesitated. I found, however, that it would take one year to procure it here and eight months at Galveston. I employed her the best lawyer at Galveston, Mr Hale (son of Mrs Sarah J.).[47] who happened to be here and the papers were at once drawn up and Mrs M[umford] signed the application to the District Court. Colonel Staniford said he would pay all costs and was much pleased. The

47. Sarah J. Hale was the editor of *Godey's Lady's Book*. See Appendix A for her son William.

case will be decided the last week in May. I stated the case to Judge Divine who is now holding his court here and he says there will be no difficulty at all. That he would give it at once if the case were brought before him. In her petition the only grounds on which she asks for a divorce is that her husband has given her no support for three years and by the laws of Texas this is sufficient to obtain a divorce.

Having disposed of that business, Jennie as she now wishes everybody to call her, desired my advice in another matter. She then told me that Dr Jarvis had offered himself and his $40,000 just before she left San Antonio. He desired no answer at this time and Jennie only listened to him. He desired her to consult you in the matter. He told her that he had written me a long letter on this subject, but I have never received it. I advised her to accept provided the Doctor settled $25,000 on her before marriage. She will probably do it. But she said she wished he was not quite so old and had better teeth and would wear gold spectacles. Colonel Staniford is evidently gratified and told me that he had made his will and gives all his property ($40,000) to little Tommy. I told Jennie that there was $80,000 between the three, but perhaps there would have to be another division of one of the forty thousand dollars. She laughed and said she reckoned not.[48]

The doctor has a little Chihuahua dog at San Antonio which he was patting all the time and when he proposed Jennie, in all innocence of her heart, said, "Well, Doctor, I suppose you have got tired of patting nothing but your little dog." The doctor laughed heartily, Jennie blushed but did not explain that she only meant that he wanted a wife to pet. I laughed at her more than the Doctor did. She looks a little older and Tommy is a very sweet child.

I reminded Jennie of your remark that there was sunshine in the future for her yet. She said she would prefer to marry a young man. I told her that she could hardly expect that as she was 30 and had one child. She will take the Doctor if your advice coincides with mine. I have no doubt it will. Of course, Ella, this matter must remain a profound secret until after the divorce is obtained.

Colonel Staniford purchased 8 building lots for $400 and 50 acres of land which will also make building lots for $250. I told him to reserve 4 of his building lots for Dr Jarvis to build a pretty cottage on for Jennie. He

48. As it turned out, William's suggestion was a good one. Nathan and Jennie Jarvis had a child whom they named William Chapman Jarvis, born on May 15, 1855 (N. S. Jarvis to HBC, Sept. 3, 1855, CC).

promised to do so. I have a great deal more to tell you about this but will reserve it until I can tell you in person the 9th of October.

Good night, dearest Ella. The 9th of October, then my wife, my child, kisses, happiness!

Sept. 23. This is a bright beautiful morning and I have promised to go fishing with a talented minister who is here for his health. He has hemorrhage of the lungs.

Our yard and garden look well since the rains. I pay $30 per month, the same that the Government allows me. General Smith asked me to hire him a house much inferior to ours: the old lady asks $50 per month.

General Smith has purchased 100 acres nearer town than Colonel Staniford's. General Harney has 1000 acres below Colonel Staniford's. General Smith has purchased several building lots nearer the water below my office. If the town extends very much, General Smith's 100 acres will be worth a fortune.

William

My dear Mother, Point Isabel, Texas

Sept. 28. I am not very well today. The whole month has been damp and rainy and I have been a little asthmatic—not bad, but enough to make much exertion impossible. I am living here very quietly and pleasantly and rather dread tearing up and making another move.

General Smith is so pleased with Corpus Christi that he is going to make it his headquarters. He will have his staff with him and I shall not have the quiet easy time I have had here. My great object is to make myself as healthy as much as possible for my baby. I avoid as much as I can all excitement and fatigue. So far, I have never known a child reared more easily.

Sept. 30. A letter comes from Corpus Christi. The Major will be here on the ninth of October.

Helen

My darling child, Point Isabel, Texas

Sept. 28. I received two letters yesterday from "Aunt Emmy;" but none from my dear boy as I had expected. It delights me to hear such a good account of you. How I would like to share your berries and apples and milk, but I am compelled to be so very moderate in such enjoyments that it is better for me to be out of the way of temptation.

We expect your dear father on the 9th October. He will be delighted with his dear little Ella and with the house. I think Jane will go over to Corpus Christi with us. Little Jimmy Stillman has a little baby sister.[49]

Your ever affectionate,
Mother

My dear Mother, Corpus Christi, Texas

Nov. 1, 1852. We buy a great many books, lend a great many and lose a great many, but I consider it money well expended. It is seldom a good book is actually *consumed* and so long as it lies about in the world— on dusty shelves where reading is rare, on counters; in bar rooms, everywhere it is an effective missionary. In this Western world too there are so many men of cultivated intellect and [a] craving for general reading who scarce ever get sight of anything but [cheap] novels and that but seldom. Oh! this Western life, how little understood! How miserable and paltry all efforts for its amelioration!

But I must save this much of my page to tell you something of Corpus Christi. It is a beautiful quiet spot, that is, for the Gulf Coast. There is no rugged scenery about the Southern as the Northern bays and with this exception the shores are perfectly flat. We leave the schooner thirty miles below and ascend in small sail boats to Corpus Christi. The bay is navigable only for very small sailing vessels or light draught steamers. For steamers there is not yet sufficient business. The mail is brought regularly once a week by way of Indianola.[50] The village is built on a flat plain and directly behind it, facing the bay thirty miles across, is quite a bold green bluff on which the best residences are built. There is far more beauty of scenery here than on the Rio Grande, quite an important element of happiness with me. We live in a much more retired regular fashion than formerly. Altogether the change to me is a pleasant one and I think will act favorably on my health.

49. This was Isabel (christened Elizabeth) Goodrich Stillman, born September 22, 1852, in Brownsville. She died unmarried on August 16, 1894, in New York City. Jimmy Stillman was born on June 9, 1850, in Brownsville. Wise in the ways of business, he left Brownsville to amass one of the great American fortunes during his career (Stillman, *Charles Stillman*). See Appendix A.

50. The port of Indianola, on the western end of Matagorda Bay, was an army depot and shipping line stop in the 1850s. It disappeared in the 1880s, after being visited by several disastrous hurricanes and by-passed by major railroads (*Handbook of Texas,* I, 883).

We have the best improved and prettiest place. A small cottage in a yard ornamented with choice and beautiful shrubbery. Most of the houses on the bluff are engaged for the Officers; General Smith, Major Deas, Captain Blair, all with families. Dr Jarvis also comes with the General, two unmarried officers, and the band of the Rifle Regiment. I am very glad to have Dr Jarvis among us again, not [only] professionally, but as a friend.

There is no church—only the occasional services of a Methodist minister. There is, however, a very good day school kept by a New England man, a Mr Taylor, and a flourishing little Sunday school started and sustained by two excellent Christian ladies from the North.

Love to all.
Helen

My dear Willie, Corpus Christi, Texas

Nov. 7. Mother and I intended to write you long letters by this mail but we have been so busy in getting things to rights in the new cottage that we have not had time. Mother says I must write you a short letter by this mail and she will write you by the next.

I promised to tell you something of my ride down Padre Island. We started from Corpus Christi at 4 o'clock in the morning and rode 16 miles before we came to the place where we crossed the Laguna Madre at the upper end of Padre Island. We were two hours and a half in crossing the water and it must be a good seven miles; the water in some places came up to the bottom of the body of our old ambulance.

After we got onto Padre Island, we rode that day about six miles and encamped, or rather stopped on the beach as we had no tents. Peter Rouche watered the horses while Curry made the coffee. We had a nice supper of cold roast beef, cold boiled eggs and bread. After supper we all "turned in." I had my little iron bedstead and the old shawl, the boys lay down on the sand. The next morning we had breakfast and were off by 3 o'clock. We rode that day 45 miles along the beach over a beautiful road as hard as on Brazos Island. We passed the wreck of the schooner *Colonel Cross*.

The next day we rode 40 miles: meals all the same as the first. The next and last day we rode 35 miles and got to the Brazos. I make the length of Padre Island 125 good miles: they certainly were long ones to me as there was such a perfect sameness along the beach, nothing but logs and sandhills and besides, Billy, you know my face was homeward. Perhaps if I had been going the other way the distance would not have seemed so long. Our horses were pretty well tired out. I had two horses. I got to "Blair Cottage" about an hour before sun down the fourth day after leaving Corpus Christi.[51] Mother was just going to ride in the carriage with Governor Henderson. I think she was glad to see me and I do believe the baby half knew me or recognized my voice for she came to me at once. I remained there 9 days and then we started back in the *Major Barbour.*

Mother and Janie and Mrs Foley send much love to Willie. Mother unites with me in love to you and all.

Your affectionate Father

My dear Mother, Corpus Christi, Texas

Nov. 19. Moving to a new place and setting up housekeeping involves a great amount of labor, and, though I have had abundant and efficient assistance, my mind and thoughts, at least, have been in the arrangements.

The baby cannot be left out of sight a moment. She is quick and nervous in all her motions and creeps with incredible velocity about the house. She is cutting her teeth regularly in orthodox fashion and she now has four full grown teeth and two others fairly cut through. They seem to cause her but little pain and no sickness. Altogether *as my child*, I consider her a sort of living miracle.

Though I have not been exactly sick I have not been very well. For the last fortnight I have felt better and can attend to my house and prepare sewing and such things very comfortably, but anything like mental effort is altogether out of the question.

It is unfortunate that I have so completely lost my taste for light reading. I cannot read a novel for the story alone; there must be something suggestive or provocative of thought in some way to make me enjoy it and therefore in certain conditions, I shrink from all reading much probably as you shrink from walking.

By great good luck, since I came to Corpus Christi, I have seen a copy of "*Uncle Tom's Cabin.*" I do not think it is sold in the Southern book stores and I believe this is the only copy in Texas. It was brought from New Jersey where everybody was reading it at the time by a young man whose parents were originally from New England, but are now residents of this place. I had been very curious to see it, not for its views on the slavery question for my mind has long since been made up on that subject, but I was curious

51. This is the Chapmans' house at Point Isabel.

to judge of the literary merits of a work that has created such excitement.

She certainly to my mind has great artistic power. It is the only book I have seen for a long time where the plot excited me. Generally the machinery of a story is nothing to me, the delineation alone interests me, but this book I could not let alone after once opening it. The Major commenced reading it aloud evenings but I could not resist my desire to look over the pages and find out if George and Eliza got safe to Canada, then the fate of Eva, then St. Clair, then Uncle Tom. So the book was all read in that way by fragments seized from the hurry of many pressing occupations.

She has shown her strong good sense in scorning a romance writer's license in exaggeration. To Southern residents it seems altogether more natural probably than to you at the North. You only know the African race as stupid, indolent, poor, pariahs among you as most of the free Negroes are, but I have seen enough myself to convince me that, in moral nobility, there may be many Uncle Toms in the lighter shades of the mulatto population. I have seen that rare blending of physical and intellectual beauty, so unusual in the pure European races, enough to convince me that George and Eliza are more than poetical creations and I have seen many a little ebony imp bearing a most wonderful family resemblance to Topsey.

Marie is a capital specimen of a selfish weak-minded indolent Southern woman; St Clair of a noble nature obscured and darkened by the tendencies of a life such as that in New Orleans where the universal principle seems to be "Let us eat and drink for tomorrow we die." Tom Loker is a genuine product of Western life and Legree is not painted in colors too detestable to describe that most detestable monster, a *wholly unprincipled Yankee*. The cold calculating Northern blood that keeps them smooth and respectable at home seems to make them devils incarnate in the backwoods. The Major is enthusiastic about the book and I am very glad he has read it.

The Dix family who lent the book do, as almost all Northern people do, keep some slaves for house purposes and would not hesitate to buy or sell.[52] The daughter who is Southern born and with Southern feelings on the subject told me she considered it a very fair representation of slavery as she had seen it rather than something written as exceeding the truth.

Your ever affectionate,
Helen

52. This is probably the family of Captain John James Dix.

13.
EPILOGUE

The Chapmans' fascination with *Uncle Tom's Cabin,* their opposition to slavery, and their Northern affiliations would have necessitated that they leave Texas during the Civil War. But the Army made the decision for them, and the Chapmans unknowingly closed their Texas frontier sojourn when their tour of duty in Corpus Christi ended in April 1857. During William's tenure as quartermaster in Corpus Christi, he continued to engage in various business ventures. He acquired a number of tracts of land and engaged in sheep and cattle ranching.[1]

As for Helen, the chronicler of the Chapman family life and life in Brownsville, the Rio Grande frontier had left an indelible mark on her character. Although occupied with raising her daughter in the new setting, she continued many of the civilizing efforts she had pursued in Brownsville. She conceived it her duty to combat ignorance, injustice, and oppression and to promote religion. An example of this may be found in a draft of a letter seeking funds for Henderson Laffarty's new Methodist church in Corpus Christi.

1. The famous Chapman Ranch outside Corpus Christi was not owned by the William Chapman family mentioned in this book. In addition to owning residential lots in Corpus Christi, William Chapman purchased two larger tracts known as Las Comitas and Palo Alto in partnership with Francis Morris of New York (see warranty deed dated June 23, 1853, and recorded July 14, 1853, in Book E, p. 263, Deed Records of Nueces County, Texas, as to the former, and warranty deed dated Aug. 10, 1853, and recorded Aug. 17, 1853, in Book E, p. 300, Deed Records of Nueces County, Texas, as to the latter). Later, in 1856, Chapman purchased a half interest in the Rincon de Santa Gertrudis, which became the headquarters of the King Ranch (see special warranty deed from Richard King and his wife, Henrietta, to William Chapman, dated Apr. 25, 1856, and recorded Feb. 3, 1857, in Book F, p. 458, Deed Records of Nueces County Texas, for a 1/4 undivided interest, and deed from Hamilton P. Bee as administrator of the Estate of Gideon K. Lewis, dec'd. to William W. Chapman and Richard King, dated Aug. 1, 1856, recorded Oct. 20, 1904, in Book 13, pp. 117–119 of the Record of Deeds, Nueces County, Texas, for another 1/4 undivided interest).

Laffarty was cut of the same cloth worn by poor and humble Cravens of Brownsville.[2]

Dear Sir,[3]

Corpus Christi, Texas
September 17, 1853

A few hours after closing my letter [to you], I saw Mr Laffarty, and was told by him that the school master is fairly starved out of his school, and has abandoned it.

This, of course, throws him out of any place to preach; and, in an interview with the man who rents the room and keeps the tavern underneath, the landlord told him frankly, that it was a great loss to him in money to have a church over his bar room, and desired him to go some where else.

He said the more respectable dram drinkers had still such a lingering regard for the church, that they preferred going somewhere else for their Sunday drinks, and he added that for himself, his grandfather was a Methodist minister, and he still retained such respect for religious services, that when the people in the bar room got noisy and riotous, he couldn't help trying to shut them up, telling them they would disturb the congregation.

This invariably made them angry, and they too would go off somewhere else to drink. He seemed to think that grog shops and meeting houses could not exist harmoniously together, so he desired Mr. Laffarty to depart and thus we are begging once more.

These surrounding counties of Refugio, Nueces and San Patricio, cover an immense tract of country, and its scattered population can only be reached by travelling missionaries. In this wide extent of country, there is not a single church, Catholic or Protestant, and unless some external aid arrives, for the completion of this Methodist Church, already commenced, there may not be one for years to come. Must it fail?

2. Henderson S. Laffarty, born about 1798, was admitted into the Texas Conference at Bastrop, Texas, on December 22, 1852. He died in June, 1870, in Dewitt County, Texas. After being evicted from the rented church premises, Laffarty built the first Methodist church in Corpus Christi, Texas. See Vernor G. Woolsey, *History of the First United Methodist Church* (Corpus Christi: Artcraft Printing, 1978); Homer S. Thrall, *History of Methodism in Texas* (Houston: E. H. Cushing, 1872), 171; Nail, *The First Hundred Years*, 119–120.

3. The letter, of which only a draft remains, was probably addressed to Dr. Baird or Mr. Fairchild of the *Christian Union*.

As I have told you, Mr Laffarty is obscure and humble; he has no influential friends abroad, and never admits to the possibility of any foreign aid. He has no knowledge or hint of what I am doing.

Whatever be the result, my dear sir, I shall never for a moment doubt your own sympathy with my wishes, and once more entreating your patience in this occupation of your time, I remain

Helen Chapman also made a public defense of the rights of Mexicans living in Texas, a cause with few supporters at the time. In a letter to the *Indianola Bulletin* of October 1853, her statement that she wished to use her pen to serve the weak and oppressed came to a searing fruition.[4] In this document, Chapman, employing arguments not commonly advanced until a century later, showed herself to be one of the early advocates of full civil rights for Mexican Americans. The *Indianola Bulletin* letter was prompted by an editorial proposing relocation of the Mexican Americans of Matagorda County, Texas:[5]

Messrs. Editors, Corpus Christi, Texas

The following is the comment of the *Indianola Bulletin* on the most cruel and outrageous act of the citizens of Matagorda County.

"To strangers it may seem wrong."

Most assuredly it will and how does the *Indianola Bulletin* make it right? There are none but the lower class of Peon Mexicans in the county, none but the lower class! and this is the reason why, under the protection of a free government professedly respecting the rights of the poorest and humblest, this is made a reason for sending them forth into a wild unsettled region where even strong armed men do not travel without the protection of numbers.

"They have no fixed domicile."

This is not at all likely since they have been cheated out of their land and hacales by the grasping and unscrupulous conduct of their white masters.

4. HBC to EWB, May 5, 1848, CC.

5. The original editorial has not survived in microfilmed issues of the *Indianola Bulletin*.

"Thirdly, they often steal horses and girls and endeavor to run them to Mexico"

And so the innocent must suffer with the guilty. Instead of sending off the offenders, they must all go, old men, women and little children from lands that were once their own. The county of their enforced adoption drives them from here and where shall they go. No town or city will receive them and in the waste country of Texas they will starve. If they do, after long wanderings, find their way back into Mexico what must be their story to their Mexican brethren? Oppressive wrong and outrage will be the burden of their tale and if any spirit is left in this unfortunate race they will resolve in the sad event of another war to stand shoulder to shoulder and die every one rather than resign themselves to the sure extinction that must follow Annexation.

The spirit of this outrage is not confined alone to the citizens of Matagorda County. Nothing but the restraint of public opinion prevents the same course everywhere and in many places this even is ineffectual. At Austin, Mexican men, women and children were driven out of the town and subjected to great distress and suffering for no other crime that I can learn than for the reasons that they offered to work on the State buildings for lower wages thereby reducing the price of labor among the white mechanics. I give this from hearsay and good authority though I should be most happy to be contradicted and apprized that I am wrong.

I am not mistaken, however, in the feeling that exists among older Texans especially towards this unfortunate race. It may be excused, in a measure, when we consider how fresh in their minds are the fearful memories of the savage, relentless barbarity that made them struggle for independence. Still the time has gone by when they may allow their private feuds to derange the whole course of justice and force onto a comparatively unoffending class, the sins of their fathers.

The *Indianola Bulletin* gives the ostensible reasons for this outrage but the real reason is "*They are in the way.*" They are an unsightly blot on a flourishing community. They dislike the sight of them. The races do not harmonize and so the weak and the helpless must give way.

While on a land journey this spring to Galveston, I crossed Matagorda bay from the towns of Matagorda to the peninsula whence a stage runs to Velasco. The boatman was an old settler of Dutch origin but had lived in Texas from his boyhood. He was a small, sharp, shrewd man, a successful settler and decidedly felt himself to be one of the sovereign people. Among other questions I asked him if there were many Mexicans about Matagorda.

"Well, a pretty smart chance," he said, "but they know their place; they keep mostly with the niggers and they don't show us any of their sass."

And then with a scowl and such a shrug of aversion as we would speak of some venomous reptile, he exclaimed, "Oh! I hate the sight of a Mexican like poison." This is the real feeling and from a long residence among the Mexicans, I do not hesitate to say, it is more for their father's sins than their own that they are so regarded. As the Dutch boatman said they don't dare show any "sass." They are a cowed, timid, abject race, living apart, outcast from intercourse and sympathy and only stealing, I believe, when driven to it by hunger or extremity of some kind. I have lived in the neighborhood of Mexicans for years, sleeping at night with doors and windows wide open and never lost an article. Their pilfering is of the most limited kind and it is absurd to make their thieving propensities a pretext for banishment.

And now let me ask is not the most degraded Peon Mexican a citizen of the United States? Is he not entitled to its protection? And have the citizens of Texas a right to drive them from point to point? Is this a question solely of state sovereignty about which the General government has nothing to say. Inquire of all candid and intelligent men what is the condition of naturalized Mexicans in Texas. Are they to be deprived of the protection of all laws?

Let the press, at least, and public sentiment frown on this outrageous act of oppression.

Helen Chapman sent a letter to editors of the *Intelligencer,*[6] dated approximately October 1853[7] on a similar theme.

Gentlemen: Corpus Christi, Texas

I trust for the sake of humanity you will allow the accompanying article a place in your columns. Every candid sensible man must know that the Texan Mexicans are too poor and too powerless to make their presence dangerous and I know you will agree with me that only the sternest necessity of self preservation can justify such a general and criminal sentence of banishment.

6. This may be the *National Intelligencer,* published in Washington, D.C.

7. The draft of the letter from Chapman is undated.

My name has no prominence to give the communication any force but I sign it to this private note lest you might be unwilling to publish an article of this nature without the true name of the writer.

It is a very common idea in Texas that it is no wrong to kill a Mexican and I have often heard it said that it would be impossible to find a jury who would convict an American for such a crime and yet in the face of these well known facts as to the conditions of the Texan Mexicans, we are told that Annexation to us would be a *great blessing to Mexico.*

Is Mexico an abstraction? or when we speak of a blessing to Mexico, do we speak of the people of Mexico. If the people be meant, may God mercifully spare them the infliction of such a blessing. Their situation truly is bad enough now but it would be a thousand times worse then. It would be the old story of Indian wrongs, driven before the superior race, or trampled under foot. The American Flag would wave over them as a Uper tree is said to wave over those who seek its shade. And the national crime in this case would be tenfold greater because the Mexicans, it cannot be denied, are partially civilized.

The great first difficulty is already overcome. They know *how to labor* and under a suitable system they might be made peaceful unoffending citizens. The experiment has been successfully and fairly tried by individuals.

They are among us and there are two courses for us to pursue. Either carry on this unrelenting system of banishment and extinction or to give them teachers, employment, protection and, by means of all good Christian arts, draw them from barbarism and elevate them to enlightened enjoyment of freedom.

Let the world judge which of these is the wiser and more Christian mode of action.

In the spring of 1857, William Chapman was ordered to Benicia, California, but he was allowed to return to Washington en route to settle his accounts and to protest the proposed transfer. He hoped to avoid California and remain in Texas, but his effort was only partially successful. Although he was not assigned to California, he remained in the East. The year 1858 was spent in Fort Schuyler in New York City and he was assigned to Fort Monroe, Virginia, the following year. William Chapman died unexpectedly on September 28, 1859, at Old Point Comfort, Virginia. Helen was in Westfield, Massachusetts, at the time, and Willie Chapman was a cadet at West Point.

With his father's demise, Willie decided against a military career and resigned from the Point. But when the Civil War began, Willie joined a company of New York volunteers. Willie served in the Union Army on Folly's Island, South Carolina, and later throughout the Virginia campaign. Helen continued her residence in the North during the Civil War and often visited with Jennie (Mumford) Jarvis in Baltimore while Willie was fighting in Virginia.

Willie was severely wounded at Gravelly Run in Virginia and was breveted for gallant and meritorious services at the battle of White Oak Road near the end of the war. He returned to Corpus Christi after the war and remained a citizen of Texas for the rest of his life. He married Jessie Rankin, a native of Glasgow, Scotland, in 1868. The couple named two of their three children after Willie's parents.[8] Emily Blair died "of Cansor" on June 13, 1869, and Welles Ellsworth Blair, Helen's brother, lived out his life in Wisconsin with his wife Lucy and their two children.[9]

Although Helen Chapman visited Corpus Christi on many occasions after the Civil War, she moved with her daughter, Nellie, as her namesake was called, to Aiken, South Carolina, in the 1870s. Nellie married Ellery Brayton of nearby Augusta, Georgia, in a ceremony at Corpus Christi on July 17, 1878.[10] The Braytons and Helen Chapman moved to Columbia, South Carolina, soon

8. Willie died on December 9, 1907, and Jessie on August 15, 1920. Their children were Jessie Blair Chapman (Furman), Helen Blair Chapman (Philibert), and William Warren Chapman.

9. Welles Blair and his branch of the family did not fare well. Welles died August 6, 1886, at age sixty-eight in Kenosha, Wisconsin, and Lucy, his wife, died March 23, 1916 at age ninety-four in Neenah, Wisconsin. In a sad letter written in 1922, Welles's son, Thomas Blair, then elderly, told of failure on the Wisconsin frontier, exacerbated by Welles's continued alcoholism, and Lucy's resultant shame. Their family lived in poverty and remained isolated from the general population of Kenosha. The Blair daughter became a librarian; the son, a real estate broker. Neither child ever married because, according to Thomas, they never felt socially adequate (Thomas B. Blair to Marion Barron, Mar. 30, 1922, CC).

10. They had two children, Marion Paine Brayton Barron (b. June 23, 1879, d. Aug. 9, 1956) and Helen Isabel Brayton Freeman (b. Dec. 13, 1881, d. Apr. 13, 1946), who were lifelong residents of Columbia, S.C.

after the wedding. Brayton, originally from Fall River, Massachusetts, attended Brown University and graduated from Harvard Law School. He practiced law and had a distinguished political career in Columbia, South Carolina.

During the Civil War, the Confederate States of America had confiscated certain of the Chapman properties in Texas on the grounds that Helen was an alien enemy. When Helen returned to Corpus Christi after the war, she was forced to litigate to recover her sequestered property. Although she incurred some losses, she was, for the most part, successful in this effort. The Chapmans' interest in the King Ranch property was not confiscated, but since no moneys or profits had been paid to the Chapmans since the beginning of the partnership, Helen desired to obtain a division of the property. She "made persistent and repeated efforts to communicate with [King] directly. He promised on two occasions to call on me, but the first appointment was not kept and a promise to call and see me on his return from Kansas was never performed."[11] While in Texas for the nuptials, Helen Chapman hired the law firm of Lackey and Stayton to sue King to recover her interest in the Rincon de Santa Gertrudis, headquarters of the King Ranch.[12]

Helen died on December 10, 1881, in Columbia, South Carolina. Soon after her death, a new attorney with the Lackey, Stayton & Kleberg law firm, Robert J. Kleberg, wrote the executor of Helen Chapman's estate, Ellery Brayton, and said, "There is a suit pending in the District Court of Nueces County instituted by Mrs. Ella Chapman, now dec'd, against Richard King involving

11. See Helen Chapman's sworn testimony in answer to interrogatory (the fifth cross interrogatory) of March 22, 1881, in the case of *Helen B. Chapman vs. Richard King*, Case No. 1279, in the District Court of Nueces County, Texas. William Chapman was King's second partner, having purchased the interest of Gideon K. (Legs) Lewis, King's original partner, from the Lewis estate. William Chapman's financial records of the transaction indicate that he had paid to King as of August 4, 1856, the sum of $1,000 to cover the purchase of one half of King's interest ($100.00), to pay for Chapman's half of the amount due the Lewis estate ($787.50), and to pay some incidental expenses ($112.50). Chapman also paid out an additional $6,218.00 to build the ranch house ($441.57), to stock the ranch with cattle ($2,339.50), horses ($248.00), sheep ($2,218.00), oxen, mules, and saddles ($288.00), as well as other expenses totaling $682.93 (WWC Record Book of Rancho Expenses, Apr. 1 through Aug. 4, 1856, CC).

12. Lea, *King Ranch*, I, 334.

the title to a tract of land."[13] Kleberg asked Brayton to provide authorization from Helen Chapman's South Carolina probate proceedings so that he could continue the lawsuit. Kleberg said he was hopeful that the matter could be settled amicably.[14]

In April 1883, the Texas court ruled in favor of Helen Chapman's estate, upholding its interest in the King Ranch.[15] However, Kleberg wrote Brayton that, rather than take the land, he was compelled by emergency circumstances to accept Richard King's offer of $5,811.75 plus court costs to acquire the Chapman interest in the real property. The emergency, according to Kleberg, was that the King offer had to be entered in open court before the end of the term in order to be binding on the parties. Otherwise, he wrote, the court would not have acted on the matter until the fall of 1883. Kleberg said that the terms of settlement called for payment of the agreed sum in four installments at six, twelve, eighteen, and twenty-four month intervals.

When Brayton wrote to object to the results obtained, Kleberg responded, "As to the settlement, we have simply to say that it was to the interest of counsel as well as the estate of Chapman to get all we possibly could, as their interests were identical.[16] This we

13. Robert J. Kleberg (hereafter RJK) to Ellery M. Brayton (hereafter EMB), July 24, 1882, CC. Although a lawyer, Brayton, busy with his own law practice and involved in South Carolina politics, was not familiar with his mother-in-law's business affairs in Texas. Kleberg never revealed to Brayton that the property in question was the headquarters of the King Ranch. (It is also the site of present-day Kingsville, Texas.) The Rincon de Santa Gertrudis was approximately 15,500 acres of land. The Chapman one-half interest in the property should have been 7,749 acres, but Kleberg advised Brayton in his letters that he could only prove ownership to 3,874½ acres (RJK to EMB, Apr. 23, 1883, CC). Interestingly, Richard King, for reasons known only to him, had not recorded the Lewis Estate deed, which proved William Chapman's ownership of the other one-quarter interest in the property. That deed was recorded in 1904, forty-eight years after original delivery. See n. 1, above.

14. RJK to EMB, Aug. 17, 1882, CC.

15. The Chapman lawsuit was based solely upon the special warranty deed of April 25, 1856, from Richard King and Henrietta King to William Chapman (see n.1, above, Book F, p. 458, Deed Records of Nueces County, Texas). "The deed held up in court," according to Lea (*King Ranch*, 334). The deed for Chapman's remaining one-quarter undivided interest, still in the possession of Richard King, had not been recorded at the time of this suit, and neither Helen Chapman, nor her estate, nor presumably her attorney Kleberg, knew of its existence at the time of the settlement. See n. 13 above.

16. Kleberg was working for the Chapman estate on a contingency fee basis (RJK to EMB, Apr. 23, 1883). However, according to Tom Lea, the King Ranch biographer, Richard King

think we succeeded in doing. Our next court convenes in December [1883] & we could not see any advantage of delaying until then when we probably could not have done as well. While the money was not paid at once, the sum is bearing interest. We feel that we have done what was best for our client, Mrs. Chapman, now dead, in this matter & regret that you should not seem satisfied."[17]

If one could have asked Helen Chapman about this lost legacy, she might have assigned little value to it in the overall scheme of things. After all, the acquisition of wealth and property was William's ambition, not hers. She hoped "to improve the condition of those less fortunate,"[18] and to provide nurture and love to her family. Her letters reveal how she endeavored to achieve these goals. Those letters, she might have said, were her legacy.

began paying Robert Kleberg a $5,000 annual retainer to represent his interests in 1881, two years before Kleberg settled the case on behalf of the Chapman estate. This relationship was never disclosed to Brayton. See Lea, *King Ranch*, I, 339–340.

17. RJK to EMB, June 22, 1883, CC. On an ironic note, had it not been for the personal efforts of Helen Chapman and her letters to the Home Missionary Society beseeching them to send a missionary to Brownsville, it is unlikely that Hiram Chamberlain would have ever found his way to Brownsville. In that event, Richard King would never have met his beloved wife, Henrietta Maria Morse Chamberlain King.

18. HBC to EWB, Jan. 5, 1851, above.

APPENDIX A

Military Personnel and Major Figures

The following abbreviations are used in citations for the entries in this appendix:

CC	Chapman Family Collection, Eugene C. Barker Texas History Center, University of Texas at Austin.
CS	Chauncey D. Stillman, *Charles Stillman, 1810–1875* (New York: n.p., 1956).
DAB	Dumas Malone (ed.), *Dictionary of American Biography* (11 vols.; New York: Charles Scribner's Sons, 1932).
EW	Martha A. Sandweiss, Rick Stewart, and Ben W. Huseman, *Eyewitness to War: Prints and Daguerreotypes of the Mexican War, 1846–1848* (Fort Worth: Amon Carter Museum, 1989).
GR	Paul Horgan, *Great River: The Rio Grande in American History* (New York: Rinehart & Company, 1954).
H	Frances B. Heitman, *Historical Register and Dictionary of the United States Army, September 28, 1789 to March 2, 1903* (2 vols.; Washington, D.C.: Government Printing Office, 1903).
HT	Walter Prescott Webb, H. Bailey Carroll, and Eldon Stephen Branda (eds)., *Handbook of Texas* (3 vols.; Austin: Texas State Historical Association, 1952, 1976).
KR	Tom Lea, *The King Ranch* (2 vols; Boston: Little Brown and Company, 1957) .
NCAB	*The National Cyclopaedia of American Biography* (Ann Arbor: University Microfilms, 1967).
ZT	Zachary Taylor, *Letters of Zachary Taylor from the Battlefields of the Mexican War* (1908; reprint, New York: Kraus Reprint Co., 1970).

Abadie, Eugene Hilarian. Medical doctor and a native of France; joined army as assistant surgeon July 4, 1836; became brevet colonel during Civil War; died Dec. 22, 1874 (H, 149).

Abercrombie, John Joseph. Lieutenant colonel from Tennessee; West Point, 1822; breveted for service in Florida and at Monterey; attained rank of brigadier general during Civil War; retired June 12, 1865; died Jan. 3, 1877 (H, 150).

Anderson, Nathaniel. Major from Tennessee; became quartermaster at Mouth of the Rio Grande June 1847; honorably discharged Mar. 3, 1849 (H, 164).

Arista, Mariano. Mexican Military leader, 1802–1855; entered Mexican army c. 1819; general and commander at battles of Palo Alto and Resaca de la Palma; commandant of Matamoras Apr. 1846–May 18, 1846; Mexican secretary of war, June 1848; president of Mexico, 1850–1853; banished from Mexico 1855 (*Encyclopedia Americana*, II, 283; HT, I, 68).

Avalos, Francisco. Mexican general and commandant of Matamoras, assumed command of garrison at Matamoras Dec. 10, 1848 (*American Flag*, Dec. 27, 1848, as quoted in the New Orleans *Daily Delta*, Jan. 3, 1849).

Babbitt, Edwin Burr. Captain from Connecticut; West Point, 1826; chief quartermaster for the San Antonio district; later chief quartermaster in Oregon and Pacific departments; died Dec. 10, 1881 (H, 177–178).

Bainbridge, Henry. Colonel from New York; West Point, 1821; breveted at Monterey, Contreras, and Churubusco; appointed lieutenant colonel of the First Infantry, June 11, 1851; died in the burning of a steamer on Galveston Bay, May 31, 1857 (H, 182).

Baird, Robert. Presbyterian minister from New York; 1798–1863; prominent author and clergyman; associated with a number of missionary societies (Henry Warner Bowden, *Dictionary of Religious Biography* [Westport, Conn.: Greenwood Press, 1977], 24).

Baker, Daniel. Presbyterian minister from Midway, Georgia; 1791–1857; educated at Hampden-Sydney and Princeton; ordained 1818; a leading evangelist; from distinguished pastorates in Harrisonburg, Virginia, Washington, D.C. and Savannah, Georgia; visited the Lower Rio Grande in 1849; president of Austin College, 1853–1857 (Ernest Trice Thompson, *Presbyterians in the South, 1607–1861* [Richmond: John Knox Press, 1963], I, 428-430; HT, I, 98–99).

Bangs, Caroline. A poet using the nom de plume Cora Hargrave; known as "the Poetess of the Rio Grande"; married Samuel Bangs in 1838 as his second wife; died 1858 (*American Flag*, May 17, 1848; Lota M. Spell, *Pioneer Printer* [Austin: University of Texas Press, 1963], 128–151).

Bangs, Samuel. Printer from Boston, Massachusetts; 1794–1854?; came to Texas in 1816 as a printer for the Mina Expedition; first printer in the state; moved from Corpus Christi to Matamoras with Taylor's army; printed in Victoria and Saltillo, Mexico, and worked on the *Galvestonian*, the *Telegraph*, and the *Texas Register* in Houston, the *San Luis Advocate*, the *Musquito*, the *Commercial Chronicle*, the *Galveston News*, the *Daily Globe*, the Corpus Christi *Gazette*, and the Matamoros *Reveille*; moved to Point Isabel 1848; operated a hotel (Lota M. Spell, *Pioneer Printer* [Austin: University of Texas Press, 1963], 128–151; Verna Jackson McKenna, *Old Point Isabel: Lighthouse Beacon of Brazos Santiago* [Harlingen, Texas: 1956], 23–24; HT, I, 106).

Barnes, Joseph K. Medical doctor from Pennsylvania; joined army as assistant surgeon June 15, 1840; attained rank of brigadier general surgeon general Aug. 22, 1864; promoted to brevet major general, Mar. 13, 1865; died April 5, 1883 (H, 192).

Belden, Samuel A. Merchant from New Orleans; a member of the firm of Stillman and Belden; one of the founders of Brownsville (CS, 9).

Benham, Henry Washington. Captain from Connecticut; led his class at West Point, 1837; Corps of Engineers; retired 1882; died June 1, 1884 (H, 210).

Bennett, Albert Gallatin. Colonel from Delaware; joined the army as paymaster Aug. 14, 1846; breveted lieutenant colonel at National Bridge, Mexico, June 11, 1847; died Feb. 28, 1857 (H, 211).

Blair, William B. Captain from Virginia; West Point, 1838; attained rank of captain, Commissary of Subsistence, Sept. 27, 1850; resigned May 14, 1861; served as major, Commissary of Subsistence, in Confederate Army; died March 23, 1883 (H, 222).

Blair, William W. Attorney from Westfield, Massachusetts; Nov. 24, 1781–Apr. 4, 1851; married Emily Welles Dec. 24, 1814; two children, Helen Ellsworth Blair Chapman and Welles Ellsworth Blair.

Bliss, William Wallace Smith. Major from New York; West Point, 1833 at age of 18; nicknamed "Perfect Bliss"; married Mary Elizabeth Taylor, Zachary Taylor's fifth daughter; died Aug. 5, 1853 (H, 225; ZT, xii–xiii).

Borginnis, Sarah. Irish laundress nicknamed "The Great Western"; possessed of large size and great physical strength; married to a soldier in the Seventh Infantry; served food and tended wounded soldiers during the bombardment of Fort Texas, May 1846; achieved national acclaim as "the Heroine of the Mexican War"; established a hotel in El Paso after the war; died 1866 in Arizona (Robert W. Johannsen, *To the Halls of Montezuma, the Mexican War in the American Imagination* [New York: Oxford University Press, 1985] 139–141; HT, III, 96–97).

Brewerton, George Douglas. Lieutenant from Rhode Island; promoted to first lieutenant June 26, 1850; resigned from army Dec. 31, 1852; died Jan. 1, 1901 (H, 243).

Brice, Benjamin Wilson. Major from Virginia; West Point, 1829; temporarily served as acting assistant quartermaster at Matamoras; paymaster general with rank of brigadier general 1864–1872; died Dec. 5, 1892 (H, 244).

Britton, Forbes. Captain from Virginia; born 1812; West Point, 1834; served in Seminole Wars in Florida; promoted to captain Feb. 16, 1847; resigned July 16, 1850; established a freight line from Corpus Christi; state senator, 1857–1861; died Feb. 14, 1861 (H, 246; HT, I, 218–219).

Brooke, George Mercer. Major general from Virginia; joined the army May 3, 1808; became lieutenant colonel 1819; made brevet major general 1848; commander of the Department of Texas, 1849–1851; died Mar. 9, 1851 (H, 248; HT, I, 220).

Brown, Jacob. Major from Massachusetts; born 1788; enlisted in the War of 1812; rose through the ranks to major, Seventh Infantry, Feb. 27, 1843; died May 9, 1846, from wounds received in the defense of Fort Texas, renamed in his honor (H, 252; HT, I, 224).

Bryan, Francis Theodore. Lieutenant from North Carolina; born 1823; West Point, 1846; served on Taylor's staff in Mexican War; breveted first lieutenant at Buena Vista; explored travel routes west of San Antonio 1849; promoted to captain 1860; resigned from army June 10, 1861; died 1917 (H, 257, HT, I, 232).

Caldwell, James Nelson. Lieutenant from Ohio; West Point, 1840; attained rank of brevet lieutenant colonel Dec. 31, 1862 at Murfreesboro; resigned disabled 1863; died Mar. 12, 1886 (H, 273).

Calhoun, Patrick. Lieutenant from District of Columbia; West Point, 1841; son of John C. Calhoun, senator from South Carolina; promoted to first lieutenant July 29, 1847; captain, Sept. 6, 1853; died June 4, 1858 (H, 274).

Campbell, Nicholas. Medical doctor from New York; assistant surgeon, 1847; dismissed Aug. 1852 (H, 278).

Carpenter, Stephen Decatur. Captain from Maine; West Point, 1840; appointed captain Oct. 17, 1851; breveted at Shiloh and Murfreesboro; died Dec. 31, 1862 at Murfreesboro (H, 284).

Casey, Silas. Captain from Rhode Island; born 1807; West Point, 1826; breveted at Contreras, Churubusco, and Chapultepec; led one of the "Storming Parties" at Chapultepec and was severely wounded; attained rank of breveted major general in Civil War; died Jan. 22, 1882 (H, 289).

Cass, Lewis, Jr. Major from Ohio; 1814–1878; honorably mustered out July 20, 1848 (H, 289; for picture, see EW, 220–222).

Cazneau, Jane McManus Storms (Jane McManus). Author from New York, born 1807; divorced William Storms c. 1831; originally came to Texas with her brother, 1832; ardent expansionist; wrote for New York and Washington, D.C., newspapers; spent the 1840s in New York, Washington, and Mexico; married William Cazneau and returned to Texas; published *Eagle Pass*, 1852, under pseudonym Cora Montgomery; performed several diplomatic missions; died 1878 (HT, II, 122; *Notable American Women: 1607–1950*, ed. Edward T. James [Cambridge: Belknap Press, Harvard University, 1971], I, 315–317).

Chamberlain, Hiram. Presbyterian minister from Vermont; 1793–1866; educated at Middlebury College and Princeton and Andover theological seminaries; associated with the Home Missionary Society; called to South Texas in response to Helen Chapman's requests to the society for the establishment of a church in Brownsville; came to Texas with third wife, Anna Adelia Griswold; founded First Presbyterian Church of Brownsville Feb. 23, 1850; father of Henrietta Maria Morse (from first marriage), who later married Richard King (KR, I, 63).

Chapman, Thomas Finley. From Springfield, Massachusetts; William Chapman's older brother; born July 20, 1812; resident of Austin, Texas, in the 1840s and 1850s (E. Swift to WWC, Apr. 27, 1850, CC).

Churchill, Sylvester. Inspector general from Vermont; born Aug. 2, 1783; inspector general June 1841–Sept. 1861; breveted at Buena Vista; died Dec. 17, 1862 (H, 301).

Churchill, William Hunter. Lieutenant from New York; West Point, 1840; breveted at the battles of Palo Alto and Resaca de la Palma; died Oct. 19, 1847, at Point Isabel (H, 301).

Cooke, Louis P. Born 1811 in Tennessee; served as army lieutenant colonel in Texas, 1836–1837; member of the Third Congress of the Republic; secretary of the Texas navy, 1839–1841; died of cholera 1849 (HT, I, 406).

Cooper, Samuel. Colonel from New York, West Point, 1815; acting inspector general; adjutant general, July 15, 1852–Mar. 3, 1861; resigned to serve in same capacity in Confederate Army; died Dec. 3, 1876 (H, 326).

Craig, Presley H. Medical doctor from Pennsylvania; joined the army July 6, 1812, as surgeon's mate; died Aug. 8, 1848, with rank of major surgeon (H, 333).

Cravens, Neamiah A. Methodist minister from Virginia; born c. 1808; came to Brownsville in 1850 from Alabama (Olin W. Nail, *The First Hundred Years of the Southwest Texas Conference of the Methodist Church: 1858–1958* [Austin: Capital Printing Co., 1958], 64–65).

Cushing, Caleb. General from Massachusetts; born Jan. 17, 1800; raised a regiment of Massachusetts volunteers Jan. 1847; promoted to brigadier general Apr. 14, 1847; commandant at Matamoras, 1847; conducted the Court of Inquiry in the dispute between Scott and Worth, Pillow, and Duncan, Nov. 1847; died Jan. 2, 1879 (H, 347).

Daniels, Charles Belding. Captain from New Hampshire; West Point, 1836; died Oct. 27, 1847, of wounds received Sept. 8, 1847, at El Molino del Rey, Mexico (H, 353).

Davenport, William. Colonel from Pennsylvania; joined the army 1812; served with distinction in the Florida Seminole Wars; military commandant at Matamoras, 1847–1848; retired Jan. 31, 1850; died Apr. 12, 1858 (H, 355).

Deas, George. Major from Pennsylvania; joined army as second lieutenant, Aug. 1, 1838; breveted Major at Contreras and Churubusco, Mexico; resigned Feb. 25, 1861; lieutenant colonel in Confederate Army, 1861–1865; died May 21, 1870 (H, 363).

Denman, Frederick John. First lieutenant from New York; West Point, 1842; accidentally killed at Fort Terrett, Texas, Mar. 2, 1853 (H, 367).

Duncan, James. Colonel from New York; born Sept. 29, 1811; West Point, 1834; breveted from captain to colonel for his actions at Palo Alto, Resaca de la Palma, and Monterey; in battles leading to the capture of Mexico City; involved in "Leonidas letter" affair and was court-martialed with Generals Pillow and Worth; died July 3, 1849 (H, 387).

Early, Jubal Anderson. Major from Virginia; West Point, 1837; honorably mustered out Aug. 3, 1848; lieutenant general in Confederate Army, 1861–1865; died Mar. 2, 1894 (H, 393).

Eastland, Thomas B. Major from Kentucky; assistant quartermaster at Brazos Santiago from June 1846; honorably discharged Mar. 3, 1849 (H, 394).

Eaton, Amos Beebe. Captain from New York; West Point, 1826; breveted at Buena Vista; served in the Commissary of Subsistence Department; became brigadier general in Civil War; died Feb. 21, 1877 (H, 395).

Fay, John J. Colonel from New York; served with the Thirteenth Infantry; honorably mustered out July 15, 1848 (H, 415).

Fraser, William Davidson. Captain from New York; West Point, 1834; aide-de-camp to General Wool during the Mexican War; breveted major May 30, 1848; died July 27, 1856 (H, 434).

Gareschè, Julius Peter. Lieutenant and a native of Cuba; West Point, 1841; first lieutenant until 1856; died a lieutenant colonel Dec. 31, 1862 at the battle of Murfreesboro (H, 446).

Garland, Rice. Attorney from Virginia; born c. 1795; admitted to the bar; practiced law in Louisiana; member of Congress, 1834–1840; judge on Louisiana Supreme Court, 1840–1846; practiced law in Brownsville after 1846; died 1861 (*Who Was Who in America: Historical Volume, 1607–1896* [rev. ed.; Chicago: A. N. Marquis Company, 1967], 267).

Garnett, Robert Seldon. Major from Virginia; West Point, 1841; breveted at Monterey and Buena Vista; served as brigadier general in Confederate Army; killed July 13, 1861, at Carrick's Ford, Virginia (H, 447).

Gibbon, John. Lieutenant from Pennsylvania; West Point, 1847; corps commander and brigadier general in early years of Civil War; became major general; stationed in Montana after the war; retired Apr. 20, 1891; died Feb. 6, 1896 (H, 452).

Gilbert, Charles Champion. Lieutenant from Ohio; West Point, 1846; served as brigadier general of volunteers during Civil War; breveted for actions at Shiloh and Richmond, and Perryville, Kentucky; retired as colonel of Seventeenth Infantry Mar. 1, 1881; died Jan. 17, 1903 (H, 455).

Glen, John C. Medical doctor from South Carolina; joined the army June 22, 1839; served in the Seminole Wars; died Feb. 14, 1848, in Matamoras, Mexico (H, 460).

Hale, William G. Attorney from New Hampshire; born 1822; graduated from Harvard 1842; came to Texas 1846; practiced law in Galveston, specializing in land suits; moved to New Orleans 1873; died 1876 (HT, I, 754).

Harney, William Selby. General from Tennessee; born 1800; joined army 1818; breveted at Cerro Gordo; commander of Eighth Military Department, 1852; commanded Department of the West 1860; retired Aug. 1, 1863, with rank of brevet major general; died May 9, 1889 (H, 502; HT, I, 772).

Henderson, James Pinckney. Attorney by training; came to Texas in 1836; led a regiment at Monterey in Mexican War; named major general in the U.S. Army; elected the first state governor of Texas 1846–1848 (HT, I, 795–796).

Hill, John Christopher Columbus. Student from Georgia; 1827–1904; moved to Texas 1835; member of the Mier Expedition, 1842; credited with great bravery during battle at Mier; adopted by Santa Anna 1843; schooled in Mexico; graduated as civil engineer from the Mineria 1855; married and had four children; returned to Texas 1880; died in Monterey, Mexico (Jacob Lee Stambaugh and Lillian J. Stambaugh, *The Lower Rio Grande Valley of Texas* [San Antonio: Naylor Company, 1954], 59, 60; HT, I, 813).

Holabird, Samuel Beckley. Lieutenant and army scout from Connecticut; West Point, 1849; commanded a mounted company on the Rio Grande; served with distinction in the Civil War; retired June 16, 1890, as quartermaster general of the army (H, 536).

Holmes, James. Lieutenant from North Carolina; West Point, 1848; second lieutenant with Fourth Artillery, Apr. 24, 1849; first lieutenant, July 15, 1852; died May 27, 1854 (H, 538).

Hudson, Walter W. Lieutenant from Kentucky; severely wounded at Fort McIntosh, near Laredo, Texas, while pursuing Indians on Apr. 7, 1850; died Apr. 19, 1850 (H, 551).

Hunt, Henry Jackson. Captain from Michigan; West Point, 1839; breveted at Contreras, Churubusco, Chapultepec, Gettysburg, and Petersburg; attained rank of major general in Civil War; retired Sept. 14, 1883; died Feb. 11, 1889 (H, 556).

Hunter, David A. Major from Washington, D.C.; born 1803; socially prominent as son of George Washington's chaplain and grandson of Richard Stockton, a signer of the Declaration of Independence; West Point, 1822; rose to rank of captain in 1833; served as General Wool's paymaster in Mexican War; later stationed in New Orleans, Washington, Detroit, St. Louis, and on the frontier; commanded the main column of

McDowell's army in the Manassas campaign; a hero at Bull Run; rose to major general in command of the Western Department, 1862; later commanded Department of the South and organized the first South Carolina Volunteers, the first all-black regiment in the Federal Service; commander of the Department of West Virginia during the battles at Piedmont and Lynchburg; served as president of the commission that tried the conspirators in the Lincoln assassination; died Feb. 2, 1886 (NCAB, IV, 264; GR, 737–738; H, 557).

Hunter, Maria. Army wife from Illinois; spouse of Major David A. Hunter (see above) and the daughter of John Kinzies, the founder and first permanent citizen of Chicago; the only officer's wife in the northern Mexico campaign to travel with the troops; frequently mentioned in the press coverage of the war (GR, 737–738; NCAB, IV, 246).

Jarvis, Nathan Sturges. Medical doctor from New York; joined the army as assistant surgeon on March 2, 1833; promoted to surgeon July 7, 1838; married Jenny Mumford after her divorce, moved to Baltimore, Maryland, and fathered a son, William Chapman Jarvis, who became a distinguished doctor; died May 12, 1862 (H, 571; N. S. Jarvis to HBC, Sept. 3, 1855, CC; DAB, IX, 625).

Jarvis, Samuel M. Captain from New York; served with Scott's army as it traveled from Vera Cruz to Mexico City; clerk for William Chapman in Quartermaster's office at Fort Brown in 1850 (HBC to Valeria Merchant, May 28, 1850; HBC to EWB, Mar. 5, 1851, CC).

Jesup, Thomas Sidney. General from Virginia; joined the army as a second lieutenant May 3, 1808; appointed quartermaster general March 8, 1818; commander in second Seminole War in Florida, 1837; later served as quartermaster general until his death on June 10, 1860 (H, 573).

Johnson, Richard W. Lieutenant from Kentucky; West Point, 1849; promoted to second lieutenant of the Tenth Infantry, June 10, 1850; rose to major general during Civil War; breveted at Chickamauga, Chattanooga, and Nashville; retired Oct. 12, 1867; died Apr. 21, 1897 (H, 577).

King, John Haskell. Captain from Michigan; joined the army as second lieutenant, Dec. 2, 1837; became captain Oct. 31, 1846; rose to major general during Civil War; breveted at Chickamauga and Ruff's Station, Georgia; retired Feb. 20, 1882; died Apr. 7, 1888 (H, 599).

King, Henrietta Chamberlain. Schoolteacher and later ranch owner from Missouri; born 1832; attended Female Institute in Holly Springs, Mississippi, for two years; moved to Brownsville 1849; taught at Rio Grande

Female Institute; married Richard King 1854; assumed control of King Ranch 1885; promoted settlement of area around the ranch with generous gifts of land and investments in businesses, churches, and schools; died 1925 (HT, III, 475–476).

King, Richard. Steamboat captain and later rancher from New York, born 1824; stowed away on a Gulf-bound ship 1835; steamboater in Alabama until 1841; served in Seminole War; ran steamboat business on the Rio Grande during and after the Mexican War with Mifflin Kenedy; bought land grant which became the King Ranch, 1852; died 1885 (HT, I, 959; HT, III, 476).

Kinney, H. L. "Colonel" from Pennsylvania; born 1814; established a trading post on his ranch, which became Corpus Christi, 1838; promoted the town for seventeen years; state senator for first four legislatures; went to Nicaragua for three years to promote a colony there; killed in Matamoras, 1862 (KR, I, 155; HT, I, 962).

Larned, Benjamin Franklin. Major from Massachusetts; served as paymaster general from 1854 to 1862; died Sept. 6, 1862 , in Washington, D.C. (H, 616).

Lee, Robert Edward. Captain from Virginia, born 1807; West Point, 1829; Chief Engineer's Office, Washington, D.C., 1834–1837; stationed at Fort Hamilton, New York, 1841–1846; served with generals Wool and Scott in Mexican War, 1846–1847; friend of the Chapmans during this period; superintendent of West Point, 1852–1855; served with A. S. Johnston's regiment in Texas, 1856–1857, 1860–1861; commanded Confederate Army 1861–1865; died 1870 (HT, II, 44–45) (see also Douglas Southall Freeman, *R. E. Lee: A Biography* [4 vols.; New York: Charles Scribner's Sons, 1934, 1935]; Carl Coke Rister, *Robert E. Lee in Texas* [Norman: University of Oklahoma Press, 1946]).

Levely, William. Medical doctor from Maryland; joined the army as an assistant surgeon Sept. 30, 1841; died Nov. 24, 1848 (H, 629).

Lewis, Gideon K. ("Legs"). Man of many trades from Ohio; born c. 1823; an active businessman and printer along the Rio Grande; survived Mier Expedition 1842; founded the Matamoras *Reveille* with Samuel Bangs 1846; a Mexican War hero; an editor; a lawyer; an agent to Washington; a candidate for Congress; a Texas Ranger; a merchant; first partner of Richard King in the King Ranch; shot by an irate husband in Corpus Christi Apr. 14, 1855, because "he seduced Mrs. Yarrington from me and my children"

(J. T. Yarrington to the Gonzales *Inquirer*, Apr. 17, 1855; KR, I, 132–134; HT, II, 52).

Love, Harry. Army express rider from Vermont; born 1810; sailor; stevedore; volunteer soldier from Mobile, Alabama; came to Texas in 1846 and served in the Mexican War; Texas Ranger; Army express rider; Indian Scout; leader of the first American exploration of the Rio Grande; distinguished himself on the Texas frontier by many feats of bravery in wartime and during subsequent years; went to California 1851; in 1853, led twenty California Rangers who killed the notorious Joaquin Murieta and his gang of cutthroats (who reputedly had robbed and killed more than 30 people in the California gold fields during the first three months of 1853); served briefly as a cavalry first lieutenant in the U.S. Army 1855–1856; became a logger in the coastal mountains of Santa Clara County in the late 1850s, residing at Ben Lomond; married Mary Bennett, a woman logger twelve years his senior, noted for her loud, untempered language, her immense size, and the sobriquets, "Mother" and, "The Strong Woman of Santa Clara"; shot when the marriage faltered in 1868 by a man in his wife's employ, Christian Elversen, at the family home in Santa Clara; died from wounds received May 30, 1868 (H, 643; William B. Secrest, *Joaquin* [Fresno: Saga-West Publishing Company, 1970]; San Jose *Mercury*, May 4, 1988; Santa Clara *Journal*, Oct. 31, 1962; Remi Nadeau, *The Real Joaquin Murieta* [Corona Del Mar, Calif.: Trans Anglo Books, 1974]).

McClellan, George Brinton. Captain from Philadelphia; born 1826; West Point, 1846; breveted at Contreras, Churubusco, and Chapultapec in Mexican War; chief engineer for General P. S. Smith 1852; resigned 1857; appointed major general of Ohio volunteers, Apr. 1861; appointed major general, U.S. Army, May 1861; general-in-chief Nov. 1861–Mar. 1862; resigned Nov. 8, 1864; Democratic Party candidate for president, 1864; died Oct. 29, 1889 (H, 656; DAB, VI, 581).

McDowell, Irvin. Captain from Ohio; West Point, 1838; General Wool's personal staff officer 1848; later assistant adjutant general in the War Department; promoted to major Mar. 31, 1856; to brigadier general, May 14, 1861, in command of the Department of Northern Virginia; to Major General, Nov. 25, 1872; breveted at Buena Vista and Cedar Mountain, Virginia; retired Oct. 15, 1882; died May 4, 1885 (H, 664).

McIntosh, James Simmons. Lieutenant colonel from Georgia; born 1786; nicknamed "Old Tosh"; commanded the Fifth Infantry at Palo Alto and

Resaca de la Palma; was pinned to the ground in the latter battle with two Mexican bayonets (one in the arm, the other through the hip) until rescued; commanded the Sixth Infantry at El Molino del Rey Sept. 8, 1847; died of wounds received Sept. 26, 1847; honored with the naming of Fort McIntosh at Laredo (H, 669).

McLean, Eugene Eckel. Lieutenant from Washington, D.C.; West Point, 1842; served as General Wool's staff officer after McDowell's departure in Matamoras and at Troy, N.Y.; attained rank of captain Aug. 29, 1855; resigned from army Apr. 25, 1861; became a major in the Confederate Army (H, 675).

McPhail, Leonard C. Medical doctor from Maryland; joined the army Nov. 30, 1834; resigned Apr. 30, 1849 with rank of assistant surgeon ; died Mar. 23, 1867 (H, 681).

Madison, Thomas C. Medical doctor from Virginia; joined the army Feb. 27, 1840; served in the battle of Buena Vista as assistant surgeon; later served as surgeon in the Confederate Army; died Nov. 7, 1866 (H, 683).

Merchant, Charles George. Lieutenant from New Hampshire; West Point, 1839; breveted first lieutenant at El Molino del Rey; captain at Chapultepec; died 1855 (H, 703).

Michler, Nathaniel. Lieutenant from Pennsylvania; West Point, 1848; served with Topographical Engineers; attained rank of brevet brigadier general, Apr. 2, 1865; died July 17, 1881 (H, 708).

Montgomery, William Reading. Brevet lieutenant colonel from New Jersey; West Point, 1825; breveted at Palo Alto, Resaca de la Palma, and El Molino del Rey; colonel in New Jersey infantry, 1861; became brigadier general of New Jersey volunteers May 17, 1861; died May 31, 1871 (H, 720; HT, II, 226).

Mumford, Ferdinand Suydam. Captain from New York; West Point, 1838; attained rank of captain on Mar. 15, 1848, but resigned Aug. 31, 1849; married to Jennie Mumford; died Oct. 1, 1872 (H, 735).

Nauman, George. Brevet lieutenant colonel from Pennsylvania; West Point, 1823; breveted for conduct at Cerro Gordo, Contreras, and Churubusco; attained rank of colonel of the Fifth Artillery, Aug. 1, 1863; died Aug. 11, 1863 (H, 741).

O'Brien, John P. J. Brevet major from Pennsylvania; West Point, 1836; served in Fourth Artillery; breveted major at Buena Vista; achieved distinction with Scott's army in battles leading to Mexico City; served as assistant quartermaster at Indian Point, Port Lavaca, Texas; died March 31, 1850 (H, 755).

Ogden, Richard L. Merchant from New York; in Brownsville 1848–1849; after leaving Texas, went into business in San Francisco under the name of Ogden & Haynes, Wholesale and General Commission Merchants; during the Civil War served in the Fourteenth Infantry rising to Captain and assistant quartermaster; resigned from army, May 14, 1864 (H, 757).

Paine, Robert Treat. Colonel of North Carolina volunteers; 1812–1872; left Mexico June 28, 1848, with six companies of North Carolinians and returned to Smithfield, North Carolina. Paine's Mutiny was a widely publicized incident of Aug. 15, 1847, in which the North Carolina volunteers rebelled against Paine's harsh discipline (William S. Hoffman, *North Carolina in the Mexican War, 1846-1848* [Raleigh, N.C.: State Department of Archives and History, 1969] 16–21; for picture, see EW, 59).

Passmore, William. Episcopal minister from North Carolina; came to Brownsville 1851; organized Episcopal Church of the Advent, Brownsville, 1851; raised funds in the North to build the church, completed in 1854 at Washington and Tenth streets (W. H. Chatfield, *The Twin Cities of the Border* [New Orleans: E. P. Brandao, 1893], 8, 9).

Paul, Gabriel René. Major from Missouri; West Point, 1834; served in Florida, 1839–1842; breveted at Chapultepec, Mexico, for his actions in leading the storming party that captured the enemy's flag; later served in the Southwest; led an expedition on the Rio Grande that captured Carvajal, in 1852; promoted to lieutenant colonel in the regular service 1862; breveted brigadier general for service at Gettysburg July 1, 1863, where he was blinded; served as deputy governor of the Soldier's Home and later was in charge of the military asylum; retired with rank of brigadier general, 1866; died May 5, 1866 (NCAB, XII, 242–243).

Phelps, John Wolcott. Captain and the son of a Vermont senator; West Point, 1836; a strict abolitionist; resigned Nov. 2, 1859, to campaign against slavery; rose to brigadier general in the Civil War; commanded the Union forces at Newport News, Virginia, and Ship Island, Mississippi; resigned Aug. 21, 1862; died Feb. 2, 1885 (H, 788; *Appleton's Cyclopaedia of American Biography*, ed. James G. Wilson and John Fiske [1888; reprint Detroit: Gale Research Company, 1968], IV, 751).

Pillow, Gideon Johnson. Major general from Tennessee; 1806–1878; law partner of James K. Polk; brigadier general of Tennessee volunteers 1846;

major general of volunteers 1847; fought at Vera Cruz, Cerro Gordo, Contreras, and Chapultepec; twice wounded; charged by General Winfield Scott with authorship of "Leonidas letter" in New Orleans *Daily Delta* of Sept. 10, 1847; brigadier general in Confederate Army (H, 792; DAB, VII, 603).

Pillsbury, Timothy. Texas congressman from Massachusetts; born 1780; served in Maine legislature; came to Brazoria County, Texas, 1837; served in fifth, sixth, and ninth legislatures of the Republic of Texas; U.S. senator, 1846–1849; died 1858 (HT, II, 379).

Porter, Giles. Major from New York; West Point, 1818; post commander at Fort Brown, 1850; retired Sept. 3, 1861; died May 31, 1878 (H, 799).

Pratt, Henry Clay. Captain from Massachusetts; West Point, 1837; breveted at Atlixco, Mexico, Oct. 10, 1847; breveted lieutenant colonel May 13, 1865; died Feb. 14, 1884 (H, 804).

Prentiss, James Henry. Captain from Massachusetts; West Point, 1830; died of yellow fever at Point Isabel, Texas, Sept. 22, 1848 (H, 805).

Prevost, Grayson M. Medical doctor from Pennsylvania; served as assistant surgeon at Buena Vista, resigned from the army June 7, 1848; married a woman named Anita from Parras, Mexico; died May 1, 1896 (H, 806).

Ramsay, Albert C. Colonel from Pennsylvania; honorably mustered out Aug. 14, 1848; died March 9, 1869 (H, 813).

Scott, John Benjamin. Major from Connecticut; West Point, 1821; breveted at Palo Alto and Resaca de la Palma; died Nov. 22, 1860 (H, 869).

Scott, Winfield. Major general from Virginia; born 1786; appointed captain 1809; lieutenant colonel 1812; brigadier general 1814; general-in-chief 1841; successfully led U.S. Army and volunteers from Vera Cruz to Mexico City 1847; preferred charges against Generals Gideon Pillow and William J. Worth and Colonel James Duncan for their complicity in the "Leonidas letter" affair; Whig candidate for president in 1852; resigned Oct. 31, 1861; died May 29, 1866 (H, 870; DAB, VIII, 505).

Sibley, Ebenezer Sprote. Captain from Ohio; West Point, 1827; breveted major at Buena Vista; attained rank of colonel in Civil War; resigned Apr. 15, 1864; died Aug. 14, 1884 (H, 885).

Smith, Buckingham. Born 1810 in Georgia; graduated from Cambridge Law School 1836; practiced law briefly in Maine; married Julia G. Gardner of Concord, New Hampshire; secretary of legation in Mexico City Sept. 9, 1850–Jan. 26, 1851; then charge d'affaires until Oct. 8, 1851; secretary of legation in Spain, 1853–1859; historical publications include "Narrative of Cabeca de Vaca" (1851); died 1871 (DAB, II, 836; DAB, XVII, 242).

Smith, Charles Ferguson. Colonel from Philadelphia; West Point, 1825; during Mexican War, commanded four companies of artillery that acted as infantry known as Smith's Light Battalion; served with distinction at Palo Alto, Resaca de la Palma, and Monterey; under Scott's command, participated in the battles leading to the capture of Mexico City; died Apr. 25, 1862 (H, 895).

Smith, Persifor Frazer. General from Pennsylvania; born 1798; graduated from College of New Jersey (later Princeton); studied and practiced law in New Orleans; served in Seminole War; judge in Lafayette, Louisiana; commissioned a colonel in the Mexican War; breveted at Monterey under Taylor; served with distinction in all battles from Vera Cruz to Mexico City; commander of the Department of Texas, 1851–1856; attained rank of brigadier general Dec. 30, 1856; died May 17, 1858 (H, 902; HT, III, 894–895).

Snelling, James G. Soulard. Captain from Minnesota; West Point, 1845; breveted at Contreras, Churubusco, and El Molino del Rey; promoted to rank of captain of the Tenth Infantry, Mar. 3, 1855; died Aug. 25, 1855 (H, 906; HT, II, 631).

Staniford, Thomas. Colonel from Connecticut; joined the army Oct. 12, 1812; promoted to lieutenant colonel of the Eighth Infantry June 29, 1846; breveted for conduct at Palo Alto, Resaca de la Palma, and Monterey; died Feb. 3, 1855 (H, 915).

Steiner, Josephus M. Medical doctor from Ohio; assistant surgeon, 1847; discharged May 1856; died 1873 (H, 920).

Stewart, Joseph. Lieutenant from Kentucky; West Point, 1842; became lieutenant colonel July 18, 1879; retired Aug. 25, 1879 (H, 925).

Stillman, Charles. Merchant from Connecticut; born 1810; in Matamoras from 1828; donated townsite for Brownsville, 1848; shipping merchant on the Rio Grande; married Elizabeth Pamela Goodrich 1849; moved to New York City 1866; died 1875 (HT, II, 673).

Stillman, James. Financier from Brownsville; 1850–1918; raised in Connecticut and New York; founded the National City Bank in New York, which served the industrial and financial giants of the late nineteenth century; five children (CS, 35–37, 45, 46).

Street, Washington Posey. Lieutenant from Illinois; West Point, 1847; died Sept. 13, 1852 (H, 931).

Swift, Ebenezer. Medical doctor from Massachusetts; born 1817; joined army as assistant surgeon Aug. 30, 1847; breveted lieutenant colonel and colonel during Civil War and breveted brigadier general on July 20, 1867, for services rendered voluntarily during a cholera epidemic at Fort Harker, Kansas; died Dec. 24, 1885 (H, 940; NCAB, V, 177).

Taylor, Richard. Son of Zachary Taylor. Yale, 1845; left his father's camp on the Rio Grande in 1848 for health reasons; Mississippi cotton planter until 1849; served as lieutenant general in the Confederate Army, commanding the Departments of Alabama and Mississippi; died Apr. 12, 1879 (ZT, xiii).

Taylor, Zachary. Major general from Virginia; commanding general in Seminole War; commanding general at Palo Alto, Resaca de la Palma, Monterey, and Buena Vista; president of the United States, 1848–1850; died July 9, 1850 (H, 949; HT, II, 716–717; for a brief biography, see ZT, xiii-xxvi).

Temple, Robert Emmet. Colonel from Vermont; later a resident of Albany, New York; West Point, 1828; honorably discharged Aug. 26, 1848; died July 20, 1854 (H, 950).

Ten Broeck, Peter G. Stuyvesant. Medical doctor from Maine; joined the army as assistant surgeon, Dec. 13, 1847; attained rank of brevet lieutenant colonel during Civil War; died Dec. 19, 1867 (H, 950).

Thomas, George Henry. Major from Virginia; born 1816; West Point, 1840; served with the Third Artillery at Buena Vista; breveted at Monterey and Buena Vista; commanded second Cavalry, 1857–1860; Major general during Civil War; nicknamed "The Rock of Chickamauga" for refusing to yield his position during that battle; died Mar. 28, 1870 (H, 953–954; HT, II, 772).

Tompkins, Daniel D. Brevet colonel from New York; West Point, 1820; quartermaster in New Orleans; in San Antonio, 1852; attained rank of colonel Dec. 22, 1856; died Feb. 26, 1863, in Brooklyn (H, 965).

Totten, James. Lieutenant from Pennsylvania; West Point, 1841; saw action at Booneville and Wilson's Creek, Missouri, and Mobile, Alabama, in Civil War; retired a brigadier general; died Oct. 2, 1871 (H, 966).

Townsend, Edward Davis. Captain from Massachusetts; West Point, 1837; became a general in the Civil War; died May 10, 1893 (H, 967).

Trevitt, John. First lieutenant from New Hampshire; West Point, 1844; attained rank of captain Dec. 31, 1856; resigned Apr. 17, 1861; died Mar. 24, 1893 (H, 970).

Twiggs, David Emanuel. General from Georgia; born 1790; entered the army 1812; served in the Seminole War; promoted to brigadier general June 30, 1846; served under Taylor and then led one of Scott's divisions; served with distinction in every battle of the Mexican War except Buena Vista; head of Department of the West, 1857; major general in Confederate Army; died July 15, 1862 (H, 976; HT, II, 812).

Van Vliet, Stewart. Captain from New York; West Point, 1840; promoted to captain and assistant quartermaster June 4, 1847; at Fort Brown, 1852; became brigadier general of volunteers Mar. 13, 1865; mustered out Sept. 1, 1866; died Mar. 28, 1901 (H, 984).

Vielé, Egbert Ludovickus. Lieutenant from New York; born 1825; West Point, 1847; resigned, 1853; chief engineer of Central Park in New York City, 1856–1857; Brigadier general of volunteers for Union Army; New York parks commissioner, 1863–1884; U.S. congressman, 1885–1887, died Apr. 22, 1902 (H, 987; DAB, X, 267–268).

Vielé, Teresa Griffin. Army wife from New York; born 1831; married Egbert Vielé 1850; came to Texas; published *Following the Drum* in 1858; divorced in 1870s; moved to Paris for remainder of her life; traveled widely; died 1906 (Teresa Griffin Vielé, *Following the Drum: A Glimpse of Frontier Life,* foreword by Sandra L. Myres [Lincoln: University of Nebraska Press: 1984], 3–4, 8).

Waldradt, William W. Captain and attorney from New York; served on military commission in Matamoras from early 1847 until war's end, trying civil cases under the terms of martial law (*American Flag*, June 28, 1848).

Washington, John Macrae. Major from Virginia; West Point, 1817; commanded Company B, Fourth Artillery at Buena Vista; breveted lieutenant colonel, Feb. 23, 1847; drowned at sea en route to California, Dec. 24, 1853 (H, 1007; for picture, see EW, 195–196).

Webb, Nathaniel Seymour. Captain from Connecticut; entered army Mar. 16, 1847; breveted major for service at Chapultepec; mustered out Aug. 26, 1848 (H, 1011).

Webster, Joseph Dana. First lieutenant of the Topographical Engineers; born 1811 in New Hampshire; attained rank of brevet major general in Civil War; died Mar. 12, 1876 (H, 1013).

Weld, Thomas Bradford Jones. Major from Maine; West Point, 1845; served with the Second Artillery, stationed at Fort Brown; died Sept. 10, 1850 (H, 1016).

Whiting, Henry. General from Massachusetts; born Nov. 28, 1788; chief quartermaster of Taylor's column; breveted brigadier general at Buena Vista; published several books and poems; died Sept. 16, 1851 (H, 1030).

Whiting, Henry Macomb. Lieutenant from Massachusetts; West Point, 1842; breveted first lieutenant at Buena Vista; assistant quartermaster at Point Isabel; died Oct. 8, 1853 (H, 1030).

Wilson, Henry. Lieutenant colonel from Pennsylvania; joined the army May 17, 1813; breveted at Monterey in Mexican War; resigned Feb. 25, 1861; died on Feb. 21, 1872 (H, 1046).

Wool, John Ellis. Brigadier general from Newburgh, New York; born Feb. 20, 1784; raised a company and obtained a captain's commission in the War of 1812; inspector general of the army, 1816–1841; promoted to brigadier general June 25, 1841; to major general, May 16, 1862; retired Aug. 1, 1863; died Nov. 10, 1869 (H, 1059–1060).

Wooster, Charles F. Captain from New York; West Point, 1837; breveted captain at Sacramento near Chihuahua, Mexico, Feb. 28, 1847; died Feb. 14, 1856 (H, 1060).

Worth, William Jenkins. Major general from New York; born 1794; appointed first lieutenant Mar. 1813; served as aide-de-camp to General Winfield Scott as a young soldier; served as West Point commandant 1820–1828; promoted to colonel July 1838; served at Palo Alto, Resaca de la Palma, Monterey, and all engagements from Vera Cruz to Mexico City; turned against mentor Winfield Scott in the "Leonidas letter" affair; later appointed by Scott to command the Department of Texas; died of cholera May 7, 1849 (H, 1061; DAB, X, 536).

APPENDIX B

Newspaper Articles Pertaining to the Chapmans and the Frontier

1847–1848

American Flag, Dec. 30, 1847: We publish today the several orders for the levying and collecting taxes or military contributions. It will be perceived that the entire fiscal concerns of the country [Mexico], so far as they can be, are to be controled by the officers of the United States army. . . . We feel great confidence that, under the management of the present energetic Quarter-master, Capt. Chapman, the Orders will be strictly enforced; and we anticipate therefrom a surplus of revenue, which is intended to assist in defraying the expenses of the war. At the same time, we sincerely believe that the order of things to grow out of the new arrangement, will promote the general welfare.

American Flag, Jan. 3, 1848: On Thursday our Commandant, Col. Davenport and Capt. Chapman, Quarter Master, accompanied by the first Alcalde, Sr. Lo. Valdez, visited the Public Schools of this city. These Schools had been discontinued since our occupation, until within about six months. They found the acquirements of the scholars highly creditable to both pupils and teachers, and the supervision and management of the Schools, equally creditable to the gentlemen composing the Ayuntamiento, during whose administration they were re-established. It also appears that the utmost liberality within their power has been extended for the support of the Schools. In a few days, however, under the new arrangement, the supervision of the Schools will be shared by officers of our Government, and the funds necessary for their maintainence will be by them appropriated. The deep interest already exhibited by Capt. Chapman, shows his just appreciation of the responsibility of the duty imposed on him—also shows that our Governor has wisely chosen in the selection of so fit an officer to carry into effect the instructions from Washington. Although it is adding to the multitude of Capt. C.'s duties, we feel great confidence that this branch of duty will receive from him, as well as from the Commandant of the District, the attention that its vital importance demands.

American Flag, Jan. 9, 1848: We mentioned in our paper of the 3rd instant, that a lot of silver valued at ninety thousand dollars arrived here on the 1st instant. The duties on this (seven per cent) will amount to about seven thousand dollars. It was consigned to Mr. J. P. Schatzell, Ex-United States Consul. As money appears somewhat difficult to raise here on short notice, our Commandant allowed him to take the silver on his giving his written promise for the amount of the duties payable on demand. Yesterday, (the 7th) the payment of the duties were formally demanded, but were not met. Our active and efficient Collector, Captain W. W. Chapman, was compelled by Tariff regulations dated March 30, 1847, to place a sentinel over the silver. Mr. Schatzell most unaccountably refused to pay the duties, refused to deposit a number of bars of the silver equal to the value of duties—would not tell where the silver was, nor give the key to any of his rooms. This is the more strange after the indulgence shown him by our worthy Commandant, Col. Davenport. Capt. Chapman had no other course left but to force a door, which he promptly did, found the silver, and placed a strong guard over it. We understand that the sentinel will remain until the duties are paid. We also understand that the Captain posts every relief of Sentinel himself, and counts the bars (85) each visit. Different conduct or example might have been expected from Mr. Schatzell, who has been for several years the representative of our Government at this post—were it not (to use the mildest term applicable) for his wayward disposition, so notorious.

American Flag, Feb. 2, 1848: CITY IMPROVEMENTS.—It is gratifying to notice—as a consequence of the new order of things which places the municipal taxes of the city under the control of the Quartermaster, Capt. Chapman—that this public spirited and energetic officer, is making use of the city funds in a manner creditable to himself, advantageous to the city, and highly conducive to the comforts and pleasures of the citizens. But a few days have elapsed since he assumed the management of the finances of the city, and what do we see as the result? An efficient civil police have been appointed, who are ever on the alert to protect the property of citizens, arrest offenders, and preserve order and quiet. The streets, late so drear and dark after nightfall, are now hung with lamps from one extreme to the other, presenting a very pleasing sight, and giving a sense of security not wont to be felt by the wayfarer. As far as time and circumstances would permit, (the late heavy rains having proved an insurmountable obstacle) the streets and crossings have been improved, and such regulations adopted as will prevent the accumulation of dirt and filth calculated to engender disease. And last, though not least, the once beautiful Plaza, which, through neglect, since the Americans have occupied Matamoros, has been despoiled of its beauty and made an eye-sore to the citizen and stranger, is now undergoing such improvement as will, when finished, place it in better condition than when the Mexicans viewed it as an ornament to their city. The whole square is being encircled with a neatly painted railing, to prevent intrusion from horses and other animals—the trees, which had nearly all been broken down or injured, have been replanted, and other improvements are in progress highly creditable to the taste and judgment of Capt. Chapman, and which will place him in an enviable light before the citizens of Matamoros and strangers visiting here. Much remains to be done in repairing the streets which it will take time to accomplish, but we are confident that the work commenced, will progress as fast as circumstances will permit.

The *Jackasses* who interfere with and bray out against the progressing improvements will be served but right if they meet the fate of their brothers who invaded the Plaza the other night.

American Flag, Mar. 1, 1848: The Ball on the night of the 22nd of February, in commemoration of Washington's Birthday, we understand passed off very pleasantly. We were only present a short time, but long enough to observe the elegant and tasteful decorations of the dancing room, hung with flags of the different nations, and ornamented with several fine pictures. The Consuls of the different nations, the President of the Ayuntamiento with his charming and accomplished lady; Sr. Menchaca, a distinguished Mexican lawyer; Sr. Arguilles, Notary Public of the city; Colonel Davenport, Civil and Military Governor of Matamoros; Major Hunter, Paymaster, and his lady; Captain Chapman, Q. M. and his lady; Major Anderson, Q. M. at the Mouth of the River and his lovely daughters; the accomplished Major McCarty, with the officers of the 10th Regiment generally—several officers of the old army—the inhabitants of Matamoros, both Mexican and American—alike united in the festivities.

American Flag, Mar. 1, 1848: We learn with sincere regret, and venture to say there is not a resident in Matamoros but will sympathize with us, that Capt. Chapman is soon to be relieved as Quarter Master at this post, being ordered to Washington City, as we understand, to fill a post in the office of the Quartermaster General. Capt. Chapman has so identified himself with Matamoros during his brief residence here, by his many prominent and praiseworthy acts, that he seems as one, the chief amongst us—the fount from which has emanated all the improvements which now grace our city, and all our present enjoyments. Praise of him as an officer or a gentleman would be fulsome. His successor here, as we learn, is to be Capt. Sibley, now A. Q. M. at Monterrey. Several weeks will probably elapse before the change takes place.

American Flag, Mar. 29, 1848: Ourselves in common with the entire community have been much gratified in learning by last mail, that Capt. W. W. Chapman, by order from Washington, is continued in his present position as Quartermaster at this post. We hope that a honorable Ayuntamiento will, when the existing Armistice shall be promulgated, carry out the vigorous plan of municipal and general improvements that this gentleman has so creditably commenced—always excepting the capitation tax and the tax on our printing office, those not being an improvement by any means, but an unheard of exaction.

American Flag, May 17, 1848:

CAMERON COUNTY

This county, formed at the last session of the Legislature of Texas, is already attracting considerable attention from persons desirous of making permanent locations. It embraces Brazos Island, a part of Padre Island, Point Isabel and a large extent of country between the Mouth of the Rio Grande and Reynosa, extending to within about fifteen miles of the latter place, with a present population of, not less than four thousand persons, out of which, there are probably seven hundred legally qualified voters. . . . Every male Mexican twenty-one years of age, who resided in Texas six months immediately preceding the adoption of the present Constitution, will have an undoubted right to vote. This section of the Constitution was wisely incorporated, as without it great injustice would be done to Mexicans residing in the Western part of the State, by subjecting them to the burdens of taxation, while they would be deprived of the elective franchise.

A large addition to the present population of this section of country may be expected during the coming fall and winter from the United States, numbers of Germans and French having signified their intention of seeking a home in the valley of the Rio Grande. The lands upon this river, in most parts, are of a desirable quality, and delightfully situated for residences. In addition to the fertility of the soil, its elevated character and the salubrity of its climate—the contiguity of this section of country to the stock raising districts of Mexico, whereby settlers will be enabled to purchase all kinds of stock in large or small quantities, at low prices, without inconvenience, together with the convenient communication with the Gulf, offers advantages to settlers which cannot be realized in any other portion of the State.

These lands are well adapted to the growth of corn, cotton, sugar, rice, hemp, and *especially tobacco*, being very similar to the celebrated Rose Oak lands in Virginia, which are declared by agriculturalists to be equal to any in the world. Another important advantage will accrue to settlers on the Rio Grande from their having a ready market for all their produce at their own doors, at high prices, as the demand is, and will be for many years, in advance of the productions.

With these advantages what may we not predict for Cameron county? In a very short time, we expect to see well cultivated plantations, with sugar mills and cotton gins—smiling villages, churches, school houses, &c., spring up at various points on the river. Such are some of the blessings that will grow out of this war.

American Flag, May 24, 1848: "WOLF!"—. . . A few days ago a wolf of enormous size was discovered making depredations upon a sheepfold near the Mouth of the River. He was chased away, but not until after he had destroyed thirty of the flock. He took his course directly up the river, until within a few miles of Matamoros, where he killed forty more of the mutton tribe. After this bloody feat he concluded to pay our good friends of Santa Rita a visit, and introduced himself while they were indulging in a general waltz at a fandango. The *Senoritas* just screamed, then fainted; the *Hombres*, thinking the *Diablo* was turned loose among them, sprang toward the chaparral. His wolfship, discovering that he was not in a sheep corral, but among their owners and tenders, bounded off, upsetting in his flight two old coffee women, and a man and horse, just after the former had mounted. The wolf was fortunately shot and killed, before he had succeeded in making off. After he was dead, he measured, from the point of his nose to the tip of his tail, twelve feet and *some* inches, and from the point of his shoulder to the bottom of his paw, 2 feet and 9 inches. The extraordinary size of the animal, as stated by Mr. Perine, we know, will excite doubt in the minds of many, but Mr. P. is a man of veracity, and refers to numerous witnesses, who were present at the fandango, which was held in an open space, outdoors, in the town.

American Flag, June 14, 1848:

Peace!—Peace!

The roar of artillery and the ringing of bells has announced to us the restoration of Mexican authority in this city. It remains to be seen how it will be exercised towards American citizens now subject to it. From the chief military authority of the United States on this line, (if the future can be divined from the experience of the past) American citizens cannot expect much protection; it therefore behooves them to look out for themselves. We advise all Americans to pursue an orderly and peaceable course, as long as they remain on the south side of the Rio Grande, but at the same time be prepared to defend their rights if invaded. If the Mexican authorities shall pursue an impartial and just course towards the American residents here, until they shall have time to withdraw from the country, all will be well.

American Flag, June 24, 1848: The Quartermaster's Department here is busily engaged in erecting buildings and temporary sheds on the opposite bank of the river, preparatory to the transfer of quarters from this city. The place selected for the new quarters—which we suppose will remain a permanent military establishment—is about half a mile above Fort Brown, on an elevated ridge beyond the reach of overflow from the river. The spot is well selected, and just the place according to our way of thinking, where is to be the great commercial emporium on the Rio Grande. Uncle Sam, being a large capitalist, a public spirited, liberal and enterprising old gentleman, will give such a start to this new city that its future importance requires no prophet to foresee—"*Athens*" (the embryo city is so christened) already appears to us with its thousands of magnificent houses, its thousands upon thousands of industrious and enterprising inhabitants, and a trade hardly excelled by the great emporium of the Mississippi.

American Flag, June 28, 1848 [letter to the editors]:

For the American Flag.

Gentlemen:—You are rather too fast in giving a name to the location of the Quarter Master's Depot on the other side. Furthermore, it is not intended that any private buildings shall be erected at that point. But should it chance that a town spring up there, a national name for it would be more befitting than the stale and worn out name of "Athens"—a name given to so many country Post offices and "Cross Roads" in the United States, that a letter directed to Athens, generally makes the circuit of the whole Union in search of its proper destination—"Brownsville" occurs to me as being the most appropriate name for this place, in memory of the gallant Major Brown, who fell in defence of the spot on which it is located.

C.

[Editor's response:] We stand corrected and rebuked, and promise not to meddle in future with other people's business.

American Flag, July 5, 1848: FOURTH OF JULY IN MATAMORAS—The evacuation of the city and consequent occupation of all classes in preparation for a move, prevented anything like a formal celebration yesterday of the 72d anniversary of our national independence. . . . During this ceremony of Flag raising, the 10th regiment U.S. Infantry, Col. Temple commanding, marched in detached companies along the street leading to the beautiful plain back of the city, for review and inspection by Major General Wool. The regiment, 900 strong, made a display of its efficiency in tactics and drill eliciting the admiration of all. Gen. Wool and staff, with a number of officers and citizens on horseback dashed down the streets to the parade. . . . After going through various evolutions in a masterly manner, firing by files, by wings and by battalion, the parade was dismissed, and the General and staff with Col. Temple and a number of other officers, returned to Col. Davenport's quarters, where, after partaking some refreshments, the gentlemen paired off to enjoy the hospitalities and kind attentions to be met with in the generous and lively families of this city.

New Orleans *Daily Delta*, Aug. 29, 1848: On the 16th ult., as we learn from the *Flag*, the Quartermaster removed from his quarters in Matamoros to the Government Depot, near Fort Brown, in Texas, taking with him the last of the Government Property which was remaining in Mexico—so Maj. Chapman can boast that, if he was not the first in the war, he was the last officer out of it, or rather the country in which it was waged. The *Flag* says: "Industry, economy and order mark every branch of the public service at the new Depot. The necessary buildings are in rapid progress towards completion, and the whole business of the Quartermaster's Department is conducted with a due regard to the public interest. Without the lines houses are springing up in every direction. Take it altogether, and Brownsville bids fair to become a town of no trifling importance."

The *Flag* has a highly complimentary notice of Maj. Chapman, an officer whose services in the field and as Quartermaster at Matamoros have earned him well-merited distinction, while the many and great benefits he has conferred upon the people of Matamoros, in the improvement of their city, by aiding in the reestablishment and care of their public schools, and in many other ways have endeared him to them, and elicited from the Ayuntamiento of the city a complimentary letter of thanks, on his retirement from the scene of his arduous duties. Maj. Chapman's departure, says the *Flag*, is regarded with unfeigned regret by all the citizens of Matamoros.

[Resolution of the Ayuntamiento, or city council of Matamoras, addressed to William Chapman, Aug. 3, 1848, which was not requoted in the preceding extract]: It having come to the knowledge of this corporation that the day on which you move your residence to the other side of the river is very near and considering that the amicable feelings you leave in this city by the manner in which you have comported yourself during the period of your command both as a government agent and soldier, may make you occasionally desire to return to this city, the corporation has resolved in an extraordinary session held today, to manifest to you that for such occasions you have permission to land on this side of the river. Assuring you that this is not mere ceremony, but that the desire to cultivate the most friendly relations with you has been the cause of proposing this exception.

New Orleans *Daily Delta*, Sept. 27, 1848 [reporting the city's first news of the gold discovery in California]: *Gold in California.*—An immense bed of gold, one hundred miles in extent, it is said, has been discovered in California, on American Fork and Feather rivers, tributaries of the Sacramento, near Monterey. Mr. Colton, the alcalde of Monterey, states that the gold is found in the sands in grains resembling squirrel shot, flattened out. Some grains weigh an ounce each. It is got by washing out the sand in any vessel, from a tea saucer to a warming pan. A single person can gather an ounce or two a day, and some even a hundred dollars' worth. Two thousand whites and as many Indians are on the ground. All the American settlements are deserted, and farming nearly suspended. The women only remain in the settlements. Sailors and captains desert the ships to go to the gold region, and laborers refuse ten dollars a day to work on the farms.

New Orleans *Daily Delta*, Oct. 4, 1848: *Severe Gale—Brazos Island Overflowed.*—Capt. Otway, of the U.S. Transport Steamer *Maria Burt*, arrived yesterday from the Brazos, reports that a severe gale raged at that place from the 16th to the 23d ult., the wind blowing from all points of the compass, accompanied with heavy rains, in consequence of which the whole of the Island was overflowed. On the 23d, the inhabitants took refuge on board the steamers and vessels in port, for safety, until the flood subsided. [There were sixteen vessels in port at Brazos Santiago and seven steamers at the Mouth of the River during the storm.]

New Orleans *Daily Delta*, Oct. 21, 1848 [extracting from the *Matamoros Flag* of Oct. 9, 1848]: Mr. Henry [Harry] Love, well known as having proved himself a good and faithful soldier, and one of the most trustworthy and fearless express-riders on this line, arrived at Fort Brown on the 4th inst., from Chihuahua. . . . This side of Parras, Mr. Love was detained for twenty-four hours, at a rancho, being surrounded by a band of Cumanche Indians, who, after stealing a lot of horses and mules and wounding several Mexicans, finally retired. Mr. Love, in company with Mr. Sherman, came across a party of Apache Indians, in the desert known as the *Travesia*, at about eight o'clock on a dark night. They hailed these Indians, supposing them to be Mexicans, and were in turn saluted with a shower of arrows. They returned the fire, and retreated on the same road a short distance, then, by taking the mountains they avoided the Indians during the next day, but on returning to the road the Indians took their trail, and followed them to an arroyo, or ravine, swelled by recent rains and of difficult passage. Here they made a stand, and when the Indians arrived within reach of their rifles, fired on them, killing their chief, whom they saw fall; they then dashed across the arroyo. In crossing, Mr. Sherman's horse, which had been wounded by the Indians the night before, and being too weak, from loss of blood to stem the current, was instantly swept from under him, and was dashed over a fall of about seventy feet. Mr. Love threw his lariat over Mr. Sherman, and brought him safely to the shore. Mr. Love, who has made several excursions on this route, as also others, states that he has uniformly met with kind and hospitable treatment from the higher classes of the inhabitants.

1849

New Orleans *Daily Delta*, Apr. 26, 1849 [quoting from the *American Flag* of Apr. 11 and 18, 1849]: Indians, supposed to be about one hundred in number, made a foray in the vicinity of Santa Rita district, . . . twelve miles from this place, where they stole and drove off a large number of horses and mules. As far as heard from we learn of the murder of two women, and the carrying off a number of children. They have been committing depredations with impunity on the ranchos throughout this line. Many Mexicans have lost their entire property. . . .

On Saturday last, the 14th instant, quite an excitement was created in our town by the arrival of an express from Palo Alto, about 11 miles distant, (the famous battlefield,) with accounts that the Mexicans were arriving there in numbers for security and protection against bands of marauding Indians, who are prowling about the Mexican ranchos, murdering, robbing, and burning. Immediately on the arrival of this intelligence, a party of our fellow citizens well mounted, started in search of these marauders. About eight miles from here, the party met with three Mexicans coming in for protection, having been robbed of all they possessed. They brought in a shield and other articles which convinced us that these Indians were Camanches. Our party remained at Palo Alto during the night of the 14th, it raining heavily. Early next morning they set out, and found about twelve miles distant from Palo Alto, a Mexican camp that had been robbed. After examining the premises our party took the Indian trail, and followed it some twelve miles further, when they met another party of Mexicans and Americans, also in pursuit. Four miles further, our party met a Mexican who had escaped from the Indians, having been their prisoner, (he had been sorely whipped, and barely escaped with life.) He stated that the party of Indians that had taken him had thirty odd fresh scalps, and a large number of horses and mules. Our party here learned that the Indians were so far in advance, with the advantage of fresh horses which they had stolen, that further pursuit would be useless, and therefore returned.

New Orleans *Daily Delta*, Apr. 13, 1849: . . . We learned that the depredations of the Indians on the Mexican Territory have become even more extensive since the conclusion of the late war. . . . The terror and affliction of the Mexicans in the frontier towns [is] approaching to absolute despair. Even in towns of considerable size, they are kept in constant dread of the sudden inroad of these savages, who rush in upon them with the quickness of lightning, and seizing their wives and children, their cattle and movable property, disappear as mysteriously and suddenly as they come, bearing their spoils afar off to their distant camping grounds. The scenes of distress, of barbarous violence, of cruel and remorseless ravages, . . . exceed even the records of any thing that can be found in the settlement of our own country. . . .

It was with a view to putting an end to these distressing scenes, that certain clauses were introduced into the late treaty of Guadalupe [Hidalgo], by which our government solemnly pledged its faith to restrain the depredations of the Indians on our border, compel them to surrender their Mexican prisoners, and to punish them for any barbarities against the Mexicans, which might come under the observation of our authorities. . . .

The great body of both the Camanches and Apaches, the constant and most formidable of these savage depredators upon the Mexican territory, reside within our territory, chiefly on the Western plains of Texas and in the valley of the Rio Grande. Here, they find themselves pressed on one side by the vast, sterile plains of the West, and on the other by the advancing settlements of our own people. Game is yearly growing scarce. The buffalo has, in a great measure, abandoned the dry plains of the South. Thus, then, these Indians find themselves driven either to steal or to work for a bare subsistence. The former pursuit is much more congenial to their tastes and religion than the latter. . . .

If the Indians are prevented from depredating on the Mexicans, they will be thrown back upon our own settlements, and will transfer to our own territory those distressing events of which Mexico is now the scene. . . . These Indians, too, unlike those which have successively disappeared before the civilization and settlement of the whites on this continent, have no territory to fall back on. . . . Whither then can they go, and how can they be supported without depredating upon their neighbors, are questions which should employ the most anxious concern and investigations of our Home Department.

Some mode by which agriculture may be introduced and the peaceful arts inculcated, is the only means by which these savages can be induced to abandon their hereditary habits of plunder and war. The bayonet will be found inefficacious. . . . Now and then we might possibly be able to capture and punish them. But these cases would bear but a small proportion to the number or extent of their depredations. They would, too, arouse a deep feeling of revenge, which in the Indian is not easily sated. The Camanches have two main points in their religious creed, two virtues which they cultivate more ardently and devotedly than most Christians do the articles of their faith; they are Theft and Revenge. A wrong is never forgotten or forgiven by them. It may not be to-day, to-morrow, this year, the next, or ten years hence, but sooner or later, the Camanche's revenge will fall upon his enemy, when he least expects.

At present these Indians profess a friendly disposition for our Government and people. But this feeling proceeds from an apprehension that our hostility might seriously interfere with their depredations upon the Mexicans, and cannot be confided in. It will therefore be necessary for the Government to increase our force on the Southwestern frontier . . . and thus to terminate the most distressing scenes of barbarity and cruelty which have ever been exhibited on this continent.

New Orleans *Daily Delta*, May 24, 1849 [extracting from the *American Flag* of May 16, 1849]: We notice a petition, from citizens residing on the Rio Grande, to the President of the United States, published in the Flag, informing him of their exposed condition, and asking him for a body of calvary sufficiently large to afford them the protection which they conceive they have a right. . . .

On Thursday last [May 10] our town was thrown into great excitement by the arrival of an express from Palo Alto, announcing . . . that a numerous and formidable band of Indians had just made a descent upon that place, and had already committed many acts of startling and savage barbarity. The stage from Point Isabel had been intercepted, and the proprietor, Mr Bangs, and Mr Lombardo, a passenger, were taken prisoners. A train of transport wagons had also been captured between Brownsville and Point Isabel, containing much valuable merchandise. . . . [By the newspaper account, four were killed, one was wounded, an additional seven were taken captive, and seventy horses were stolen. Bangs and Lombardo escaped]. They were, however, reduced to a state of nudity. . . . The aged mother of Mrs. Willsey persisted in following her children, and did so for some distance, regardless of savage menace, when the Indians, seizing her, tied her hands behind her, pierced her with their lances and arrows, and left her on the ground weltering in her blood, as they supposed, dead. This poor woman, however, succeeded in reaching a neighboring rancho in a most shocking and mutilated condition, and is now, we understand, a maniac.

New Orleans *Daily Delta*, June 7, 1849: Brazos Santiago, May 27, 1849. *Editors Delta*: About half past two o'clock on Sunday Morning, the 26th ultimo, a tornado swept over this part of the world, causing great loss of property, and what is more to be regretted, two valuable citizens lost their lives at Point Isabel, by having the respective houses blown down upon them, in which they had taken shelter. . . .

At Point Isabel, the list of disasters are as follows: a fine storehouse owned, and occupied by Mr. J. H. Levi, was blown to pieces; a portion of the heavy rafters falling upon him, crushed him in a shocking manner, and causing almost instant death. He has left a large family to mourn his irreparable loss. Another fine building, used as a warehouse, was blown down, killing a Mexican gentleman who was engaged in the transportation of goods across the country from the Point to Brownsville. There were several other houses blown to pieces, and a portion of the fragments scattered hundreds of yards and almost every building was more or less injured.

Truly the people of Point Isabel have a hard time of it. I can scarcely describe my feelings at witnessing, but a few days ago, the frantic grief of a mother, who had her three daughters, (blooming young ladies) torn from her by the Indians, and that within a few miles of the embryo city "Fronton" [Point Isabel]. The destruction of property, though great on the Brazos, was not attended by any loss of life or limb; a number of buildings were blown down, which will be a serious drawback to the prosperity of the place. [Five vessels were severely damaged but survived the storm.]

New Orleans *Daily Delta,* Dec. 23, 1849, Brownsville correspondent: The steamboat, *J. E. Roberts,* was lost on the beach near Boca Chica, on the 8th . . . . Many packages that came ashore were stolen or buried in the sand hills, and boxes and trunks were completely rifled. . . . The people of Brownsville have christened the inhabitants of Brazos Island and Mouth of Rio Grande, "The Sandhill Thieving and Wrecking Crew". . . . Capt. Ben Moses, who combines an assortment, and in whom is concentrated all the offices and honors that could be heaped on one individual, has, in his capacity of justice of the peace, first alcalde, high constable, sheriff, administrator, notary public, merchant, doctor, manufacturer of impunados, and head hombre of Odd Fellows, exerted himself to his utmost to save property and bring to justice the thieves, but, as yet, with little success, as they have decamped into the chapparal or elsewhere with their booty.

1850

New Orleans *Daily Delta*, Mar. 9, 1850 [extracting from the Brownsville *Rio Grande Sentinel*, Feb. 27, 1850]: We are gratified at being able to announce that a Protestant church was organized at this place on Saturday, the 23d instant, under the pastoral care of Rev. Hiram Chamberlain, a clergyman who has recently come among us with his family, under the auspices of the Board of Missions of the Grand Assembly of the Presbyterian church. Last Sabbath the ceremony of a formal and public organization [First Presbyterian Church of Brownsville] was witnessed by our citizens, after which the sacrament of the Lord's Supper was administered to the members present and to a considerable number of the members of churches of other denominations, who, being also present, were cordially invited to participate. The services were solemn and deeply interesting. The Pastor announced the names of nineteen members—five of whom, having formerly belonged to other denominations, united with the privilege of withdrawing to join their own peculiar denominations when an opportunity should occur.

New Orleans *Daily True Delta*, Mar. 10, 1850 [from the Matamoras correspondent's letter of Mar. 4, 1850]: Buildings are going up every day; goods arriving, steamboats loading and unloading, and every person seems engaged to some useful employment. The Mexicans are perfectly astonished at the growth of Brownsville, Not yet two years old, and numbering 2500 inhabitants;. . . .

New Orleans *Daily Delta*, Mar. 22, 1850 [from the Brownsville correspondent's letter of Mar. 12, 1850]: The population of Brownsville, of all colors, at the present time is 5000. It is a right bustling, business place; every one seems to have something to do, and to be intent on doing it. Several two and three story brick houses are going up. . . .

A bad feeling had for some time existed between G. M. Armstrong and E. B. Scarborough, editor of the [Rio Grande] *Sentinel*, in consequence of an article published in that paper reflecting on the former. They met accidentally in the Garrison, when Scarborough told Armstrong that he intended to shoot him that evening. Armstrong thereupon drew his "Texas Code of Practice"—a six shooter—and discharged four of the barrels at Scarborough, every shot taking effect. The wounds are not considered mortal, and Scarborough is doing well.

New Orleans *Daily Delta*, Mar. 28, 1850: Late from the Rio Grande.—Heavy Norther at the Brazos—Brazos Island Overflowed—Marine Disasters—Five Hundred Indians Encamped near Roma—General Alarm of the Inhabitants—Indian Murders and Depredations, etc.

. . . there was a heavy norther at the Brazos on the 22d, which caused an overflow of the whole island, with the exception of the sand hills, and continued for forty-eight hours. [Three schooners went ashore and were lost.]

New Orleans *Daily True Delta*, Apr. 17, 1850 [extracting from the *Rio Grande Sentinel*, Apr. 10, 1850, which reported a town meeting held in Brownsville on April 8 at which resolutions were passed and an agent, G. K. Lewis, was selected to appeal directly to the U. S. Congress for additional protection from Indian raids]: . . . The horrors of Indian warfare were truthfully depicted by men who have been eye-witnesses of the heart-rending scenes of cruelty which are continually practised upon the unprotected settler on this frontier. We say unprotected, for with the limited number of U.S. troops stationed here, and from the nature of these troops, the settler is as insecure as though no regular force existed; in proof of which we will state some few facts. Last summer, when the Indians were down in force on the Lower Rio Grande, and at Palo Alto, but a few miles from two U.S. Military Stations—the one of this place and the other at Point Isabel—application was made to them for assistance and, in justice to the officers in command, we must say that it was promptly granted. Assistance was sent to the sufferers with all the dispatch that lay in their power, but how ineffectual: This relief consisted in a company of Infantry, who, in one instance, marched to the scene of outrage *on foot*! and, on another occasion, were dispatched in quest of the enemy *in wagons*! Assistance was thus sent, intended to afford relief against an enemy whose movements are as fleet almost as the winds!

. . . We understand that experienced engineers have been ordered to examine the river with an eye to its navigation. Suitable boats are being constructed at the Brasos for this expedition, and the early arrival of the officers to take command of them is expected. In fact an expedition has already been put under way by Major W. W. Chapman, U.S. Quartermaster—a man for whose indefatigable enterprise and gentlemanly courtesy this whole section of country is indebted. This last mentioned expedition consists of a light draught boat, with a compliment of some fifteen or twenty men, under command of that experienced frontiersman, Harry Love, who is as much of an adept on land as he is on water, and "at-home" in either place. Harry has, we are informed, instructions to take his boat as high up the river as he can float her, and we feel confident that Captain Love will make report of having traveled many miles of the Rio Bravo del Norte.

New Orleans *Daily Delta*, June 12, 1850 [from the Rio Grande correspondent's letter of June 4, 1850]: Capt. Glover, the American Consul at Monterey, had $33,000 seized a few days ago, a short distance below Camargo, by a party of Banditti, belonging to the Avalos Brigade. This gang demanded Capt. Glover's papers, alleging that the money was intended to be smuggled into Texas. The papers being produced, the officer declared them to be illegal; and immediately, without further ado, took possession of the conducts and brought it with all haste to Matamoros, and delivered it over to Gen. Avalos. Never were dollars more eagerly clutched than those of Capt. Glover by the ex-captain of the Puebla robbers. He made no concealment of his joy, declaring that as he was made Lieutenant for successful robbery on the Puebla road, he would now attain the Presidency or a Generalship of the line, by virtue of this big haul. The *Bandera Mexicana*, published in Matamoros, appeared in brilliant colors, in honor of the deeds of the brave General; a *salvo* of artillery was fired from all the batteries; the greasy buzzard of Mexico [The Mexican flag]—the same which lay salted up in a barrel, during the war—was unfurled, and floated insultingly from the battlements of the Pintos Castle. But, alas! This dream of happiness was too short to last long. The legality of the decree confiscating Capt. Glover's property, was questioned, and decided by higher authority against the exultant Avalos, and he is compelled to disgorge the spoils. The General has not smiled since the decision was given, and it is said he kicked his Adjutant down stairs three times the day it was announced. Were he not such a coward, fears would be entertained that he would commit suicide. . . .

A few nights ago, I was at a party given by Mrs. Maj. Chapman, in honor of a young couple that came all the way from the interior of Mexico to get married. There were at least one hundred gentleman and ladies present. Among the guests, I noticed the same Pinto General, Avalos, and the notorious scamp Col. Postillo, the villain who was engaged in the massacre of Fanning's men in 1836, at Goliad. When their presence was announced, the band involuntarily struck up the Rogue's March. Several respectable Mexican families that were present retired. Through the efforts of our kind host and hostess, the affair was made a very merry and pleasant one, and the festivities were continued till three o'clock in the morning.

Brownsville is growing very fast, there is a great deal of business going on and no small quantity of rascality [which included Mrs. R. D. Denton's overdosing on arsenic and laudanum; a convicted murderer escaping from jail and fleeing to Matamoras; a Mexican raping his six-year-old daughter and the "inhuman monster, after being well cowhided by his better half, took refuge on the other side of the river"; and D. W. Shropshire and J. Van Alsten having an affray in which the former was killed; "bowie knives, five shooters, and double-barreled guns being the weapons used."]

New Orleans *Daily True Delta*, June 18, 1850 [quoting the *Rio Grande Sentinel*, June 12, 1850]: Every one has heard of the silver plate captured in the pavilion of Gen. Arista, at the battle of Resaca de la Palma, and about which the papers spoke so much at the time. This plate has been given up by the American authorities at Fort Brown, to the agent of the original owner, and by him sold, as per order from Gen. Arista, for the benefit of the Mexican soldiers who were wounded in the engagement in which it was captured. One of our enterprising merchants, Mr. John E. Garey, has become the purchaser.

New Orleans *Daily True Delta*, July 9, 1850 [extracting from the *Rio Grande Sentinel*, July 3, 1850]: On Sunday evening last, at about dusk, the law and order abiding portion of our citizens were surprised at the intelligence that the notorious Kellogg, who was imprisoned awaiting his trial before the district court, under some dozen charges, and among them several of highway robbery, had escaped. . . . Several attempts were made, we are told, by the jailer to arrest the prisoner, after he had escaped the enclosure of the prison walls, but he was deterred from doing so by the hoots and threats of the unprincipled rabble who had gathered around him. He assures us that he does not believe that he would have been permitted to have taken his prisoner back to jail, had he succeeded in recapturing him.

[*Daily True Delta* editorial comment]: If escapes from the Brownsville jail continue to be as frequent as for some time past, we shall begin to think that the "law and order abiding portion" of the citizens are but a minority of the population of that thriving town.

New Orleans *Daily Delta*, July 10, 1850 [from the Brownsville correspondent's letter of July 4, 1850]: *An act of Heroism worthy a Great General.*—Last Sunday evening a peaceable man, (a Frenchman) by the name of Duval, and citizen of Matamoros, was returning to that place from this city, and when within a short distance of the town was overhauled by one of the Avalos Banditti. While thus engaged, the Prieta General, who chanced to be passing by with his Adjutant, seeing that Mr Duval was unwilling to be searched—for he had nothing—and refusing to follow the robber to the Custom House, *gallantly* descended from his carriage, and with one of Colt's revolvers in each hand, (the other fellows doing likewise,) levelled them at the breast of this unarmed man, struck him on the head with one of the pistols; and inflicting this treatment while he was a prisoner. Was not this *noble* of the *Prieta* General?—The man who occupies at present the proud position of a General, commanding the Mexican forces on the Rio Grande. This is not the only act he has been guilty of. His history is well known to every man, woman and child of Matamoros. Not even later than the last trip of the steamship *Globe*, from your city [New Orleans], a young lady, (a *brunette*) came passenger by her. She is familiarly known as the "Widow Garcia," and formerly lived in Matamoros. Report has it that an intimacy existed between her and General Avalos; in fact, she openly confessed that she considered it a duty incumbent upon the sex, to make any sacrifice to the man she loved; and that she loved the General no one can doubt. She suddenly left Matamoros in February last, much to the surprise of her friends, and under circumstances unknown to any body save a few. The *Mobile Advertiser*, contained an account of a horrible infanticide, committed in that city by a Mexican lady, who was examined and acquitted upon the evidence of two physicians. Every one here is of the opinion that Alabama has had the high honor of giving birth, and likewise death, to a young Avalos. She is again, I understand, under his charge and protection. . . .

Two things are most difficult for Avalos to do
Tis to be honorable, and be honest too.

I visited Matamoras some two days ago, It is a very dull place, as it ever will be, until it casts off the tyranny by which it is enthralled. The grand Plaza is the only ornament it possesses. This place, through the kindness and untiring energy of Major Chapman and his fair lady, has become the admiration of all. Not that it surpasses any thing of the kind among you [in New Orleans] but that it should exist, is a wonder to all. The war closed too soon for the Major to enjoy the reward of his industry, or to carry out his generous intentions; and now, the only consolation he has, is to visit it occasionally, in company with his fair and generous-hearted companion, and pluck a golden orange from the tree his industry planted, or a rose from the scrub which the delicate fingers of his lady so carefully nurtured. But he threw his pearls before swine.

New Orleans *Daily True Delta*, July 10, 1850: Many think that, owing to the nature of the country prowled over by the Comanche, and other equally warlike tribes, a war there must be speedily brought to a close, particularly if the invading force be properly mounted: but appear to forget that the movements of the Indians are entirely unimpeded by a cumbrous commissariat, and the other impediments to celerity inseparable from the movements of regular troops on active service in the field. . . . The Quartermaster's Department, on the intelligence direction of which so much depends, was never in more efficient working, or in better hands, . . . and Major Chapman, an able and excellent officer, has charge of the Department at that important point the Brazos. It is to be hoped the Government will put it in the power of their able military officers to proceed vigorously to work and, instead of spinning out to a wearisome length this miserable war, from which there is no way to escape, bring it quickly to an end, honorable, humane, and definitive.

New Orleans *Daily Delta*, July 23, 1850 [extracting from the *American Flag* and *Rio Grande Sentinel*, July 17, 1850]: From these papers we take the following report of two cases, in both of which summary vengence was taken on two individuals. However well deserved may have been their punishment, there is no justification for resorting to popular retaliation, in a country where the law should be supreme. We have already stated in this paper that a desparate character, Bill Hardy, had wantonly murdered, at Brownsville, a Capt. Brennan [of the Schooner *Spray*] who had just traveled from Galveston with him.

He was arrested and after his arrest and imprisonment [quoting from the *Flag*], it became known that he had killed a man in St. Louis, another on the Arkansas River, and that he had attempted to take the lives of several men in San Antonio, Austin and Galveston, from which place Capt. Brennan paid his passage, and that he was sent in irons from Monterey, during the war, but effected his escape by jumping overboard somewhere between this place and Reynosa, and swimming ashore. On learning his past history, and knowing the unsafe condition of our jail, our citizens were generally of the opinion that it was best to cut short his murderous career, while they had it in their power. With this understanding a large concourse of citizens assembled in the vicinity of the jail. Some few were in favor of going through the form of a trial, but the majority looked upon such a proceeding as a mere farce, since the Coroner's inquest and the prisoner's own admission had established his guilt beyond doubt or cavil. To test the sense of the meeting, it was proposed that all in favor of hanging, step out. The result was an almost entire change of places on the part of the crowd, which then proceeded to the jail and demanded the culprit. The deputy sheriff remarked to the crowd, that he held the keys of the jail, and it was his duty to safely keep the prisoner, but he did not feel disposed to resist the demands of so large a portion of the citizens of the county. He would, therefore, deliver up the keys, with the request that the prisoner be permitted to make any statement in extenuation, or otherwise, he might wish. This was readily acceded, when the prisoner was unfettered and brought forth, and in that condition permitted to walk to the place of his execution. It was proposed to tie him, but on his assuring that he would not attempt to run, he was suffered to go free and untrammeled in any way. On reaching the spot selected for this tragic scene, he remarked that he knew he had to die, and intended to die like a man; but would rather be shot than hung. The crowd assembled to witness the solemn tragedy was quite large, but orderly and quiet, with a few exceptions. No one volunteering to shoot the guilty, hardened wretch, it was decided that he must hang. Rev. Mr. Cravens then came forward and introduced himself, and asked Hardy if he desired any preparation or had any statement to make, He said he had nothing to say except as to the disposition of his effects and requested the writing of a few letters to his friends. He then requested Mr. Cravens to pray for him. During all this time, and even while the arrangements were making for launching him into eternity, where he would meet with a more dread tribunal than any on earth, he evinced the most perfect indifference as to his fate, not suffering a muscle of his face or limbs to betray the least emotion. And even took the rope that was to hang him, and tied the hangman's knot to show how it was done, without the slightest perceptible tremor of the nerves. Those managing the matter fearing the knot was not well tied, untied it for the purpose of retying, in which they failed, when he remarked to a gentleman standing near him that he would have to tie it again. This kind office, the individual addressed, promised to perform for him. The doomed man then got into a cart, mounted on a plank which rested on the wheels, without any resistance or assistance, and, while the rope, which was suspended from a beam used for hoisting beeves, was being adjusted around his neck, asked to have his hands tied behind him. There he stood, high above the crowd, his hands tied, the noose close about his neck, death staring him in the face, calm, cool, and collected. The cart moved from under him, and, in this condition, he was hurled into eternity. Such a spectacle we never witnessed before—may we never again. It was evidently his intention to have leaped from the cart, but was prevented from so doing by some one attracting his attention as it started, which caused his feet to drag from the tail. He died after a slight struggle, and thus terminated the earthly career of the notorious Bill Hardy, who had been the terror of every community in which he lived. . . .

Another Brutal Assassination and Speedy and Summary Justice.—We were yesterday, says the *Sentinel*, shocked with the report of another frightful assassination in our city, and, on inquiry, found the particulars to be as follows: A party of men were gambling at a low groggery, or "hell," kept by a man named McKee, on Levee Street, when a dispute arose between two persons, Mexicans, in relation to a bet of twelve and a half cents. A few words were passed between the parties, when one of them, named Francisco Flores, drew a pistol and deliberately fired it full in the face of his adversary. The pistol was loaded with three buckshot, only one of which took effect, in the shoulder of the intended victim, the others lodging in the neck of another person, named Delesforo Liundo, causing his death in a few hours. After this savage act, the murderer fled, running on board a steamboat which was lying at the wharf, from whence he jumped into the river, and attempted to escape, by swimming to the other side. He was pursued and arrested when about midway of the stream and brought back. By this time the indignation of the populace had arrived at a degree wholly beyond control, and he was taken by them to the outskirts of the city, where a fearful, though just and summary punishment stopped his further career of crime. He died upon the scaffold while his hands were yet wet with the blood of his victim.

New Orleans *Daily True Delta*, Aug. 6, 1850 [from a letter from an "intelligent correspondent at Brownsville" of July 31, 1850]: Our city was again the scene of another murder. On Thursday last, an altercation sprung up on the levee between one Howard Slaughter, a notorious character employed on the Steamer *Tom McKinny*, and Solomon Debart, when Slaughter picked up a bar of iron, which was lying close by, and struck Debart several blows on the head, fracturing his skull in two places, from the effects of which he died the same night, at 11 o'clock. On Friday an inquest was held over the body, and the jury returned a verdict in accordance with the facts. The deceased was a native of Pennsylvania. Slaughter has been arrested and is now in jail, heavily ironed, and will be tried for manslaughter at the October term of the Circuit Court of Cameron County. It was with difficulty that a large portion of the citizens were prevented from taking him to the limits of the city and hanging him, so strong have they of late imbibed a mob feeling. . . .

Temperance is making rapid progress in this place. A society has been organized within the last three weeks and already numbers about 35 members. . . .

Within the last week our Chief Magistrate [Israel Bigelow] has twice exhibited his pugilistic powers, in the shape of *rough and tumble fights*—once with a Justice and once with a member of the learned profession. In the last case he is said to have got the worst of it, as he was not seen in the streets for four days afterwards, and a certain druggist reports having sold a quantity of sugar of lead. The principal officer should not set such *pug*nacious examples: but the people are satisfied that the Mayor has turned out to be a *perfect horse*. . . .

The city is infected with lewd and abandoned women, who keep their dens of corruption in the most public and central part of the city, and it is impossible for any respectable lady to walk out in the evening, without being made an eye-witness to the most disgraceful and disgusting scenes. . . .

New Orleans *Daily True Delta*, Aug. 20, 1850 [from the Brownsville correspondent on Aug. 15, 1850]: The drinking houses are not doing much—nearly every person has joined the temperance society; you hear nothing but temperance, temperance from morning til night. Success to the cause, it is a noble one. . . .

The election for State, District and county officers held on the 5th, passed off with more quiet than was anticipated. The election was not on party grounds, but rather of clique. The men elected are, with one or two exceptions, able and good men, and will no doubt discharge the duties of their respective offices with much credit. There was some tall voting done at some of the precincts of the county . . . . at one place, where there were only eight persons living, more than ninety votes were polled. The Mexican population on that day deserted their homes in Matamoros, and crossed over to avail themselves of the glorious privileges of the ballot box. . . .

The city is remarkably healthy; the weather during the day is excessively warm, and the least breeze raises a cloud of dust, but the nights are the most pleasant I have experienced any where, and if it were not for the mosquitoes and the thousands of the canine race that bark and howl at night, there would be a chance to sleep.

New Orleans *Daily Delta*, Aug. 27, 1850 [extracting from the *Rio Grande Sentinel*, Aug. 17, 1850]: HARRY LOVE'S EXPLORING EXPEDITION UP THE RIO GRANDE. We learn from the Brownsville Sentinel that Harry Love, the famous frontiersman, arrived in that city on the 17th instant, after an absence of over six months, upon an exploring expedition up the Rio Grande. The Sentinel says:

Six months ago this adventurous man left here with a small keel-boat, manned with twelve hands, with orders from Major Chapman to ascend the river as far as he could find it practicable. We than stated that Harry would push this enterprise as far as it could be taken by any other man, and we are pleased to find that we were not mistaken in our predictions. We are informed by him that he has ascended the Rio Grande to the immense distance of 1400 miles from its mouth, being, as at present computed, 1000 miles above its present head of navigation—and again descended the stream in safety. . . .

. . . One act of this daring man we cannot refrain from noticing here. After having, at great labor and mental trouble, carried his frail bark far up into the mountains through which our noble river holds its way, and having come to obstructions which it was beyond the power of man to overcome, and at which his ascent by water must stop, he planted, fast in the solid rock, a staff, bearing proudly to the winds, the stars and stripes of his country's banner—fit momento of the gallant daring of himself and his brave little band.

New Orleans *Daily Delta*, Sept. 4, 1850 [from Brownsville correspondent's letter of Aug. 28, 1850]: Business is quite dull—that is, retail business—in consequence of the restrictions imposed by Gen. Avalos, upon the intercourse between the citizens of Matamoros and Brownsville. Under his instructions, men are seized and searched, and plundered of the smallest article purchased on this side. Men have had as low as three dollars in money taken from their pockets. Our merchants say this is in consequence of the interference of the papers of this city with the acts of this Knight of the Highway. . . . And now he finds the revenue received at the custom house opposite this place, insufficient to satisfy his avaricious desires, administer to his licentiousness and keep up his seraglio, he has resorted to his old method of raising means.

New Orleans *Daily True Delta*, Sept. 25, 1850 [from the Brownsville correspondent's letter of Sept. 19, 1850]: . . . The river has fallen again and is very low. Indeed these are what may be styled starving times. Money is scarce. The market is well stocked with goods, except some groceries, which are in demand.

A few days since, Major Chapman, quartermaster at this port, succeeded in arresting four negroes who had escaped from Calcacieu, La., and crossed the Sabine, and were in a canoe in Boca Chica. When caught, they were in a canoe pulling as hard as they could for the Mexican shore, which they would have reached in ten or twelve minutes. They were, I believe, sent to New Orleans on the *Yacht*. Great praise is due to Major Chapman for his energy as manifested in the matter. . . .

But faint hopes are entertained for Capt. Glover ever getting back the amount ($55,000) seized by the Mexican authorities, notwithstanding it is generally believed that a decision has been rendered in his favor. Avalos says he will not give up the *rhino* though every tribunal in the world should decree it. Indeed I think it would embarrass him to do so, for a certain widow, who, some three months since was arrested on well grounded suspicion of having given birth to a young hero and destroyed its life, is said to have a large portion of it. It took part of it to get her clear of the Mobile authorities.

New Orleans *Daily Delta*, Oct. 11, 1850: MAJOR CHAPMAN AT FORT BROWN. We have received a letter from this gentleman, contradicting certain statements which have appeared in our Rio Grande correspondence, as well as elsewhere, in regard to him. The following extracts from the Major's letter embrace the gist of his contradiction:

"Statement one was, that at a party given at my house, and attended by a large number of American and Mexican citizens, General Avalos, the Commander of the Mexican troops at Matamoros, was publicly insulted on his entrance, by the band commencing to play the Rogue's March. It is due to the respectable portion of the community, as well as to myself, to say that from the time of General Avalos' entrance to the moment of his departure, nothing occurred that could, by any possibility, give foundation for such a disgraceful story. It is an insult to the large and respectable body of American citizens in Brownsville, to suppose they would have countenanced such a gross violation of the laws of hospitality and good breeding. You will do me the favor, therefore, to contradict, most positively, the statement of the correspondent of the Delta."

Referring to another statement respecting his reputed agency in recovering certain fugitive slaves, the Major says;

"Whatever credit is due in the transaction, belongs wholly and exclusively to Capt. Edward M. Anderson, commander of the U.S. Steamer, *Mentoria*. At the time of the capture, I was thirty miles distant, and had no possible connection with the seizure or transportation to New Orleans.

Allow me to repeat once more, that in *my house* at all times, General Avalos has invariably received the treatment due *from gentlemen to a gentleman*, and that I had no part whatever in the seizure of four slaves from Calcacieu, La."

New Orleans *Daily Delta*, Oct. 11, 1850 [from the Brownsville correspondent's letter of Oct. 1, 1850]: Yesterday, (Tuesday,) a Mexican came to this side and swore out a warrant against another Mexican, who had robbed a store on the Mexican side. Part of the goods stolen were found on this side, through the revelations of an accomplice, who was frightened to disclose all he knew. The deputy sheriff, in company with said accomplice, and the owner of the goods, went in quest of the burglar, and succeeded in overhauling him, some twenty miles above here. At the time they approached him, he was dismounted. The officer rode up and asked his name, which he gave. The deputy sheriff then informed him that he was an official, and wanted him to go to Brownsville. The prisoner, as he was then claimed to be, made towards his horse, where he had a knife. This he did not succeed in getting, doubtless being deterred by the appearance of shooting irons in the hands of the officer. He then attempted to run, when he was shot through the neck, which caused his death. The body was thrown across a saddle, on a mule belonging to deceased, and in this way conveyed to this place, where an inquest was held upon it. The verdict of the coroner's jury was that the deceased come to his death by a pistol ball through his neck, shot by the deputy sheriff, in discharge of his duty. The occurrence occasioned some excitement, and led to an examination of the facts before a justice of the peace, which resulted in the justification of the act. The whole transaction has been an unwarrantable stretch of power. In the first place, all the parties concerned in the robbery belonged on the other side of the river, and consequently were answerable to the laws of Mexico, and not to the laws of Texas. The deputy sheriff done what he conceived to be his duty, in obeying the order of the justice of the peace and attempting to arrest the culprit. But it is questionable whether he was justifiable in shooting him down, because he attempted to escape, and that, too, before he had served the warrant upon him in due form. The community justifies the act, because deceased was a bad man and a greaser.

Rio Grande Sentinel, November 27, 1850: From the Washington Republic. EXPLORATION OF THE RIO GRANDE. *Report of Exploration of the Rio Grande, made by* H. LOVE, *in the keel-boat Major Babbitt, with a map of the river—Navigation of the river—Military posts, Soil, Products, &c.*[1]

ASSISTANT QUARTERMASTER'S OFFICE,
BRAZOS SANTIAGO, TEXAS,
Sept. 5, 1850.

General: I have the honor to report that Captain Love has returned from his explorations of the Rio Grande.[2]

1. This report on the expedition, dated September 5, 1850, was published in Washington, Brownsville, New Orleans, and even Mexico City.

2. Harry Love had recently served as a civilian express rider for the U.S. Army, earning $75.00 per month plus expenses. The names of the twelve men who accompanied Love are unknown.

He left Ringgold Barracks, Texas, (nearly opposite Camargo, Mexico,) with the keel-boat "Major Babbitt," and a crew of twelve men, on the 11th of March, 1850. The "Major Babbitt" was fifty feet long, sixteen feet wide, and drew, with her crew, provisions, arms, &c., on board, eighteen inches of water.[3] Captain Love was instructed to carry her to the highest attainable point on the Rio Grande; and I am satisfied he faithfully complied with the orders received. He found this point at a distance of nine hundred and sixty-seven miles from Ringgold Barracks, where his further progress in the keel-boat was stopped by impassable falls, which he named "Brooke's Falls."[4] On arriving at this point Captain Love carried the skiff which accompanied his boat around these falls, launched her, and rowed her 47 miles to other falls, which he named "Babbitt's Falls."[5] These are 1,014 miles above Ringgold Barracks, about 150 by land below El Paso, 25 by land below the mouth of the Conchos,[6] and 291 by water above the mouth of the Puerco, sometimes called the Pecos.

Beyond this point he found it impossible to proceed with the skiff, either by land or water, and left it the 15th of July on his return. He arrived at Ringgold Barracks on the 11th of August, where he turned over his boat to the Quartermaster, and reported to me at this post on the 25th of August.

From Captain Love's rough notes, and from frequent conversations with him, I am enabled to present the following report of his expedition. I would here observe that his distances were not taken with mathematical

3. Love designed and constructed the keel boat *Major Babbit* and a similar boat or barge named the *Harry Love*. William Chapman wrote, "I have Love's model boat in hand and it will be completed in 15 days. It is a beautiful model, 50 feet by 13. It will carry 100 barrels of flour, and draw but 13 inches of water. It draws but 4 inches light. As soon as it is done, I shall send him to Presidio with it and if it answers my expectations I shall immediately, with your approval, construct four others. If these boats can be used it will be a much cheaper mode of supplying Laredo and Presidio than by the train. . . . In regard to manning the keelboats, I would respectfully suggest that each boat should have such a man as Love for Captain and eight good soldiers or hired citizens. If the boat's crew were well armed, no other guard would be necessary" (WWC to Capt. E. B. Babbitt, Jan. 24, 1849, CC).

4. General George M. Brooke was the commander of the Military Department for Texas at the time. This waterfall may have been the rock-fall in Santa Elena Canyon in the Big Bend of the Rio Grande. Generally speaking, there are rapids on the Rio Grande, but not waterfalls in the sense the term is usually used (Dr. Curtis Tunnell, Executive Director of the Texas Historical Commission, to Caleb Coker, Dec. 1, 1989).

5. Babbitt's Falls may have been Las Cascadas in Canyon Colorado west of Big Bend National Park (ibid.). Edwin Babbitt was the quartermaster at the army headquarters in San Antonio.

6. Rio Conchos enters the Rio Grande from Mexico across from Presidio, Texas.

precision, yet I believe them to be sufficiently accurate for all practical purposes.[7] All the distances given are by the river, unless specially mentioned as being by land. On the accompanying map, (the skeleton of which was taken from Emery's, published in 1844,)[8] I have put down the towns on both sides of the river, the rivers and creeks emptying into the Rio Grande, coal mines, &c., and the distance of every important point from Ringgold Barracks.

NAVIGATION OF THE RIVER

It would here be proper to remark that Captain Love made his expedition at a time when the water was lower in the Rio Grande than had been known for several years, and therefore it was a most favorable season to ascertain the practicability of its navigation at all times.

From Ringgold Barracks to Kingsbury's Fall's, which are 169 miles above Fort McIntosh, (near Laredo,) and eleven below Presidio Rio Grande, (where General Wool's column crossed into Mexico in 1846,)[9] there are obstructions in the river which would prevent its navigation about seven months of each year by steamboats of the class which now run between its mouth and Ringgold Barracks. During the other five months, from June to November, when the river is generally high, steamboats of the largest class now running on the Lower Rio Grande, could go without difficulty to

7. The report contains some inaccuracies, especially with regard to distances (see n.9 below), but is relatively error free as to places lying below the mouth of the Pecos River (Tunnell to Coker, Dec. 1, 1989).

8. This is W. H. Emory's *Map of Texas and the Countries Adjacent: compiled in the Bureau of Topographical Engineers from the best Authorities of the State Department under the direction of Col. J. J. Abert* (1844). It was not prepared from an actual survey, but was a compilation from several preexisting "authorities," and was based primarily on the map of John Arrowsmith of London in 1841. In both maps, the upper valley of the Rio Grande and western Texas were narrowly distorted. The Emory map showed the Puerco entering into the Rio Grande and referred to the upper reaches of the Puerco as the Pecos. Devil's River was shown but not named. Actually both rivers enter the Rio Grande from a more perpendicular direction and do not run closely parallel to the Rio Grande as Emory's map suggested. Chapman's use of Emory's map detracted from the clarity of his report with respect to points upriver from the Pecos. However, by using the scale on the Emory Map and measuring downriver from El Paso, Babbitt's Falls would be on the western upswing of Big Bend National Park (See Robert Sidney Martin and James C. Martin, *Contours of Discovery: Printed Maps Delineating the Texas and Southwestern Chapters in the Cartographic History of North America, 1513–1930* (Austin: Texas State Historical Association, 1986), 54.

9. This is Presidio San Juan Bautista, located between Eagle Pass and Laredo, Texas.

Kingsbury's Falls. During the seven months of low, or rather ordinary water there are three and a half feet of water in the channel, which is about 22 feet wide. A smaller class steamboat could be constructed (iron would probably be the best,) to navigate the channel at all seasons of the year. Those adapted for towing keel-boats would perhaps be preferable. This narrow channel only occurs at intervals, and Captain Love is of opinion that it could be widened to admit the passage of the largest class steamboats now on the river, say of the size of the United States "Corvette," or "Major Brown," which are about 150 feet long, 46 wide, and draw, loaded, three and a half feet—for $10,000. As Captain Love is a better sailor and frontiersman than a civil engineer, probably a nearer approximation to the truth would be arrived at by doubling or trebling his estimate. Private steamboats of about the size of the above mentioned Government boats run at all seasons as high as Guerrero, 103 miles above Ringgold Barracks.

KINGSBURY'S FALLS

These falls entirely obstruct the navigation of the river for steamboats. Two keel-boats—the "Harry Love" and "Major Babbitt"—have been hauled over them with much difficulty. They are about 200 feet long, with a fall of four feet, and the rock which forms them is argillaceous limestone, which is easily removed with a crow-bar. Captain Love is of opinion that a channel could be cut through them, or rather that the present channel could be widened to admit the passage of the steamboats "Corvette" or "Major Brown," for about $3,000. Captain Kingsbury, (a practical engineer,) who made an examination of them in 1849 under my instruction, (see my report dated May 16, 1849,) assured me that a channel could be cut through them to allow the passage of the keel-boat "Harry Love," (which was 75 feet long, 20 wide, and drew 18 inches of water,) for less than $500.

Captain Love was informed, by an American merchant residing at the town of Presidio, Mexico, (six miles from the falls,) that during the five months of last year, when the water was unusually high, a steamboat drawing three and a half feet could have run over them; this I think doubtful.

From Kingsbury's Falls up to the mouth of the San Pedro or Devil's river, a distance of 232 miles, there is nothing to obstruct the navigation of the river with steamboats of the largest class running on the lower Rio Grande. Although the river was at its lowest known stage when Captain Love passed up, there were nearly four feet of water, with a wide channel.

The mouth of Devil's river, which is about 100 miles below the mouth of the Puerco, and 617 above Ringgold Barracks, is the head of steamboat navigation. Above this, the Rio Grande runs between high mountains, is deep, rapid, crooked, and narrow. It, however, could be navigated with some difficulty by keel-boats, to a point 56 miles above the "Grand Indian Crossing," or about 283 miles above the mouth of Devil's river.[10]

The garrison at Fort McIntosh (Laredo) is now supplied by keel-boats, and a train of from 30 to 40 six-mule teams; the latter also supplies Fort Duncan, (near Eagle Pass,) which is 100 miles by the road above Laredo, and 65 by the river above Kingsbury's Falls. If the obstructions at Kingsbury's Falls were removed, Fort Duncan could be furnished by keel or steamboats, thus obviating the necessity of an expensive wagon train. Should the river be rendered navigable, at the trifling expense above mentioned, to the mouth of Devil's river, it would then become an important question, whether it might not be judicious economy to establish a depot at that point, and transport our stores from thence, by land to El Paso, instead of, as at present, transporting them by wagons, at an immense expense, from Lavaca, on the Gulf of Mexico, to El Paso, a distance of 850 miles.[11] Captain Love, who rode from El Paso to San Antonio about a year since, with despatches, believes that a good road could be made, without much labor or expense, from the mouth of Devil's river to El Paso, and that the distance would not exceed 300 miles.[12] This estimate is, of course, in a measure conjectural, but I think the route indicated well worth an examination; and, if Captain Love's opinion should prove to be correct, the subject of a change in the manner of supplying El Paso, and perhaps Santa Fe, which is 320 miles above El Paso, would be well worthy the attention of the Department.

10. The location of the "Grand Indian Crossing" mentioned is not clear. Actually, the Comanche Trail from Texas into Mexico split just north of the Chisos Mountain Range in present-day Big Bend National Park with the western branch crossing the Rio Grande at Lajitas, Texas, and the eastern branch crossing near the curve of the Big Bend (Park Ranger Gus Sanchez to Caleb Coker, Dec. 17, 1990).

11. The actual distance is approximately 700 miles.

12. In January 1849, Chapman hired Love at $75.00 per month and all expenses to deliver dispatches from General Worth at headquarters in San Antonio to Colonel J. M. Washington, the commanding officer at Santa Fe (WWC to J. M. Washington, Jan. 31, 1849, CC). Love traveled alone to Santa Fe and was ordered to return to San Antonio via El Paso and report in person to Major General Worth respecting the best route, including "the roads, the water and grass and the resources and character of the country" (WWC to H. Love, Jan. 30, 1849, CC).

MILITARY POSTS, TOWNS, SOILS, PRODUCTS, ETC.

Ringgold Barracks is the first military station on the Rio Grande above Fort Brown, and is garrisoned by two companies of the First Infantry, under the command of Major Lamotte. This is a depot from which are supplied Fort McIntosh, Fort Duncan, the Texas Rangers, and other mounted troops stationed temporarily in the vicinity of those posts. All the supplies from [for][13] this depot are transported from Fort Brown at present by the United States Steamboat Corvette.

The next military post on the Rio Grande is Fort McIntosh, situated near the old town of Laredo, and is garrisoned by two companies of the first Infantry, under the command of Captain Burbank.

Between Ringgold Barracks and Fort McIntosh are several towns, viz: Camargo, situated on the San Juan River, three miles from its junction with the Rio Grande, having a population of about two thousand; Rio Grande City, a new and flourishing place on the American side, one mile above Ringgold Barracks; Roma, a new town on the Texas side, with a population of about five hundred, among whom are several enterprising merchants, who carry on considerable trade with the neighboring Mexican States; Mier, situated two miles from the Rio Grande, on the river Alcantro, with a population of about two thousand; Guerrero, six miles from the Rio Grande, on the Salado, with a population of about four thousand.

The soil on both sides of the Rio Grande, between Ringgold Barracks and Fort McIntosh, is very fertile, and under cultivation. The principal products are corn, beans, melons, &c. Some tobacco, planted this year for the first time, looks well. Ebony, willow, musquit, and hackberry, grow along its banks. The grazing is excellent, supporting immense flocks of sheep and goats, and vast herds of cattle are seen in every direction. Game is very abundant. There are large mines of bituminous coal near Guerrero. The distance between these two points, Ringgold Barracks and Fort McIntosh, is one hundred and twenty miles by land, and two hundred and sixteen by water.

The next military post is Fort Duncan, (near Eagle Pass,) garrisoned by three companies of the First Infantry, under the command of Colonel Morris. It is about one hundred miles by land, and two hundred and thirty four by water, above Fort McIntosh. The only town of any size between Forts

13. WWC margin note, correcting article.

McIntosh and Duncan is Presidio, situated six miles from the Rio Grande, opposite the Fort at Presidio Rio Grande, and about thirty miles from Fort Duncan. It contains two thousand inhabitants, and has a garrison of two hundred men.

A little town is springing up just below Fort Duncan, which will probably become one of considerable commercial importance, as it is near that point where the roads from Mapimi, Parras, Monclova, Santa Rosa, San Fernando, Nava, Presidio, &c., strike the Rio Grande.

The soil between Fort McIntosh and Fort Duncan is excellent; but, in consequence of the frequent incursion of the Indians, only a small portion is under cultivation. The farmers turn their attention on a grand scale to the raising of sheep and goats—animals which the Indians never steal. Wild horses and game are abundant. Timber the same as below Fort McIntosh, with the addition of pecan.—There are two inexhaustible mines of bituminous coal of superior quality on the Texas side of the river—specimens of which, brought down by Captain Love, I have tested

There are several rich silver mines on the Mexican side, some forty or fifty miles back from Presidio Rio Grande, which were worked to advantage by the Spaniards before their expulsion in 1829,[14] even after paying a handsome percentage of the nett proceeds to the Mexican government and the owners of the land.—Nothing presents [prevents][15] their being worked now but the want of capital, and, perhaps, energy.

There are no settlements, either American or Mexican, above Fort Duncan; neither will there be any until settlers are appointed [afforded][16] some permanent protection against the Indians.

The country and soil between Fort Duncan and the mouth of Devil's river, are represented by Captain Love as beautiful and rich beyond description, and watered by numerous streams flowing into the Rio Grande from both sides. The principle are the Escondido or San Fernando, Elm, Moret, Las Moras, Pecan, San Fillipe, Bear, and Turkey. The whole country is susceptible of irrigation, but from a single visit, it of course could not be decided whether a scarcity of rain in that region would render this mode of watering the soil necessary. The lands are well timbered at intervals with live oak, pecan, mulberry, hackberry, ash, musquit, &c. There are many fine

14. Mexico won its independence from Spain in 1821.

15. WWC margin note, correcting article.

16. WWC margin note, correcting article.

mill-sites on the streams, as nearly all have excellent water-power. They abound with perch and the regular speckled trout of our northern mountain streams. The bear, antelope, deer, jaguar, ocelot, ounce, puma, catamount, wildcat, wolf, turkey, goose, duck, grouse patridge, pigeon, squirrel, *chuchalaca*, &c., &c., were round in great abundance. Captain Love says that he frequently saw herds of black-tailed deer numbering two or three thousand. He also saw immense droves of wild horses and cattle. He describes this country as the finest in the world for grazing, and believes it capable of sustaining *almost any given number* of sheep and goats. From the mildness of the climate, sheep in this region, and, in fact, along the whole valley of the Rio Grande to its mouth, require no sheds during the winter months, and it is also unnecessary to cut hay for them, as they can graze the entire year. The sheep along the valley of the Rio Grande seem to be free from the diseases so common at the North. From this fact, the small expense in taking care of them, and the first cost, (about fifty cents per head,) this will become a very lucrative business.

There is an extensive mine of bituminous coal on the Texas side, about twelve miles above Fort Duncan.

The face of the country between the mouth of Devil's river and Babbitt's Falls is generally mountainous and barren along the river, though portions of it back from the Rio Grande, between the Devil's river and the Puerco, are good for grazing or cultivation. A valley about ten miles wide, covered with fine musquit grass, stretches for hundreds of miles between the Puerco and Rio Grande.[17]

Captain Love saw no Indians during his expedition, but passed many places where they had recently been, with large numbers of horses and mules, and saw numerous small fires at night in the mountains, probably indicating their presence.[18]

About fifty miles below the mouth of the Puerco there is a large cave containing several rooms, with natural arches overhead, and capable of holding one thousand men. A narrow passage leading from it probably

17. Emory's map indicated a valley at this location.

18. Although Love reported that he did not see Indians, Theresa Viele, the wife of Lieutenant Egbert Viele, stationed at Fort McIntosh near Laredo, commented that Love did leave the river briefly to help LieutenantsViele and Hudson chase Indian horse thieves. The pursuers split into two parts and Love remained with Vieles troop. Lieutenant Hudson, leading the other troop, was mortally wounded by Indians on April 7 and died on April 19, 1850. Love did not participate in the action (Viele, *Following the Drum*, 233–234).

terminates on the other side of the mountain, as a strong current of air rushed through the entrance.[19] A short distance above the cave there are thirteen natural towers, about 2,000 feet high, and 200 in diameter.[20]

The "*Grand Indian Crossing*" is 121 miles above the mouth of the Puerco.[21] This is the ford where the Camanche and other tribes of Indians pass the Rio Grande when making their incursions into Mexico, and is the only crossing place for more than 400 miles, as the river from the mouth of Devil's river to Babbitt's Falls (and probably a long distance above,) is from 12 to 18 feet deep.—There are four feet of water at the crossing.—The city of Chihuahua is only 150 miles from this point.[22] The road leading to the "Crossing" runs along the valley between the Rio Grande and Puerco mentioned above, is very wide, well beaten, and resembles a much travelled thoroughfare. It runs up this valley some two hundred miles, when it crosses the Puerco, and goes off into the Indian Summer range. It can be seen from the mountains ten or fifteen miles, winding along the valley.

A garrison stationed at this point would enable us to prevent the passage of the Indians into Mexico, and materially aid in carrying out our treaty stipulations with that nation relative to this subject. It could be supplied with some difficulty by keel-boats.

The Indian appears to be the natural enemy of the Mexican, for he kills him whenever he can find him, and frequently with no possible reason. The Mexicans have such a dread of Indians that they never stand their fire, but run at the very first indication of their presence. The Indians have been very troublesome to the Mexicans for the last two years, and have appeared in large bodies as far south as Durango. The military commander of that place, about a year since, hired at an extravagant compensation a company of Americans, who were on their way to California, to fight a party of some two

19. This would be Parida Cave, which is on Lake Amistad. It is 300 feet wide, 100 feet high, and 200 feet deep. It is near the mouth of the Pecos River (Tunnell to Coker, Dec. 1, 1989).

20. These "Towers" do not exist (ibid.).

21. The Emory map shows the overland straight-line distance between the mouth of the Pecos and Lajitas, Texas, as being slightly in excess of 100 miles.

22. See n. 10 above. The present depth of the Rio Grande along the portion mentioned is much shallower, based upon the editor's personal observations (in Big Bend National Park in December 1990). It is evident that irrigation demand along the upper Rio Grande has decreased the water flowing through this area substantially in the last 140 years. Ease of access to the river and availability of water from springs along the route of the migrating Indians probably contributed more to the location of the Indian crossings than depth of the river (Sanchez to Coker, Dec. 17, 1990). The linear distance from Lajitas, Texas, to Chihuahua, Mexico, is approximately 150 miles.

hundred who were in the neighborhood: this at a time when there was a large garrison of regular troops in the city, and several thousand citizens capable of bearing arms.

The establishment of another military post at the mouth of Devil's river, and one or two between it and Fort Duncan, (Eagle Pass,) would enable us not only more faithfully to perform our treaty stipulations with Mexico, but would cause that fertile country below the Devil's river to be settled by a peaceful population, and the rich prairies whitened by the flocks of pioneer farmers from the old States.

I have the honor to be, General, most respectfully, your obedient servant,

W. W. CHAPMAN
Brevet Major and Assistant Quartermaster,

Major General T. S. Jesup,
Quartermaster General
Washington, D.C.

[The following editorial appeared in the same issue.]

The Rio Grande.

We call the attention of our readers to the able report of the late exploration of our river by HARRY LOVE, which we publish today, formed into eloquent facts from the rude notes of the explorer, by Major W. W. Chapman, U.S. Quartermaster, under whose auspices the expedition was organized.

The inhabitants upon the banks of the Rio Grande have much cause to thank this enterprising officer for thus properly representing to his Government the practicability of opening the river to navigation, and the extraordinarily small cost attending such a result. With steamboat navigation on the Rio Grande to the distance reported as practicable by Major Chapman, the benefits that would result to those who reside in the Valley would be almost incalculable. A complete revolution in transportation of Merchandise would follow; all that portion of Santa Fe trade, which now finds its way into the country from Missouri over almost interminable plains, would be taken to the very doors of the consumers by means of the river, and the trade greatly enlarged and the demand increased in consequence. Every protection would be afforded to the pioneer settler, through the establishment of necessary military posts, and the whole Valley would be enlivened with growing villages and teeming farms. Possessing, as we do, a climate perennial, and lands unsurpassed in fertility by any in the world, our beautiful Valley would soon become a favorite resort for the industrious immigrant from the overstocked nations of the Old World, and its many advantages would also offer great inducements to the enterprising farmer and tradesman from the older States of our own loved Union."

1851

New Orleans *Daily Delta*, Jan. 10, 1851 [quoting from the *Rio Grande Sentinel*, Jan. 1, 1851]: Howard Slaughter, and the two Mexicans who were severally convicted of murder at the late session of the District Court, and sentenced to be hung on Friday last, were accordingly executed. They all confessed their guilt on the scaffold, and repented the crime they had committed. The Rev. Mr. Chamberlain, of the Presbyterian Church, at the request of Slaughter, made an impressive prayer in behalf of the prisoner, and the officiating priest of the Roman Catholic church, addressed the multitude in Spanish and English, expressing the deep sorrow and regret of the culprits for their offences against the laws of the country. The last words of Howard Slaughter were—"Beware of Liquor, for it has brought me to this."

1852

New Orleans *Daily True Delta*, May 18, 1852 [quoting from an unidentified issue of the Brownsville *American Flag*]: Never since the close of the late war with Mexico, has the condition of this frontier presented so lamentable an aspect as at the present, or an occasion which demanded more clearly the united and prompt action of its citizens. . . .

Within the past week we have the startling news of the death of ten persons—one American and nine Mexicans—without the sanction of any law, save that of a hastily assembled and incensed multitude. Everywhere the public mind is greatly excited in consequence of these alarming prospects and no one can foretell the fearful consequences that may ensue.

New Orleans *Daily Delta*, June 22, 1852 [from the Brownsville correspondent's letter of June 15, 1852]: You will see in the Rio Bravo and American Flag accounts of numerous murders and wholesale plunder on this frontier. If those journals were published daily, they could fill their pages with like horrid accounts.

New Orleans *Daily Delta*, Aug. 31, 1852 [from a letter by Captain G. K. Lewis of Aug. 4, 1852]: "A man by the name of Peter, a servant of Major Chapman, was killed by ——— Thibault, at Point Isabel on Monday last. The circumstances, as far as I have been able to learn them, are as follows: Peter went into the house of Thibault and committed some indecencies, when T. put him out. He afterwards returned, and repeated what he had previously done, upon which T. pushed him off the counter, on which he was seated, and, falling on his head, broke his neck. Thibault will be bound over or committed to stand trial in the next term of District Court.

New Orleans *Daily Delta*, Sept. 8, 1852, Brownsville correspondent [Captain G. K. Lewis]: Here in this county, they provided against any such inconvenience to the voters, by taking the ballot box, accompanied by judges and clerks, and traveling up and down the river, some twenty-four miles, receiving the votes of the sovereigns wherever they found them. They do not say that they crossed into Mexico, but they say that if they did, it was only because they river was so confounded crooked that they would have lost too much time by keeping around the bends, and if they got any votes in Mexico, it was entirely accidental, and, therefore, it being considered unavoidable, must be legal. What do you think of that?

BIBLIOGRAPHY

NEWSPAPERS

American Flag, 1846–1848.
New Orleans *Daily Delta*, 1848–1853.
New Orleans *Daily True Delta*, 1848–1853.
Rio Grande *Sentinel*, 1850.
San Jose *Mercury*, May 4, 1988.
Santa Clara *Journal*, October 31, 1962.

PRIMARY SOURCES

Audubon, John Woodhouse. *Audubon's Western Journal: 1849–1850.* Ed. Frank Heywood Hodder. Glorieta, N.M.: Rio Grande Press. 1969.

Calderon de la Barca, Frances. *Life in Mexico.* New York: Doubleday. 1843.

Cazneau, Mrs. William L. *Eagle Pass or Life on the Border.* Ed. Robert Crawford Cotner. Austin: Pemberton Press. 1966.

Chapman Family Collection. Eugene C. Barker Texas History Center. University of Texas at Austin.

Domenech, Abbe Emanuel. *Missionary Adventures in Texas and Mexico. a personal narrative of six year's sojourn in those regions.* Translated from the French under the author's superintendence. London: Longsmans, Brown, Greene, Longmans and Roberts. 1858.

Fisher, Howard T., and Marion Hall Fisher, eds. *Life in Mexico: The letters of Fanny Calderon de la Barca.* Garden City, N.Y.: Doubleday & Company. 1966.

Ford, John Salmon. *Rip Ford's Texas.* Ed. Stephen B. Oates. Austin: University of Texas Press, 1987.

Gregg, Josiah. *Diary and Letters of Josiah Gregg: Excursions in Mexico and California. 1847–1850.* Ed. M. G. Fulton. Norman: University of Oklahoma Press. 1944.

———. *Diary and Letters of Josiah Gregg: Southwestern Enterprises. 1840–1847.* Ed. M. G. Fulton. Norman: University of Oklahoma Press. 1941.

Kendall, George Wilkins. *Narrative of the Texan Santa Fe Expedition.* New Orleans: New Orleans Picayune. 1844.

McCutchan, James D. *Mier Expedition Diary.* Ed. Joseph Milton Nance. Austin: University of Texas Press. 1978.

Register of the Department of State, Corrected to July 1, 1871. Washington, D.C.: Government Printing Office. 1871.

Regulations for the Army of the United States. New York: Harper & Brothers. 1857.
Taylor, Zachary. *Letters of Zachary Taylor from the Battlefields of the Mexican War*. 1908. Reprint. New York: Kraus Reprint Co. 1970.
United States Seventh Census (1850). Counties of Cameron, Starr, and Webb, Texas. Schedule I, Free Inhabitants. Microfilm. Barker Texas History Center. University of Texas at Austin.
Vielé, Teresa Griffin. *Following the Drum: A Glimpse of Frontier Life*. 1858. Reprint. Lincoln: University of Nebraska Press. 1984.

SELECTED SECONDARY SOURCES

Allhands, J. L. *Gringo Builders*. Iowa City, Iowa: N.p. 1931.
Appleton's Cyclopaedia of American Biography. Ed. James G. Wilson and John Fiske. 7 vols. 1888. Reprint. Detroit: Gale Research Company. 1968.
Bauer, K. Jack. *The Mexican War, 1846–1848*. New York: Macmillan. 1974.
Bell, Florence. *A History of the First Presbyterian Church of Brownsville, Texas*. N. p., n.d.
Bender, A. B. "Opening Routes across West Texas, 1848–1850." *Southwestern Historical Quarterly*, XXXVII (Oct. 1933), 116–135.
Bill, Alfred Hoyt. *Rehearsal for Conflict: The War with Mexico, 1846–1848*. New York: Alfred A. Knopf. 1947.
Bowden, Henry Warner. *Dictionary of Religious Biography*. Westport, Conn.: Greenwood Press. 1977.
Briscoe, Eugenia Reynolds. *City by the Sea: A History of Corpus Christi, Texas 1519–1875*. New York: Vantage Press. 1985.
Brown, John Henry. *The Indian Wars and Pioneers of Texas*. Austin: L. E. Daniell, Publisher. [1880].
Callcott, Wilfried Hardy. *Santa Anna*. Hamden. Conn.: Archon Books. 1964.
Camp, Yvette, and Andre Camp. *The Nagel Travel Guide Series, Mexico*. Geneva: Nagel Publishers. 1960.
Chamberlain. Samuel E. *My Confession*. New York: Harper & Brothers. 1956.
Chatfield. W. H. *The Twin Cities of the Border*. New Orleans: E. P. Brandao. 1893.
Cortez, Carlos E. *Juan N. Cortina, Two Interpretations*. New York: Arno Press. 1974.
Covarrubias, Miguel. *Mexico South*. New York: Alfred A. Knopf. 1967.
Crawford, Anne. *The Europa Biographical Dictionary of British Women*. London: Europa Publications. 1983.
Crow, John A. *The Epic of Latin America*. Garden City, N.Y.: Doubleday & Company. 1946.
Cullum, George W. *Biographical Register of the Officers and Graduates of the U. S. Military Academy at West Point, N.Y.* 7 vols. Boston and New York: Houghton, Mifflin. 1891–1930.
Daly, Loraine, and Pat Reumert. *The Padre Island Story*. San Antonio: Naylor Company. 1971.
Daniell, Lewis E. *Personnel of the Texas State Government, with Sketches of Representative Men of Texas*. San Antonio: Maverick Printing House. 1892.

Davenport, Harbert. "General Jose Maria Jesus Carabajal." *Southwestern Historical Quarterly*, LV (Apr. 1952), 475–483.

Davis, Ellis A., and Edwin H. Grobe, eds. *The New Encyclopedia of Texas*. Dallas: Texas Development Bureau. N.d.

Diamond Jubilee October 4–11, 1925, Celebrating the Organization of the First Presbyterian Church Brownsville, Texas, 1850–1925. Brownsville: First Presbyterian Church. N.d.

Dictionary of American Biography. Ed. Allen Johnson and Dumas Malone. 12 vols. New York: Charles Scribner & Sons. 1958–1973.

Dufour, Charles L. *The Mexican War: A Compact History, 1846–1848*. New York: Hawthorn Books. 1968.

Encyclopedia Americana. International Edition. 30 vols. Danbury, Conn.: Grolier. 1989.

Fergueson, Harvey. *Rio Grande*. New York: A. A. Knopf. 1933.

Friend, Llerena. *Sam Houston, The Great Designer*. Austin: University of Texas Press. 1954.

Gilpin, Laura. *The Rio Grande*. New York: Duell, Sloan and Pearce. 1949.

Graf, Leroy P. "The Economic History of the Lower Rio Grande Valley 1820–1875." Ph.D. diss., Harvard University. 1942.

Heitman, Frances B. *Historical Register and Dictionary of the United States Army, September 29, 1789 to March 2, 1903*. 2 vols. Washington, D.C.: Government Printing Office. 1903.

Hoffman, William S. *North Carolina in the Mexican War, 1846–1848*. Raleigh: State Department of Archives and History. 1959.

Hogner, Dorothy C. *South to Padre*. New York: Lothrop, Lee and Shepard. 1936.

Hoover, Mildred Brooke, Hero Eugene Rensch, and Ethel Grace Rensch. *Historic Spots in California*. 3rd. ed. Revised by William N. Abeloe. Palo Alto: Stanford University Press. 1966.

Horan, James D. *The Authentic Wild West: The Outlaws*. New York: Crown Publishers. 1977.

Horgan, Paul. *Great River: The Rio Grande in North American History*. New York: Rinehart & Company. 1954.

Hughes, John Taylor. *Doniphan's Expedition*. 1847. Reprint. New York: Arno Press. 1973.

Impeachment of Judge Watrous, etc.. 34th Cong. 3rd sess. House Reports. Vol II. 1856–1857.

Jenkins, John S. *History of the War between the United States and Mexico*. Philadelphia: Keystone Publishing Company. 1890.

Johannsen, Robert W. *To the Halls of Montezuma: The Mexican War in the American Imagination*. New York: Oxford University Press. 1985.

Kearney, Milo, ed. *More Studies in Brownsville History*. Brownsville: Pan American University at Brownsville. 1989.

———, ed. *Studies in Brownsville History*, Brownsville: Pan American University at Brownsville. 1986.

Keller, Helen Rex. *The Dictionary of Dates*. New York: MacMillan. 1934.

Kelsey, Anna M. *Through the Years.* San Antonio: Naylor Company. 1952.

Ladd, Horatio O. *History of the War with Mexico.* New York: Dodd, Mead and Company. 1883.

Lanman, Charles. *The Biographical Annals of the Civil Government of the United States.* New York: J. M. Morrison. 1887.

Lea, Tom. *The King Ranch.* 2 vols. Boston: Little, Brown and Company. 1957.

Lewis, Tracy H. *Along the Rio Grande.* New York: Lewis. 1916.

Lott, Virgil N., and Virginia M. Fenwick. *People and Plots on the Rio Grande.* San Antonio: Naylor Company. 1957.

Manning, William R., ed. *Diplomatic Correspondence of the United States, Inter American Affairs, 1831–1860.* Washington, D.C.: Carnegie Endowment for International Peace. 1932–1939.

Marett, Robert. *Mexico.* New York: Walker and Company. 1971.

Martin, Robert Sidney, and James C. Martin. *Contours of Discovery: Printed Maps Delineating the Texas and Southwestern Chapters in the Cartographic History of North America, 1513–193*0. Austin: Texas State Historical Association. 1986.

McCoy, Charles A. *Polk and the Presidency.* Austin: University of Texas Press. 1960.

McKenna, Verna Jackson. *Old Point Isabel: Lighthouse Beacon of Brazos Santiago.* Harlingen, Tex.: Port Isabel Press. 1956.

Merk, Frederick. *Manifest Destiny and Mission in American History.* New York: Alfred A. Knopf. 1963.

Nadeau, Remi. *The Real Joaquin Murieta.* Corona Del Mar, Calif.: Trans-Anglo Books. 1974.

Nail, Olin W. *The First Hundred Years of the Southwest Texas Conference of the Methodist Church 1858–1958.* Austin: Capital Printing. 1958.

Nance, Joseph Milton. *Attack and Counterattack: The Texas-Mexican Frontier, 1842.* Austin: University of Texas Press. 1964.

The National Cyclopaedia of American Biography. 63 vols. Ann Arbor: University Microfilms. 1967.

Neale, William. "History of the City of Brownsville, from 1848 to 1876." *Evening Ranchero*, July 5, 1876.

Nevins, Allan. *Ordeal of the Union.* New York: Scribner's Sons. 1947.

Peterson, Charles J. *The Military Heros of the War with Mexico.* Philadelphia: J. B. Smith & Co. 1858.

Peterson, Harold L., and Robert Elman. *The Great Guns.* New York: Grosset & Dunlap. 1971.

Pierce, Frank Cushman. *A Brief History of the Rio Grande Valley.* Menasha, Wisc.: George Banks. 1917.

Purcell, Anita, ed. *Frontier Mexico: 1875–1894.* San Antonio: Naylor Company. 1962.

Ray, Worth S. *Austin Colony Pioneers, Including the History of Bastrop, Fayette, Grimes, Montgomery and Washington Counties, Texas and their Earliest Settlers.* Reprint. Austin: Pemberton Press. 1970.

Ridge, John Rollin ("Yellowbird"). *The Life and Adventures of Joaquin Murieta, the Celebrated California Bandit.* Reprint. Norman: University of Oklahoma Press. 1955.

Sandweiss, Martha A., Rick Stewart, and Ben W. Huseman. *Eyewitness to War, Prints and Daguerreotypes of the Mexican War, 1846–1848.* Fort Worth: Amon Carter Museum. 1989.

Scott, Florence Johnson. *Historical Heritage of the Lower Rio Grande, etc., 1747–1848.* San Antonio: Naylor Company. 1937.

Secrest, William B. "HELL for Leather Rangers." *True West*, Mar.–Apr., 1968.

——— *Joaquin.* Fresno, Calif. Saga-West Publishing Company. 1970.

Singletary, Otis A. *The Mexican War.* Chicago: University of Chicago Press. 1960.

Smith, George Winston, and Charles Judah. *Chronicles of the Gringos.* Albuquerque: University of New Mexico Press. 1968.

Sowell, A. J. *Early Settlers and Indian Fighters of Southwest Texas.* Austin: Ben C. Jones & Co. 1900.

Spell, Lota M. *Pioneer Printer.* Austin: University of Texas Press. 1963.

Stambaugh, Jacob Lee, and Lillian J. Stambaugh. *The Lower Rio Grande Valley of Texas.* San Antonio: Naylor Company. 1954.

Stapp, William Preston. *The Prisoners of Perote.* 1845. Reprint. Austin: University of Texas Press. 1977.

Stephens, Sir Leslie, and Sir Sidney Lee, eds. *The Dictionary of National Biography.* Vol. 2. London: Oxford University Press. 1921.

Stephenson, Nathaniel W. *Texas and the Mexican War: A Chronicle of the Winning of the Southwest.* New York: United States Publishers Association. 1921.

Stillman, Chauncey Devereux. *Charles Stillman, 1810–1875.* New York: N.p. 1956.

Thompson, Ernest Trice. *Presbyterians in the South, 1607–1861.* Vol. 1. Richmond, Va.: John Knox Press. 1963.

Thrall, Homer S. *History of Methodism in Texas.* Houston: E. H. Cushing. 1872.

Toor, Frances. *New Guide to Mexico.* New York: Crown Publishers. 1948.

Trager, James. *The Peoples Chronology.* New York: Holt, Rinehart and Winston. 1979.

Turner, Martha Anne. *Texas Epic, An American Story.* Wichita Falls, Tex.: Nortex Press. 1974.

Webb, Walter Prescott, H. Bailey Carroll, and Eldon Stephen Branda, eds. *The Handbook of Texas.* 3 vols. Austin: Texas State Historical Association. 1952, 1976.

Webb, Walter Prescott. *The Texas Rangers, A Century of Frontier Defense.* 1935. Reprint. Austin: University of Texas Press. 1965.

Wilbarger, J. W. *Indian Depredations in Texas: Reliable Accounts of Battles, Wars, Adventures, Forays, Murders, Massacres, Etc., Etc., Together with Biographical Sketches of Many of the Most Noted Indian Fighters and Frontiersmen in Texas.* 2nd ed. Austin: Hutchings Printing House. 1890.

Wildwood, Warren [pseud.]. *Thrilling Adventures Among the Early Settlers, Embracing Desperate Encounters with Indians, Tories, and Refugees; Daring Exploits of Texas Rangers and Others.* Philadelphia: J. E. Potter. 1862.

Wilson, Robert A. *Mexico.* 3rd ed. New York: Harper & Brothers. 1855.

Woolsey, Vernor G. *History of the First United Methodist Church.* Corpus Christi: Artcraft Printing. 1978.

World Book Encyclopedia. 22 vols. Chicago: World Book. 1989.

INDEX

C

D

E

M

N

V

W

Y

Caleb Coker, the great-great-grandson of Helen and William Chapman, lives in Jacksonville, Florida. He is a graduate of Stanford University and Duke Law School.